Real Estate Training Institute – Pre Exam Workbook

Pre Exam Course Workbook
Real Estate Training Institute

Leslie Clauson

Real Estate Training Institute – Pre Exam Workbook

My 5-year-old son has just started reading. Every night, we lie on his bed and he reads a short book to me. Inevitably, he'll hit a word that he has trouble with: last night the word was "gratefully." He eventually got it after a fairly painful minute. He then said, "Dad, aren't you glad how I struggled with that word? I think I could feel my brain growing." I smiled: my son was now verbalizing the tell-tale signs of a "growth- mindset." But this wasn't by accident. Recently, I put into practice research I had been reading about for the past few years: I decided to praise my son not when he succeeded at things he was already good at, but when he persevered with things that he found difficult. I stressed to him that by struggling, your brain grows. Between the deep body of research on the field of learning mindsets and this personal experience with my son, I am more convinced than ever that mindsets toward learning could matter more than anything else we teach.

Researchers have known for some time that the brain is like a muscle; that the more you use it, the more it grows. They've found that neural connections form and deepen most when we make mistakes doing difficult tasks rather than repeatedly having success with easy ones.

What this means is that our intelligence is not fixed, and the best way that we can grow our intelligence is to embrace tasks where we might struggle and fail.

Salman Khan

Khan Academy

Real Estate Training Institute – Leslie Clauson

Copyright © 2014 Leslie Clauson

All rights reserved.

SBN-13:
978-1500804909

ISBN-10:
1500804908

This book is not intended to replace any books or materials used in the classroom setting or online of any school, training facility or university. It is intended to reinforce some of the most important areas of real estate that a pre exam student would need to know. It's used in addition to the instruction at the Real Estate Training Institute in Mississippi. Persons who did not attend the RETI School may not understand some of the content.

To prepare pre licensees to excel on their state real estate exam, there's only one way to go. GO RETI!

Mississippi Real Estate License Law can be found at http://www.mrec.state.ms.us/
The Mississippi Real Estate License Law found in this book was copied and pasted from the MREC site. It has been altered to help students understand the breakdown of the exam and to clearly grasp the scope of what is expected from them while practicing real estate in the state of Mississippi You may always consult an attorney. If you have any questions about Mississippi Real Estate License Law or Mississippi Real Estate Commission forms, you can contact the Mississippi Real Estate Commission at:

Physical Address:
Lefleur's Bluff Tower, Suite 300
4780 I-55 North
Jackson, MS 39211(601) 321-6970 - Office
(601) 321-6955 - Fax

Mailing Address:
P.O. Box 12685
Jackson, MS 39236

Phone: 601-932-6770
Fax: 601-932-2990

Email: info@mrec.state.ms.us

Real Estate Training Institute – Pre Exam Workbook

From Broker/Dean Leslie Clauson
Real Estate Training Institute

The pre exam courses taught at the Real Estate Training Institute are tough to pass. Above average reading comprehension and vocabulary skills are necessary to achieve success.

Please observe the following practices:

1. Class room time will not be allotted for student's personal stories.

2. Questions that are above the knowledge needed to pass the MREC/PSI exam will be identified as such and the student asking the question will be told to come back after they pass the exam for the answer.

3. When filling out the MREC application, please read the questions carefully. Do not ask a RETI associate how to complete it. (The associates at RETI agree that if a student cannot comprehend clear and concise questions on the application, he/she is not qualified nor ready to be a real estate professional.)

4. Please sign in and out daily. Hours are monitored.

The Finals – Exit Exams

There are three exit exams. All three exams will be given out in advance. There will be two exams concentrating on the national portion of the PSI exam and there will be one exam focusing on the MS state license law portion. You must pass all exams at a 90% correct rate or higher to receive a diploma from the Real Estate Training Institute.

What to expect:
Day 1: Complete Shock and Horror!
Day 2: After lunch you will start recognizing repeated information.
Day 3: Most students by the end of the day will prove to themselves that they can pass the national portion.
Day 4: MS State License Law preparation begins.
Day 5: Most students feel confident they can pass both exams.
Day 6: At this time, courses are adjusted to fit the needs of the students.
Day 7: Review
Day 8. Review
Day 9: Finals

There is no short cut.
No one can just "Slide By" and pass this course or the exam.

If a student does not demonstrate the ability to pass the MREC/PSI exam by the end of their course, he/she may be invited back to repeat an identical class. (Limited to three consecutive classes.)

Real Estate Training Institute – Pre Exam Workbook

CONTENTS

1. Student to Student — Pg 1
2. Organized Chaos — Pg 37
3. PSI Candidate Information — Pg 74
4. National Exams — Pg 84
5. MREC License Law — Pg 124
6. MREC Rules and Regulations — Pg 153
7. MREC Professions and Occupations — Pg 194
8. PSI State Content Outline — Pg 202
9. Forms — Pg 263
10. State Exams — Pg 294
11. Blank Answer Sheets — Pg 340
12. Reciprocal States — Pg 413
13. The Final Steps — Pg 415

Real Estate Training Institute – Leslie Clauson

Chapter 1

STUDENT-TO-STUDENT

Pre licensees are not told what areas of real estate they got incorrect on the Mississippi real estate exam after they pass it.

The Real Estate Training Institute strives to send new licensees into the real estate profession with a correct understanding of real estate concepts. Students who contact the school after they pass the MS exam are asked if there is anything still unclear. At that time, we correct any misunderstandings.

The following statements and notes were written by students who took the exam. Corrections were made if necessary.

Originally this section was not intended to be part of this workbook until it was remembered that there is no better teacher than a student.

From Ginger, Jason, Kari and Wyatt

1. It is unethical for a broker representing the seller to tell the buyer the lowest price a seller will accept.

2. Whenever money is transferred into a client's **trust account**, **accurate records** must be kept.

3. **Standard Accounting Practices** are used for keeping records.

4. The phrase **"procuring cause"** is most important to the broker and seller in an open listing contract. "Procure the Buyer"

5. **The Real Estate Settlement Procedures Act (RESPA)** is designed to regulate disclosure of closing information.

6. An owner's **title insurance** protects the owner from loss to a claimant with superior right of title. Title insurance insures up to the date it's issued.

7. A building constructed off site is a **modular home.**

8. The disadvantage in investing in real estate is that the money is not easily accessible. It is not easily liquid.

9. Regardless of how many loans a person takes out on their property, tax liens take priority. **Ad Valorem**

and **Special Assessment**s are both taxes. Non-payment of either can force a tax sale. Taxes get paid first when there is a foreclosure sale. Taxes get paid first in probate before a **devisee** can take title to real estate.

10. **An assessment** is a tax. Taxes take priority in getting paid off first after a foreclosure.

11. **Zoning** changes require a public hearing first and then council vote.

12. When an agent collects money from a tenant, the agent gives it to her broker, not the owner.

13. **USPAP** relates to the appraisal specialty of real estate.

14. The least obvious lead product to be found on a property is a lead pipe. It's a **latent defect**.

15. A **lead based paint disclosure** gives buyers 10 days to inspect the property at their cost.

16. Banks don't like to take a **deed in lieu of foreclosure** because they may have to pay off the junior loans. The legal event of a **Judicial Foreclosure** by the first lien holder kills the subordinated loan (the second).

17. Each **discount point** equals 1% of the loan not the sales price.

18. **Puffing** is not illegal. Puffing can lead to misrepresentation. An exaggerated opinion.

19. A broker or agent should caution the seller not to respond to all multiple offers at the same time.

20. A **counter offer** voids an offer.

21. The agent's obligation to the seller in regards to disclosure is to have him disclose all **material defects**.

22. An agent gets to keep his commission if the seller lied about a **material fact** and the buyer finds out after the close. **The Purchase Agreement** was between the Seller and Buyer. Neither agent was a party to that contract.

23. An **open agreement** is when the seller hires multiple agents. The agent that gets paid is the one that procures the buyer. (The **procuring cause**)

24. An **abstract of title** is the history of the recorded documents on the property.

25. The attorney reads the **abstract of title**. **Abstract and Opinion**.

26. A salesperson can get leases for the broker and direct customers to the broker. An **unlicensed personal assistant** can refer buyers and sellers to her broker. She is usually also the

one that answers the phone. (Receptionist)

27. Once planted oranges and apple trees are **real estate**.

28. A **lessee** and a **vendee** have possession of property but not legal title. They have an **equitable position – title** until the deed is transferred. An **equitable title** is considered an insurable interest.

29. A **lease** is personal property. (**Leasehold**) It's a piece of paper that gives a lessee the right to live in a landlord's real property. You can pick up a piece of paper and move it. **Real property** is immovable.

30. Dogs are allowed to live in non-pet apartments for handicap purposes including "**comfort pets**". **Americans with Disability Act**. A landlord cannot charge an extra pet fee for a comfort dog.

31. **Broker Protection Clause is a clause in the Listing Agreement** that protects the broker after the listing expires. It's already written into the listing agreement. It says something to the effect that if the seller sells the property who the agent introduced them to, they owe the agent a commission because they were the **procuring cause**. It has a time limit. (One month, six months…it's negotiable.)

32. **UFF (UFFI) or Urea Formaldehyde Foam** is pumped between the walls and banned in the 70's.

33. The **Grantor** signs the **Deed**.

34. Sharing a driveway is an **encumbrance**.

35. In a **sales comparison approach** to appraisal, you subtract or add from the comparable, not the subject property.

36. **Subletting** is when a tenant rents his place to another tenant.

37. What is not covered on a home warranty? The quality of workmanship.

38. The death of an associated broker does not cancel a contract. Associated brokers are broker agents. The death of the Responsible Broker kills the deal. Agents can die and the deal stills lives.

39. When a salesperson doesn't know something but should have, he did not practice care. **Negligent Misrepresentation**. (If an agent tells a client that her fireplace will add ambiance in winter and the client buys the property and then finds out the fireplace is actually just a fake fireplace front, it is **Negligent Misrepresentation**.) OR (A buyer tells her agent she wants to purchase a home in order to have a beauty salon in her garage. She would like to

have a home-based business. The agent shows the buyer a home with the garage big enough for the home-based salon. The buyer purchases the property. When the new homeowner was moving in her salon equipment, the city code enforcer pulls up and tells her the neighborhood was not zoned for home based business'. The agent did not practice care. (**Negligent Misrepresentation**) The agent is responsible for actual damages. Her **E and O insurance** will help her pay for her mistake.

40. The agent will be responsible for **Actual Damages**. Her **E and O insurance** will cover it.

41. The best reason for buying real estate is appreciation.

42. Real Estate is not easily liquid. If you need money it will take some time to get the money out of real estate. (Example: re-finance or sell it or new loan.)

43. A Reverse Amortization Loan is a **reverse mortgage**. It is for older people who would like to have tax-free income. (Seniors, retired couple)

44. **Novation**: an agreement to replace an old debtor with another one. (Used when assuming a loan.)

45. When the developer of an apartment complex is forced into having two parking spaces for each unit, it is a building code. It is **police power**.

46. When a seller gives an agent a bonus check, the agent must turn it over to her broker. An agent can only take compensation from her broker.

47. A **subordination agreement** is a release to take a second position. The second loan on your house is a **subordinated loan** to the first lien holder (loan, lender).

48. **Land** is not a fixture. **Land** is **real property**. **Fixtures** are attached to the land. (Trees, fences, shrubs or an attached door, doorknob, window, awning, faucet, sink.

49. **Straight line method of depreciation** is dividing the adjusted basis of a property by the estimated remaining useful life.

50. **PUD: Planned Unit Development**, A project or subdivision that has individually owned parcels and homes, together with recreational or landscaping elements owned by a homeowners association and managed for the mutual benefit of all homeowners.

51. The most **Trade Fixture** used in a course of business is a bowling alley.

52. A vineyard (grapes) is real property. Apple trees and orange trees are real property. They are **Fructus Naturales**. (Natural Fruit)

53. Fructus Industriales: crops (as wheat, corn) produced by labor on the part of man for industry.

54. **Emblements** are personal property. **Emblements** are crops such as tomatoes, corn, and cucumbers. They need to be planted and cultivated yearly. (If a renter farmer is evicted from his property after his crops are planted, he is allowed to harvest those crops. A farmer is entitled to the fruits of his labor.)

55. Standing timber is considered **real property**.

56. **IDX** technology is the technology that allows agents to link to the **MLS** on their web page.

57. **Title insurance** insures up to the date the policy is issued. It extends to unrecorded documents.

58. A property manager's duties do not include investing the property owner's funds.

59. If Sam and Joe own property as **joint tenants**, when Joe dies, Sam will hold title in **Severalty**. **JTWROS - Joint Tenancy with Rights of Survivorship**.

60. When a **tenant in common** tries to convey 100% title to a property without the knowledge of the other owner. He has violated the **Covenant of Seisen**. The property was not seized by him. You can't sell what you don't own. The transaction will fail because of **Impossibility of Performance**.

61. The term that best describes a tenant's interest in property is **Lease Hold Estate**. It is **personal property**. It's a reversionary estate since it reverts back to the owner.

62. A prospective buyer has the right to demand his deposit money back before the offer is accepted. If a buyer makes an offer and on her way home she finds a property she likes better and wanted to make an offer, she can withdraw the first offer before it's accepted and purchase the other property.

63. An option contract is a **unilateral contracted**. In a "rent to own", the renter need not buy but if he chooses to buy, the seller must sell. A **Listing Agreement** is a unilateral contract also. The **Listing Broker** may not sell the property but if he brings a **ready, willing and able buyer that meets the terms of the contract**, the seller must pay a commission.

64. A written and signed real estate contract may be voided if one of the parties is an **unmarried minor**. It's a **voidable contract**. A married minor is considered an adult and the contract is valid. An adult in the deal cannot force an **unmarried minor** to complete the deal.

65. If a tenant signs a five-year lease and the owner dies in 3 years with will (**testate**) the lease is valid. The **devisees** cannot kick out the tenant.

66. When a property reaches a physical condition where a tenant can no longer live there (unsafe), he may move and it is called **Constructive Eviction**.

67. The first person to record the deed is the owner. An **unrecorded deed** is valid only between the parties involved and to those who have been given notice.

68. You are assured you are getting **fee simple ownership** when the seller can furnish title insurance.

69. When a person dies **testate** (test ate – two syllables = with will – two syllables), his will passes by **devise**. Before his heirs can take possession, there must be probate. Taxes get paid first.

70. When a person dies **intestate** (in test ate – three syllables = with out will – three syllables), his property passes by descent and distribution.

71. When a commercial property is in a neighborhood that gets downzoned, the property gets **grandfathered in** and is of **non-conforming use**. If the property burns down or gets destroyed, it cannot be built back with getting a **variance** or a **conditional use permit**.

72. The economic life of a building has come to an end when the value of the land and the building equals the value of the land only. It's a tear down.

73. A **capitalization rate** incorporates return on land and building and recapture of the building.

74. A mortgage broker cannot take a kick back for an appraisal.

75. When **a FHA or DVA-VA** buyer wants to take out a loan, he must go to a qualified lender. **FHA and DVA** do not lend money. **FHA** is an insurance company and **DVA-VA** is a guarantee company.

76. The mother or father of an active military person cannot get a **DVA-VA** loan.

77. The **Truth in Lending Act (Regulation Z)** is designed to disclose the true cost of lending.

78. Agents can't go around the neighborhood inducing fear to get commissions. It is called **panic peddling** and **blockbusting**.

79. Agents can- not steer people into neighborhoods where they believe people should live. It's called **steering**.

80. When three banks independently turn down a loan for a consumer based on

the property's neighborhood economic factors, it is not **redlining**.

81. Refusing to rent to someone based on race is a violation of the **Fair Housing Act**. A landlord cannot segregate all the families with children in one area of the complex.

82. When a brokerage does not predominately display the **Equal Housing Opportunity (EHO) Poster**, it is called **Prima Facie** Discrimination. (Prima Facie=Prime Face=in your face.)

83. The best way to appraise a single-family home is **Comparative/Comparable Market Analysis – Market Data**. (The date a comparative is sold is an important factor.)

84. A broker's **trust account (escrow account)** is a non-interest bearing checking account.

85. Monies in a **trust account (escrow account)** are not assets of the broker. It is the client's funds and **accurate records** must be kept.

86. A broker may deposit his own funds into a **trust account (escrow account)** to open the account and to pay any fees associated with it. A broker cannot use trust-escrow funds, which are client funds to pay his office bills. It is called comingling.

87. Brokers are not responsible to identify **latent defects**.

88. A loan with a partial payment is a **partially amortized loan**. There is a **balloon payment**.

89. A loan that only interest is paid and at the end has a **balloon payment** is a **straight loan**.

90. Disadvantages of a bank taking **a deed in lieu of foreclosure** are that it is not a legal event and they will be responsible for **junior loans**.

91. The primary responsibility of a property manager (**general manager**) is to get the highest NET return for the owner.

92. When you want to extend your patio, check **setback limits**.

93. When a **co-op (cooperative)** owner defaults on his payment, the others in the complex must pay his share. **Co-op** ownership is personal property. The owner owns stock in a **cooperative** It is the only personal property that has property disclosures. (1 to 4 units only.)

94. A condo owner's title is **fee simple**, the highest form of ownership.

95. Owners of a **time-share** hold title as **tenants in common**. Interests are unequal. One person can have a timeshare for two weeks in a two bedroom and someone else could

have five days in a three bedroom and so on.

96. **Trigger terms** for **Regulation Z** are a percentage, down payment, number of payments, starting amount of payments and service charge. (It's the stuff you need a magnifying glass to read.)

97. When a broker receives an **earnest money deposit check**, he must deliver it to the **trust account – escrow account** by the end of the next business or banking day.

98. Brokers cannot get together and price fix commissions, fees or boycott other agents. **(Sherman Anti Trust Act)**

99. A handicapped person may make **Reasonable Alterations or Accommodations** to an apartment or rental at his cost but he must return the apartment to its original condition at the end of the lease (also at his cost). The least likely thing to be brought back to its original condition is the handrail screwed into tile in the shower. (They are left because it will do more damage to remove them.)

100. **Regulation Z** requires that the buyer have a three day right of rescission if the loan is on his personal residence.

101. A bank that substitutes it's judgment on behalf of another bank is a **bank intermediary**.

102. **HUD** protects people dealing with **Fair Housing** complaints. You have one year to file a complaint. Some people will take their complaint to the courts because the courts do not cap rewards.

103. **Laches** is when you waited too long to sue someone. (Laches=locks=locked out of suing) (For instance, if you wait one year and three days to file a Fair Housing Suit, the doctrine on Laches has taken over. You are locked out of suing because you attempted your suit after the one year allowance time to sue.)

104. **Caveat Emptor** means Buyer Beware.

105. **Pur Autre Vie** means "for the life of another". It's a life estate based on another's life.

106. **Private Mortgage Insurance (PMI)** is not needed when you put 20% down.

107. A **Writ of Execution** is a court order to allow the sheriff to seize property because it's suspected that a person will be transferring property out of his name during a **Lis Pendens**. (Lawsuit Pending)

108. **A government entity can take your property by eminent domain.** (They pay just compensation and condemn the property.) The only person who can do **Reverse**

Real Estate Training Institute – Pre Exam Workbook

Condemnation is the property owner.

109. A **CMA and BPO** differ from an appraisal in that the appraisal can determine more. An appraisal can determine value while a **BPO and CMA** estimates a selling price.

110. Sending in a partial payment on your mortgage will still cause a default.

111. A **Power of Attorney** allows someone to act for someone else. If an **unmarried minor** was given a power of attorney by his brother to sign on his behalf, only the **unmarried minor** needs to sign. The contract is also a voidable contract.

112. When in doubt as to where money should go, turn it over to the courts to determine. The form you use will be an **Interpleader**.

113. A seller is not obligated to accept a price lower than the asking price.

114. An **Exclusive Agreement** does not guarantee you a commission but an **Exclusive RIGHT Agreement** does. A broker will spend more money on advertising with an **Exclusive RIGHT Agreement**. The **Exclusive Agreement** allows the seller to sell it him or herself without paying a commission. (If it doesn't RIGHT, then it's wrong for you.)

115. A condo complex would like to eminent domain three houses adjacent to their property in order to expand the Condominiums parking spaces. The complex is not allowed to do it. Only government agencies can **eminent domain**.

116. When an investor would like to purchase a property to build a casino in a non-casino state, the contract will fail because of **Impossibility of Performance**. When a person would like to purchase an unlicensed whiskey store in order to run a whiskey store, the contract will fail for Impossibility of Performance.

117. When a person records a **deed**, it is said to be giving **Constructive Notice to the World**.

Real Estate Training Institute – Pre Exam Workbook

From Jason, Leanna and Rachel

1. **Seisen** is legal ownership. To be **seized** in property means you own it.

2. When an elderly couple gifts a property to a hospital but reserve the right to have a **life estate**, the hospital is said to be the **Remainder Man**.

3. A **Less Than Freehold** Estate is **Leasehold**. Not a **life estate**.

4. **General Warranty Deed = Fee Simple**. The **deed** with the highest form of protection.

5. To find an **encroachment** hire a surveyor.

6. The furniture in your house is **personal property**.

7. A **beneficiary rights** to a property is **personal property**. It's a **will**. A **will** can be picked up and moved like a lease. The **real estate** itself is **real property**.

8. **Real property** is land and the area below and above the surface to infinity and all of the improvements thereon.

9. The intention of the party who attached a **fixture** is the most important factor in determining if something is real or personal. (Example: Was the freestanding refrigerator enclosed into cabinets meant to be a permanent fixture? The intention of the owners who moved it into place and installed it will determine the answer.

10. A landowner who sells their farm must specifically reserve the **mineral rights** or they will automatically pass to the buyer.

11. An example of a right, improvement or privilege that belongs to and conveys with a property is an **appurtenance**. Means "In addition to". (Example an **easement appurtenant** is ownership of a property with a **right of way** over someone else's property in addition to the ownership of their property.)

12. **Trade fixtures** are **personal property**. **Trade Fixtures** are a commercial tenant's **personal property**.

13. **Intestate** = with out will – without will.

14. The last entities to receive money after **probate** are the **heirs**. The first **liens** to be paid are taxes. (Taxes include **Ad Valorem** and **Special Assessments**.)

15. Ownership by **Joint Tenancy** has an advantage because a person can avoid the expense **and delay of probate**. **Joint** Tenancy with Rights of Survivorship = JTWROS

16. The buyer and attorney can decide and determine the method of

ownership. The attorney is the **Conveyancer**. A **Conveyancer** is a legal position. Brokers and agents cannot practice law. If a Client or customer asks an agent how they should take title, you tell to ask an attorney.

17. When one co-owner wants to sell his interest in real estate and the other co-owners don't, he may bring a legal action to the courts to sell his interest. It's called a **Suit for Partition** or **Partition the Property**. His interests will be sectioned off (partitioned from the rest of the property) and can be sold.

18. **Severalty** – to own to the exclusion of anyone else. Own it by yourself.

19. When there is a **Tenants by the Entirety** ownership, a broker should get both husband and wife to sign the listing. With **Joint Tenancy** and **Tenancy in Common**, you only need one person to list a property. All owners must sign to actually sell it.

From Todd, Oscar and Ronnie

1. A **Principal-Client** is the person or entity that delegates authority in order to create an agency relationship.

2. **Delegated Authority** is the Principal's act that creates agency.

3. To create agency the principal **Delegates Authority**, and the broker must **Consent to Act**.

4. **Fiduciary** is the type of relationship based on trust and confidence.

5. A duty to a **principal** that includes **confidentiality is loyalty**.

6. Representing both sides of the same transaction with written permission explaining what is due each party is **Dual Agency**.

7. Unlawful mixing of the broker's money and his client's funds is **Commingling**.

8. **The Protection Clause** extends the period of time that a seller agrees to pay a commission.

9. A relationship where an agent represents only one party is **Single Agency**.

10. A **Subagent** is an agent's agent. The agents of the responsible broker are sub agents.

11. **Puffing** is an agent's exaggerated opinion. Not illegal. **Puffing** could lead to **misrepresentation**.

12. **Fraud** is intentional misrepresentation. **E and O insurance** will not help an agent when an agent commits intentional fraud.

13. **REALTORS Code of Ethics** is the standard of ethical behavior for Realtors. (*National Association of Realtors Trademark)

14. **Boycotting** is the illegal action where two or more brokers agree not to cooperate with a third broker. One broker may decide on his own to not pay another agent the same commission split as he offers others.

15. **A Tie In - Tying Arrangement (tie-in)**: Requiring a buyer to list his or her current home with the same agent in order to purchase the desired new home the buyer wants.

16. **Obedience** is the type of duty required of an agent when asked by an owner not to place a "Seller Financing" sign in the yard. (Or any sign)

17. Giving a seller Estimation of Proceeds from an income property to determine their net profit before listing the building for sale in an example of **Care**.

18. A **General Agent** is a **property manager** who has several duties to perform for his or her principal/client. The **primary duty of a property manager** is to get the highest net return for the owner.

19. **Agency Disclosure** is informing clients/fiduciaries and customers of your relationships which each person.

20. A **Latent Defect** is not discoverable by an ordinary inspection. (Lead pipes in the wall, bad electrical wiring in the kitchen, boards ruined from a fire painted over and covered.)

21. **Seller's Property Disclosure Act** is legislation requiring the seller to reveal the honest condition of the property whether a defect is seen or a **Latent Defect**.

22. **CERCLA** is associated with **Superfund** and holds the responsible polluting party for the clean up or liability **without excuse**.

23. **SARA** is for innocent landowners who find themselves in possession of a polluted property.

24. **Brownfields Legislation** helps revitalize defunct and polluted areas of contamination.

25. **Strict Liability** is when the owner of a polluted property is responsible for the cleanup **Without Excuse**. **CERCLA**

26. **Joint and Several Liability** is when a single person and a group is held liable for damages.

27. **Retroactive Liability** is liability extending back to the previous owners of a parcel of land.

28. **Lead Poisoning** is a potential cause of mental retardation in children.

29. Undisclosed **dual agency** is an illegal form of real estate representation.

30. **Lead Based Paint Disclosure Act** is a federal law that gives the buyer 10 days after an accepted offer to inspect the homes built **before 1978**.

31. **Consideration** is a legal requirement of agency. (cash or equivalent)

32. **Earnest Money** can be used as **liquidated damages** if it is stated in the contract. **Earnest money** is put up by the buyer in order to show his true intention to move forward with the transaction.

33. An **Expressed Contract** is parties stating the exact terms. (Something in writing.) An example is going to the drive through EXPRESS Lane at McDonalds, ordering food, driving to the first window and paying. At that window you receive a receipt. Then, you pull up to the second window with your receipt. Only after you have a receipt in hand will you be able to get food. (Something in writing.)

34. **Implied Contract** is like eating dinner in a restaurant before paying. It's going to a fancy restaurant where a host will seat you. After seated you order dinner and the waitress brings the food to you before you pay for it. By your actions of ordering food and eating it you are implying you will pay for it. There is nothing in writing.

35. An **Option** and a **Listing** are both **Unilateral Contracts**. ("I will do something if you do something first.") Only one person is forced into doing something.

36. A contract with an **unmarried minor** is a **Voidable Contract**. At any time the minor can change his mind. An adult cannot force a minor to complete a transaction.

37. Violation of **Specific Performance** is when the seller took the drapes and water softener which were fixtures attached to the property. A court order requiring a promise to be carried out is a suit for **Specific Performance**.

38. **An Open Listing** is hiring multiple agents. Only the real estate firm who procures the buyer gets paid by the seller.

39. **Exclusive Right to Sell** is a listing stating the listing agent will get paid regardless of who procures the buyer. (Procuring Cause)

40. **Net Listings** are prohibited in most states because of the uncertainty of the selling price. When your Client calls you up and says to you that he needs $500,000 from the sale of a property and you as his agent can keep anything you can get above that.

41. **Listing Contracts** are the property of the **broker**.

42. **Stature of Frauds** requires all real estate contracts regardless of what type to be in writing.

43. **Equitable Title** is also known as an insurable interest of real estate. It's the Buyer, Optionee or Vendee. It can be willed.

44. Delivery of the Deed gives **Legal Title** to the Buyer.

45. An Offer becomes the **Purchase Agreement/Contract** once it's accepted. It is the same document.

46. For an offer to be accepted it must be **Delivered and Accepted**.

47. **Devise** is the transfer of real property by a will. (A **Codicil** is used to change a will.)

48. **Divisor** is the giver of the property when he dies.

49. **Township**- 36 Sections with each section having 640 acres.

50. **JTWROS**- Joint tenancy with the right of survivorship.

51. **Ad Valorem**- " According to value" TAXES- Your property taxes.

Real Estate Training Institute – Pre Exam Workbook

From Tim, Carl, Tai and Lisa

1. **Covenant of Seisin**- the grantor's expression that he or she has possession and the right to convey the property. Example: When there are three partners who own an apartment complex and one of the partners is trying to sell 100% ownership of the property without the other two **partners knowing it, he has violated the Covenant of Seisen. In this case the deal will fail because of Impossibility of Performance.**

2. **Constructive Notice**- By recording a **deed** a person has given **Constructive Notice to the worl**d. Once the deed is recorded everyone has been given notice whether they know about it or not. An unrecorded deed is valid only to those parties involved and to those who actually know about it.

3. **Grantor**- The person who sells the property. The one conveying the property to the **Grantee** by deed. It's the seller. The **Granto**r is the only person(s) who signs the deed.

4. OR-OR-OR is the GIVOR

5. EE-EE-EE is the gimmee gimmee gimmee the propertee

6. **Grantee**- The person who receives the title by deed. It's the buyer.

7. **Abstract of title**- a history of recorded documents on the property. The attorney reads the **Abstract of Title**. **Abstract and Opinion**

8. **Title Insurance**- When issued, it insures that the title is free of all encumbrances, defects and liens except for those listed. It protects against loss from title defects. **Title Insurance** extends to unrecorded documents.

9. **Trust deed**- most often seen in seller financing situations. A way of conveying real estate by the **trustor.**

10. **Covenant of Quiet Enjoyment**- The **Grantor** guarantees that title is good and is insuring against other parties who might claim superior title.

11. **Testate**- dying "with will". (Two syllables: Test-Ate and With-Will)

12. **Intestate**- Dying "with out will". (Three syllables: In-Test-Ate and With-Out-Will)

13. **IRS Code 1031**- IRS code governing **tax-deferred exchanges.**

14. **RESPA- Real Estate Settlement Procedures Act. Settlement** of cost legislation. Prohibits undisclosed kickbacks.

15. **Quitclaim deed**- the deed that gives the least protection. A deed that offers the **grantee** no warranty as to the status of the property title.

Quitclaim deeds are used to remove a **cloud on title**. (Quiet a Title)

16. **HUD Form 1- Uniform Settlement Statement**: A government form which itemizes services and all fees charged to the borrower by the lender or mortgage broker/banker and the real estate broker when a consumer is applying for a loan for the purpose of purchasing or refinancing real estate.

17. **Independent Contractor**- 90% of his earnings (a very high percentage) and income is based on sales production.

18. **Civil Rights Act of 1866**- Prohibits property discrimination based on race.

19. **HUD**- The enforcement agency that oversees **fair housing**. A person has one year to file a housing complaint with **HUD**. If a person waits too long to file (after one year), the doctrine of **laches** kicks in and the aggrieved party is locked out of suing. Some people will take a housing complaint to the federal courts instead of **HUD** because in a federal court, damages (dollar value) from the violating party are not capped.

20. AIDS and a convicted drug user are protected under disability.

21. A handicapped tenant may make **Reasonable Alterations or Accommodations** to his rental. It must be done at the tenant's expense but before the tenant vacates the property, the property must be returned to the original condition. The least likely thing a tenant will put back to its original condition are grab bars put into the shower tile. It will do more damage to remove them than to leave them there.

22. **Familial Status**- A protected class that includes women who are pregnant or have children under 18. It's the status of the family. An unmarried woman with kids is protected. Children under 18 are protected. An owner of an apartment complex cannot segregate families with children into certain buildings within a complex. A landlord cannot decide to NOT rent to an unmarried woman with kids or a pregnant woman based on **Familial Status** unless the landlord/owner lives in the 1-4 unit building. Senior complexes built for a segment of the population who are 55 years of age and older may discriminate based on familiar status. A senior complex can choose not to rent to someone based on the age of the children. When the senior complex bases the decision not to rent because of familiar status, **Fair Housing Laws** protect the senior complex.

23. **Title VIII**- The Federal Fair Housing Act of 1968

24. **EHO Poster- The Equal Housing Opportunity Poster** must be conspicuously displayed in all real estate, appraising and lender offices.

If the poster is not conspicuously displayed, it is considered, **"Prima Facie Discrimination"**.

25. **62 years and older**- Senior Housing exempt from **familial status** discrimination.

26. **Blockbusting**- Trying to Induce owners to sell their property because minorities or any protected group is moving into their neighborhood. Also called **Panic Peddling**.

27. **Redlining**- when a lending institution decides NOT to lend money within a neighborhood "in transition" or a neighborhood with a heavy population of a protected class.

28. **Steering**- when an agent shows minority buyers properties only in certain neighborhoods instead of the entire market. **Steering** is when an agent shows a buyer properties only in neighborhoods where the agent believes the buyer should live.

29. **Federal Trade Commission- FTC** the agency that enforces **Regulation Z and Truth in Lending**.

30. **Regulation Z**- Disclosure of the true cost of credit. Includes **Trigger Term**s and a **Three Day Right of Rescission**.

31. **Annual Percentage Rate**- A **Trigger term**, which must be, clearly stated for comparative purposes for the true the cost of loans.

From Barbie, Sharon and Ashlynne

1. **Trigger Terms**- The amount or percentage of any down payment, the number of payments or period of repayment, the amount of any payment and the amount of any finance charge.

2. **ECOA – Equal Credit Opportunity Act**. Legislation preventing discrimination in lending.

3. Religious organizations and other private clubs may be allowed to discriminate under certain circumstances. Considered a Private Club)

4. **Special Agent**- A listing-Seller's Agent or a Buyer's Agent. They are hired to do one specific act.

5. **Estate for years**- a lease with a definite beginning and a definite end. It doesn't have to be a year. It can be three days, two days, one week, six months or any amount of time along as it has a definite beginning and a definite end.

6. **General agent**- is a property manager. A property manager's primary responsibility is to get the highest net return for the property owner. The property manager doesn't give the rent collected to the owner but gives it instead to his broker. Hired to do general duties.

7. **Cooperative- Co-op**: A form of stock ownership or ownership in **stock** that allows for a person to occupy a unit. The owner/tenant is a stockholder. It is personal property. A **Co-op** is the only personal property that has a **property condition disclosure statement** before the transfer to a new owner of the **stock.**

8. **Condominium- Fee-simple** (the highest form of ownership) with an ownership share in the common elements. It's a condo. You own your unit and what's in it. You also own a portion of the common areas like the pool, elevators, hallways, and entryway.

9. **Net lease**- when a tenant pays all or some of the landlord's operating expenses.

10. **Percentage Lease**- Used for shopping centers or stores, sometimes restaurants. The rent includes a percentage of the tenant's sales receipts. An example would be "$2000 a month plus 2 percent of the store's sales total".

11. **Mission Statement**- "To exceed our customer's expectations."

12. **Time Shares**- Multiple owners owning the same parcel of real estate with a different ownership interest and at different time intervals. Title is owned as **Tenants in Common/Tenancy in Common**.

13. **Emblements**- Crops that require annual planting and harvesting. Examples are corn, peas, beans, tomatoes, cucumbers, and squash.... They are personal property. If a tenant farmer has planted his yearly crops but gets evicted before the crops are ready for harvest, the landlord cannot touch the crops. The crops of the evicted farmer tenant's are his personal property. The farmer is allowed to maintain the crops and harvest them. A farmer is entitled to the fruits of his labor.

14. **Sub-divider**- An investor who buys undeveloped land and divides it into smaller tracts. Each tract is then recorded. Often a sub-divider will obtain a **blanket mortgage** that covers his entire property. When he subdivides the property and would like to sell an individual parcel, the investor will get a **Partial Release Claus**e from the lender in order to sell that parcel.

15. **Zoning Ordinance**- Defines how property in specific geographic zones can be used regulates lot sizes, density, height structures and purpose. Government Law. **Police Power**.

Real Estate Training Institute – Pre Exam Workbook

From Terry, Shawn, Tammy, Edna and Marie

1. **UCC- Uniform Commercial Code** regulates the sale of personal property apart from the real estate being sold when a business transfers ownership. Personal property should be transferred with a **Bill of Sale**.

2. **Chattel**- French word for cattle. Cattle are movable. **Chattel** is **personal property**.

3. **Leverage**- using other people's money. Financing by using borrowed funds.

4. **Capital gain**- Used for your personal residence. Must have lived there for at least two years out of the last five. Capital Gains exclusion is: **$250,000** for a single person and **$500,000** for a married couple. Capital Gains are computed on the difference between the net adjusted basis (cost) and the selling price.

5. **Land**- Real Estate, Real Property. Land does not depreciate.

6. **Corporation**- A legal entity that never dies. "**Double Taxation**."

7. **S. Corporation**- Ownership is limited to 35 shareholders. "A Pass Through Company."

8. **General Partnership**- Every partner has a personal liability.

9. **Limited Partnership**- The Limited Partners has limited liability in the amount of their investment. The **General Partners** have unlimited liability.

10. **Franchise**- Examples are Century 21, Tarbell, Keller Williams, Prudential. Members pay a percentage of their earning to the franchise for expertise and/or advertising and branding.

11. **100% commission plan**- a **landlord broker** that makes his money on desk fees. A **landlord broker** is renting out the space in the office but in exchange to the agent, the agent is allowed to keep 100% of his earned commissions.

12. **Habendum clause**- "To have and to Hold" A granting clause in the deed.

13. **Independent Contractor**- At least 90% of his income must be made by commissions and sales. Has an agreement with his broker to produce certain results without being told how to do the job. The broker cannot offer a health insurance or retirement plan. Will get a **1099misc** from his broker yearly with the amount of commission received from the broker in order to pay his taxes.

14. **Employee**- At least 90% of his income must come from salary and wages. Can be told what to do and exactly how to do it.

15. A **Broker** is responsible for the direct supervision of a brokerage firm. A broker is **responsible for the real estate activities of his salespeople.** A broker is not responsible for everything his salespeople do in their day-to-day lives.

16. **Sherman Antitrust Act**- Commission cannot be fixed amongst brokers. Brokers cannot get together and boycott another broker out of business. Cannot fix fees with other brokerages. Prohibits price fixing.

17. **ADA- American with Disability Act**- Prohibits discrimination based on disability. An office with 15 or more employees must be accessible to those with disabilities.

18. A **good training program** creates a **high morale** in the brokerage.

19. **Unlicensed Personal Assistant's** duties must be defined in the **broker's policy and procedures manual**. An unlicensed personal assistant can refer buyers and seller to their broker. They can carry paper. Most times they are receptionists and part of their job is to answer the phone. If a buyer or seller asks to speak to a salesperson, the unlicensed personal assistant can refer that person to his broker.

20. **Commingling**- mixing the broker's personal funds with the client trust account funds.

21. **Trust Account– Escrow Account**- A checking account (demand account), non-interest bearing. The funds deposited belong to the clients and customers. **Trust Account Funds** are not the assets of the broker.

22. **Company dollar**- Gross income minus all commissions. (Basically it's what's left over after the agents are paid.) After finding the Company Dollar, then the bills are paid.

23. **Desk Cost**- Even though it's called "Desk Cost or Desk Fee", it is not based on the amount of desks in the office. It is based on the amount of salespeople. The broker divides the operating expenses (rent, gas, electric, business license etc.) by the number of active salespeople.

24. **CMA- Comparative Market Analysis**- Benefits the Seller. It helps agents determine a price range for a property to list. It doesn't determine value. Only an appraisal can determine value.

25. **Substitution**- what an appraiser uses to determine value by comparing equally desirable substitutes nearby.

26. **Diminishing Returns**- The point in time when improvements can't add value to a property anymore. The property is over built or over improved.

27. **Assemblage**- The act of assembling or putting together contiguous lots to

Real Estate Training Institute – Pre Exam Workbook

increase the value of the combined property.

28. **Plottage**- The increased value from assemblage. The result of assemblage. **Assemblage creates plottage.**

29. **Progression**- the least expensive or smallest home in the neighborhood made up of larger and more expensive homes. Regression is the largest and most expensive home in a neighborhood containing smaller and less expensive homes.

30. **Land**- Land does not depreciate.

31. **Physical Deterioration**- a leaky roof, a cracked foundation wall, worn out window tracks.

32. **Functional Obsolescence**- a four bedroom two story home with one bathroom. A home with three bedrooms on the second floor and one bathroom on the first floor.

33. **External Obsolescence**- Loss in value due to an airport expanding it's runway and now planes fly over a neighborhood at a low altitude. A deteriorating neighborhood with UN maintained buildings.

34. **Capitalization**- A investors return rate.

35. **Tenancy at Sufferance**– A tenant possessing a property without the landlord's consent. An eviction is on the way. The landlord wants the tenant gone. The landlord is suffering.

36. **GRM**- Sold price divided by monthly rents.

37. **Amenities**- Value is enhanced by a home's proximity to bike trail, a community pool or a beautifully shaded park. Things OFF the property....Amen.

38. **Comparable**- a name for sold home used in an appraisal or a CMA. The comparable gets adjusted when comparing it to the subject property.

From Joe, Rico and Eddie

1. A **Client** is someone you work for.

2. A **Customer** is someone you work with.

3. **Joint Tenancy**- The last one living owns in severalty. **JTWROS**: Joint Tenancy with Rights of Survivorship.

4. **Co-operative** owners are shareholders of the corporation.

5. **Civil rights act of 1866** prohibits discrimination on race.

6. **General lien vs. specific lien**.

7. **Undue influence**.

8. When an agent wants to do a **CMA** in a neighborhood of mostly foreclosures he will take the actual arm's length (or more) **sales comparisons** from the bank selling to a party.

9. **Regression vs. Progression**.

10. Leases and agreements must be in writing to bring action. Everything in real estate has to be in writing to be enforceable in court according to the **Statue of Frauds**.

11. When **title** is granted in a **life estate** the person will own the property until he dies.

12. When a seller accepts an offer from a buyer who needs to sell his or her own home first, to keep from being caught in a lengthy transaction the seller can add an escape clause to the contract.

13. A condo complex can't **eminent domain** a house to expand parking.

14. If an incompetent person signs a lease, the lease is void.

Real Estate Training Institute – Pre Exam Workbook

From Stephanie, Lebron and Jill

1. When a tenant vacates their lease because the landlord will not fix the heat, it is **constructive not**ice or **constructed eviction**.

2. **Holdover tenancy**.

3. **Fair housing act of 1968**.

4. An owner's death kills the listing.

5. **Remainder- remainder man-** in a life estate.

6. **Reversion** in a life estate.

7. **Commission** is negotiable.

8. **Subletting**.

9. There can be **discount points** on a **VA** or **FHA** loan.

10. Capital gains exclusion- single at **250,000** and married **500,000**.

11. **Squatters rights-** open, notorious and hostile..... Time = **Adverse Possession.**

12. Public assistance is considered when deciding to rent to someone.

13. An **easement** terminates with the **merger of titles**.

14. **Liquidated Damages- Earnest Money** can become **Liquidated Damages** if the buyer **breaches** the **Purchase Contract**.

15. **Tenancy for years-** lease begins and ends on definite dates.

16. When a landlord does not buy insurance and instead he installs a platform to raise the air conditioner, he is **controlling the ri**sk.

Real Estate Training Institute – Pre Exam Workbook

From Bill, Tylor, Rider and Grant

1. **Equal Credit Opportunity Act** does not allow for discrimination against an old person. **Equal Credit Opportunity Act** does not address interest rates. Banks set their own rates.

2. A man going door-to-door in an older neighborhood and telling the residents that children or a family from another country will be moving into their quiet neighborhood is guilty of **blockbusting/panic peddling**.

3. **Deed Restriction**: Limitation on Use

4. An owner of a property can discriminate if he lives on his 1-4 unit property.

5. **FHA = 3.5% down**.

6. You can have points on both **FHA** and **VA**. Both are assumable. A non-veteran can assume a VA loan.

7. **Home Owners Association– CC and R's**. At the close the buyer will receive additional paperwork.

8. If a local **zoning** law and a **deed restriction** contradict each other which one takes precedence? The stricter rule or law.

9. **Civil Rights Act of 1968** is also known as the Fair Housing Act.

10. A buyer has 10 days to inspect for lead on the property. **Lead Disclosure**.

11. What should an agent tell a buyer if the buyer would like to have a test for radon done? Hire a professional.

12. What should a broker tell a buyer about a house that only flooded once during "the great flood"? Disclose it.

13. **Married couple capital gains: $500,000 – Single $250,000**

14. When a buyer signs an agreement to pay a broker for the broker finding a property for him to buy, it is an **expressed contract** and a **unilateral contract**.

15. What can cancel all contracts? Mutual consent and the acts of all parties.

16. A couple makes an offer and before it was accepted they make another offer on another house. They can either back out of the first offer if it is not accepted or buy both.

17. **Easement by Necessity**– A property cannot be land locked.

18. When **title** is granted in a life **estate** the person will own the property until he dies.

19. When a seller accepts an offer from a buyer who needs to sell their own home first, to keep from being caught in a lengthy transaction the seller can

add an escape clause to the contract or offer the buyer the **First Right of Refusal** if another offer comes in.

20. The seller took the ceiling fan before he moved out; did he have a right to take it? NO sue for **specific performance**.

21. Do not **comingle**.

22. **Principal**- The person or entity that delegates authority in order to create an agency relationship. It's the **Client**.

23. **Delegated authority**- the principal's act that creates agency.

24. **Consent to act**- to create agency the principal delegates authority, and the broker must do this.

25. **Fiduciary**- a type of relationship based on trust and confidence.

26. **Commingling**- Unlawful mixing of the broker's money and his client's funds.

27. **Protection clause**- extends the period of time that a seller agrees to pay a commission.

From Dot, Tatiana and Peter

1. Before extending your patio in the front yard, you should check **set back limits** first.

2. When a **CMA** is done, nearby homes are used for the **comparables**. Not a home in another town, township or city even if the same builder using the same materials built it.

3. Inventory and equipment are personal property. **Personal Property** is transferred by a **"Bill of Sale"**.

4. **Franchises** like Century 21, Tarbell and Prudential have **Volume Advertising**. It is an advantage.

5. When an appraiser is doing an appraisal, he does not use 'land depreciation'.

6. **Avulsion**- a tearing away of land due to a violent event. I.e.; a sweeping swollen river swept away an outcropping of land or an earthquake tore away some land.

7. Who keeps the **Listing Agreement**? The **Seller** and the **Listing Agent**.

8. Who keeps the **Purchase Contract**? Both Seller and Buyer and Both Agents.

9. A **"Purchase Money Mortgage"** is a form of Seller Financing.

10. **Radon Gas** can be Easily Mitigated. It enters the house through the basement.

11. A **trade fixture** is a commercial renter's personal property attached to the landlord's real property. At the end of the lease, the tenant removes the **trade fixture** and takes it with him.

12. The attorney reads the **Abstract of Title**.

13. **Regulation Z** gives the Borrower **three (3) days to rescind** the financing loan if it is based on his primary residence. **Three Day Right of Rescission.**

14. If someone discriminates but they don't know they did because they are just basically ignorant or stupid, it is still a violation.

15. A Fully **Amortized Mor**tgage has the same payment each month with the amount going to interest decreasing monthly and the amount going toward principal each month increasing. No **balloon payment**. It reverses over time.

16. The best way to find or verify an **encroachment** is with a survey. (Hire a surveyor.)

17. An Oak Tree, rock or a man made monument: A landmark and directions used in the measurement of land when using the "**metes and**

bounds" approach. **Point of Beginning or POB.**

18. The area of the country that uses **metes and bounds** are the **original 13 colonies and the older parts of the United States. It might say the original 13 states.**

19. In a house built before **1978,** check for **lead based paint**.

20. Know: **In Severalty, In Common, Joint Tenancy and Entirety.**

21. A. A husband and wife own a property and when the husband died, one third of his interest went to each of his children and one third went to his wife. What form of ownership did he and his wife most likely have? **In Common.**

22. B. A husband and wife own property as **Joint Tenants**. The husband's will gave his interest to his property to his son. Upon his passing, how is **title** held? The wife owns the property In **Severalty**.

23. How does an owner of an apartment complex and a real estate broker enter into an agreement for the broker to manage the property? Through the use of a **Property Management Agreement**.

24. **Zoning** is local government police power. "**State Enabling rights**".

25. A man signed a 5-year lease and in year 3 he died. His sons inherited the property and want to move into the leased property. What is the status of the lease? It's Valid.

26. A broker and her **unlicensed assistant** were travelling to deliver a signed counter offer to their client. They got into a terrible car crash and the broker was rushed to the hospital. What should the unlicensed assistant do? Carry the counter offer to the client before going to the hospital.

27. The primary duty of the **property manager (General Agent)**? The Net Income for the Owner. (Getting leases or Chose the activity that increases income.)

28. A **trust account** is a checking account. A demand Account.

29. Offers and Counteroffers must be delivered ASAP.

30. **Gross Rent Multiplier** = Gross Rent Monthly

31. Pre-payment penalties or the total amount of interest paid does not have to be disclosed with **Regulation Z**.

32. A seller does not have to accept an offer lower than the asking price.

33. Where are loans bought from on the **secondary mortgage market**? Banks. A formal **appraisal** has to be

Real Estate Training Institute – Pre Exam Workbook

done when one bank buys a loan from another.

34. Who does the listing agent owe **fiduciary duties** to? **The Client**.

35. It is illegal for a broker to supply health insurance or a retirement plan to an **independent contractor**. YES and 90% (a high percentage) of his income has to come from sales or commission.

36. The value of a property at **250,000** or more is when an appraiser needs a higher license.

37. An agent does not have to disclose if a felony was committed on a property.

38. How many square feet in an acre? **43560**. (4 old guys driving 35 in a 60.)

39. **Usury** Laws protect the consumer.

40. A woman applied to rent an apartment in a **Senior Complex** (age 55 and above). She was turned down based on the age of her children. In this situation, who does federal **Fair Housing Laws** protect? The Senior Complex.

41. Commission is negotiated. Local boards do not set it.

42. The "**Procuring Cause**" is the person who will get paid in an "**Open Listing**".

43. **Eminent Domain, Condemnation and Just Compensation** are words that go together. One will be in the question and one of the others will be in the answer.

44. Who is the only person that can do "**Inverse/reverse Condemnation**"? The Owner.

45. The deed that gives the least protection is the "**Quit Claim**" Deed.

46. A lender can decline a loan based on the applicant's income. It would not be a violation of **Fair Lending Laws**.

47. **Co-op vs. Condo**. (You have to know the differences.)

48. Keep all records for **3 years**.

49. A **convicted drug dealer** is not protected under federal fair housing laws. A convicted drug user may be protected under the **American with Disabilities A**ct.

50. **FHA** is insured. **DVA** is guaranteed.

51. Banks sometimes will not take a **Deed in Lieu of Foreclosur**e because **junior liens** may need to be paid off.

52. A Listing gent noticed shingles that were broken on the roof. He should **disclose** that defect.

53. A **Buyer's Agent** was told a property had no defects. Upon his inspection, he found several problems. The agent

should **disclose the defects** to his buyer.

54. **E and O Insurance** will not cover an agent who makes a deliberate falsehood or tries to deceive someone on purpose.

55. **A trade fixture** is a renter's personal property attached to the landlord's real property. At the end of the lease, the tenant removes the trade fixture and takes it with him.

Real Estate Training Institute – Pre Exam Workbook

From Penney, Sarah, Linda and Michael

1. Definition of **Points**.

2. Credits and Debits are shown on the **HUD One**.

3. What is listed on the **HUD-1** statement? Choices were property items to be sold, credit/debits of buyer seller…etc. Answer is Credit/Debits

4. Know what **1099 S** and **1099 MISC.**

5. Several questions on the broker relationship with salespersons/independent contractors and clients

6. Two questions on **Regulation Z**.

7. What is the advantage of a **joint-tenancy** when one dies and the other person is left. Avoids probate.

8. **Metes and Bounds** question. = "**Point of Beginning**"

9. Does agent have to tell buyer there was felony on the property? No. It is not a **material fact**.

10. What is caused by decaying material etc……? Answer: **Radon**

11. What term is most closely associated with land being taken for public purposes? **Eminent domain** was not listed. **Condemnation** was listed and the next best choice.

12. **FHA** loan = **3.5% down**. **FHA** is an insurance company. It insures the bank will get its money.

13. **Title insurance** extends to unrecorded instruments.

14. What is the **protection clause** for…(question was much more long-winded than this)? The answer was long and basically described the broker being protected for multiple things.

15. Know at what point a broker earns his commission. When he brings **a ready willing and able buyer who can meet the terms of the listing agreement**.

16. What method is most likely to identify encroachments on a property? Answer: something with "survey".

17. A **Condo** is **real property**.

18. Standing timber is **real property**.

19. Complicated funds question about broker handling funds. Where does a broker send funds to when he can't determine where they belong? Answer: money should go to courts to determine. The form is an INTERPLEADER.

20. Person wants to start business in a residential **zoning** what do they need

32

to get. Answer: **conditional use permit or a variance.**

21. Salesperson's death does NOT kill the deal.

From Snooki, Izzie and Sandra

1. Flood insurance is required when a property is in a **SFHA. Special Flood Hazard Area. (FEMA flood area)**

2. When a large company moves away from a town and takes 3000 jobs with them, the price of homes for sale decreases. **(Supply and Demand)**

3. A real estate licensee with many years of practice became a **real estate counselor** to help people make real estate decisions.

4. A large landowner sold his property to a home developer who plans on **subdividing** it and building single-family residences. The term that best describes either the process or result would be called a **subdivision**.

5. When overbuilding commercial office space continues, the cost of a company renting an office decreases. **(Supply and Demand)**

6. The renter is responsible for insuring his personal property. Renter's Insurance.

7. When farmers and ranchers are afraid the people upstream will be taking too much water and there will be none left for them, they may be protected by **prior appropriation**. Found in the drier areas of the country and the desserts. It is the only water right that can sold away from the deed to the rest of the property.

8. **Immobility** is the **physical characteristic** in which a city, county or state would depend on in order to predict future tax income from property owners.

9. When lumber or bricks are left on a driveway in order for the homeowner to build a new fence, while the products are on the driveway, they are considered **personal property**.

10. **Dower** is woman and **Curtesy** is man.

11. A county airport took several streets of homes in order to expand its runway through the government power of **eminent domain**.

12. When the county took several streets through eminent domain to extend an airport runway, they left one house, which is now experiencing extreme noise and shaking due to the expansion. The homeowner may be able to get the county to take her property through the use of **reverse condemnation**.

13. Mary was granted a life estate for her life. Upon her passing the property will pass to her child. The type of ownership the child has is **remainder. (Remainder man)**

14. When Joe inherited a piece of land from his father, he immediately began digging up the topsoil and sold it to a

landscaping company. He then dug out the gravel and sold it to someone else. He then found clay, dug it out and sold it also. He has a will giving the property to his daughter upon his passing. When he dies his daughter will inherit a big hole in the ground.

15. When a gas company would like to bury its pipes over the property of several homes, they will apply for an **easement in gross**.

16. **Homestead Exemption** may protect a portion of the homeowner's property from unpaid credit card bills.

17. **Home Affordable Modification Program**: Helps homeowners avoid foreclosure by lowering their monthly payment. (Making monthly payments affordable)

18. When a town installs sidewalks, gutters and lighting down a dirt road. The added tax increase levied on the property owners in that city is called a **special assessment**.

19. **Specific lien** is on the property. A **voluntary specific lien** would be financing a swimming pool. An involuntary specific lien would be taxes.

20. A truck driver has an **easement** over his neighbor's property in order to store his large truck when he is not working. The **easement** may be terminated if the man sells his truck and would like to terminate the **easement**. (Or the merging of titles.)

21. Other owners in a **subdivision** with a **homeowners association** are the people who enforce the **CC and R's**.

22. A public limitation on use would be caused by **police power**. (Eminent domain – zoning)

23. The natural forces of **accretion** or when sand is moved from one side to another on a barrier island, the result of the land addition is called **alluvion**.

24. **Adverse Possession** = open, notorious, hostile and continuous possession.

25. Title to property transfers only when the **deed** is **delivered and accepted**.

26. An **executor** of a **devisor's estate** would most likely give the **devisee** a **special warranty deed**.

27. A **notary** does establish that the person signing is who she claims she is. The MOST important thing for a notary to do is to make sure the person is signing **without duress or undue influence**. (Voluntary)

28. **Joint tenancy**: Time, title and interest

29. The disadvantage of a corporation is **double taxation**. When a corporation owns a shopping mall or

high-rise or income property, double taxation still exists.

30. **REIT: A syndication or conglomerate of investors who pool their money** to buy investments such as residential income property, high rises, malls, commercial buildings…

31. Spanish Common Law is usually found in the western states. It would be a **community property state**. Property a couple acquires after marriage is the property of both husband and wife. (Does not include inheritance)

32. Unless specified, partners (brothers) will automatically take title as **tenants in common**.

33. A **corporation** can title as **SEVERALTY or Tenants in Common.**

34. **Joint Tenants and Tenants in Common are co-ownership.**

35. You are not a **REALTOR** until you join the National Association of Realtors. It's trademarked. They subscribe to a Code of Ethics. (**Realtists** are a parallel organization who also subscribes to a code of ethic.)

Real Estate Training Institute – Pre Exam Workbook

CHAPTER 2

ORGANIZED CHAOS

This book is not intended as a substitute for the books and materials used in a classroom or online. It is intended to reinforce what pre licensees have to learn and to reinforce some of the most important topics on the exam.

Easements

Easements "run with the land", meaning that when a property owner sells, the easement automatically transfers with the property.

Easement by Necessity: A person needed access to his property. There can't be a landlocked property. The owner of the property needed access. Needed = Necessity

Easement by Prescription: Time will always be stated. It's when someone has been doing something for a long period of time. It's based on Adverse Possession.

Adverse Possession: A way in which to obtain title through continuous or continual use of a property which is open and notorious (not hiding it) and it would be hostile if the true owner knew about it.

Bob was driving over the northeast corner of Al's property for 10 years. Al knew about it but didn't like it. Al never said anything to Bob. One day, Al decided he wanted to build a home for his daughter on that portion of land that Bob has been driving over. Al asked Bob to stop using his property. Bob took Al to court and was granted permission to continue to drive over Al's property and Al's intention to build his daughter a new home on that section of land had to be abandoned.

Bob was granted by the court an **Easement by Prescription**. When **Easement by Prescription** is the correct answer, the question will have a time factor. (Examples: For a long period of time Sam was…..For several years, Carl was,…..Since 1909 Pam was…..)

Think about someone doing something for a long period of time as becoming addicted to something and now they need a prescription.

An **Easement Appurtenant**: Something in addition to.

Example: Carl owns his home in the lake front community in addition to a non-contiguous easement appurtenant for access to the lake. Or Carl owns his home in addition to a right of way over my neighbor's property in order to access my property. (For ingress and egress.)

Real Estate Training Institute – Pre Exam Workbook

An easement is most like a Right of Way. An easement is recorded and in your deed. An easement can end with the Merging of Titles. Merging of Titles means that one person bought or now owns both properties. An easement can also end if the Dominant Tenement Easement User releases the easement in favor of the owner of the servient tenement.

Dominant vs. Servient

The property the easement is on is the **Servient Tenement**.

The property that benefits from the easement is the **Dominant Tenement**.

(The Servient Tenement is SERVING the Dominant Tenement.)

An easement is an encumbrance on the Servient Tenement.

Encumbrance means "something burdensome" or something that bothers something.

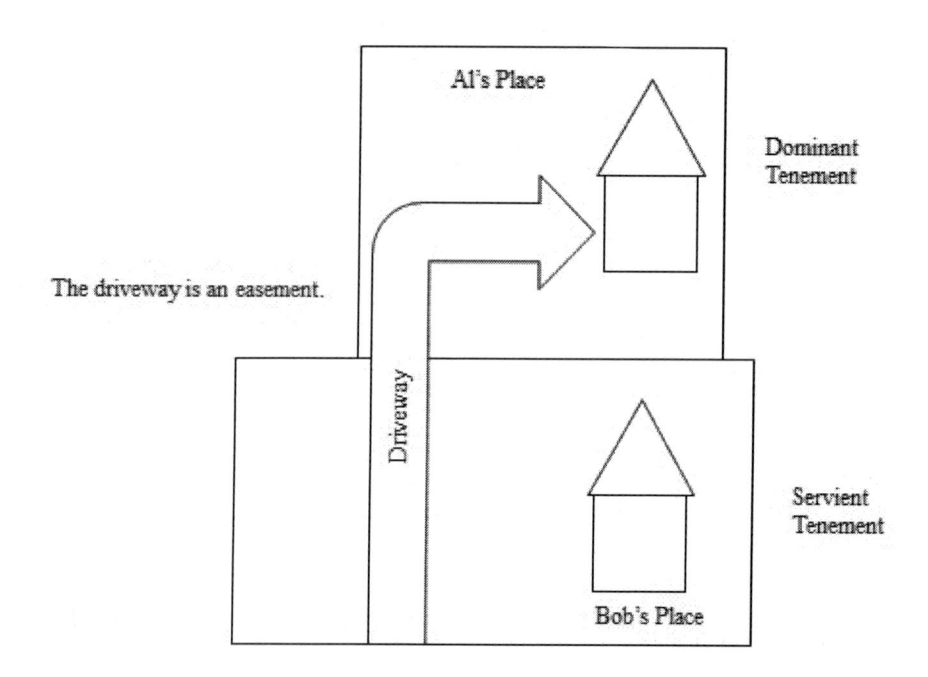

Noncontiguous Easement Appurtenant

If Bob buys a home in a lakefront community but two streets from the lake and is granted an easement over another lakefront property in order to access the lake, It is called a Noncontiguous Easement Appurtenant.

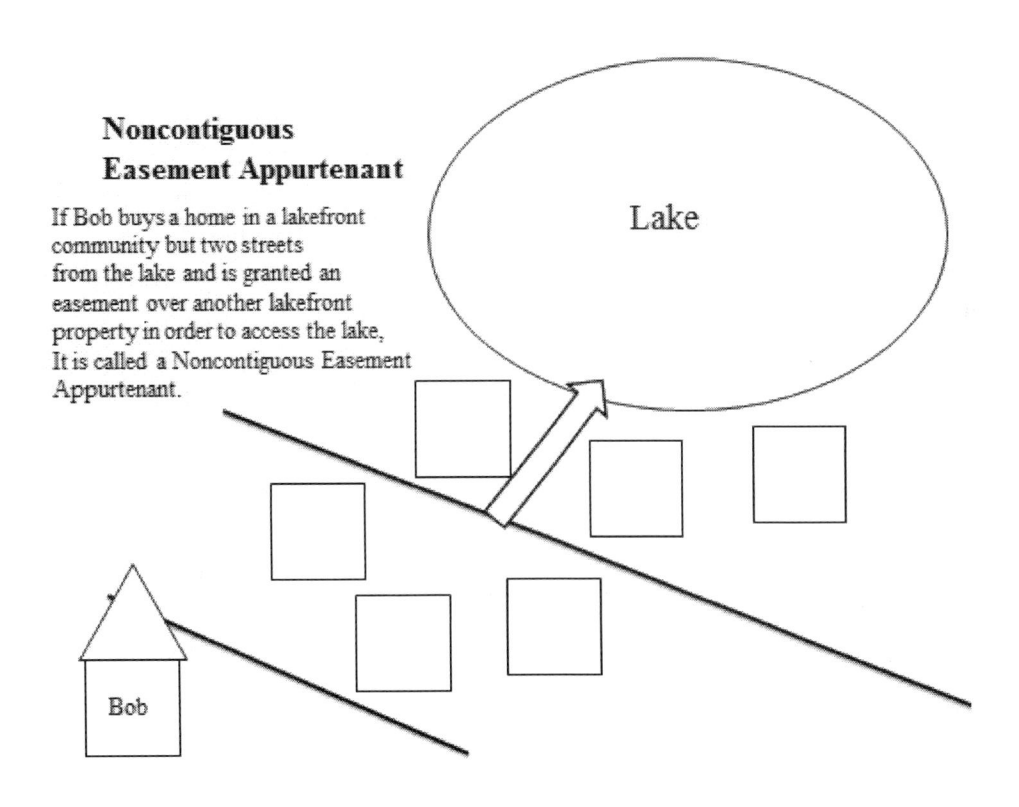

Noncontiguous properties are properties that don't touch each other. They don't share a real property border. They are not side by side.

Real Estate Training Institute – Pre Exam Workbook

An **Easement in Gross** would be used in a situation when a utility company needs to bring electric wires over a long distance. Or a gas company needs to bury a gas line, or some other utility company or drainage system. There is no Dominent Tenement. There are only Servient Tenements.

Gross Easements

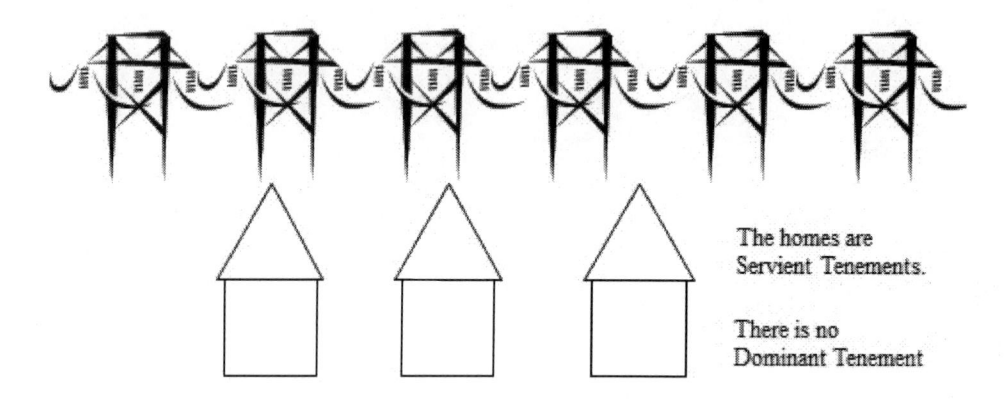

The homes are Servient Tenements.

There is no Dominant Tenement

Land

Economic Characteristics of Land	**Physical Characteristics of Land**
Situs – area preference (location)	Immobility
Scarcity	Indestructability
Permanence	Nonhomogeneous (uniqueness)

Liens

Specific Liens – Against the property	**General Liens**
Real estate taxes	Judgment
Special Assessments – a tax	Court Degree
Mechanics liens	

Real Estate Training Institute – Pre Exam Workbook

Government Control on Real Property (PETE)

Police Power

Eminent Domain

Taxation

Escheat

Police Power vs. Deed Restriction

Police Power	Deed Restriction
Protects the health, safety, welfare and morals of the public.	*A limitation of use upon an individual's real estate.*
Zoning	Obstructing a view of a neighbor
Building codes	How *and* where to build a fence
EPA	Removing trees
	Color homes, pet restrictions, vehicles…………

Eminent Domain – and – Reverse Condemnation

Eminent Domain

The government takes your property for the use of the public.

The owner is paid Just Compensation

through Condemnation.

Reverse Condemnation is when the homeowner is forcing the government to use Eminent Domain to take their property.

A man at the end of an expanded airport runway could try Reverse Condemnation.

Escheat

When a person dies intestate and no heirs can be found, property will escheat to the state. It becomes the property of the state. Land cannot be ownerless.

Taxation

Ad Valorem (according to value)

Special Assessments

Property taxes

Taxes always take priority over other liens. They get paid first.

Real Estate Training Institute – Pre Exam Workbook

Freehold Estates – How to Hold Title (Ownership) *partial list

In Severalty
Tenancy In Common
Joint Tenancy
Tenancy of the Entirety

Severalty: One person – To Sever all Ties (SEVER al ty)

In Common: Co Ownership – Each owner can dispose of his interests without the approval of the other owners. Owners can "will it" to their heirs.

Owners who would like to sell their interest can file a Suit for Partition, allowing them to sell their interests.

Interests can be unequal. **The only form of ownership that can be unequal.**

Timeshare owners all own their title as Tenants in Common

Joint Tenancy: Co Ownership. JTWROS – Joint Tenancy With Rights of Survivorship. The last surviving member will own the property in Severalty. This form of ownership can't be "willed".

Interests are always equal. If there are two owners, it will be 50/50. If there are three owners, each owner will own 1/3. If there are four, each owner will own ¼ and so on.

Each owner can file for a Suit for Partition in order to sell their interests.

The Four Unities of Title are: Title, Time, Interest and Possession are required.

Entirety: Husband and Wife Only. They are treated as one person.

Real Estate Training Institute – Pre Exam Workbook

Testate: Two syllables – Test ate	Intestate: Three syllables – In test ate
Two syllables – With will	Three Syllables – With out will

Testate: Devise
The person who passes and leaves the will is the **Devisor**. (or is the givor)
The person who is left the property is the **Devisee**.
In a will, the Divisor specifically states who is going to get what.
Probate. Before the Devisees can get anything, probate makes sure all the taxes are paid first.

Intestate: Property passes by **Descent and Distribution**. If no heirs can be found, real estate will **escheat** to the state because land can-not be ownerless.

Water Rights

Riparian
Littoral
Prior Appropriation

Riparian: access to and use of the water. rivers and streams
Runs with the land. (Meaning it stays with the deed when the property is sold.)

Littoral: Large lakes and ocean. NAVIGABLE Ownership of the property is up to the high tide water mark.

Ownership to the mean high tide mark. When the tide is low, the public is allowed to walk between your property and the ocean.

Runs with the land. (It stays with the deed when the property is sold.)

Prior Appropriation: The right to use water is controlled by the state. Usually found in the drier areas or deserts.

The rights can be sold seperatly away from the land.

Prior Appropriation: (The First in Use and Beneficial Purpose.)

If farmers believe that the new farmer up stream will be taking too much water out of a stream leaving no water for the downstream farmers, they can be granted Prior Appropriation. (First in Use will limit or stop the upstream farmer from taking water.)

OR – OR - OR is the GIVOR

EE - EE – EE is the Gimmee – Gimmee – Gimmee the Propertee

OR – OR – OR – is the Givor	EE – EE – EE is the Gimmee the Propertee
Grantor	Grantee
Vendor	Vendee
Lessor	Lessee
Optionor	Optionee
Mortgagor	Mortgagee

Grantor: The Giver on the Deed. The Grantor signs the Deed – The Seller

Vendor: The person who is offering something for sale.

Lessor: The person who grants a lease. The Landlord. The givor.

Optionor: The person who grants an option.

Mortgagor: The person making the payment. The givor of the payment.

Grantee: Gimmee the Deed. The Buyer.

Vendee: The purchaser – Gimmee the Propertee.

Lessee: The person to who the lease is granted. The Tenant.

Optionee: The person who holds the option.

Mortgagee: The entity that takes back the propertee if the Mortgagor stops making the payment

Real Estate Training Institute – Pre Exam Workbook

If It Doesn't Say
<u>Right</u>
Then It's Wrong For You

Listings

Exclusive; An exclusive listing agreement where the Seller hires only one agent but reserves the right to sell it herself without having to pay the agent a commission. An agent may not be paid at all if the seller procures the buyer.

Exclusive Right: An exclusive listing agreement whereas the agent will get paid no matter who procures the buyer. You always get paid even if the Seller sells it herself. (Thus, if it doesn't say RIGHT, then it's wrong for you.)

Open: Any number of agents. The agent that can prove they were the procuring cause is the agent who will be paid.

All listings are **Unilateral Contracts**. (A promise of one person to do something if another person completes an act.) The agent may not procure a buyer but if the agent does bring a <u>ready, willing and able buyer who can meet the terms of the listing agreement</u>, the agent has earned her commission.

When the agent earns her commission by bringing a <u>ready, willing and able buyer who can meet the terms of the listing,</u> the seller is obligated to pay a commission whether the seller decides to sell or not.

A listing is an employment contract. The listing is between the Seller-Client-Principal and the Seller's Agent.

The Seller delegates' authority to the agent and the agent consents to act.

A Listing agreement makes a Seller's Agent a **Special Agent**. A Seller's Agent has been hired to do one specific act. As opposed a Property Manager who is **a General Agent** and hired to do general duties and whose primary responsibility is to get the highest net return for the owner.

Agency

The Offer becomes the Purchase Agreement/Contract once it is accepted. The Purchase Agreement/Contract defines the legal rights of the Buyer and Seller.

The Purchase Agreement/Contract is between the Buyer and Seller.

A counter offer voids the original offer.

Seller

Client – Principal

Seller's Agent

The Seller's Agent owes the Client – Principal Fiduciary Duties. COLD AC They are:

Confidentiality

Obedience

Loyalty

Disclosure

Accountability

Care

The Seller's Agent has earned a commission when he brings a ready, willing and able buyer who can meet the terms of the listing agreement.

The Listing Agreement is between the Seller and the Seller's Agent.

Buyer

Customer

Selling Agent

The Buyer is due Fair and Honest Dealings.

A Customer is not represented.

The Buyer deposits an <u>earnest money</u> deposit when making an offer to show his true intentions to follow through with the transaction.

Once the offer is accepted, the <u>earnest money</u> deposit may become money set aside in case the Buyer <u>breaches</u> the Purchase Agreement. It is called <u>Liquidated Damages</u> and is given to the Seller if the Buyer does in fact breach the Purchase Contract.

A Customer could be a buyer, seller, landlord or tenant.

```
                    Responsible Broker
                        (The Boss)
                   The Broker owns all
                    the listings and
                         deals.
                            |
              ┌─────────────┴─────────────┐
      Agent License.                Broker License.
      Salespeople are              Salespeople are
      Sub Agents of the            Sub Agents of the
          Broker.                      Broker.
```

When a Sub Agent of the Broker gets a listing, the Broker owns the listing. The Broker becomes the Agent for that listing and the Salespeople become the Sub Agent of the Seller.

If a Sub Agent has a listing and decides to move to the office of another Broker, the listing will stay with the original Broker.

The Broker and the Sub Agents have an employment contract that defines what is expected of each party.

The Broker and the Sub Agents work for the Seller/Client/Principal and they work with the Buyer/Customer.

If the Broker in the deal dies, all deals and listings die. The Sub Agents would need to move to another responsible Broker and execute all new contracts and disclosures because one of the parties in the transaction have changed.

If a Sub Agent in a deal dies, it has no effect on any listings or transactions.

The Sub Agents are responsible mainly to their Broker.

A Broker cannot pay another responsible Broker's Sub Agent unless the deal on which the Broker is paying was generated while the Sub Agent was under the direct supervision of that responsible Broker.

A Sub Agent can-not accept any payment or bonus unless it is from the responsible Broker to which their license is held. If a client or customer gives a Sub Agent a bonus, the Sub Agent has to turn that bonus over to her responsible Broker.

A responsible Broker is responsible for the real estate activities of his agents.

Real Estate Training Institute – Pre Exam Workbook

Dual Agency

Dual Agency is when an Agent represents both Buyer and Seller with the written expressed acceptance of both the Buyer and Seller.

The Seller is the Client and the Buyer is the Customer.

Example of a Dual Agency

Broker Bob

Sub Agent Sally – Sally is a Sub Agent of Broker Bob.

Sally got a listing at 1234 Park Street. The listing will belong to Broker Bob.

Sally and the Client/Principal decided to have an Open House on Saturday.

1234 Park Street

On Saturday morning, Broker Bob got a call at his office from a potential Buyer who asked Broker Bob to meet him at 1234 Park Street. Two hours later Broker Bob met the potential Buyer. The potential Buyer loved the property and asked Broker Bob to write the Offer to Purchase.

Who does Broker Bob represent?

Real Estate Training Institute – Pre Exam Workbook

Broker Bob represents the Seller.

The Seller/Principal is due the Fiduciary Duties of: COLD AC

Confidentiality
Obedience
Loyalty
Disclosure
Accountability
Care

The Buyer/Customer is due Fair and Honest Dealings.

When Broker Bob met with the potential Buyer, Broker Bob needed to make his relationship disclosure known to the Buyer.

Broker Bob would need to tell the Buyer, "Don't tell me anything you don't want the seller to know." Or "You should keep to yourself any information you would not like the Seller to know."

Before the Potential Buyer was making the offer, he asked Broker Bob if he knew the lowest price the Seller would accept. Broker Bob cannot disclose that information.

If the potential Buyer tells Broker Bob to make an offer lower than asking price but if it were rejected, he would raise his price to the asking price, what should Broker Bob do? Broker Bob would need to disclose that information to the Seller/Client/Principal.

Broker Bob works _for_ the Seller/Client/Principal and works _with_ the Buyer/Customer.

Legal Descriptions

Metes and Bounds

Rectangular Survey System

Lot and Block (Plat Map)

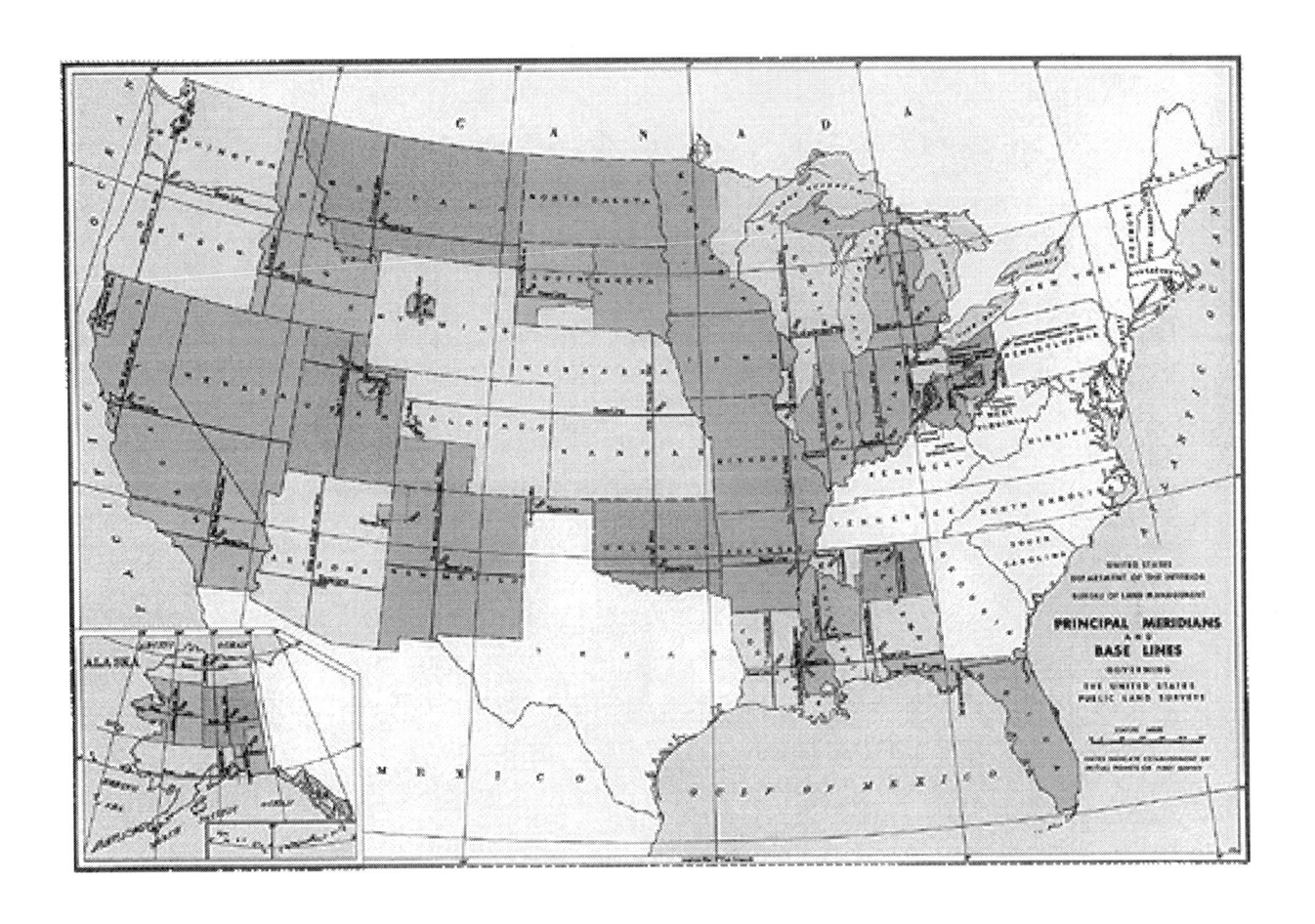

The **Metes and Bounds** system of measurement is used in the Original 13 Colonies, the older parts of the country and Texas.

The other parts of the country use the **Rectangular Survey System**.

Metes and Bounds

Waterway or River

Starting at the old oak tree –POB- walk north until coming to the river – turn right until the old fence – turn right on School Street and come back to the POB.

Point of Beginning

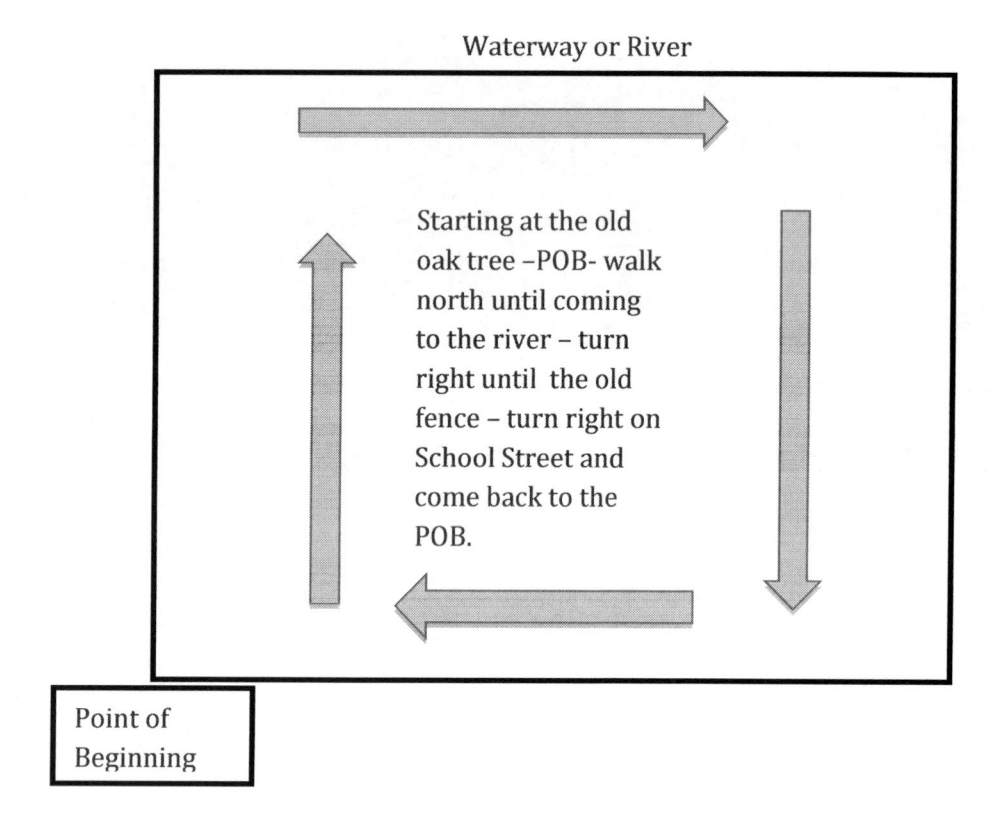

Metes and Bounds starts at the **Point of Beginning**. It can be an old oak tree, a manmade monument, a rock or some other physical feature of the land.

Real Estate Training Institute – Pre Exam Workbook

Rectangular Survey System

The Principle Meridian runs north and south.

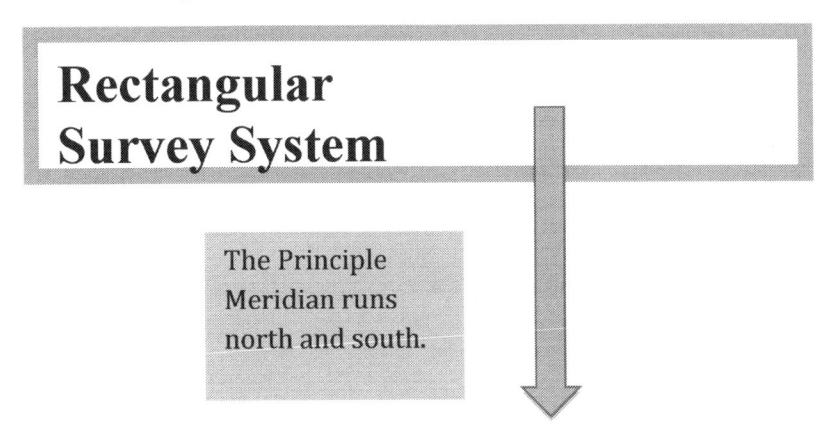

Range Lines run north and south parallel to the Principle Meridian.

EXAMPLE 2
TOWNSHIP DIVIDED INTO SECTIONS

←ONE MILE→					
6	5	4	3	2	1
7	8	9	10	11	12
18	17	16	15	14	13
19	20	21	22	23	24
30	29	28	27	26	25
31	32	33	34	35	36

←ONE MILE→ (left side), SIX MILES (right side), SIX MILES (bottom)

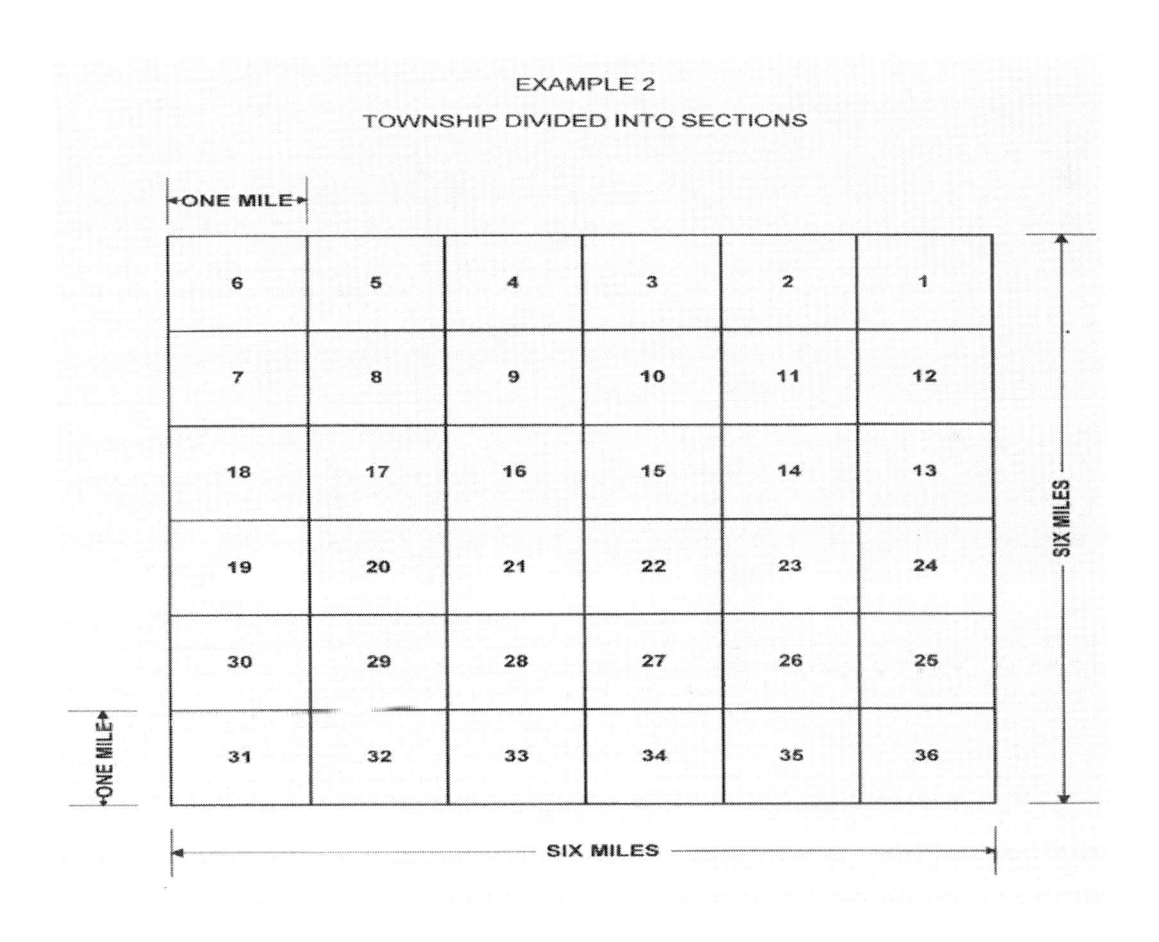

Baselines run east and west.

59

Real Estate Training Institute – Pre Exam Workbook

Range lines run parallel to Meridians.
Township Lines run east and west parallel to the Baseline.

A Township has 36 sections.

Each section is one square mile.

One square mile is 640 acres.

There are 43,560 square feet in each acre.

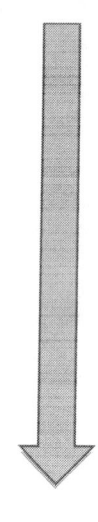

⬇

4 Old Ladies Driving 35 in a 60.

43560

Real Estate Training Institute – Pre Exam Workbook

6	5	4	3	2	1
7	8	9	10	11	12
18	17	16	15	14	13
19	20	21	22	23	24
30	29	28	27	26	25
31	32	33	34	35	36

6	5	4	3	2	1
7	8	9	10	11	12
18	17	16	15	14	13
19	20	21	22	23	24
30	29	28	27	26	25
31	32	33	34	35	36

Every 5th Township shifts over. It is called a Correction Line. It is to offset the curvature of the earth.

6	5	4	3	2	1
7	8	9	10	11	12
18	17	16	15	14	13
19	20	21	22	23	24
30	29	28	27	26	25
31	32	33	34	35	36

Section 16 in each Township is set aside for schools.

Real Estate Training Institute – Pre Exam Workbook

The Principle Meridians and the Baselines in the United States.

Real Estate Training Institute – Pre Exam Workbook

Lot and Block

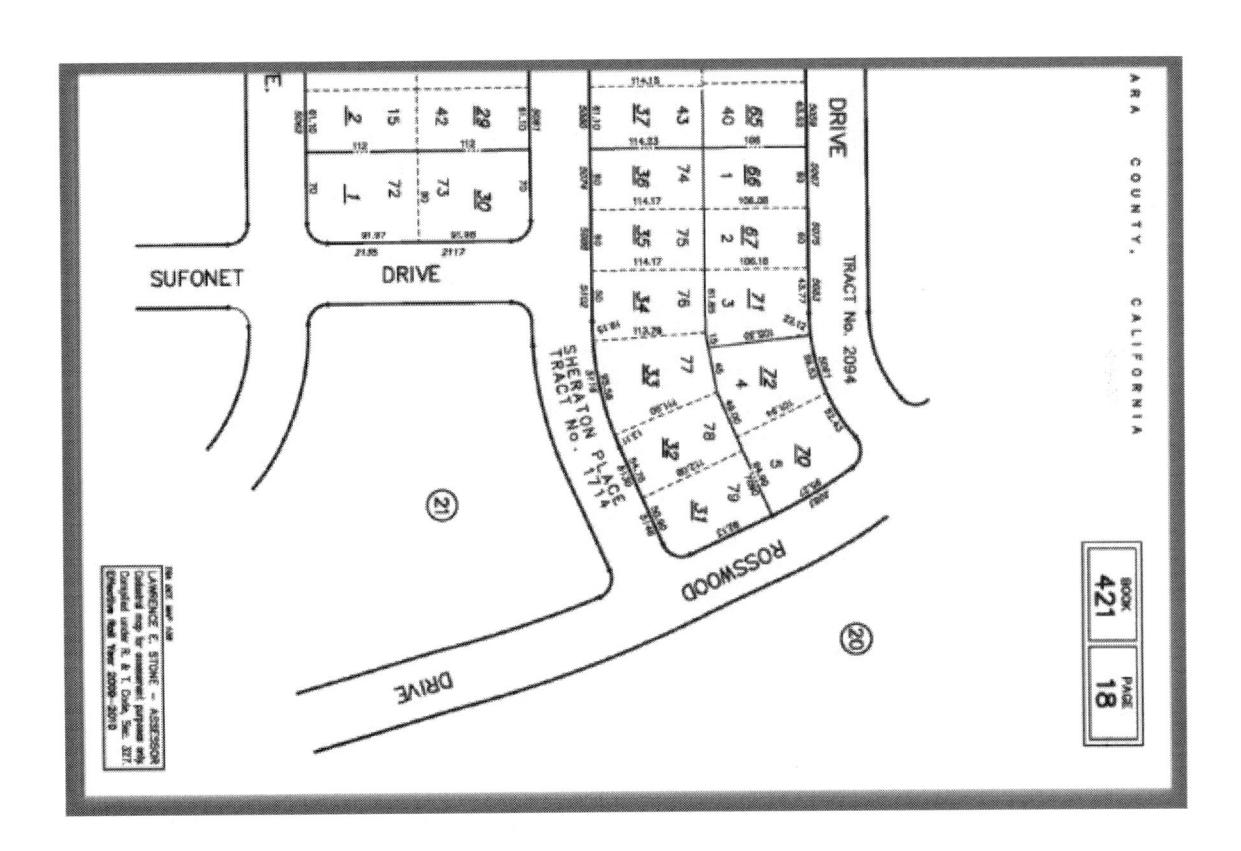

Lots and Block are used is small towns and communities.

A subdivision plat
is prepared by a licensed surveyor or engineer.
The Plat divides the land into
numbered or lettered lots and blocks.

Real Estate Training Institute – Pre Exam Workbook

Regulation Z

The (TILA) Truth in Lending Act is intended to ensure that credit terms are disclosed in a meaningful way so consumers can compare credit terms more readily and knowledgeably.

Protects consumers against inaccurate and unfair credit billing and credit card practices:

- Provides consumers with rescission rights;
- Provides for rate caps on certain dwelling-secured loans;
- Imposes limitations on home equity lines of credit and certain closed-end home mortgages;
- Provides minimum standards for most dwelling-secured loans; and
- Delineates and prohibits unfair or deceptive mortgage lending practices.

The TILA and Regulation Z do not, however, tell financial institutions how much interest they may charge or whether they must grant a consumer a loan.

**From: https://www.fdic.gov/

RESPA
Resl Estate Settlement Procedures Act

The HUD 1 itemizes all charges imposed upon a borrower and seller for a real estate transaction.

Real Estate Training Institute – Pre Exam Workbook

A. Settlement Statement (HUD-1)

OMB Approval No. 2502-0265

B. Type of Loan

1. ☐ FHA	2. ☐ RHS	3. ☐ Conv. Unins.	6. File Number:	7. Loan Number:	8. Mortgage Insurance Case Number:
4. ☐ VA	5. ☐ Conv. Ins.				

C. Note: This form is furnished to give you a statement of actual settlement costs. Amounts paid to and by the settlement agent are shown. Items marked "(p.o.c.)" were paid outside the closing; they are shown here for informational purposes and are not included in the totals.

D. Name & Address of Borrower:	E. Name & Address of Seller:	F. Name & Address of Lender:

G. Property Location:	H. Settlement Agent:	I. Settlement Date:
	Place of Settlement:	

J. Summary of Borrower's Transaction

100. Gross Amount Due from Borrower
101. Contract sales price	
102. Personal property	
103. Settlement charges to borrower (line 1400)	
104.	
105.	

Adjustment for items paid by seller in advance
106. City/town taxes to	
107. County taxes to	
108. Assessments to	
109.	
110.	
111.	
112.	

120. Gross Amount Due from Borrower

200. Amount Paid by or in Behalf of Borrower
201. Deposit or earnest money	
202. Principal amount of new loan(s)	
203. Existing loan(s) taken subject to	
204.	
205.	
206.	
207.	
208.	
209.	

Adjustments for items unpaid by seller
210. City/town taxes to	
211. County taxes to	
212. Assessments to	
213.	
214.	
215.	
216.	
217.	
218.	
219.	

220. Total Paid by/for Borrower

300. Cash at Settlement from/to Borrower
301. Gross amount due from borrower (line 120)	
302. Less amounts paid by/for borrower (line 220)	( )

303. Cash ☐ From ☐ To Borrower

K. Summary of Seller's Transaction

400. Gross Amount Due to Seller
401. Contract sales price	
402. Personal property	
403.	
404.	
405.	

Adjustment for items paid by seller in advance
406. City/town taxes to	
407. County taxes to	
408. Assessments to	
409.	
410.	
411.	
412.	

420. Gross Amount Due to Seller

500. Reductions In Amount Due to seller
501. Excess deposit (see instructions)	
502. Settlement charges to seller (line 1400)	
503. Existing loan(s) taken subject to	
504. Payoff of first mortgage loan	
505. Payoff of second mortgage loan	
506.	
507.	
508.	
509.	

Adjustments for items unpaid by seller
510. City/town taxes to	
511. County taxes to	
512. Assessments to	
513.	
514.	
515.	
516.	
517.	
518.	
519.	

520. Total Reduction Amount Due Seller

600. Cash at Settlement to/from Seller
601. Gross amount due to seller (line 420)	
602. Less reductions in amounts due seller (line 520)	( )

603. Cash ☐ To ☐ From Seller

The Public Reporting Burden for this collection of information is estimated at 35 minutes per response for collecting, reviewing, and reporting the data. This agency may not collect this information, and you are not required to complete this form, unless it displays a currently valid OMB control number. No confidentiality is assured; this disclosure is mandatory. This is designed to provide the parties to a RESPA covered transaction with information during the settlement process.

Previous edition are obsolete

HUD-1

Real Estate Training Institute – Pre Exam Workbook

L. Settlement Charges

700. Total Real Estate Broker Fees

	Paid From Borrower's Funds at Settlement	Paid From Seller's Funds at Settlement

Division of commission (line 700) as follows:
- 701. $ _____ to _____
- 702. $ _____ to _____
- 703. Commission paid at settlement
- 704.

800. Items Payable in Connection with Loan

- 801. Our origination charge $ _____ (from GFE #1)
- 802. Your credit or charge (points) for the specific interest rate chosen $ _____ (from GFE #2)
- 803. Your adjusted origination charges (from GFE #A)
- 804. Appraisal fee to (from GFE #3)
- 805. Credit report to (from GFE #3)
- 806. Tax service to (from GFE #3)
- 807. Flood certification to (from GFE #3)
- 808.
- 809.
- 810.
- 811.

900. Items Required by Lender to be Paid in Advance

- 901. Daily interest charges from ____ to ____ @ $ ____ /day (from GFE #10)
- 902. Mortgage insurance premium for ____ months to ____ (from GFE #3)
- 903. Homeowner's insurance for ____ years to ____ (from GFE #11)
- 904.

1000. Reserves Deposited with Lender

- 1001. Initial deposit for your escrow account (from GFE #9)
- 1002. Homeowner's insurance months @ $ ____ per month $ ____
- 1003. Mortgage insurance months @ $ ____ per month $ ____
- 1004. Property Taxes months @ $ ____ per month $ ____
- 1005. months @ $ ____ per month $ ____
- 1006. months @ $ ____ per month $ ____
- 1007. Aggregate Adjustment -$

1100. Title Charges

- 1101. Title services and lender's title insurance (from GFE #4)
- 1102. Settlement or closing fee $
- 1103. Owner's title insurance (from GFE #5)
- 1104. Lender's title insurance $
- 1105. Lender's title policy limit $
- 1106. Owner's title policy limit $
- 1107. Agent's portion of the total title insurance premium to $
- 1108. Underwriter's portion of the total title insurance premium to $
- 1109.
- 1110.
- 1111.

1200. Government Recording and Transfer Charges

- 1201. Government recording charges (from GFE #7)
- 1202. Deed $ ____ Mortgage $ ____ Release $ ____
- 1203. Transfer taxes (from GFE #8)
- 1204. City/County tax/stamps Deed $ ____ Mortgage $ ____
- 1205. State tax/stamps Deed $ ____ Mortgage $ ____
- 1206.

1300. Additional Settlement Charges

- 1301. Required services that you can shop for (from GFE #6)
- 1302. $
- 1303. $
- 1304.
- 1305.

1400. Total Settlement Charges (enter on lines 103, Section J and 502, Section K)

Comparison of Good Faith Estimate (GFE) and HUD-1 Charges		Good Faith Estimate	HUD-1
Charges That Cannot Increase	HUD-1 Line Number		
Our origination charge	# 801		
Your credit or charge (points) for the specific interest rate chosen	# 802		
Your adjusted origination charges	# 803		
Transfer taxes	# 1203		

Charges That In Total Cannot Increase More Than 10%		Good Faith Estimate	HUD-1
Government recording charges	# 1201		
	#		
	#		
	#		
	#		
	#		
	#		
	#		
	Total		
	Increase between GFE and HUD-1 Charges	$ or %	

Charges That Can Change		Good Faith Estimate	HUD-1
Initial deposit for your escrow account	# 1001		
Daily interest charges $ /day	# 901		
Homeowner's insurance	# 903		
	#		
	#		
	#		

Loan Terms

Your initial loan amount is	$
Your loan term is	years
Your initial interest rate is	%
[illegible]	$ [illegible] ☐ [illegible] ☐ [illegible] ☐ [illegible]
[illegible]	○ No ○ Yes, [illegible]
[illegible]	○ No ○ Yes, [illegible] $
[illegible]	○ No ○ Yes, [illegible] $
[illegible]	○ No ○ Yes, [illegible] $
[illegible]	○ No ○ Yes, [illegible] $ [illegible] years
[illegible]	○ [illegible] ○ [illegible] $ [illegible] ☐ [illegible] ☐ [illegible] ☐ [illegible] ☐ ☐ ☐

Note: [illegible]

[illegible] Page 3 of 3 HUD-1

Real Estate Training Institute – Pre Exam Workbook

Pre-Qualification Letter
ABC Bank of Mississippi
Gopher Toes, Mississippi

1. Sale Price: $300,000.00

2. Down Payment: 20%

3. Interest Rate: 6.5%

4. Terms: 30 years

5. Homeowner's Insurance: $1850.00 per year

6. Property Tax: Assessed at 70% of its purchase price and $2.84 per $100.00.

7. What is the monthly payment?

Real Estate Training Institute – Pre Exam Workbook

1. **Sale Price: $300,000.00**

2. **Down Payment: 20%**

3. **Interest Rate: 6.5%**

4. **Terms: 30 years**

5. **Homeowner's Insurance: $1850.00 per year**

6. **Property Tax: Assessed at 70% of its purchase price and $2.84 per $100.00.**

7. **What is the monthly payment?**

> $300,000 x .8 = $240,000 * Loan Amount
>
> (Use Amortization Table) 6.5 at 30 years = 6.32
>
> $240,000 divided by 1000 – 240
>
> 240 x 6.32 = **$1516.80** * monthly loan payment
>
> 1850 divided by 12 months = **154.16** * insurance per month
>
> 300,000 x .70 = 210,000
>
> 210,000 divided by 100.00 = 2100
>
> 2100 x 2.84 = 5964 divided by 12 months = **497**
>
> **Add: $1516.80 + 154.16 + 497 = 2167.96**

Real Estate Training Institute – Pre Exam Workbook

Amortization Table - Monthly Payment per $1,000 of loan

Rate Per Year	5 years	10 years	15 years	20 years	25 years	30 years	35 years	40 years
5	18.88	10.61	7.91	6.6	5.85	5.37	5.05	4.83
5 1/2	19.11	10.86	8.18	6.88	6.15	5.68	5.38	5.16
6	19.34	11.11	8.44	7.17	6.45	6	5.71	5.51
6 1/2	19.57	11.36	8.72	7.46	6.76	6.32	6.05	5.86
7	19.81	11.62	8.99	7.76	7.07	6.66	6.39	6.22
7 1/2	20.04	11.88	9.28	8.06	7.39	7	6.75	6.59
8	20.28	12.14	9.56	8.37	7.72	7.34	7.11	6.96
8 1/2	20.52	12.4	9.85	8.68	8.06	7.69	7.47	7.72
9	20.76	12.67	10.15	9	8.4	8.05	7.84	7.72
9 1/2	21.01	12.94	10.45	9.33	8.74	8.41	8.22	8.11
10	21.25	13.22	10.75	9.66	9.09	8.78	8.6	8.5
10 1/2	21.5	13.5	11.06	9.99	9.45	9.15	8.99	8.89
11	21.75	13.78	11.37	10.33	9.81	9.53	9.37	9.29
11 1/2	22	14.06	11.69	10.67	10.17	9.91	9.77	9.69
12	22.25	14.35	12.01	11.02	10.54	10.29	10.16	10.09
12 1/2	22.5	14.64	12.33	11.37	10.91	10.68	10.56	10.49
13	22.76	14.94	12.66	11.72	11.28	11.07	10.96	10.9
13 1/2	23.01	15.23	12.99	12.08	11.68	11.46	11.36	11.31
14	23.27	15.53	13.32	12.44	12.04	11.85	11.76	11.72
14 1/2	23.53	15.83	13.66	12.8	12.43	12.25	12.17	12.13
15	23.79	16.14	14	13.17	12.81	12.65	12.57	12.54
15.5	24.06	16.45	14.34	13.54	13.20	13.05	12.98	12.95

Real Estate Training Institute – Pre Exam Workbook

Fair Housing

HUD investigates complaints of housing discrimination based on race, color, religion, national origin, sex, disability, or familial status.
A person has one year to file a fair housing complaint.

Fair Housing Act
Title VIII of the **Civil Rights Act of 1968** (Fair Housing Act), as amended, prohibits discrimination in the sale, rental, and financing of dwellings, and in other housing-related transactions, based on race, color, national origin, religion, sex, familial status (including children under the age of 18 living with parents or legal custodians, pregnant women, and people securing custody of children under the age of 18), and disability.

The Civil Rights Act of 1866, 14 Stat. 27-30, enacted April 9, 1866, was the first United States federal law to define US citizenship and affirmed that all citizens were equally protected by the law.[1] It was mainly intended to protect the civil rights of African-Americans, in the wake of the American Civil War.

Every real estate office and lending office must predominantly display the **Equal Housing Opportunity** poster. If the EHO poster is not predominantly displayed, it is called prima facie discrimination.

Title VIII – 68
Title Eight – Sixty Eight

Real Estate Training Institute – Pre Exam Workbook

Equal Housing Opportunity Notice/Poster

A true and correct copy can be found at
www.hud.gov

U.S. Department of Housing and Urban Development

The EHO notice (poster) must be predominantly displayed in every real estate office or it is considered to be **prima facie discrimination**.

Real Estate Training Institute – Pre Exam Workbook

U. S. Department of Housing and Urban Development

EQUAL HOUSING OPPORTUNITY

We Do Business in Accordance With the Federal Fair Housing Law

(The Fair Housing Amendments Act of 1988)

It is illegal to Discriminate Against Any Person Because of Race, Color, Religion, Sex, Handicap, Familial Status, or National Origin

- In the sale or rental of housing or residential lots
- In advertising the sale or rental of housing
- In the financing of housing
- In the provision of real estate brokerage services
- In the appraisal of housing
- Blockbusting is also illegal

Anyone who feels he or she has been discriminated against may file a complaint of housing discrimination:
    1-800-669-9777 (Toll Free)
    1-800-927-9275 (TTY)
    www.hud.gov/fairhousing

U.S. Department of Housing and Urban Development
Assistant Secretary for Fair Housing and Equal Opportunity
Washington, D.C. 20410

Previous editions are obsolete

form HUD-928.1 (6/2011)

Real Estate Training Institute – Pre Exam Workbook

CHAPTER 3

PSI CANDIDATE INFORMATION

MISSISSIPPI REAL ESTATE CANDIDATE INFORMATION BULLETIN FROM PSI SERVICES, LLC ON STATE TESTING

Can be found and downloaded for free at http://www.mrec.state.ms.us

The PSI Information Bulletin clearly shows the categories that you will be tested on.
A copy of the outline has been copy and pasted here.
The corresponding page numbers are the pages where the answers can be found.
The book Guide to the PSI Real Estate Exam (seventh edition update) will be used.
*If no page number is found, feel free to look it up on the internet.

Property ownership (Salesperson 7 items/Broker 6 items)

1. Classes of property - page 21
a. Real versus personal property
b. Defining fixtures – page 21

2. Land characteristics and legal descriptions - pages 21 -22
a. Physical characteristics of land - 21
b. Economic characteristics of land –21
c. Types of legal property descriptions - page 22
d. Usage of legal property descriptions - page 23
e. Physical descriptions of property and improvements - page 28
f. Mineral, air and water rights

3. Encumbrances and effects on property ownership – page 23
a. Liens (types and priority) - page 23
b. Easements and licenses – page 23-24
c. Encroachments - page 24

4. Types of ownership – page 25
a. Types of estates - *Freehold and non-freehold* – page 25
b. Forms of ownership - page 27
c. Leaseholds – page 28
d. Common interest ownership properties 28
Condominiums, co-operatives and planned unit developments
Condos 28
e. Bundle of rights: possession, control, exclusion, enjoyment and disposition. The bundle of rights is what you have when you own real estate. They are sometimes referred to as sticks. Page 29

Real Estate Training Institute – Pre Exam Workbook

Land use controls and regulations (Salesperson 5 items/Broker 5 items)

1. Government rights in land – page 39
a. Property taxes and special assessments – page 39
b. Eminent domain, condemnation, escheat - page 40
c. Police power - page 40

2. Public controls based in police power – page 40
a. Zoning and master plans – page 40
b. Building codes – page 41
c. Environmental impact reports - page 41
d. Regulation of special land types (floodplain, coastal, etc.) – page 41

3. Regulation of environmental hazards – 42
a. Abatement, mitigation and cleanup requirements page - 42
CERCLA – page 42
b. Restrictions on sale or development of contaminated property
Lead paint disclosure –page 43
c. Types of hazards and potential for agent or seller liability - 44

4. Private controls – page 47
Deed restrictions and homeowners associations
a. Deed conditions or restrictions – page 47
b. Covenants, conditions and restrictions (CC&Rs) – page 47
c. Homeowners association (HOA) regulations – page 47

Valuation and market analysis (Salesperson 8 items/Broker 6 items)

1. Value - *appraisal FIRREA – page 55*
a. Market value and market price - page 56
b. Value - page 56
i. Types and characteristics of value – page 56
ii. Principles of value – page 56
iii. Market cycles and other factors affecting property value – 57

2. Methods of estimating value/appraisal process – 57
a. Market or sales comparison approach – page 57
b. Replacement cost or summation approach - page 58
c. Income approach – page 59
d. Basic appraisal terminology (e.g., replacement versus reproduction cost – page 60
And page
Reconciliation – page 60
Depreciation – page 60
Kinds of obsolescence -)

Real Estate Training Institute – Pre Exam Workbook

3. Competitive/Comparative Market Analysis (CMA) page 60
a. Selecting and adjusting comparables – page 60
b. Contrast CMA and appraisal page 61
Appraisal determines value and a CMA benefits the seller by estimating a range for a selling price
i. Price per square foot – page 61
ii. Gross rent and gross income multipliers - page 61
iii. Capitalization rate - page 61

4. Appraisal practice; situations requiring appraisal by a certified appraiser – page 61 *USPAP, $250,000*

Financing (Salesperson 6 items/Broker 7 items)

1. General concepts – page 71
a. LTV ratios – page 71
points – page 71
origination fees,
discounts - page 71
broker commissions
b. Mortgage insurance (PMI) – page 71
c. Lender requirements, equity, qualifying buyers, loan application procedures 71

2. Types of loans - page 72
and sources of loan money
a. Term or straight loans – page 72
b. Amortized – page 72
partially amortized (balloon) loans - page 72
c. Adjustable rate mortgage (ARM) loans – page 72
d. Conventional versus insured – page 72
e. Reverse mortgages – page 72
equity loans – page 72
subprime – page 72
and other nonconforming loans = page 72
f. Seller/owner financing - 73
purchase money mortgage page 73
g. Primary market page 73
h. Secondary market – page 74
i. Down payment assistance programs – page 74

3. Government programs
FHA, VA, Rural Economic and Community Development, Rural Development and Farm Agency – page 75
a. FHA - 75
b. VA - 75
c. Other federal programs – 75

Real Estate Training Institute – Pre Exam Workbook

4. Mortgages/deeds of trust
owner assisted - 76
a. Mortgage clauses
(assumption - 76
due-on-sale - 76
alienation same as due on sale - 76
acceleration – 76
prepayment - 77
release - 77
b. Lien theory versus title theory - 77
In the United States, slightly more states are "title theory" states than are "lien theory" states. In lien theory states, a mortgage or a deed of trust will create a mortgage lien upon the title to the real property being mortgaged, while the mortgagor still holds both legal and equitable title. In title theory states, a mortgage is a transfer of legal title to secure a debt, while the mortgagor still retains equitable title.
c. Mortgage/deeds of trust and note as separate documents - 777

5. Financing/credit laws - 77
a. Lending and disclosures
regulation z - 77
i. Truth in lending -
ii. RESPA - 78
closing statement – settlement sheet
iii. Equal Credit Opportunity 78
ECOA – 78
b. Fraud and lending practices - 78
i. Mortgage fraud - 78
ii. Predatory lending practices (risks to clients) - 79
iii. Usury lending laws - 79
iv. Appropriate cautions to clients seeking financing
Real Life Situations – graduated payment
Pre payment penalties........ 79
Regulation Z 79

General principles of agency (Salesperson 10 items/Broker 11 items)

1. Nature of agency relationships – 89
Principal - 90
a. Types of agents and agencies 90
special - 90
general - 90
designated - 96
subagent, sub agency - 91
etc.)
b. Nonagents (transactional/facilitational) - 91

Real Estate Training Institute – Pre Exam Workbook

c. Fiduciary responsibilities – COALD or COLD AC – page 91

2. Creation and disclosure of agency and agency agreements (general, not state specific) – 91
a. Agency and agency agreements 91
b. Disclosure when acting as principal or other conflict of interest – 92

3. Responsibilities of agent/principal – *COLD AC or COALD*
Fiduciary Duties – Fiduciary Relationship - 92
a. Duties to client/principal (buyer, seller, tenant or landlord) 92
b. Traditional common law agency duties; effect of dual agency on agent's duties * drawn out on board 92

4. Responsibilities of agent to customers and third parties, including disclosure, honesty, integrity, accounting for money - 93

5. Termination of agency Page 94
a. Expiration 94
b. Completion/performance 94
c. Termination by force of law 94
d. Destruction of property/death of principal 94
e. Mutual agreement 94

Mandated disclosures (Salesperson 8 items/Broker 9 items)

1. Property condition disclosure - 103
a. Property owner's role regarding property condition – 103
b. Licensee's role regarding property condition – 103

2. Warranties – *103*
a. Purpose of home or construction warranty programs 103
b. Scope of home or construction warranty programs - 104
3. Need for inspection and obtaining/verifying information - 104
a. Explanation of property inspection process and appropriate use - 104
b. Agent responsibility to inquire about "red flag" issues - 104
c. Responding to non-client inquiries 104

4. Material facts related to property condition or location - 105
a. Land/soil conditions 105
b. Accuracy of representation of lot or improvement size, encroachments or easements affecting use
c. Pest infestation, toxic mold and other interior environmental hazards – 105
mold - 105
d. Structural issues such as roof, gutters, downspouts, doors, windows, foundation 105
e. Condition of electrical and plumbing systems, and of equipment or appliances that are fixtures 106
f. Location within natural hazard or specifically regulated area, potentially uninsurable property 105

Real Estate Training Institute – Pre Exam Workbook

g. Known alterations or additions

5. Material facts related to public controls, statutes of public utilities
a. Zoning and planning information - 107
b. Boundaries of school/utility/taxation districts, flight paths -107
c. Local taxes and special assessments, other liens - 107
d. External environmental hazards - 107
e. Stigmatized/psychologically impacted property - 108
Megan's Law issues - 108

Contracts (Salesperson 11 items/Broker 12 items)

1. General knowledge of contract law - 115
a. Requirements for validity - 115
b. When contract is considered performed/discharged – 115
c. Assignment and novation - 116
d. Breach of contract and remedies for breach -116

2. Contract clauses – 116

3. Listing agreements - 117
a. General requirements for valid listing - 117
b. Exclusive listings - 117
c. Non-exclusive listings – *open listing - 117*

4. Buyer/tenant representation agreements, including key elements and provisions of buyer and/or tenant agreements - 117

5. Offers/purchase agreements - 118
a. General requirements - 118
b. When offer becomes binding (notification) *118*
c. Contingencies - 118
d. Time is of the essence – 118

6. Counteroffers/multiple counteroffers -1119
a. Counteroffer cancels original offer 119
a counter offer voids the offer
b. Priority of multiple counteroffers 119

7. Leases – 119
a. Types of leases, e.g., percentage, gross, net, ground -119
b. Lease with obligation to purchase or lease with an option to purchase - 119

8. Other real estate contracts - 119
installment contract/contract for deed/land contract
a. Options - 119

Real Estate Training Institute – Pre Exam Workbook

b. Right of first refusal 120

Transfer of title (Salesperson 5 items/Broker 5 items)

1. Title insurance - 129
a. What is insured against - 129
b. Title searches, title abstracts, chain of title - 129
c. Cloud on title, suit to quiet title 129

*The term **cloud on title** refers to any irregularity in the chain of title of property (usually real property) that would give a reasonable person pause before accepting a conveyance of title. A cloud on title reduces the value and marketability of property because any prospective buyer aware of the cloud will know that they are buying the risk the grantor may not be able to convey good title. Often, the discovery of a cloud on title will provide the grantee a reason to back out of a contract for the sale of real property.*
*Examples of clouds on title include a property's address being misspelled in a deed conveying title, a mortgage lien whose repayment hasn't been officially recorded, a deed which has been signed but hasn't been properly recorded, an easement that has not been properly recorded, unpaid property taxes, a failure to transfer property rights (such as mineral rights) to a former owner of the property, and a pending lawsuit before a court of law over ownership to the property. A cloud on title is generally considered synonymous with a **title defect**.*
The usual remedy for a cloud on title is to file a civil action to quiet title.
An **action to quiet title** is a lawsuit brought in a court having jurisdiction over property disputes, in order to establish a party's title to real property, or personal property having a title, of against anyone and everyone, and thus "quiet" any challenges or claims to the title.

2. Deeds – 130
a. Purpose of deed, when title passes – *evidence of title* – 130
b. Types of deeds (general warranty, special warranty, quitclaim) and when used - 130
c. Essential elements of deeds - *Deed Requirements* - 130
d. Importance of recording - 131

3. Escrow or closing; tax aspects of transferring title to real property – 131
a. Responsibilities of escrow agent - 131
b. Prorated items 131
c. Closing statements/HUD- 132
d. Estimating closing costs 132
e. Property and income taxes: Ad Valorem taxes are the property taxes. It means according to value. A special assessment is a tax. Only the people who benefitted by the improvement pay the special assessment. 132
1099 S - 1099Misc -
f. 1031 exchanges - 132

4. Special processes 133
a. Foreclosure/short sale – 133
Deficiency Judgment 133
b. Real estate owned (REO) 133

Practice of real estate (Salesperson 12 items/Broker 12 items)

Real Estate Training Institute – Pre Exam Workbook

1. Trust/escrow accounts (general, not state specific) - 141
a. Purpose and definition of trust accounts, including monies held in trust accounts - 141
b. Responsibility for trust monies, including commingling/conversion
The broker is responsible for trust funds at all times. Trust finds are clients and customer funds. Trust funds must be deposited into a trust/escrow account by the close of the next business or banking day once there has been a mutually acceptable contract between the buyer and the seller.

2. Federal fair housing laws - 141
a. Protected classes - 141
i. Covered transactions - 141
ii. Specific laws and their effects 141
b. Compliance 141
i. Types of violations and enforcement 142
ii. Exceptions - 142

3. Advertising and technology – 146
a. Incorrect "factual" statements versus "puffing" 146
Puffing can lead to misrepresentation
i. Truth in advertising -146 trigger terms on 146
ii. Fair housing issues in advertising 146
b. Fraud, technology issues - 146
i. Uninformed misrepresentation versus deliberate misrepresentation (fraud) 147
E and O does not include intentional misrepresentations
Uniformed misrepresentation – an agent is responsible for actual damages
ii. Technology issues in advertising and marketing
reg z - 146

4. Agent supervision – 148
a. Liability/responsibility for acts of associated licensees and employees 148
b. Responsibility to train and supervise associated licensees and employees
The responsible broker is responsible for the real estate activities of his agents. 148

5. Commissions and fees 149
a. Procuring cause/protection clauses 149
Procuring Cause: The agent that procures the buyer gets a commission.
The Protection clause is in the Listing Agreement whereas the Seller agrees to pay the Broker if the seller sells the property to someone the agent introduced the buyer to within a certain amount of time.
b. Referrals and other finder fees 149

6. General ethics - 149
a. Practicing within area of competence 150
b. Avoiding unauthorized practice of law – You can't give legal advice. Can-not be a conveyancer

7. Antitrust laws - 150
a. Antitrust laws and purpose - 150
b. Antitrust violations in real estate - 150

Real Estate Training Institute – Pre Exam Workbook

Real estate calculations (Salesperson 6 items/Broker 4 items)

1. Basic math concepts 159
a. Area
b. Loan-to-value ratios
c. Discount points
d. Equity
e. Down payment/amount to be financed

2. Calculations for transactions, including mortgage calculations

3. Property tax calculations

4. Prorations (utilities, rent, property taxes, insurance, etc.) -
a. Commission and commission splits
b. Seller's proceeds of sale
c. Transfer tax/conveyance tax/revenue stamps
d. Amortization tables - handout
e. Interest rates
f. Interest amounts
g. Monthly installment payments
h. Buyer qualification ratios

5. Calculations for valuation
a. Competitive/comparative market analyses (CMA)
b. Net operating income
c. Depreciation - land does not depreciate
d. Capitalization rate
e. Gross rent and gross income multipliers (GRM, GIM)

Specialty areas (Salesperson 2 items/Broker 3 items)

1. Subdivisions, including deed restrictions - 189
2. Commercial, industrial and income property - 189
a. Types of leases - 189
b. Trade fixtures - *commercial tenant personal property attached to the landlords real property.*
c. Accessibility – ADA 190
d. Tax depreciation – *straight line method of depreciation – business property*
e. 1031 exchanges - 190
f. Trust fund account - Client funds 190

Real Estate Training Institute – Pre Exam Workbook

CHAPTER 4

National Exams

Exam One ***This is one of the finals.

USE ANSWER SHEETS – DO NOT WRITE the answers on this exam
THIS IS A FINAL EXAM. You will need to get 90% correct.

1. A written agreement or contract between a buyer and seller when the buyer wants to buy and the seller is wanting to sell, after a meeting of the minds is called?
1. A BPO.
2. An appraisal.
3. A contract.
4. A disclosure agreement.

2. An appraiser must be licensed or certified to handle Federally related work on residential, residential income, commercial and all other real estate properties valued at
1. $1,000,000.
2. $550,000.
3. $250,000.
4. $525,000.

3. Which of the following homeownership costs and expenses may be deducted on Federal Income Taxes?
1. Repairs to the exterior building, assessments and purchasing fees.
2. Cost of purchase including commissions paid premiums on title insurance and deed encumbrances.
3. Mortgage loan origination fees, mortgage loan interest and local property taxes.
4. Repairs, insurance premiums and interest.

4. Which type of ownership is most often used for a timeshare?
1. Stock Cooperative.
2. Tenancy in common.
3. Tenancy in severalty.
4. Joint.

5. How is title held when a person owns a cooperative?
1. Tenancy in common.
2. Tenancy by the entirety.
3. Joint tenancy.
4. Stock.

Real Estate Training Institute – Pre Exam Workbook

6. The sellers and buyers have a contract in which the seller will convey title to the buyer if the buyer comes up with $35,000 before February 1st. What type of contract is this?
1. Installment.
2. Option contract.
3. Variable.
4. A buy - sell contract.

7. The closing agent must give information as to the sales price and seller's social security number to the
1. bank in which the new mortgage is.
2. HUD office.
3. National Home Mortgage Association.
4. IRS.

8. A broker has supplied the money for a developer to build a new neighborhood with the stipulation that the broker becomes the sole agent for the builder when the properties are ready for sale. This is a
1. specific agency.
2. riparian rights.
3. agency coupled with an interest.
4. open agency.

9. A Real Estate Broker has given a developer the money to build a new community in return for the developer to give the broker an Exclusive Right to Sell Agreement. This is a/an
1. open agency coupled with financing.
2. agency coupled with financing.
3. open Listing Agreement.
4. agency coupled with an interest.

10. In a transaction what type of legal description is used in most cases?
1. The street address only.
2. The same one used in prior transactions, verified by a surveyor.
3. The metes and bounds if the property is west of the Mississippi River.
4. The one the seller guesses is correct.

11. Assuming all factors are the same, which location would probably bring the highest price for a parking lot for sale?
1. Business district zoned for one story small businesses.
2. Recreational area.
3. Residential area zoned for single family homes.
4. Business zoned for 20 story high rises.

12. An arrangement in which an elderly homeowner borrows against the equity in his home and in return receives a regular monthly tax free payment from the lender is a
1. Back Load Mortgage.
2. Front Load Mortgage.
3. Reverse Annuity.
4. Inverse Annuity.

13. A mentally disabled person that was declared incompetent can't enter into a contract unless
1. a person appointed by a parent can sign legal contracts for the disabled person.
2. a disabled person can under no circumstances enter into a contract without the written certification acquired while in school.
3. a person appointed by the court may enter into the contract on the disabled person's behalf.
4. All of the above under certain conditions.

14. In a situation where state water rights are automatically conveyed with property is (*hint- best answer answer)
1. prior appropriation.
2. prior subjective conditions.
3. a condition stated on all loan documents.
4. alluvian.

15. A client would like to sell his house after owning it for one year. The client let the agent know that the property was treated for termites 14 months ago. What should the agent do?
1. Tell the client not to disclose the information so the agent's husband can re - treat the property and make money.
2. Tell the client to keep his car out of the garage so not to attract any new termites.
3. Tell the client that radon is nothing to be afraid of.
4. Tell the client to disclose that information.

16. Radon
1. enters the house through the roof vents.
2. is nothing to be concerned about?
3. enters the house through the basement floor.
4. is caused by friable asbestos.

17. Radon is
1. a colorless, odorless and tasteless gas occurring naturally from the decay of substances.
2. colorless, odorless and tasteless friable asbestos.
3. a lead by product.
4. a black mold infestation that has become airborne.

Real Estate Training Institute – Pre Exam Workbook

18. Friable asbestos
1. airborne asbestos.
2. airborne asbestos coupled with lead.
3. is addictive and must be avoided.
4. can be found in paint on windowsills.

19. When a judgment on a property has been properly recorded. The world has been given
1. substantive written notice.
2. construed notice.
3. construction notice.
4. constructive notice.

20. Two lots owned by the same seller and of the same size were sold two days apart. The lot directly on the sand beach was sold for $100,000 more than the lot across the highway which will have a peek a boo look at the water. What characteristic was taking effect?
1. Permanence.
2. Streetus.
3. Situs.
4. Situational indestructability.

21. The FHA is best associated with
1. a qualifying tool for mortgages.
2. a banking entity with assets.
3. a secondary market mortgage based interest indicator.
4. an insurance company.

22. Ana, a property manager, may legally refuse to rent to
1. a person unable to live alone without help.
2. a person convicted of selling drugs.
3. a person who wants to adjust the apartment and pay for it in order to fit her wheelchair.
4. Both 1 and 2.

23. Discount points
1. are the points paid on the sales price in order to reduce the price of a property.
2. are the points paid on the full price offer with a 20% down payment in order to reduce a loan.
3. are points paid on the amount of the loan in order to buy down interest rate.
4. Can be any of the above.

24. Each discount point is
1. based on 1% of the loan.
2. based on 1% of the purchase price.
3. based on 1% of the cost of repairs made by the seller.
4. based on 1% of each friable asbestos particle inhaled.

25. Ana, a property manager and who under usual circumstances would not have to give notice to vacate to a person whose one-year lease will be coming to an end in 10 days. Ana has discovered that the tenant whose situation is mentioned above has been convicted of illegal drug dealing and knows she can legally not rent to the convicted drug dealer. Ana decided to give the convicted drug dealer a Notice to Vacate just in case. The drug dealer stayed in the property for 45 more days after the expiration of the lease and attempted to pay rent in which Ana refused. The tenant has
1. a periodic tenancy.
2. tenancy in common with other tenants.
3. a tenancy in sufferance.
4. a radar problem.

26. A foremost reason for buying a condo over a luxury single family home on the ocean is
1. the back yard.
2. price.
3. loan terms.
4. discount points.

27. A woman bought a house subject to her getting approval to run her beauty shop from the city. The city refused her request. The contract was canceled because of
1. inability to pay.
2. financing based on homes rather than businesses.
3. impossibility of performance.
4. her mother.

28. A woman bought a house subject to her getting approval to run her business from her home. The city rejected her request. The woman was able to get her deposit money back because of a
1. noncompliance clause.
2. liquidated damages contingency.
3. contingency in the offer.
4. noncompliance of zoning.

29. When taking a listing, the agent should verify
1. radon.
2. lead.
3. square footage.
4. the original purchase price.

30. For federal tax purposes, the form a broker will give an agent to file their taxes is a
1. 5024 – misc.
2. 1099 misc.
3. 1099 – s.
4. 940.

31. The escrow agent or attorney at the close of escrow will file which tax form to be sent to the IRS?
1. 1099 - misc.
2. 1099 - s
3. 1040
4. 360

32. When a "trigger term" is used in an ad, The Truth in Lending Act requires the following disclosures except
1. amount of loan or cash price.
2. pre-payment penalties.
3. number, amount and frequency of payments.
4. amount of the down payment required.

33. Earnest money deposits should be
1. deposited into the broker's business account.
2. deposited into a safe deposit box.
3. deposited into a trust account by the end of the next business day.
4. be given to the agent to hold.

34. When a borrower defaults on a loan which has an acceleration clause it permits the lender
1. seize the personal assets of the borrower.
2. force the borrower to vacate his home immediately.
3. demand the entire note be paid immediately.
4. All of the above.

35. When a buyer of a four-plex refers to the property renting for 1000 dollars a month therefore the property is worth $100,000, the buyer is using the
1. IRS.
2. HUD.
3. GRM.
4. NOAA.

36. An Environmental Impact Statement
1. projects the dollar amount of an entire project.
2. summarizes the neighborhood in general terms.
3. projects the impact on the environment of a proposed project.
4. is used only for state projects.

37. A buyer wants to make an offer based on complex financing. The agent should
1. give legal advice.
2. call his broker at home.
3. suggest the buyer consult an attorney to furnish the wording.
4. drop the client.

38. The purpose of collecting an earnest money deposit is to
1. display the buyer has intention to carry out the deal.
2. insure a commission will be paid.
3. set aside funds for prorated taxes.
4. All of the above.

39. Usury laws are
1. intended to protect an agent from his broker.
2. intended to supply fair housing information.
3. intended to provide the FHA with down payment assistance.
4. intended to regulate interest charged by lenders.

40. Real Property is converted to personal property by
1. annexation.
2. severance.
3. novation.
4. laches.

41. Inducing panic selling in a neighborhood is
1. redlining.
2. steering.
3. friable asbestos.
4. blockbusting.

42. One day after a broker's listing on a property expired, the seller hired a new agent and that agent put the property on the MLS. A third agent called the broker with the expired listing and asked to see the property. The broker should respond by
1. telling the third agent who called to see the property that he no longer is the agent for the seller.
2. setting up an appointment with the seller to show the property.
3. hanging up.
4. talking bad about the seller's property.

43. Which of the following investors would like a property manager that emphasizes income and cash flow over maintenance?
1. The Dept. of Housing and Urban Development.
2. A bank owning foreclosed property.
3. An entrepreneur who owns several apartment buildings.
4. All of the above.

44. A buyer depended on his agent's information that the property the buyer is considering making an offer on is in a tax area of the lowest taxes in the city. Based on that information, an offer was made. Before the transaction closed the buyer found out the taxes in that area are some of the highest in the state. The buyer may seek to rescind the contract based on
1. redlining.
2. blockbusting.
3. misrepresentation.
4. puffing.

45. The document the buyer and seller sign to establish their legal rights is the
1. deed.
2. purchase contract.
3. listing agreement.
4. buyer's agreement.

46. Ownership of common stock in a corporation
1. can be real estate.
2. is a deed.
3. is considered personal property.
4. is required to purchase a home.

47. A homeowner paid his neighbor $10,000 in order to have access to cross over the southeast portion of his property to reach a new road. This is an easement
1. by prescription.
2. in gross.
3. appurtenant.
4. for safety.

48. Which of the following would cancel a listing agreement?
1. salesperson transferring to a new broker.
2. property owner's divorce.
3. property owner's marriage.
4. property owner's death.

49. A competitive market analysis (CMA) considers
1. demographics.
2. unknown friable asbestos.
3. original price of the property.
4. square footage of the subject property.

50. Under the Comprehensive Environmental Response, Compensation and Liability Act (CERCLA) who is liable for damages from the dumping hazardous waste on the property being sold?
1. The state government.
2. The federal government.
3. The buyer.
4. The seller.

51. Methods to calculate the reproduction or replacement cost of a building include all of the following except
1. quantity survey method.
2. straight line method.
3. unit in place method.
4. square foot method.

52. The best example of a buffer zone is
1. a warehouse between a neighborhood and strip mall.
2. garden homes between a single-family residential neighborhood and a shopping center.
3. an office building between a commercial strip mall and a school.
4. All of the above.

53. Antitrust Laws prohibit all except
1. dual representation.
2. setting commission fees with other brokers.
3. boycotting other brokers.
4. restricting competition.

54. Private homes built before 1978 may contain potentially dangerous levels of lead. The FHA
1. will not lend money on these properties.
2. require the buyer to acknowledge a disclosure of the presence of any known lead paint.
3. require the seller to remove the lead before selling.
4. require testing before the property can be sold.

55. Inverse (Reverse) Condemnation may be brought by
1. the city government.
2. the homeowner.
3. the federal government.
4. the state government.

56. The responsible broker is responsible for
1. all actions of salespeople.
2. all actions of unlicensed salespeople.
3. real estate activities of associated salespeople.
4. no acts of employees.

Real Estate Training Institute – Pre Exam Workbook

57. A salesperson told a customer that his listing has the best view of the ocean. The customer noticed that the property has a peek a boo view of the ocean. This is an example of
1. blockbusting.
2. a violation of Truth in Lending Laws.
3. puffing.
4. intentional fraud.

58. When does a lender require flood insurance?
1. When the property was flooded by a busted water line.
2. When the property is located in a Flood Hazard Zone.
3. When the seller puts down more than 20%.
4. When the buyer is using an out of state lender.

59. John bought a rental apartment building for $215,000. The assessed value is $205,000. The tax rate is $1.50 per $100 of assessed value. What is the monthly tax?
1. $3075
2. $307.75
3. $256.25
4. None of the above.

60. Ana bought a home for $165,000. Her assessed value is $160,000. She is taxed 2.25 for every $100 of assessed value. What is her monthly tax due?
1. $301.25
2. $295.87
3. 303.65
4. None of the above.

61. Under a land contract who retains equitable title?
1. Vendee.
2. Vendor.
3. Grantee.
4. Grantor.

62. Under a land contract who retains fee ownership of the property? (Title)
1. Vendor
2. Vendee
3. Grantor
4. Grantee

63. A buyer made an offer and the seller responded with a counter offer. When the buyer was reviewing the counter offer the seller received a better offer from another buyer. The seller can accept the second offer
1. if the second offer is coupled with a higher down payment.
2. if the seller withdraws the counter offer before the buyer accepts it.
3. if the first buyer has been informed in writing that the seller is going to accept the second offer.
4. the seller is forced to wait for the response of the first buyer.

Real Estate Training Institute – Pre Exam Workbook

64. A broker received a commission of 6% of the selling price from his client. The commission was $9720. The sales price of the property was
1. $160,000.
2. $158,000.
3. $162,000.
4. None of the above.

65. John listed his property with sales agent Tracy. John sold his own home to his cousin. John did not have to pay a commission to Tracy. The type of listing most likely was a/an
1. net listing.
2. gross listing.
3. exclusive Right to sell listing.
4. exclusive listing.

66. A broker has decided to buy his client's house, which the broker has listed. The broker should
1. wait six weeks.
2. buy the property through a straw man.
3. not accept any offers on the property to protect his interest.
4. make his true intention known to his client.

67. The gross rent multiplier for a duplex is calculated by dividing the sales price by
1. its gross yearly rent.
2. its gross monthly payment.
3. its gross monthly rent.
4. its net yearly income.

68. Depreciation is based on
1. land and the building.
2. land only.
3. building only.
4. economic obsolescence.

69. A minority couple asked a salesperson to find them a property worth around $500,000. The salesperson showed the couple lower priced property in integrated neighborhoods only. This may be an example of
1. blockbusting.
2. redlining.
3. steering.
4. puffing.

Real Estate Training Institute – Pre Exam Workbook

70. Mary died without a will. She has one daughter and three granddaughters. Mary's estate will be distributed by
1. statute of novation.
2. statute of reverse condemnation.
3. statute of escheat.
4. statute of descent.

71. Real Estate transactions are reported to the IRS. Required information includes
1. sales price and buyer's name and social security number.
2. seller's name, social security number(s) and price.
3. buyer's name and method of payment.
4. seller's name and address only.

72. If conditions for purchase are included in the deed and those conditions are violated
1. the violator may face jail and a fine.
2. the violator will serve jail time.
3. an injunction can be placed on the property.
4. the property reverts back to the original grantor/owner.

73. When a seller gives her broker authorization to perform a single act, it causes
1. special agency.
2. dual agency.
3. universal agency.
4. uncommon lawful agency.

74. When the government establishes legislation to preserve order, protect the public health and safety and promotes the general welfare of the public, it is called
1. lawful power.
2. police power.
3. inverse condemnation.
4. All of the above.

75. If one party in a contract does not live up to their part of the contract there is money set aside that will serve as full compensation to the aggrieved party. This is called
1. earnest money.
2. liquidated damages.
3. arbitration clause.
4. agreement pay.

76. When two parties have a verbal and a written contract and the contracts conflict, which contract takes precedent?
1. The oral agreement if it was made first.
2. The written contract.
3. Neither, new contracts must be drawn.
4. The oral agreement in all cases.

Real Estate Training Institute – Pre Exam Workbook

77. Usury Laws protect
1. the lender.
2. the seller.
3. the borrower.
4. the agent.

78. Which is the best method to appraise a single-family home?
1. Cost comparison.
2. Depreciated method.
3. Market data.
4. Tax assessment method.

79. A single woman has applied to rent an apartment in a community where 95% of the residents are over the age of 55. She has two children. One is eight and the other is three. The Federal Fair Housing Law
1. makes it mandatory that she be rented to.
2. protects the apartment owner from being forced to rent to her because over 80% of the residents are over the age of 55.
3. protects the children for familiar status.
4. All of the above could happen.

80. An agent told the buyer that the property the buyer wanted was connected to the city's sewer system. After the purchase the buyer found out that the property had a septic tank and was not connected to the city's sewer system. What protects the agent from financial loss?
1. The National Association of Realtors national protection fund.
2. E and O insurance coverage.
3. The homeowner's insurance policy.
4. Title insurance.

81. A position of trust and confidence a client puts into an agent is called
1. implied or expressed.
2. fiduciary.
3. customer loyalty.
4. It can be any of the above.

82. The owner of the property you have listed is
1. the customer.
2. the subagent.
3. the prospect.
4. the client.

83. The following is considered prima facie evidence of discrimination by a broker;
1. Failure for a customer to qualify for a loan.
2. Failure of the lender not to grant.
3. Failure to display the equal opportunity poster at the broker's office.
4. Failure to keep appointments.

84. Termination of an easement can happen
1. with a fire on the dominant property.
2. when the owner of the easement dies.
3. with the merger of titles.
4. when one property sells.

85. A contract to purchase that has not closed is
1. null.
2. void.
3. an executory contract.
4. an implied assessment.

86. An adjustable mortgage contains all of the following except
1. life of loan cap.
2. margin.
3. depreciation.
4. index.

87. Zoning Ordinances primarily
1. implements a city master plan.
2. implement the quality of workmanship.
3. control business.
4. control water quality.

88. Economic characteristics of land include
1. the metes and bounds.
2. situs or area preference, scarcity and durability.
3. the plot plan.
4. palm trees.

89. A tenant's lease expired last week. The tenant went ahead and paid next month's rent and the landlord gave him a receipt. This is a
1. net lease.
2. tenancy in common.
3. holdover tenancy.
4. tenancy at sufferance.

90. A neighbor allowed his next-door neighbor to fish from his pond in the month of July only. The neighbor with the lake granted
1. an easement appurtenant.
2. a restriction.
3. a gross easement.
4. a license.

91. A violation of The Federal Fair Housing law can be heard by either within the Dept. of Housing and Urban Development or by a Federal Judge. The Federal Court hearing has an advantage to the complaining party because
1. it's faster.
2. there is no dollar limit on damages paid.
3. it's fairer.
4. there is no advantage.

92. When a property owner dies without a will or heirs, the property
1. become at sufferance.
2. is executory.
3. becomes the property of the closest neighbor.
4. escheats to the state.

93. Ana, John and Jim bought together a property worth $675,000. John put up $337,500, Ana put up 25%. How much ownership interest does Jim have?
1. 15%
2. 25%
3. 35%
4. 45%

94. Ana, John and Jim bought together a property worth $675,000. John put up $337,500, Ana put up 25%. How much money did Jim have to come up with?
1. $172,564.
2. $158,943.
3. $168,750.
4. $89,500.

95. The amount of commission is
1. set by the Board of Realtors.
2. negotiable.
3. set by multiple brokers.
4. set by law.

Real Estate Training Institute – Pre Exam Workbook

96. A doctor built a five-bedroom house with five bathrooms on a lot in a neighborhood where all the homes are three bedrooms and one bath. The doctor's home will most likely suffer from
1. subrogation.
2. novation.
3. progression.
4. regression.

97. Which of the following owners of an apartment building would emphasize maintenance of value over income?
1. An entrepreneur who owns several income properties.
2. HUD
3. FCC
4. Dept. of the Interior

98. When several approaches of value are applied to a property, the appraiser will do which of the following?
1. Plottage
2. Reconciliation
3. Ascension
4. Round off to the highest value

99. Elevation Benchmark?
1. A seat in the community park zoned recreational.
2. Horizontal Plain used to find the legal description in high rises.
3. A mark used in a rectangular survey system measurement.
4. The measurement point as the point of beginning.

100. Jim wants to open a grocery store on a lot that is zoned for residential. Jim
1. will need to obtain a variance or a conditional use permit.
2. will need to petition the local courts to change the zoning.
3. will be able to open if the people in the neighborhood write letters to the mayor.
4. All of the above can happen.

101. The Equal Credit Opportunity Act does not address
1. factors for borrower's analysis.
2. written credit denial letters.
3. interest rates.
4. discrimination in lending.

Real Estate Training Institute – Pre Exam Workbook

102. A property went into foreclosure with a first mortgage of 158,000 and a second mortgage of 33,000. The second mortgagee will receive
1. the entire 33,000.
2. whatever is left over after paying off all other property liens.
3. one half of the amount owed.
4. nothing.

103. The government survey system is not generally used in
1. states west of the Mississippi River.
2. the southern states.
3. the original 13 states.
4. the northern states.

104. Violating Fair Housing practices, an agent
1. will lose their license only.
2. will get probation.
3. will get arrested immediately.
4. will have his license revoked and will be criminally prosecuted.

105. A very old oak tree!
1. Metes and Bounds
2. Rectangular Survey
3. Straight Line Method
4. North America

106. A CMA benefits?
1. The Buyer
2. The Seller
3. The Agent
4. The Broker

107. A contour map is used for which of the following locations?
1. Flat low-lying areas
2. Desert towns
3. A very hilly location
4. They are never used.

108. A Trustee may?
1. Sell the property
2. Lien the property
3. Do whatever is permitted in the trust agreement
4. Keep the deed after final payment

109. Prior Appropriation will most likely be found in what type of area?
1. Mountains
2. Deserts - Dry areas
3. Islands
4. Jungles

110. An Environmental Impact Statement is used for?
1. A proposed project
2. An outdated project
3. A private company
4. A quitclaim deed

111. An environmental Impact Statement is considered police power because it deals with which of the following?
1. Fish
2. Boats
3. Health and Safety
4. Pets

112. When a person dies without a will and no heirs can be found, the property
1. escheats to the state.
2. gets condemned.
3. gets reverted.
4. becomes part of the heir's estate.

113. Escheat happens
1. because property – land can not be ownerless.
2. when the heirs reject the property.
3. land reverts back to the original grantor.
4. All of the above.

114. Inverse – Reverse Condemnation may be brought by the
1. state.
2. county.
3. feds.
4. homeowner

115. Deed restrictions pertain to
1. the seller only.
2. the buyer only.
3. the future and current owners.
4. the previous grantee only.

Real Estate Training Institute – Pre Exam Workbook

116. Determinable and defeasible are best described as
1. ownership with a condition.
2. ownership with a deed.
3. dual representation.
4. single representation.

117. When a condition is violated in a deed
1. it becomes a brownfield.
2. the property becomes unusable.
3. the property reverts back to the original grantor.
4. the owner gets escheated.

118. All of the following terms deal with appraisal except?
1. Reproduction costs
2. Replacement costs
3. Straight line method of depreciation
4. Valuation

119. Usury laws
1. protect the lender.
2. protects the borrower.
3. protects the bank.
4. protects trade.

120. The clause in a contract that allows the bank to call the entire note due and payable is?
1. Acceleration Clause
2. Protection Clause
3. Defeasible Fee Clause
4. Santa Clause

121. Who would have the most options for loans and loan programs?
1. Mortgage Banker
2. Mortgage Broker
3. Mortgage Servicer
4. Mortgage Repo Guy

122. An agent brought a ready, willing and able buyer that met the terms of the contract. The broker has earned her commission
1. when the seller gives a counter offer.
2. when the buyer gives a counter offer.
3. when the seller accepts the offer.
4. when the buyer accepts the counteroffer.

Real Estate Training Institute – Pre Exam Workbook

123. The term "Remainder" is most like?
1. When an owner conveys a life estate to one party and the remainder to another.
2. When the owner conveys ½ the estate to a relative and the remainder to a friend.
3. The remainder of the Offer to Purchase that needs to be completed.
4. The remainder of the rejected offers.

124. Tenancy for years is?
1. A leasehold for at least 5 years.
2. A lease for at least two years with a definite end.
3. A lease with a definite beginning and a definite ending.
4. A lease for the remainder of a person's life.

125. Real estate contracts must be in writing to be enforceable in court according to
1. prima facie laws.
2. statue of frauds.
3. moveable chattel.
4. because Jim says so.

126. The term "Duress" is most like;
1. Durability
2. Attainability
3. Undue Influence
4. Escheat

127. When a renter finds the rental to be dangerous or unsafe to live in and the landlord refuses to make repairs needed to bring the property to a safe condition, the tenant may vacate and not be responsible for the remainder of the lease. When the tenant moves, the tenant has given the landlord
1. condemnation.
2. association.
3. constructive notice/eviction.
4. construction notice.

128. A lease on an apartment has ended yet the tenant keeps paying a monthly rent and the landlord keeps accepting the rent. This type of leasehold would be considered
1. a holdover tenancy.
2. an illegal contract.
3. unacceptable.
4. void.

129. The Civil Rights Act of 1968 was meant as a follow-up to the Civil Rights Act of 1964. It is called the
1. Fair Act.
2. Fair Housing Act.
3. Fair Housing Enactment.
4. Fair Rental Housing Act.

130. The Civil Rights Act of 1866 prohibited discrimination based on?
1. National Origin
2. Familial Status
3. Race
4. Pregnancy

131. The definition of subletting is most like?
1. The leasing of a premise by a lessee to a third party.
2. The lease leasing to the lessor.
3. The lessor leasing to a relative.
4. The least lease the lessor leased to the lease.

132. Which of the following is true for both VA Loans and FHA Loans?
1. They are both insured.
2. Both are guaranteed.
3. The buyer is insured by FHA with both.
4. Both loans could have discount points to buy down the loan.

133. Public Assistance is considered
1. lawful income.
2. income not used in calculating income for a mortgage.
3. income not used in calculating income for a rental.
4. All of the above.

134. When a landlord owns a four-plex in a FEMA designated flood plain and decides not to buy insurance but instead raise the air conditioners and heaters on high platforms, the owner
1. has forced insurance companies to accept his decision and pay him for new equipment in case of flood.
2. violated FEMA laws.
3. is said to be "Controlling his Risk".
4. is said to be "eliminating his risk".

135. A liquor store on the main highway was enjoying brisk business and substantial profits. The county decided to move the main highway ¼ mile away to the north of the store. This caused traffic to be re-routed and profits dropped significantly. This would be an example of?
1. Substantial misrepresentation
2. External or Economic obsolescence
3. Interior obsolescence
4. Functional Obsolescence

Real Estate Training Institute – Pre Exam Workbook

136. Which term describes a loan with the loan payment is less than the interest charged resulting in the outstanding balance of the loan increasing?
1. Straight Mortgage
2. Fully Amortized
3. Negative Amortization
4. Partial Payment and Interest

137. An Abstract of Title is
1. the history of the property.
2. the future recorded documents of the property.
3. the history of the recorded documents on a property.
4. an ownership title.

138. Into which bank account would a broker deposit commissions?
1. personal account
2. business account
3. escrow account
4. cash account

139. The cheapest way to handle asbestos is
1. to pull it from the floor with no protection.
2. scrap it off a building.
3. hire someone to take it out of a building.
4. encapsulation.

140. Radon
1. is an odorless colorless (radioactive) gas that may cause lung cancer.
2. is easily mitigated.
3. should be inspected and verified by a real estate broker before taking a listing.
4. Both one and two.

141. A buyer is purchasing a home in a neighborhood that has a homeowner's association. At the closing, what additional documents should the buyer receive?
1. The Neighborhood CC and R's (The covenants, conditions and restrictions) and bylaws.
2. The neighborhood nuisance disclosures.
3. The city tax disclosure and 6-month retroactive bill.
4. All of the above.

142. After the close of an escrow, who would keep for three years the Listing Agreement?
1. The customer and the client
2. The buyer and the Selling Agent
3. The Seller and the customer
4. The Client and the Seller's Agent

Real Estate Training Institute – Pre Exam Workbook

143. After the close of escrow, who would for three years keep the Purchase Agreement?
1. The Client
2. The Client, the Customer, the Selling Agent and the Seller's Agent
3. The Seller and the Buyer
4. The Customer and the Buyer's Agent

Real Estate Training Institute – Pre Exam Workbook

Answers:

1. A written agreement or contract between a buyer and seller when the buyer wants to buy and the seller is wanting to sell, after a meeting of the minds is called?
3. A contract.

2. An appraiser must be licensed or certified to handle Federally related work on residential, residential income, commercial and all other real estate properties valued at
3. $250,000.

3. Which of the following costs of homeownership may be deducted on Federal Income Taxes?
3. Mortgage loan origination fees, mortgage loan interest and local property taxes.

4. Which type of ownership is most often used for a timeshare?
2. Tenancy in common.

5. How is title held when a person owns a cooperative?
4. Stock.

6. The sellers and buyers have a contract in which the seller will convey title to the buyer if the buyer comes up with $10,000 before July 1st. What type of contract is this?
2. Option contract.

7. The closing agent must give information as to the sales price and seller's social security number to the
4. IRS.

8. A broker has supplied the money for a developer to build a new neighborhood with the stipulation that the broker becomes the sole agent for the builder when the properties are ready for sale. This is a
3. agency coupled with an interest.

9. A Real Estate Broker has given a developer the money to build a new community in return for the developer to give the broker an Exclusive Right to Sell Agreement. This is
4. agency coupled with an interest.

10. In a transaction what type of legal description is used in most cases?
2. The same one used in prior transactions, verified by a surveyor.

11. Assuming all factors are the same, which location would probably bring the highest price for a parking lot for sale?
4. Business zoned for 20 story high rises.

Real Estate Training Institute – Pre Exam Workbook

12. An arrangement in which an elderly homeowner borrows against the equity in his home and in return receives a regular monthly tax-free payment from the lender is
3. reverse annuity.

13. A mentally disabled person that was declared incompetent can't enter into a contract unless
3. a person appointed by the court may enter into the contract on the disabled person's behalf.

14. In a situation where state water rights are automatically conveyed with property is
1. prior appropriation.

15. A client would like to sell his house after owning it for one year. The client let the agent know that the property was treated for termites 14 months ago. What should the agent do?
4. Tell the client to disclose that information.

16. Radon
3. enters the house through the basement floor.

17. Radon is
1. a colorless, odorless and tasteless gas occurring naturally from the decay of substances.

18. Friable asbestos
1. airborne asbestos.

19. When a judgment on a property has been properly recorded. The world has been given
4. constructive notice/eviction.

20. Two lots owned by the same seller and of the same size were sold two days apart. The lot directly on the sand beach was sold for $100,000 more than the lot across the highway which will have a peek a boo look at the water. What characteristic was taking effect?
3. Situs.

21. The FHA is best associated with
4. an insurance company.

22. Ana, a property manager, may legally refuse to rent to
2. a person convicted of selling drugs.

23. Discount points
3. are points paid on the amount of the loan in order to buy down interest rate.

24. Each discount point is
1. based on 1% of the loan.

Real Estate Training Institute – Pre Exam Workbook

25. Ana, a property manager and who under usual circumstances would not have to give notice to vacate to a person whose one-year lease will be coming to an end in 10 days. Ana has discovered that the tenant whose situation is mentioned above has been convicted of illegal drug dealing and knows she can legally not rent to the convicted drug dealer. Ana decided to give the convicted drug dealer a Notice to Vacate just in case. The drug dealer stayed in the property for 45 more days after the expiration of the lease and attempted to pay rent in which Ana refused. The tenant has
3. a tenancy in sufferance.

26. A foremost reason for buying a condo over a luxury single family home on the ocean is
2. price.

27. A woman bought a house subject to her getting approval to run her beauty shop from the city. The city refused her request. The contract was canceled because of
3. impossibility of performance.

28. A woman bought a house subject to her getting approval to run her business from her home. The city rejected her request. The woman was able to get her deposit money back because of a
3. Contingency in the offer.

29. When taking a listing, the agent should verify
3. square footage.

30. For federal tax purposes, the form a broker will give an agent to file their taxes is a
2. 1099 misc.

31. The escrow agent or attorney at the close of escrow will file which tax form to be sent to the IRS?
2. 1099 - s

32. When a "trigger term" is used in an ad, The Truth in Lending Act requires the following disclosures except
2. pre-payment penalties.

33. **Earnest money deposits should be**
3. deposited into a trust account by the end of the next business day.

34. **When a borrower defaults on a loan that has an acceleration clause it permits the lender**
3. demand the entire note be paid immediately.

35. When a buyer of a four-plex refers to the property renting for 1000 dollars a month therefore the property is worth $100,000, the buyer is using the
3. GRM.

Real Estate Training Institute – Pre Exam Workbook

36. An Environmental Impact Statement
3. projects the impact on the environment of a proposed project.

37. A buyer wants to make an offer based on complex financing. The agent should
3. suggest the buyer consult an attorney to furnish the wording.

38. The purpose of collecting an earnest money deposit is to
1. display the buyer has intention to carry out the deal.

39. Usury laws are
4. intended to regulate interest charged by lenders.

40. Real Property is converted to personal property by
2. severance.

41. Inducing panic selling in a neighborhood is
4. blockbusting.

42. One day after a broker's listing on a property expired, the seller hired a new agent and that agent put the property on the MLS. A third agent called the broker with the expired listing and asked to see the property. The broker should respond by
1. telling the third agent who called to see the property that he no longer is the agent for the seller.

43. Which of the following investors would like a property manager that emphasizes income and cash flow over maintenance?
3. An entrepreneur who owns several apartment buildings.

44. A buyer depended on his agent's information that the property the buyer is considering making an offer on is in a tax area of the lowest taxes in the city. Based on that information, an offer was made. Before the transaction closed the buyer found out the taxes in that area are some of the highest in the state. The buyer may seek to rescind the contract based on
3. misrepresentation.

45. The document the buyer and seller sign to establish their legal rights is the
2. purchase contract.

46. Ownership of common stock in a corporation
3. is considered personal property.

47. A homeowner paid his neighbor $10,000 in order to have access to cross over the southeast portion of his property to reach a new road. This is an easement
3. appurtenant.

48. Which of the following would cancel a listing agreement?
4. Property owner's death.

Real Estate Training Institute – Pre Exam Workbook

49. A competitive market analysis (CMA) considers
4. square footage of the subject property.

50. Under the Comprehensive Environmental Response, Compensation and Liability Act (CERCLA) who is liable for damages from the dumping hazardous waste on the property being sold?
4. The seller.

51. Methods to calculate the reproduction or replacement cost of a building include all of the following except
2. straight line method.

52. The best example of a buffer zone is
2. garden homes between a single-family residential neighborhood and a shopping center.

53. Antitrust Laws prohibit all except
1. dual representation.

54. Private homes built before 1978 may contain potentially dangerous levels of lead. The FHA
2. require the buyer to acknowledge a disclosure of the presence of any known lead paint.

55. Inverse (Reverse) Condemnation may be brought by
2. the homeowner.

56. The responsible broker is responsible for
3. real estate activities of associated salespeople.

57. A salesperson told a customer that his listing has the best view of the ocean. The customer noticed that the property has a peek a boo view of the ocean. This is an example of
3. puffing.

58. When does a lender require flood insurance?
2. when the property is located in a Flood Hazard Zone.

59. John bought a rental apartment building for $215,000. The assessed value is $205,000. The tax rate is $1.50 per $100 of assessed value. What is the monthly tax?
3. $256.25

60. Ana bought a home for $165,000. Her assessed value is $160,000. She is taxes 2.25 for every $100 of assessed value. What is her monthly tax due?
4. None of the above.

61. Under a land contract who retains equitable title?
1. Vendee.

Real Estate Training Institute – Pre Exam Workbook

62. Under a land contract who retains fee ownership of the property? (Title)
1. Vendor

63. A buyer made an offer and the seller responded with a counter offer. When the buyer was reviewing the counter offer the seller received a better offer from another buyer. The seller can accept the second offer if
2. the seller withdraws the counter offer before the buyer accepts it.

64. A broker received a commission of 6% of the selling price from his client. The commission was $9720. The sales price of the property was
3. $162,000.

65. John listed his property with sales agent Tracy. John sold his own home to his cousin. John did not have to pay a commission to Tracy. The type of listing most likely was a/an
4. exclusive listing.

66. A broker has decided to buy his client's house that the broker has listed. The broker should
4. make his true intention known to his client.

67. The gross rent multiplier for a duplex is calculated by dividing the sales price by
3. its gross monthly rent.

68. Depreciation is based on
3. building only.

69. A minority couple asked a salesperson to find them a property worth around $500,000. The salesperson showed the couple lower priced property in integrated neighborhoods only. This may be an example of
3. steering.

70. Mary died without a will. She has one daughter and three granddaughters. Mary's estate will be distributed by
4. statute of descent.

71. Real Estate transactions are reported to the IRS. Required information includes
2. seller's name, social security number(s) and price.

72. If conditions for purchase are included in the deed and those conditions are violated
4. the property reverts back to the original owner.

73. When a seller gives her broker authorization to perform a single act, it causes
1. special agency.

Real Estate Training Institute – Pre Exam Workbook

74. When the government establishes legislation to preserve order, protect the public health and safety and promotes the general welfare of the public, it is called
2. police power.

75. If one party in a contract does not live up to their part of the contract there is money set aside that will serve as full compensation to the aggrieved party. This is called
2. liquidated damages.

76. When two parties have a verbal and a written contract and the contracts conflict, which contract takes precedent?
2. The written contract.

77. Usury Laws protect
3. the borrower.

78. Which is the best method to appraise a single-family home?
3. Market data.

79. A single woman has applied to rent an apartment in a community where 95% of the residents are over the age of 55. She has two children. One is eight and the other is three. The Federal Fair Housing Law
2. protects the apartment owner from being forced to rent to her because over 80% of the residents are over the age of 55.

80. An agent told the buyer that the property the buyer wanted was connected to the city's sewer system. After the purchase the buyer found out that the property had a septic tank and was not connected to the city's sewer system. What protects the agent from financial loss?
2. E and O insurance coverage.

81. A position of trust and confidence a client puts into an agent is called
2. fiduciary.

82. The owner of the property you have listed is
4. the client.

83. The following is considered prima facie evidence of discrimination by a broker.
3. Failure to display the equal opportunity poster at the broker's office.

84. Termination of an easement can happen
3. with the merger of titles.

85. A contract to purchase that has not closed is
3. an executory contract.

Real Estate Training Institute – Pre Exam Workbook

86. An adjustable mortgage contains all of the following except
3. depreciation.

87. Zoning Ordinances primarily
1. implements a city master plan.

88. Economic characteristics of land include
2. Situs, scarcity and durability.

89. A tenant's lease expired last week. The tenant went ahead and paid next month's rent and the landlord gave him a receipt. This is a
3. holdover tenancy.

90. A neighbor allowed his next-door neighbor to fish from his pond in the month of July only. The neighbor with the lake granted
4. a license.

91. A violation of The Federal Fair Housing law can be heard by either within the Dept. of Housing and Urban Development or by a Federal Judge. The Federal Court hearing has an advantage to the complaining party because
2. there is no dollar limit on damages paid.

92. When a property owner dies without a will or heirs, the property
4. escheats to the state.

93. Ana, John and Jim bought together a property worth $675,000. John put up $337,500, Ana put up 25%. How much ownership interest does Jim have?
2. 25%

94. Ana, John and Jim bought together a property worth $675,000. John put up $337,500, Ana put up 25%. How much money did Jim have to come up with?
3. $168,750.

95. The amount of commission is
2. negotiable.

96. A doctor built a five-bedroom house with five bathrooms on a lot in a neighborhood where all the homes are three bedrooms and one bath. The doctor's home will most likely suffer from
4. regression.

97. Which of the following owners of an apartment building would emphasize maintenance of value over income?
2. HUD

Real Estate Training Institute – Pre Exam Workbook

98. When several approaches of value are applied to a property, the appraiser will do which of the following?
2. Reconciliation

99. Elevation Benchmark?
2. Horizontal Plain used to find the legal description in high rises.

100. Jim wants to open a grocery store on a lot that is zoned for residential. Jim
1. will need to obtain a variance or a conditional use permit.

101. The Equal Credit Opportunity Act does not address
3. interest rates.

102. A property went into foreclosure with a first mortgage of 158,000 and a second mortgage of 33,000. The second mortgagee will receive
4. nothing.

103. The government survey system is not generally used in
3. The original 13 states.

104. Violating Fair Housing practices, an agent
4. will have his license revoked and will be criminally prosecuted.

105. A very old oak tree!
1. Metes and Bounds

106. A CMA benefits?
2. The Seller

107. A contour map is used for which of the following locations?
3. A very hilly location

108. A Trustee may?
3. Do whatever is permitted in the trust agreement.

109. Prior Appropriation will most likely be found in what type of area?
2. Deserts - Dry areas

110. An Environmental Impact Statement is used for?
1. A proposed project

111. An environmental Impact Statement is considered police power because it deals with which of the following?
3. Health and Safety

Real Estate Training Institute – Pre Exam Workbook

112. When a person dies without a will and no heirs can be found, the property
1. escheats to the state.

113. Escheat happens
1. because property – land can-not be ownerless.

114. Inverse – Reverse Condemnation may be brought by the
4. homeowner

115. Deed restrictions pertain to
3. the future and current owners

116. Determinable and defeasible are best described as
1. ownership with a condition.

117. When a condition is violated in a deed
3. the property reverts back to the original grantor.

118. All of the following terms deal with appraisal except?
3. straight line method of depreciation

119. Usury laws
2. protect the borrower.

120. The clause in a contract that allows the bank to call the entire note due and payable is?
1. Acceleration Clause

121. Who would have the most options for loans and loan programs?
2. Mortgage Broker

122. An agent brought a ready, willing and able buyer that met the terms of the contract. The broker has earned her commission
3. when the seller accepts the offer.

123. The term "Remainder" is most like?
1. When an owner conveys a life estate to one party and the remainder to another.

124. Tenancy for years is?
3. A lease with a definite beginning and a definite ending.

125. Real estate contracts must be in writing to be enforceable in court according to
2. Statue of Frauds.

126. The term "Duress" is most like
3. undue influence.

127. When a renter finds the rental to be dangerous or unsafe to live in and the landlord refuses to make repairs needed to bring the property to a safe condition, the tenant may vacate and not be responsible for the remainder of the lease. When the tenant moves, the tenant has given the landlord
3. constructive notice/eviction.

128. A lease on an apartment has ended yet the tenant keeps paying a monthly rent and the landlord keeps accepting the rent. This type of leasehold would be considered
1. a holdover tenancy.

129. The Civil Rights Act of 1968 was meant as a follow-up to the Civil Rights Act of 1964. It is called the
2. Fair Housing Act.

130. The Civil Rights Act of 1866 prohibited discrimination based on?
3. Race

131. The definition of subletting is most like?
1. The leasing of a premise by a lessee to a third party

132. Which of the following is true for both VA Loans and FHA Loans?
4. Both loans could have discount points to buy down the loan

133. Public Assistance is considered
1. lawful income.

134. When a landlord owns a four-plex in a FEMA designated flood pain and decides not to buy insurance but instead raise the air conditioners and heaters on high platforms, the owner
3. is said to be "Controlling his Risk".

135. A liquor store on the main highway was enjoying brisk business and substantial profits. The county decided to move the main highway ¼ mile away to the north of the store. This caused traffic to be re-routed and profits dropped significantly. This would be an example of?
2. External or Economic obsolescence

136. Which term describes a loan with the loan payment is less than the interest charged resulting in the outstanding balance of the loan increasing?
3. Negative Amortization

137. An Abstract of Title is
3. the history of the recorded documents on a property.

138. Into which bank account would a broker deposit commissions?
2. Business account

Real Estate Training Institute – Pre Exam Workbook

139. The cheapest way to handle asbestos is
4. encapsulation.

140. Radon
4. Both one and two.

141. A buyer is purchasing a home in a neighborhood that has a homeowner's association. At the closing, what additional documents should the buyer receive?
1. The Neighborhood CC and R's (The covenants, conditions and restrictions) and bylaws.

142. After the close of an escrow, who would keep for three years the Listing Agreement?
4. The Client and the Seller's Agent

143. After the close of escrow, who would for three years keep the Purchase Agreement?
2. The Client, the Customer, the Selling Agent and the Seller's Agent

Real Estate Training Institute – Pre Exam Workbook

Exam Two: Practice

1. An Environmental Impact Statement is used for what?
1. A proposed project.
2. An outdated project.
3. A private company project only.
4. A governmental project only.

2. An Environmental Impact Statement is considered a Police Power because it deals with
1. bridges.
2. boat docks.
3. health and safety.
4. animals.

3. When a person dies without a will and no heirs can be found, the property
1. escheats to the state.
2. condemnation occurs.
3. a suit for specific non-action is filed.
4. inverse condemnation occurs.

4. Escheat happens
1. because property can - not be ownerless.
2. because there are more than two people involved.
3. because local governments want to build a real estate portfolio.
4. All of the above.

5. Inverse (Reverse) Condemnation may be brought by
1. the state.
2. the city.
3. the seller.
4. the homeowner.

6. Which of the following persons would most likely seek a Conditional Use Permit or Variance?
1 A person wanting to build an addition to their home.
2. A school.
3. A property owner whose property is zoned for single family residences but wants to open a small grocery store on the property.
4. A government agency.

7. Which of the following pertain to the present and the future owners?
1. Family size.
2. Home Designs.
3. Deed Restrictions.
4. All of the above.

119

Real Estate Training Institute – Pre Exam Workbook

8. Determinable Fee or Defeasible Fee are
1. ownership with a condition.
2. ownership without any conditions.
3. fee Simple Ownership.
4. a property owned by a corporation.

9. When a condition in a deed is violated, what happens to the property?
1. Nothing.
2. It reverts back to the original grantor.
3. The deed gets given to a public party.
4. All of the above.

10. All of the following deal with appraisal except
1. reproduction cost.
2. replacement cost.
3. straight line method of depreciation.
4. valuation.

11. Usury Laws
1. protects the lender.
2. protects the borrower.
3. protects the government.
4. protects China.

12. When a borrower defaults on a payment, the lender will call the entire note due and payable. The clause in the contract that allows for this is called
1. Acceleration Clause.
2. Protection Clause.
3. Defeasible Fee Clause.
4. Santa Claus.

13. Who would have the most options for loans and loan programs?
1. Mortgage Banker.
2. Mortgage Broker.
3. Mortgage Servicer.
4. Mortgage Repo Guy.

14. Another term for a Straight Mortgage (interest only) is a
1. variable mortgage.
2. amortized mortgage.
3. term mortgage.
4. reverse negative mortgage.

15. An agent brought a ready, willing and able buyer to the seller. The agent has earned her commission when which of the following happens?
1. The seller gives a counter offer.
2. The buyer withdraws the offer.
3. The seller accepts the offer.
4. The broker withholds all other offers.

Real Estate Training Institute – Pre Exam Workbook

Answers:

1. An Environmental Impact Statement is used for what?
1. A proposed project.

2. An Environmental Impact Statement is considered a Police Power because it deals with
3. health and safety.

3. When a person dies without a will and no heirs can be found, the property
1. escheats to the state.

4. Escheat happens
1. because property can - not be ownerless.

5. Inverse (Reverse) Condemnation may be brought by
4. the homeowner.

6. Which of the following persons would most likely seek a Conditional Use Permit or Variance?
3. A property owner whose property is zoned for single family residences but wants to open a small grocery store on the property.

7. Which of the following pertain to the present and the future owners?
3. Deed Restrictions.

8. Determinable Fee or Defeasible Fee are
1. ownership with a condition.

9. When a condition in a deed is violated, what happens to the property?
2. It reverts back to the original grantor.

10. All of the following deal with appraisal except
3. straight line method of depreciation.

11. Usury Laws
2. protects the borrower.

12. When a borrower defaults on a payment, the lender will call the entire note due and payable. The clause in the contract that allows for this is called
1. Acceleration Clause.

13. Who would have the most options for loans and loan programs?
2. Mortgage Broker.

14. Another term for a Straight Mortgage (interest only) is
3. term mortgage.

Real Estate Training Institute – Pre Exam Workbook

15. An agent brought a ready, willing and able buyer to the seller. The agent has earned her commission when which of the following happens?
3. The seller accepts the offer.

REAL ESTATE TRAINING INSTITUTE
1636 POPPS FERRY ROAD, M1
BILOXI, MS 39532
228-354-8585

online Campus: www.goretionline.com

End of National Exam Information

Begin Mississippi Real Estate License Law Exam

Real Estate Training Institute – Pre Exam Workbook

CHAPTER 5

MREC License Law

This is not a true and correct copy. A true and correct copy can be found at:
http://www.mrec.state.ms.us

This copy of MREC License Law has been altered. For educational purposes only.

*Please give special attention to the sections that have been underlined or highlighted for your benefit.

"The Real Estate Brokers License Law of 1954"

It shall be unlawful for any person, partnership, association or corporation to engage in or carry on, directly or indirectly, or to advertise or to hold himself, itself or themselves out as engaging in or carrying on the business, or act in the capacity of, a real estate broker, or a real estate salesperson, within this state, without first obtaining a license as a real estate broker or real estate salesperson.

Definitions;

(1) The term "real estate broker" within the meaning of this chapter shall include all persons, partnerships, associations and corporations, foreign and domestic, who for a fee, commission or other valuable consideration, or who with the intention or expectation of receiving or collecting the same, list, sell, purchase, exchange, rent, lease, manage or auction any real estate, or the improvements thereon, including options; or who negotiate or attempt to negotiate any such activity; or who advertise or hold themselves out as engaged in such activities; or who direct or assist in the procuring of a purchaser or prospect calculated or intended to result in a real estate transaction.

The term "real estate broker" shall also include any person, partnership, association or corporation employed by or on behalf of the owner or owners of lots or other parcels of real estate, at a stated salary or upon fee, commission or otherwise, to sell such real estate, or parts thereof, in lots or other parcels, including timesharing and condominiums, and who shall sell, exchange or lease, or offer or attempt or agree to negotiate the sale, exchange or lease of, any such lot or parcel of real estate.

(2) The term "real estate" as used in this chapter shall include leaseholds as well as any and every interest or estate in land, including timesharing and condominiums, whether corporeal or incorporeal, freehold or non-freehold, and whether said property is situated in this state or elsewhere; provided, however, that

*the term "real estate" as used in this chapter shall not include oil, gas or mineral leases, nor shall it include any other mineral leasehold, mineral estate or mineral interest of any nature whatsoever.

Real Estate Training Institute – Pre Exam Workbook

(3) One (1) act in consideration of or with the expectation or intention of, or upon the promise of, receiving compensation, by fee, commission or otherwise, in the performance of any act or activity contained in subsection (1) of this section, shall constitute such person, partnership, association or corporation a real estate broker and make him, them or it subject to the provisions and requirements.

(4) The term "real estate salesperson" shall mean and include any person employed or engaged by or on behalf of a licensed real estate broker to do or deal in any activity as included or comprehended by the definitions of a real estate broker, for compensation or otherwise.

(5) The term "automated valuation method" means any computerized model used by mortgage originators and secondary market issuers to determine the collateral worth of a mortgage secured by a consumer's principal dwelling.

(6) <u>The term "broker price opinion" means **an estimate** prepared by a real estate broker, agent, or salesperson that details the probable selling price of a particular piece of real estate property and provides a varying level of detail about the property's condition, market, and neighborhood, and information on comparable sales, but does not include an automated valuation model.</u>

Exempt from the licensing requirements shall be

any person, partnership, association or corporation, who, as a bona fide owner, shall perform any aforesaid act with reference to property owned by them, **or to the regular employees thereof who are on a stated salary, where such acts are performed in the regular course of business**.

(a) Attorneys at law in the performance of primary or incidental duties as such attorneys at law.

(b) Any person holding in good faith a duly executed power of attorney from the owner, authorizing the final consummation and execution for the sale, purchase, leasing or exchange of real estate.

(c) The acts of any person while acting as a receiver, trustee, administrator, executor, guardian or under court order, or while acting under authority of a deed of trust or will.

(d) <u>Public officers while performing their duties as such.</u>

(e) <u>Anyone dealing exclusively in oil and gas leases and mineral rights.</u>

(9) Nothing in this chapter shall be construed to prohibit life insurance companies and their representatives from negotiating or attempting to negotiate loans secured by mortgages on real estate, nor shall these companies or their representatives be required to qualify as real estate brokers or agents under this chapter.

(10) Exempt from License Requirements: the activities of mortgagees approved by the Federal Housing Administration or the United States Department of Veterans Affairs, banks chartered under the laws of the State of Mississippi or the United States, savings and loan associations chartered under the laws of the State of Mississippi or the United States, licensees under the Small

Real Estate Training Institute – Pre Exam Workbook

Loan Regulatory Law, being Sections 75-67-101 through 75-67-135, and under the Small Loan Privilege Tax Law, being Sections 75-67-201 through 75-67-243, small business investment companies licensed by the Small Business Administration and chartered under the laws of the State of Mississippi, or any of their affiliates and subsidiaries, related to the making of a loan secured by a lien on real estate or to the disposing of real estate acquired by foreclosure or in lieu of foreclosure or otherwise held as security. No director, officer or employee of any such financial institution shall be required to qualify as a real estate broker or agent under this chapter when engaged in the aforesaid activities for and on behalf of such financial institution.

Broker's price opinion; preparation, contents and use of opinion

(1) A person licensed may prepare a broker's price opinion and charge and collect a fee for such opinion if:

(a) The license of that licensee is active and in good standing; and

(b) The broker's price opinion meets the requirements of subsections (3) and (4) of this section.

(2) Notwithstanding any provision to the contrary, a person licensed under this chapter may prepare a broker's price opinion for:

(a) An existing or potential seller for the purposes of listing and selling a parcel of real property;

(b) An existing or potential buyer of a parcel of real property;

(c) A third party making decisions or performing due diligence related to the potential listing, offering, sale, exchange, option, lease or acquisition price of a parcel of real property; or

(d) An existing or potential lienholder or other third party for any <u>purpose **other than** as the basis to determine the value of a parcel of real property, for a mortgage loan origination, including first and second mortgages, refinances, or equity lines of credit.</u>

(e) The provisions do not preclude the preparation of a broker's price opinion to be used in conjunction with or in addition to an appraisal.

(3) A broker's price opinion prepared under the authority granted in this section shall be in writing and shall conform to the standards and guidelines published by a nationally recognized association of providers of broker price opinions. The Mississippi Real Estate Commission shall promulgate regulations that are consistent with, but not limited to, the standards and guidelines of a nationally recognized association of providers of broker price opinions.

(4) A broker's price opinion shall be in writing and contain the following:

(a) A statement of the intended purpose of the price opinion;

(b) A brief description of the subject property and property interest to be priced;

(c) The basis of reasoning used to reach the conclusion of the price, including **the** applicable market data and/or capitalization computation;

(d) Any assumptions or limiting conditions;

(e) A disclosure of any existing or contemplated interest of the broker or salesperson issuing the opinion;

(f) The effective date of the price opinion;

(g) The name and signature of the broker or salesperson issuing the price opinion;

(h) The name of the real estate brokerage firm for which the broker or salesperson is acting;

(i) The signature date;

(j) A disclaimer stating that, "This opinion is **not an appraisal of the market value of the property**, and may not be used in lieu of an appraisal. If an appraisal is desired, the services of a licensed or certified appraiser must be obtained. **This opinion may not be used by any party as the primary basis to determine the value of a parcel of real property for a mortgage loan origination, including first and second mortgages, refinances or equity lines of credit.**";

(k) A certification that the licensee is covered by errors and omissions insurance, to the extent required by state law, for all liability associated with the preparation of the broker's price opinion.

(5) If a broker's price opinion is submitted electronically or on a form supplied by the requesting party: Electronic submission is allowed.

(a) **A signature may be an electronic signature.**

(b) A signature required and the disclaimer required may be transmitted in a separate attachment if the electronic format or form supplied by the requesting party does not allow additional comments to be written by the licensee. The electronic format or the form supplied by the requesting party must:

(i) Reference the existence of a separate attachment; and

(ii) Include a statement that the broker's price opinion is not complete without the attachment.

A person licensed **may not** prepare a broker's price opinion for any purpose in lieu of an appraisal when an appraisal is required by federal or state statute.

A broker's price opinion which **estimates value or worth** of a parcel of real estate rather than sales price shall be deemed to be an appraisal and may not be prepared by a licensed broker or sales agent under the authority of their licensee but may only be prepared by a duly licensed appraiser and must meet the regulations promulgated by the Mississippi Real Estate Appraiser Licensing and Certification Board.

Real Estate Training Institute – Pre Exam Workbook

<u>A broker's price opinion</u> **may not under any circumstances be referred to as a valuation or appraisal.**

Disclosure of information concerning size or area of property involved in real estate transaction; liability; remedy for violation of section

<u>(1) (a) In connection with any real estate transaction, the size or area, in square footage or otherwise, of the subject property, if provided by any real estate licensee shall not be considered any warranty or guarantee of the size or area information, in square footage or otherwise, of the subject property.</u>

<u>(b) (i) If a real estate licensee provides any party to a real estate transaction with third-party information concerning the size or area, in square footage or otherwise, of the subject property involved in the transaction, the licensee shall identify the source of the information.</u>

(ii) For the purposes of this section, "third-party information" means:

1. An appraisal or any measurement information prepared by a licensed appraiser;

2. A surveyor developer's plan prepared by a licensed surveyor;

3. A tax assessor's public record; or

4. A builder's plan used to construct or market the property.

(c) A real estate licensee has no duty to the seller or purchaser of real property to conduct an independent investigation of the size or area, in square footage or otherwise, of a subject property, or to independently verify the accuracy of any third-party information.

(d) A real estate licensee who has complied with the requirements, shall have no further duties to the seller or purchaser of real property regarding disclosed or undisclosed property size or area information, and shall not be subject to liability to any party for any damages sustained with regard to any conflicting measurements or opinions of size or area, including exemplary or punitive damages.

(2) (a) If a real estate licensee has provided third-party information to any party to a real estate transaction concerning size or area of the subject real property, a party to the real estate transaction may recover damages from the licensee in a civil action only when a licensee knowingly violates the duty to disclose the source of the information as required in this section.

<u>However, nothing in this section shall provide immunity from civil liability to any licensee who knowingly misrepresents the size or area of the subject real property.</u>

(b) The sole and exclusive civil remedy at common law or otherwise for a violation of this section by a real estate licensee shall be an action for actual damages suffered by the party as a result of such violation and shall not include exemplary or punitive damages.

(c) For any real estate transaction commenced after July 1, 2013, any civil action brought pursuant to this section shall be commenced within two (2) years after the date of transfer of the subject real property.

(d) In any civil action brought pursuant to this section, the prevailing party shall be allowed court costs and reasonable attorney fees to be set by the court and collected as costs of the action.

(e) A transfer of a possessory interest in real property subject to the provisions of this section may not be invalidated solely because of the failure of any person to comply with the provisions.

(f) The provisions of this section shall apply to, regulate and determine the rights, duties, obligations and remedies, at common law or otherwise, of the **seller** marketing the seller's real property for sale through a real estate licensee, and of the purchaser of real property offered for sale through a real estate licensee, with respect to disclosure of third-party information concerning the subject real property's size or area, in square footage or otherwise, and this section hereby supplants and abrogates all common-law liability, rights, duties, obligations and remedies of all parties therefor.

The Mississippi Real Estate Commission

The commission shall consist of **five (5) persons**, to be **appointed by the Governor** with the advice and consent of the Senate.

Each appointee shall have been a resident and citizen of this state for at least **six (6) years prior to his appointment, and his vocation for at least five (5) years** shall have been that of a real estate broker.

One (1) member shall be appointed for the term of one (1) year; two (2) members for terms of two (2) years; two (2) members for terms of four (4) years; thereafter, the term of the members of said commission shall be for four (4) years and until their successors are appointed and qualify. There shall be at least one (1) commissioner from each congressional district, as such districts are constituted as of July 1, 2002. The commissioners appointed from each of the congressional districts shall be bona fide residents of the district from which each is appointed. One (1) additional commissioner shall be appointed without regard to residence in any particular congressional district. Members to fill vacancies shall be appointed by the Governor for the unexpired term. The Governor may remove any commissioner for cause. The State of Mississippi shall not be required to furnish office space for such commissioners. The provisions of this section shall not affect persons who are members of the Real Estate Commission as of January 1, 2002. Such members shall serve out their respective terms, upon the expiration of which the provisions of this section shall take effect. Nothing provided herein shall be construed as prohibiting the reappointment of any member of the said commission.

(2) The commission shall organize by selecting from its members a chairman, and may do all things necessary and convenient for carrying into effect the provisions of this chapter, and may from time to time promulgate rules and regulations. Each member of the commission shall receive per diem as authorized in Section 25-3-69, Mississippi Code of 1972, and his actual and necessary expenses incurred in the performance of duties pertaining to his office as authorized in Section 25-3-41, Mississippi Code of 1972.

(3) The commission shall adopt a seal by which it shall authenticate its proceedings. Copies of all records and papers in the office of the commission, duly certified and authenticated by the seal of said commission, shall be received in evidence in all courts equally and with like effect as the original. All records kept in the office of the commission under authority of this chapter shall be open to public inspection except pending investigative files.

Licenses for business entities

A corporation, partnership, company or association shall be granted a license **when individual broker's licenses have been issued to every member, owner, partner or officer** of such partnership, company, association or corporation who actively participates in its brokerage business and when any required fee is paid.

Qualifications for license

Licenses shall be granted only to persons who present, and to corporations, partnerships, companies or associations whose officers, associates or partners present satisfactory proof to the commission that they are **trustworthy and competent** to transact the business of a real estate broker or real estate salesperson in such manner as **to safeguard the interests of the public**.

Broker License

Every person who applies for a resident license as a real estate broker:

(a) shall be **age twenty-one (21) years** or over.

have his legal domicile in the State of Mississippi at the time he applies.

(b) shall be subject to the jurisdiction of this state.

subject to the income tax laws and other excise laws.

subject to the road and bridge privilege tax laws thereof.

(c) shall not be an elector in any other state.

(d) shall have held a license as an active real estate salesperson for twelve (12) months immediately prior to making application for the broker's examination.

(e) shall have successfully completed a minimum of **one hundred twenty (120) hours** of courses in real estate.

(f) shall have successfully completed the real estate broker's examination.

An applicant who has not held an active real estate salesperson's license for a period of at least twelve (12) months immediately prior to submitting an application shall have successfully completed a minimum of **one hundred fifty (150) classroom hours** in real estate courses, which courses are acceptable for credit toward a degree at a college or university as approved by the Southern Association of Colleges and Schools.

Salesperson License

Every applicant for a resident license as a real estate salesperson shall be **age eighteen (18) years or over**,

be a bona fide resident of the State of Mississippi prior to filing his application,

shall have successfully completed a minimum of **sixty (60) hours** in courses in real estate

shall have successfully completed the real estate salesperson's examination.

Reciprocity

*Reciprocity varies.

The residency requirements set forth in this section shall not apply to those licensees of other states who qualify and obtain nonresident licenses in this state.

The commission is authorized to exempt from such pre-licensing educational requirements, in whole or in part, a real estate licensee of another state who desires to obtain a license provided that the pre-licensing educational requirements in the other state are determined by the commission to be equivalent to pre-licensing educational requirements in this state and provided that such state extends this same privilege or exemption to Mississippi real estate licensees.

Nonresident's license; application

A nonresident may apply for a nonresident's license in Mississippi provided the individual is

a licensed broker in another state or

is a broker/salesperson or salesperson affiliated with a resident or nonresident Mississippi broker or is a nonresident who applies for a broker's license and who will maintain an office in Mississippi.

The nonresident broker **need not maintain a place of business within Mississippi** provided he is regularly actively engaged in the real estate business and maintains a place of business in the other state.

The nonresident licensee or applicant shall be subject to all the provisions of this chapter except for the residency requirement and approved equivalent pre-licensing education.

Every nonresident applicant shall file a statement of irrevocable consent with the Real Estate Commission that legal actions may be commenced against him in the proper court of any county of this state in which a cause of action may arise or in which the plaintiff may reside by service of process or pleading authorized by the laws of this state, by the Secretary of State of Mississippi, or by any member of the commission or chief executive officer thereof, the consent stipulating that the service of process or pleading shall be taken in all courts to be valid and binding as if personal service had been made upon the nonresident licensee in this state. The consent shall be duly acknowledged. Every nonresident licensee shall consent to have any hearings conducted by the commission at a place designated by the commission.

Any service of process or pleading shall be served on the executive officer of the commission by filing duplicate copies, one (1) of which shall be filed in the office of the commission and the other forwarded by certified mail to the last known principal address of the nonresident licensee against whom such process or pleading is directed. No default in any such action shall be taken except upon an affidavit of certification of the commission or the executive officer thereof that a copy of the process or pleading was mailed to the defendant as herein provided, and no default judgment shall be taken in any such action or proceeding until thirty (30) days after the mailing of process or pleading to the defendant.

An applicant shall sign an agreement to cooperate with any investigation of the applicant's real estate brokerage activities which the commission may undertake.

Each applicant for a nonresident license must qualify in all respects, including education, examination and fees, as an applicant who is a resident of Mississippi with the exception of the residency requirement and approved equivalent pre-licensing education.

A certification from the Executive Officer of the Real Estate Commission in the state in which the nonresident maintains his principal place of business shall be required. An applicant shall disclose all states in which he has held a real estate license and furnish a certification of licensure from that state or states.

The applicant/broker shall obtain an appropriate Mississippi license for the firm through which he intends to operate as a broker.

Any nonresident broker, broker-salesperson and salesperson shall meet Mississippi continuing education requirements after becoming licensed just as any resident licensee.

A broker or salesperson licensed in this state, on inactive status in good standing and no longer a resident of this state, may, after meeting other requirements for nonresident licensees, make application for a nonresident license without being required to meet current pre-licensing educational requirements at the time of application or having to sit for the examination in order to obtain the equivalent nonresident license.

A nonresident licensee in good standing who changes his legal domicile to the State of Mississippi may obtain a resident license equivalent to his nonresident license without meeting the current educational requirements or sitting for the examination, provided other requirements set forth for residents of the state are met.

A nonresident licensee may utilize the inactive status for his license under the same requirements as a resident licensee, including but not limited to, continuing education requirements and ceasing active status under a licensed nonresident broker.

Application for license

(1) Every applicant for a real estate broker's license shall apply therefor in writing <u>upon blanks prepared by the commission</u> and shall provide such data and information as the commission may require.

(2) <u>Such application shall be accompanied by the recommendation of **at least three (3) citizens** who have been property owners **for at least three (3) years**, who have **known the applicant for three (3) years**, and who are not related to the applicant, certifying that the applicant bears a good reputation for honesty and trustworthiness and recommending that a license be granted to the applicant.</u>

(3) Every applicant for a salesperson's license shall apply therefor in writing <u>upon blanks prepared by the commission</u> and shall provide such data and information as the commission may require.

(4) <u>Each application for license shall also be accompanied by **two (2) photographs** of the applicant in such form as the commission may prescribe.</u>

(5) <u>Each application or filing made under this section shall include the **social security number(s)** of the applicant.</u>

Nonresident may not act except in cooperation with licensed broker of state

<u>It shall be unlawful for any licensed broker, salesperson or other person who is not licensed as a Mississippi resident or nonresident broker or salesperson and a licensed broker or licensed salesperson in this state to perform any of the acts regulated, except that a licensed broker of another state who does not hold a Mississippi real estate license may cooperate with a licensed broker of this state **provided that any commission or fee resulting from such cooperative negotiation shall be stated on a form filed with the commission reflecting the compensation to be paid to the Mississippi broker.**</u>

Whenever a Mississippi broker enters into a cooperative agreement under this section, the Mississippi broker shall file **within ten (10) days** with the commission a copy of each such written agreement. By signing the agreement, the nonresident broker who is not licensed in this state agrees to abide by Mississippi law, and the rules and regulations of the commission; and further agrees that civil actions may be commenced against him in any court of competent jurisdiction in any county of this state in which a claim may arise.

The Mississippi broker shall require a listing or joint listing of the property involved. The written cooperative agreements shall specify all material terms of each agreement, including but not limited to its financial terms.

The showing of property located in Mississippi and negotiations shall be supervised by the Mississippi broker.

In all advertising of real estate located in Mississippi, the name and telephone number of the Mississippi broker shall appear and shall be given **equal prominence** with the name of the nonresident broker who is not licensed in this state.

The Mississippi broker shall be **liable for all acts** of the above cooperating broker, as well as for his own acts, arising from the execution of any cooperative agreement.

The Mississippi broker shall determine that the cooperating broker is licensed as a broker in another state.

All earnest money pertaining to a cooperative agreement must be held in escrow by the Mississippi broker unless both the buyer and seller agree in writing to relieve the Mississippi broker of this responsibility.

Written examination requirement; exemption for licensee of another state; reciprocity

(1) In addition to proof of his honesty, trustworthiness and good reputation, the applicant shall take a written examination which shall be held at least four (4) times each year at regular intervals and on stated times by the commission and shall test reading, writing, spelling, elementary arithmetic and his general knowledge of the statutes of this state relating to real property, deeds, mortgages, agreements of sale, agency, contract, leases, ethics, appraisals, the provisions of this chapter and such other matters the commission certifies as necessary to the practice of real estate brokerage in the State of Mississippi. The examination for a broker's license shall differ from the examination for a salesperson's license, in that it shall be of a more exacting nature and require higher standards of knowledge of real estate. The commission shall cause examinations to be conducted at such times and places as it shall determine.

(2) In event the license of any real estate broker or salesperson is revoked by the commission subsequent to the enactment of this chapter, no new license shall be issued to such person unless he complies with the provisions of this chapter.

Real Estate Training Institute – Pre Exam Workbook

(3) No person shall be permitted or authorized to act as a real estate broker or salesperson until he has qualified by examination, except as hereinbefore provided.

Any individual who fails to pass the examination for salesperson upon two (2) occasions, shall be ineligible for a similar examination, until after the expiration of three (3) months from the time such individual last took the examination. *You need to pass the state section. If you pass the state section and fail the national, you can take the national portion as many times as possible before your time expires.

Any individual who fails to pass the broker's examination upon two (2) occasions, shall be ineligible for a similar examination until after the expiration of six (6) months from the time such individual last took the examination, and then only upon making application as in the first instance. *You need to pass the state portion. If you pass the state section and fail the national, you can take the national portion as many times as possible before your time expires

(4) If the applicant is a partnership, association or corporation, said examination shall be taken on behalf of said partnership, association or corporation by the member or officer thereof who is designated in the application as the person to receive a license by virtue of the issuing of a license to such partnership, association or corporation.

(5) Upon satisfactorily passing such examination and upon complying with all other provisions of law and conditions, a license shall thereupon be issued to the successful applicant who, upon receiving such license, is authorized to conduct the business of a real estate broker or real estate salesperson in this state.

(6) The commission is authorized to exempt from such examination, in whole or in part, a real estate licensee of another state who desires to obtain a license; provided, however, that the examination administered in the other state is determined by the commission to be equivalent to such examination given in this state and provided that such other state extends this same privilege or exemption to Mississippi real estate licensees. **Reciprocity Varies**

School, Course and Instructor Qualifications have been omitted. Not on test.

A pre-license course must meet any standards that the Association of Real Estate Licensing Law Officials (ARELLO), or its successor(s), may have for pre-license courses, including, without limitation, standards for content, form, examination, facilities and instructors. If ARELLO or its successor(s) operate a certification program for pre-license courses, a pre-license course must be certified by ARELLO or its successor(s) before the commission may approve the course.

No more than eight (8) pre-license hours may be earned in a single day.

Distance learning courses have been omitted. Not on test.

Temporary licenses; post-license education

Upon passing the Mississippi broker's or salesperson's examination and complying with all other conditions for licensure, **a temporary license shall be issued** to the applicant.

The fee for the temporary license shall also be the same for the permanent license.

A temporary license shall be valid for a period of **one (1) year** following the first day of the month after its issuance.

All Mississippi residents who apply for and receive a nonresident Mississippi broker's or salesperson's license shall be subject to the requirements, including temporary licensure and completion of a **thirty-hour** post-license course.

The holder of a temporary license shall not be issued a permanent license until he has satisfactorily completed a **thirty-hour post-license course** prescribed by the commission and offered by providers specifically certified by the commission to offer this mandated post-license education.

The holder of a temporary license shall complete the entire **thirty-hour course within twelve (12) months** of issuance of his temporary license; **otherwise this temporary license shall automatically be placed on inactive status** by the Mississippi Real Estate Commission.

If the holder of the temporary license does not complete the course and have his permanent license issued within one (1) year following the first day of the month after its issuance, the temporary license shall automatically expire and lapse. A temporary license is not subject to renewal procedures in this chapter and may not be renewed.

No more than eight (8) hours may be earned in a single day.

The holder of an active license who has satisfactorily completed the post-license course and whose permanent license has been issued shall not be subject to the sixteen-hour continuing education requirement in this chapter for the first renewal of his permanent license.

Location of business and responsible broker to be designated

Every person, partnership, association or corporation licensed as a real estate broker shall be required to have and maintain a **definite place of business,** which shall be a room either in his home or an office elsewhere, to be used for the transaction of real estate business, or such business and any allied business.

The certificate of registration as broker and the **certificate of each real estate salesperson employed** by the broker shall be prominently displayed in that office.

The place of business shall be designated in the license.

In case of removal from the designated address, the licensee shall make application to the commission before removal, or within **ten (10) da**ys after removal, designating the new location of such office, whereupon the commission shall forthwith issue a new license for the new location for the **unexpired period**.

All licenses issued to a real estate salesperson or broker-salesperson shall designate their responsible broker.

Prompt notice in writing, within **three (3) days**, shall be given to the commission by any real estate salesperson of a change of responsible broker, and of the name of the principal broker into whose agency the salesperson is about to enter; **and a new license shall thereupon be issued by the commission to such salesperson for the unexpired term of the original license** upon the return to the commission of the license previously issued.

The change of responsible broker or employment by any licensed real estate salesperson without notice to the commission as required shall automatically cancel his license.

Upon termination of a salesperson's agency, the responsible broker shall within three (3) days return the salesperson's license to the commission for cancellation.

It shall be unlawful for any real estate salesperson to perform any of the acts, either directly or indirectly after his agency has been terminated and his license has been returned for cancellation until his license has been reissued by the commission.

Real estate licensees are required to obtain errors and omissions insurance coverage.

(1) The following words and phrases shall have the meanings ascribed herein unless the context clearly indicates otherwise:

(a) "Aggregate limit" means a provision in an insurance contract limiting the maximum liability of an insurer for a series of losses in a given time period such as the policy term.

(b) "Claims-made" means policies written under a claims-made basis which shall cover claims made (reported or filed) during the year the policy is in force for incidents which occur that year or during any previous period the policyholder was insured under the claims-made contract. This form of coverage is in contrast to the occurrence policy which covers today's incident regardless of when a claim is filed even if it is one or more years later.

(c) "Extended reporting period" means a designated period of time after a claims-made policy has expired during which a claim may be made and coverage triggered as if the claim had been made during the policy period.

(d) "Licensee" means any active individual broker, broker-salesperson or salesperson, any partnership or any corporation.

(e) "Per-claim limit" means the maximum limit payable, per licensee, for damages arising out of the same error, omission or wrongful act.

(f) "Prior acts coverage" applies to policies on a claims-made versus occurrence basis. Prior acts coverage responds to claims that are made during a current policy period, but the act or acts causing the claim or injuries for which the claim is made occurred prior to the inception of the current policy period.

(g) "Proof of coverage" means a copy of the actual policy of insurance, a certificate of insurance or a binder of insurance.

(h) "Retroactive date" means a provision, found in many claims-made policies, that the policy shall not cover claims for injuries or damages that occurred before the retroactive date even if the claim is first made during the policy period.

(2) The following persons shall submit proof of insurance:

(a) Any active individual broker, active broker-salesperson or active salesperson;

(b) Any partnership (optional); or

(c) Any corporation (optional).

(3) <u>Individuals whose licenses are on inactive status are not required to carry errors and omissions insur</u>ance.

(4) All Mississippi licensees shall be covered for activities contemplated under this chapter.

(5) Licensees may obtain errors and omissions coverage through the insurance carrier approved by the Mississippi Real Estate Commission and provided on a group policy basis.

The following are minimum requirements of the group policy to be issued to the commission, including, as named insureds, all licensees who have paid their required premium:

(a) All activities contemplated under this chapter are included as covered activities;

(b) A per-claim limit is not less than <u>One Hundred Thousand Dollars ($100,000.00)</u>;

(c) An annual aggregate limit is not less than <u>One Hundred Thousand Dollars ($100,000.00)</u>;

(d) <u>Limits apply per licensee per claim</u>;

(e) Maximum deductible is <u>Two Thousand Five Hundred Dollars ($2,500.00)</u> per licensee per claim for damages;

(f) Maximum deductible is <u>One Thousand Dollars ($1,000.00)</u> per licensee per claim for defense costs; and

(g) The contract of insurance pays, on behalf of the injured person(s), liabilities owed.

Real Estate Training Institute – Pre Exam Workbook

(6) (a) The maximum contract period between the insurance carrier and the commission is to be five (5) consecutive policy terms, after which time period the commission shall place the insurance out for competitive bid. The commission shall reserve the right to place the contract out for bid at the end of any policy period.

(b) <u>The policy period shall be a twelve-month policy term</u>.

(c) The retroactive date for the master policy shall not be before July 1, 1994.

(i) The licensee may purchase full prior acts coverage on July 1, 1994, if the licensee can show proof of errors and omissions coverage that has been in effect since at least March 15, 1994.

(ii) If the licensee purchases full prior acts coverage on July 1, 1994, that licensee shall continue to be guaranteed full prior acts coverage if the insurance carriers are changed in the future.

(iii) If the licensee was not carrying errors and omissions insurance on July 1, 1994, the individual certificate shall be issued with a retroactive date of July 1, 1994. This date shall not be advanced if the insurance carriers are changed in the future.

(iv) <u>For any new licensee who first obtains a license after July 1, 1994, the retroactive date shall be the effective date of licensure.</u>

(v) <u>For any licensee who changes status of license from inactive to active, the retroactive date shall be the effective date of change to "active" licensure.</u>

(d) <u>Each licensee shall be notified of the required terms and conditions of coverage for the policy at least **thirty (30) days**</u> before the renewal date of the policy.

A certificate of coverage, showing compliance with the required terms and conditions of coverage, shall be filed with the commission by the renewal date of the policy by each licensee who elects not to participate in the insurance program administered by the commission.

(e) If the commission is unable to obtain errors and omissions insurance coverage to insure all licensees who choose to participate in the insurance program at a premium of no more than Two Hundred Fifty Dollars ($250.00) per twelve (12) months' policy period, the requirement of insurance coverage under this section shall be void during the applicable contract period.

(7) <u>Licensees may obtain errors and omissions coverage independently</u> if the coverage contained in the policy complies with the following minimum requirements:

(a) All activities contemplated under this chapter are included as covered activities; (b) A per-claim limit is not less than One Hundred Thousand Dollars ($100,000.00);

(b) A per-claim limit is not less than One Hundred Thousand Dollars ($100,000.00);

(c) The deductible is not more than Two Thousand Five Hundred Dollars ($2,500.00) per licensee per claim for damages and the deductible is not more than One Thousand Dollars ($1,000.00) per licensee per claim for defense costs; and

(d) If other insurance is provided as proof of errors and omissions coverage, the other insurance carrier shall agree to a non-cancelable policy or to provide a letter of commitment to notify the commission thirty (30) days before the intention to cancel.

(8) The following provisions apply to individual licensees:

(a) The commission shall require receipt of proof of errors and omissions insurance from new licensees **within thirty (30) days of licensure**.

Any licenses issued at any time other than policy renewal time shall be subject to a pro rata premium.

(b) For licensees not submitting proof of insurance necessary to continue active licensure, the commission shall be responsible for sending notice of deficiency to those licensees.

Licensees who do not correct the deficiency within **thirty (30) days** shall have their licenses placed on inactive status.

The commission shall assess fees for inactive status and for return to active status when errors and omissions insurance has been obtained.

(c) Any licensee insured in the state program whose license becomes inactive shall not be charged an additional premium if the license is reactivated during the policy period.

(9) The commission is authorized to adopt such rules and regulations as it deems appropriate to handle administrative duties relating to operation of the program, including billing and premium collection.

License renewal; continuing education requirements; exemptions; rules and regulations; reinstatement of expired license.

Each licensee with a MREC license shall, on or before the expiration date of his license, submit proof of completion of not less than sixteen (16) clock hours of approved course work.. ***Every 2 years. CE 16 hrs**

Exempt from CE
Broker's or salesperson's license in this state for at least twenty-five (25) years and who are older than seventy (70) years of age.

Real estate license fund

Real Estate Training Institute – Pre Exam Workbook

All fees charged and collected under this chapter shall be paid by the administrator at least once a week, accompanied by a detailed statement thereof, into the treasury of the state to credit of a fund to be known as the "Real Estate License Fund,".

All monies which shall be paid into the State Treasury and credited to **the "Real Estate License Fund"** are used for:

payment of salaries and expenses, printing an annual directory of licensees, and for educational purposes.

And **maintenance of a searchable, internet-based web site** which shall satisfy the requirement for publication of a directory of licensees under this section.

Grounds for refusing to issue or suspending or revoking license; hearing

(1) The commission may, upon its own motion and shall upon the verified complaint in writing of any person, hold a hearing for the refusal of license or for the suspension or revocation of a license previously issued, or for such other action as the commission deems appropriate.

The commission shall have full power to refuse a license for cause or to revoke or suspend a license where it has been obtained by false or fraudulent representation, or where the licensee in performing or attempting to perform any of the acts mentioned herein, is deemed to be guilty of:

****HOW TO LOSE YOUR LICENSE

Making any substantial misrepresentation in connection with a real estate transaction;

Making any false promises of a character likely to influence, persuade or induce;

Pursuing a continued and flagrant course of misrepresentation or making false promises through agents or salespersons or any medium of advertising or otherwise;

Any misleading or untruthful advertising;

Acting for more than one (1) party in a transaction or receiving compensation from more than one (1) party in a transaction, or both, without the knowledge of all parties for whom he acts;

Failing, within a reasonable time, to account for or to remit any monies coming into his possession which belong to others, or commingling of monies belonging to others with his own funds.

Every responsible broker procuring the execution of an earnest money contract or option or other contract who shall take or receive any cash or checks shall deposit, within a reasonable period of time, the sum or sums so received in a **trust or escrow account** in a bank or trust company pending the consummation or termination of the transaction.

"Reasonable time" in this context means by the close of business of the next banking day;

Entering a guilty plea or conviction in a court of competent jurisdiction of this state, or any other state or the United States of any felony.

Displaying a "for sale" or "for rent" sign on any property without the owner's consent. ***Commonly seen on the exam.**

Failing to furnish voluntarily, at the time of signing, copies of all listings, contracts and agreements to all parties executing the same.

Paying any rebate, profit or commission to any person other than a real estate broker or salesperson licensed.

Inducing any party to a contract, sale or lease to break such contract for the purpose of substituting in lieu thereof a new contract, where such substitution is motivated by the personal gain of the licensee.

Accepting a **commission or valuable consideration** as a real estate salesperson from any person, except his employer who must be a licensed real estate broker.

Any act or conduct, whether of the same or a different character than hereinabove specified, which constitutes or demonstrates **bad faith, incompetency or untrustworthiness, or dishonest, fraudulent or improper dealing.**

No real estate broker shall practice law or give legal advice directly or indirectly unless said broker be a duly licensed attorney under the laws of this state.

He shall not act as a public conveyancer nor give advice or opinions as to the legal effect of instruments nor give opinions concerning the validity of title to real estate; nor shall he prevent or discourage any party to a real estate transaction from employing the services of an attorney.

nor shall a broker undertake to prepare documents fixing and defining the legal rights of parties to a transaction.

However, when acting as a broker, he may use an earnest money contract form.

A real estate broker shall not participate in attorney's fees, unless the broker is a duly licensed attorney under the laws of this state and performs legal services in addition to brokerage services.

It is expressly provided that it is not the intent and purpose of the Mississippi Legislature to prevent a license from being issued to any person who is found to be of good reputation, is able to give bond, and who has lived in the State of Mississippi for the required period or is otherwise qualified.

In addition to the reasons to lose your license above, the commission shall be authorized to suspend the license of any licensee for being out of compliance with an order for support.

(5) Nothing in this chapter shall prevent an associate broker or salesperson from owning any lawfully constituted business organization, including, but not limited to, a corporation, limited liability company or limited liability partnership, for the purpose of receiving payments contemplated in this chapter. The business organization shall not be required to be licensed under this chapter and shall not engage in any other activity requiring a real estate license.

Powers of commission as to violations; hearings upon revocation; subpoena

The commission is hereby authorized and directed to take legal action against any violator of this chapter.

Upon complaint initiated by the commission or filed with it, **the licensee or any other person charged with a violation of this chapter shall be given fifteen (15) days'** notice of the hearing upon the charges filed, together with a copy of the complaint.

The applicant or licensee or other violator shall have an opportunity to be heard in person or by counsel, to offer testimony, and to examine witnesses appearing in connection with the complaint. Hearings shall be held at the offices of the Mississippi Real Estate Commission, or at the commission's sole discretion, at a place determined by the commission.

At such hearings, all witnesses shall be sworn and stenographic notes of the proceedings shall be taken and filed as a part of the record in the case. Any party to the proceedings shall be furnished with a copy of such stenographic notes upon payment to the commission of such fees as it shall prescribe, not exceeding, however, the actual cost to the commission. The commission shall render a decision on any complaint and shall immediately notify the parties to the proceedings in writing of its ruling, order or decision.

In addition to the authority granted to the commission as hereinabove set forth, the commission is hereby vested with the authority to bring injunctive proceedings in any appropriate forum against any violator or violators, and all judges or courts now having the power to grant injunctions are specifically granted the power and jurisdiction to hear and dispose of such proceedings.

The commission is hereby authorized and empowered to issue subpoenas for the attendance of witnesses and the production of books and papers.

The process issued by the commission shall extend to all parts of the state, and such process shall be served by any person designated by the commission for such service.

The person serving such process receive such compensation as may be allowed by the commission, not to exceed the fee prescribed by law for similar services. All witnesses who are subpoenaed and who appear in any proceedings before the commission receive the same fees and mileage as allowed by law, and all such fees shall be taxed as part of the costs in the case.

Where in any proceeding before the commission any witness shall fail or refuse to attend upon subpoena issued by the commission, shall refuse to testify, or shall refuse to produce any books and papers the production of which is called for by the subpoena, the attendance of such witness and the giving of his testimony and the production of the books and papers shall be enforced by any court of competent jurisdiction of this state in the same manner as the attendance and testimony of witnesses in civil cases are enforced in the courts of this state.

The commission may obtain legal counsel privately to represent it in proceedings when legal counsel is required.

Appeals

Any applicant or licensee or person aggrieved shall have the right of appeal from any adverse ruling or order or decision of the commission to the circuit court of the county of residence of the applicant, licensee or person, or of the First Judicial District of Hinds County, **within thirty (30) days** from the service of notice of the action of the commission upon the parties in interest.

Notice of appeals shall be filed in the office of the clerk of the court who shall issue a writ of certiorari directed to the commission commanding it, within thirty (30) days after service thereof, to certify to such court its entire record in the matter in which the appeal has been taken. The appeal shall thereupon be heard in due course by said court, without a jury, which shall review the record and make its determination of the cause between the parties.

Any order, rule or decision of the commission shall not take effect until after the time for appeal to said court shall have expired. In the event an appeal is taken by a defendant, such appeal may act, in the discretion of the court, as a supersedes and the court shall dispose of said appeal and enter its decision promptly.

Any person taking an appeal shall post a satisfactory bond in the amount of Five Hundred Dollars ($ 500.00) for the payment of any costs which may be adjudged against him.

Duties of commission

The commission is hereby authorized to assist in conducting or holding real estate courses or institutes, and to incur and pay the necessary expenses in connection therewith, which courses or institutes shall be open to any licensee or other interested parties.

The commission is hereby authorized to assist libraries, real estate institutes, and foundations with financial aid, or otherwise, in providing texts, sponsoring studies, surveys and educational programs for the benefit of real estate and the elevation of the real estate business.

Penalties for violations of chapter

*First Offense
Any person violating a provision of this chapter shall, upon conviction of a first violation thereof, if a person, be punished by a fine or not less than Five Hundred Dollars ($500.00) **nor more than One Thousand Dollars ($1,000.00), or by imprisonment for a term not to exceed ninety (90) days,**

or both; and if a corporation, be punished by a fine of not more than Two Thousand Dollars ($2,000.00).

*Second Offense
Upon conviction of a second or subsequent violation, if a person, shall be punished by a fine of not less than One Thousand Dollars ($1,000.00) **nor more than Two Thousand Dollars ($2,000.00), or by imprisonment for a term not to exceed six (6) months, or both;** and if a corporation, be punished by a fine of not less than Two Thousand Dollars ($2,000.00) nor more than Five Thousand Dollars ($5,000.00).

Any officer or agent of a corporation, or any member or agent of a partnership or association, who shall personally participate in or be accessory to any violation of this chapter by such corporation, partnership or association, shall be subject to the penalties herein prescribed for individuals.

In case any person, partnership, association or corporation shall have received any sum of money, or the equivalent thereto, as commission, compensation or profit by or in consequence of his violation of any provision of this chapter, such person, partnership, association or corporation shall also be liable to a penalty of not less than the amount of the sum of money so received and not more than four (4) times the sum so received, as may be determined by the court, which penalty may be sued for and recovered by any person aggrieved and for his use and benefit, in any court of competent jurisdiction.

No fee, commission or other valuable consideration may be paid to a person for real estate brokerage activities unless the person provides evidence of licensure or provides evidence of a cooperative agreement.

License required to sue for compensation; suit by salesperson in own name

No person, partnership, association or corporation shall bring or maintain an action in any court of this state for the recovery of a commission, fee or compensation for any act done or services rendered, the doing or rendering of which is prohibited under the provisions of this chapter for persons other than licensed real estate brokers, unless such person was duly licensed hereunder as a real estate broker at the time of the doing of such act or the rendering of such service.

No real estate salesperson shall have the right to institute suits in his own name for the recovery of a fee, commission or compensation for services as a real estate salesperson, but any such action shall be instituted and brought by the broker employing such salesperson. However, any real estate salesperson shall have the right to bring an action in his own name if the action is against the broker employing such salesperson for the recovery of any fees owed to him.

Commission to adopt rules and regulations

The commission may act by a majority of the members thereof, and authority is hereby given to the commission to adopt, fix and establish all rules and regulations in its opinion necessary for the conduct of its business, the holdings of hearings before it, and otherwise generally for the enforcement and administration of the provisions of this chapter.

Further, the commission is empowered with the authority to adopt such rules and regulations as it deems appropriate to regulate the sale of timesharing and condominium properties within the state of Mississippi and the sale of timesharing and condominium properties in other states to residents of Mississippi.

"Interest on Real Estate Brokers' Escrow Accounts Act." IREBEA

Definitions

"Interest earnings" means the total interest earnings generated by the IREBEA at each individual financial institution.

*The Three Charities a Broker can donate the interest earnings to:

 1. **Local affiliate of Habitat for Humanity International, Inc**.

 2. **Local affiliate of Fuller Center for Housing, Inc**.

 3. **"Chair of real estate"** means the endowment fund held and administered by any Mississippi university. For those universities which do not designate or which do not have a "chair of real estate," the term "chair of real estate" includes a professorship of real estate.

Interest on Real Estate Brokers' Escrow Accounts (IREBEA) program

The IREBEA program **shall be a voluntary program** based upon willing participation by real estate brokers, whether proprietorships, partnerships or professional corporations.

IREBEA shall **apply to all clients or customers** of the participating brokers whose funds on deposit are either nominal in amount or to be held for a short period of time.

No earnings on the IREBEA accounts may be made available to or utilized by a broker.

Upon the request of the client or customer, earnings may be made available to the client whenever possible upon deposited funds which are neither nominal in amount nor to be held for a short period of time; **however, traditional broker-client or broker-customer relationships do not compel brokers either to invest clients' or customers' funds or to advise clients or customers to make their funds productive.**

Clients' or customers' funds which are nominal in amount or to be held for a short period of time shall be retained **in an interest-bearing checking or savings trust account** with the interest, less any service charge or fees, **made payable at least quarterly** to **any chair of real estate, local**

affiliate of Habitat for Humanity International, Inc., or local affiliate of Fuller Center for Housing, Inc. A separate accounting shall be made annually for all funds received.

The broker shall select in writing that the chair of real estate, local affiliate of Habitat for Humanity International, Inc., or local affiliate of Fuller Center for Housing, Inc., shall be the beneficiary of such funds for the interest earnings on such funds. **The interest earnings shall not be divided between one or more beneficiaries.**

The determination of whether clients' or customers' funds are nominal in amount or to be held for a short period of time rests in the sound judgment of each broker, and no charge of ethical impropriety or other breach of professional conduct shall attend a broker's exercise of judgment in that regard.

Notification to clients or customers is unnecessary for those brokers who choose to participate in the program.

Participation in the IREBEA program is accomplished by the broker's written notification to an authorized financial institution.

That communication shall contain an expression of the broker's desire to participate in the program and, if the institution has not already received appropriate notification, advice regarding the Internal Revenue Service's approval of the taxability of earned interest or dividends to a chair of real estate, or a local affiliate of Habitat for Humanity International, Inc., or local affiliate of Fuller Center for Housing, Inc.

The following principles shall apply to those clients' or customers' funds held in trust accounts by brokers who elect not to participate in IREBEA:

No earnings from the funds may be made available to any broker.

Upon the request of a client or customer, earnings may be made available to the client or customer whenever possible upon deposited funds which are neither nominal in amount nor to be held for a short period of time; however, traditional broker-client or broker-customer relationships do not compel brokers either to invest clients' or customers' funds or to advise clients or customers to make their funds productive.

Clients' or customers' funds which are nominal in amount or to be held for short periods of time, and for which individual income generation allocation is not arranged with a financial institution, shall be retained in a **noninterest-bearing demand trust account**.

The determination of whether clients' or customers' funds are nominal in amount or to be held for a short period of time rests in the sound judgment of each broker, and no charge of ethical impropriety or other breach of professional conduct shall attend a broker's exercise of judgment in that regard.

Real Estate Training Institute – Pre Exam Workbook

Real Estate Transfer Disclosure requirement provisions

apply only with respect to transfers by sale, exchange, installment land sale contract, lease with an option to purchase, any other option to purchase or ground lease coupled with improvements, of real property on which a dwelling unit is located, or residential stock cooperative improved with or consisting of not less than one (1) nor more than four (4) dwelling units, when the execution of such transfers is by, or with the aid of, a duly licensed real estate broker or salesperson.

Real Estate Transfer Disclosure Exclusions

Transfers pursuant to court order, including, but not limited to, transfers ordered by a probate court in administration of an estate, transfers pursuant to a writ of execution, transfers by any foreclosure sale, transfers by a trustee in bankruptcy, transfers by eminent domain, and transfers resulting from a decree for specific performance.

Transfers to a mortgagee by a mortgagor or successor in interest who is in default, transfers to a beneficiary of a deed of trust by a trustor or successor in interest who is in default, transfers by any foreclosure sale after default, in an obligation secured by a mortgage, transfers by a sale under a power of sale or any foreclosure sale under a decree of foreclosure after default in an obligation secured by a deed of trust or secured by any other instrument containing a power of sale, or transfers by a mortgagee or a beneficiary under a deed of trust who has acquired the real property at a sale conducted pursuant to a power of sale under a mortgage or deed of trust or a sale pursuant to a decree of foreclosure or has acquired the real property by a deed in lieu of foreclosure.

Transfers by a fiduciary in the course of the administration of a decedent's estate, guardianship, conservatorship or trust.

Transfers from one co-owner to one or more other co-owners. *Seen often on the exam

Transfers made to a spouse, or to a person or persons in the lineal line of consanguinity of one or more of the transferors. *Seen often on the exam

Transfers between spouses resulting from a decree of dissolution of marriage or a decree of legal separation or from a property settlement agreement incidental to such a decree. *Seen often on the exam

Transfers or exchanges to or from any governmental entity.

Transfers of real property on which no dwelling is located.

Delivery of written statement required; indication of compliance; right of transferee to terminate for late delivery

The transferor of any real property shall deliver to the prospective transferee the written property condition disclosure statement as follows:

Real Estate Training Institute – Pre Exam Workbook

In the case of a sale, as soon as **practicable** before transfer of title. * keyword: **Practicable**

In the case of transfer by a real property sales contract, or by a lease together with an option to purchase, or a ground lease coupled with improvements, as soon as **practicable** before execution of the contract. For the purpose of this paragraph, execution means the making or acceptance of an offer. *keyword: Practicable

The transferor shall indicate compliance either on the receipt for deposit, the real property sales contract, the lease, or any addendum attached thereto or on a separate document.

If any disclosure, or any material amendment of any disclosure, required to be made is delivered after the execution of an offer to purchase, the transferee shall have three (3) days after delivery in person or five (5) days after delivery by deposit in the mail, to terminate his or her offer by delivery of a written notice of termination to the transferor or the transferor's agent.

Limit on duties and liabilities with respect to information required or delivered

Neither the transferor nor any listing or selling agent shall be liable for any error, inaccuracy or omission of any information delivered if the error, inaccuracy or omission was not within the personal knowledge of the transferor or that listing or selling agent, was based on information timely provided by public agencies or by other persons providing information that is required to be disclosed and **ordinary care** was exercised in obtaining and transmitting it.

The delivery of any information required to be disclosed to a prospective transferee by a public agency or other person providing information required to be disclosed shall be deemed to comply with the requirements and shall relieve the transferor or any listing or selling agent of any further duty under with respect to that item of information.

The delivery of a report or opinion prepared by a licensed engineer, land surveyor, geologist, structural pest control operator, contractor or other expert, dealing with matters within the scope of the professional's license or expertise, shall be sufficient compliance for the exemption.

If the information is provided to the prospective transferee pursuant to a request therefor, whether written or oral. In responding to such a request, an expert may indicate, in writing, an understanding that the information provided will be used in fulfilling the requirements of Disclosure Law and, if so, shall indicate the required disclosures, or parts thereof, to which the information being furnished is applicable.

Where such a statement is furnished, the expert shall not be responsible for any items of information, or parts thereof, other than those expressly set forth in the statement.

Approximation of certain information required to be disclosed; information subsequently rendered inaccurate

Real Estate Training Institute – Pre Exam Workbook

If information disclosed is subsequently rendered inaccurate as a result of any act, occurrence or agreement subsequent to the delivery of the required disclosures, the inaccuracy resulting therefrom does not constitute a violation.

If at the time the disclosures are required to be made, an item of information required to be disclosed is unknown or not available to the transferor, and the transferor or his agent has made a reasonable effort to ascertain it, the transferor may use an approximation of the information, provided the approximation is clearly identified as such, is reasonable, is based on the best information available to the transferor or his agent, and is not used for the purpose of circumventing or evading.

Form of seller's disclosure statement

The disclosures required pertaining to the property proposed to be transferred shall be set forth in, and shall be made **on a copy of a disclosure form**, the structure and composition of which shall be determined by the Mississippi Real Estate Commission.

Disclosures to be made in good faith

Each disclosure and each act which may be performed in making the disclosure, shall be made in good faith; **"good faith" means honesty**.

Provisions not exhaustive of items to be disclosed

The specification of items for disclosure does not limit or abridge any obligation for disclosure created by any other provision of law or which may exist in order to avoid fraud, misrepresentation or deceit in the transfer transaction.

Amendment of disclosure

Any disclosure made may be amended in writing by the transferor or his agent. ***A Buyer can cancel the transaction without penalty if the Transfer Disclosure is amended.**

Delivery of disclosure

Delivery of disclosure shall be by personal delivery to the transferee or by mail to the prospective transferee. **Delivery to the spouse of a transferee shall be deemed delivery to the transferee, unless provided otherwise by contract.**

Agent; extent of agency

Any person or entity, other than a duly licensed real estate broker or salesperson acting in the capacity of an escrow agent for the transfer of real property shall not be deemed the agent of the transferor or transferee for purposes of the disclosure requirements unless the person or entity is empowered to so act by an express written agreement to that effect. The extent of such an agency shall be governed by the written agreement.

Delivery of disclosure where more than one agent; inability of delivering broker to obtain disclosure document; notification to transferee of right to disclosure

If more than one (1) licensed real estate broker is acting as an agent in a transaction, the broker who has obtained the offer made by the transferee shall, except as otherwise provided, deliver the disclosure required to the transferee, unless the transferor has given other written instructions for delivery.

If a licensed real estate broker responsible for delivering the disclosures cannot obtain the disclosure document required and does not have written assurance from the transferee that the disclosure has been received, **the broker shall advise the transferee in writing of his rights to the disclosure.**

A licensed real estate broker responsible for delivering disclosures under this section shall maintain a record of the action taken to effect compliance.

Noncompliance with disclosure requirements not to invalidate transfer; liability for actual damages

No transfer shall be invalidated solely because of the failure of any person to comply with any provision of Disclosure Law. However, any person who willfully or negligently violates or fails to perform any duty prescribed by any provision of Disclosure Law shall be liable in the amount of **actual damages** suffered by a transferee.

Enforcement by Mississippi Real Estate Commission

The Mississippi Real Estate Commission is authorized to enforce the provisions of MS Real Estate Law. Any violation shall be treated in the same manner as a violation of the Real Estate Broker License Law of 1954, and shall be subject to same penalties.

Failure to disclose nonmaterial fact regarding property as site of death or felony crime, as site of act or occurrence having no effect on physical condition of property, or as being owned or occupied by persons affected or exposed to certain diseases; failure to disclose information provided or maintained on registration of sex offenders

The fact or suspicion that real property is or was:

The site of a natural death, suicide, homicide or felony crime (except for illegal drug activity that affects the physical condition of the property, its physical environment or the improvements located thereon);

The site of an act or occurrence that had no effect on the physical condition of the property, its physical environment or the improvements located thereon;

Owned or occupied by a person affected or exposed to any disease not known to be transmitted through common occupancy of real estate including, but not limited to, the human immunodeficiency virus (HIV) and the acquired immune deficiency syndrome (AIDS);

does not constitute a material fact that must be disclosed in a real estate transaction. A failure to disclose such nonmaterial facts or suspicions shall not give rise to a criminal, civil or administrative action against the owner of such real property, a licensed real estate broker or any affiliated licensee of the broker.

A failure to disclose in any real estate transaction any information that is provided or maintained, or is required to be provided or maintained, shall not give rise to a cause of action against an owner of real property, a licensed real estate broker or any affiliated licensee of the broker. Likewise, no cause of action shall arise against any licensed real estate broker or affiliated licensee of the broker for revealing information to a seller or buyer of real estate. Any factors related to this paragraph, if known to a property owner or licensee shall be disclosed if requested by a consumer.

Failure to disclose any of the facts or suspicions of facts above shall not be grounds for the termination or rescission of any transaction in which real property has been or will be transferred or leased. This provision does not preclude an action against an owner of real estate who makes intentional or fraudulent misrepresentations in response to a direct inquiry from a purchaser or prospective purchaser regarding facts or suspicions that are not material to the physical condition of the property including, but not limited to, those factors listed above.

CHAPTER 6

Mississippi Real Estate Commission

Mississippi Real Estate Commission Rules and Regulations

Professions and Occupations

<u>The following is not an exact copy. This copy has been altered for educational purposes.</u>

Licensing

Applying for a License

A. An applicant for a broker's license must pass the National Portion of the broker's examination with a grade of at least 75% and must pass the State Specific Portion of the examination with a grade of at least 80%.

B. An applicant for a salesperson's license must pass the National Portion of the salesperson's examination with a grade of at least 70% and must pass the State Specific Portion of the examination with a grade of at least 75%.

C. An application fee must accompany the application and will not be refunded after the applicant is scheduled for the examination.

D. The approved Examination Testing Provider will administer examination in various locations in and near the State of Mississippi. Applicants will arrange the time and place of their examination with the Testing Provider.

E. When an applicant is approved for either examination, applicant has **two months** in which to take and pass both the National Portion and the State Specific Portion of the examination. If the applicant fails to appear for the examination within the two months allowed, applicant's fee will be forfeited and their file closed. If the applicant fails to pass the first examination, applicant will be allowed to take the next examination with the payment of an additional fee to the Testing Provider. If the applicant fails to appear for the second examination, fees will be forfeited and their file closed.

F. If a corporation has been chartered by the state of Mississippi, the license will be issued in the corporate name except that no license will be issued for a corporation, company, or trade name where there exists in that county or trade area a real estate broker or real estate agency having a substantially similar name.

G. A real estate licensee of another state who desires to obtain a license under this chapter shall be exempt from the examination provided the examination administered in the other state is determined by the Commission to be equivalent to such examination given in this state and provided that such other state extends this same privilege or exemption to Mississippi real estate licensees. Real estate education courses obtained through sources (providers) other than those set forth in Section 73-35-7 of the statute but which are accepted in the state where the applicant is licensed, may be accepted by the Commission provided the state where the applicant is licensed has entered into a reciprocal agreement with this state.

Changing the Status of a License

A. To change a license from active to inactive status, licensee shall notify the Commission in writing, shall insure that the license is returned to the Commission and shall pay the appropriate fee. A licensee who is on inactive status at time of renewal may renew the license on inactive status by filing a renewal application and paying the renewal fee. A broker who terminates a real estate business may place the business license on inactive status. To return to active status, a salesperson or broker/salesperson must file a transfer application. A broker and/or a business license may be activated by notifying the Commission by letter or transfer application including required fee.

B. When a licensee wishes to transfer from one broker to another, the transferring licensee must file a transfer application signed by the new broker accompanied by the transfer fee and must furnish a statement that the licensee is not carrying any listings or pertinent information belonging to the former broker unless that broker so consents.

C. Any licensee who has entered active duty military service due to draft laws or national emergency shall, upon his return to civilian life and within twelve (12) months after honorable discharge, be considered, so far as this Commission is concerned, to have been continuously engaged in the real estate business in the same capacity as when the licensee entered military service.

Fees

The following fees are set by the Commission in accordance with Section 73-35-17:

A. Application and one year's use of license:

(1) Broker.. $150.00

(2) Salesperson... $120.00

Real Estate Training Institute – Pre Exam Workbook

B. Application for license as a real estate broker issued for partnership, association, or corporation and one year's use of license:

(1) Partnership, association or corporation.. $ 75.00

(2) Branch Office...$ 50.00

C. Renewal fees for two-year period (Maximum):

(1) Broker (individual)... $150.00

(2) Broker (partnership, association, corporation)................................ $150.00

(3) Salesperson.. $120.00

(4) Branch Office.. $100.00

Penalty for late renewal within grace period - 100%

D. Changes:

(1) Place of business change (active license only)............................... $ 50.00

(2) Each duplicate license... $ 50.00

(3) Each transfer of license... $ 50.00

(4) Status change from active to inactive status................................. $ 25.00

(5) Status change from inactive to active status................................. $ 50.00

E. Check charge:

(1) Each check returned not paid to the Commission............................$ 25.00

All fees are the same for both Resident and Nonresident Licenses.

Fees and monies payable to the Mississippi Real Estate Commission may be by personal check, cash, cashier's check or money order. All personal checks shall be made payable to the Mississippi Real Estate Commission. Any personal checks returned not paid or for any other reason shall constitute justifiable grounds for refusing, suspending or revoking a license.

Non-sufficient fund (NSF) checks, if not made good by renewal deadline, will cause the licensee to be in non-renewal status and necessitates the payment of a penalty (100%) by licensee.

Real Estate Training Institute – Pre Exam Workbook

Administration/Conducting Business

General Rules

*Please pay attention to the next few sections. I suspect ALL of it has been specifically placed here because it is information that would make sense to put on the state exam. Leslie

A. It shall be the duty of the responsible broker to instruct the licensees licensed under that broker in the fundamentals of real estate practice, ethics of the profession and the Mississippi Real Estate License Law and to exercise supervision of their real estate activities for which a license is required. **(It is not the duty of the responsible broker to make sure the salespeople have kept up on their Post Licensing and CE courses.)**

B. A real estate broker who operates under the supervision of a responsible broker must not at any time act independently as a broker. The responsible broker shall at all times be responsible for the action of the affiliated broker to the same extent as though that licensee were a salesperson and that affiliated broker shall not perform any real estate service without the full consent and knowledge of his employing or supervising broker.

However, should the responsible broker agree that a broker under his supervision may perform certain real estate services outside the responsible broker's supervision or direction, the responsible broker shall notify the Commission in writing as to the exact nature of such relationship and the names of the broker or brokers involved. The responsible broker shall immediately notify the Commission in writing upon the termination of such relationship.

C. **A licensed Mississippi broker may cooperate with a broker licensed in another state who does not hold a Mississippi license through the use of a cooperative agreement.** A separate cooperative agreement must be filed for each property, prospective user or transaction **with said writing reflecting the compensation to be paid to the Mississippi licensed broker. The listing or property management agreement for the Mississippi real property shall in such cases remain in the name of the Mississippi licensed broker.**

The commissions or other compensation resulting from the sale/rent/lease/property management or auction of the Mississippi real property and which are earned during the period the cooperative agreement is in force shall be divided on a **negotiable basis** between the Mississippi broker and the nonresident broker.

A responsible (principal) nonresident broker described herein is defined as an active, licensed responsible real estate broker of another state who does not possess an active responsible nonresident real estate broker's license issued by the Mississippi Real Estate Commission (MREC).

A Mississippi broker described herein is a responsible (principal) real estate broker whose license is on active status and whose license was issued by MREC either as a responsible resident Mississippi broker or as a responsible nonresident Mississippi broker.

The responsible nonresident broker cannot place any sign on real property located in the state of Mississippi without the written consent of the cooperating responsible Mississippi broker. When the consent is obtained, the sign of the responsible Mississippi broker must be **placed in a prominent place and in close proximity** to the responsible nonresident broker's sign. Any licensed responsible Mississippi broker assisting or cooperating in the sale, lease, property management, rental or auction of real property within the state of Mississippi with a responsible nonresident broker who fails or refuses to list his or her name in such advertisement, or fails or refuses to cross-list such property with him or her, in writing, shall be deemed in violation of the Real Estate Broker's License Act, and shall be subject to a revocation or suspension of his or her license. In such instance herein where a responsible Mississippi broker enters into a cooperative agreement with a responsible nonresident broker pertaining to the sale of real property within the state of Mississippi, **the responsible Mississippi broker must file two copies of the cooperating agreement with the Mississippi Real Estate Commission. *Two Copies in Ten Days.**

D. **A responsible broker must maintain an office and display the license therein.** If the broker has more than one office, **the broker shall display a branch office license in each branch office.**

The broker is responsible for the real estate practices of those licensees.

E. **No licensee shall pay any part of a fee, commission, or other compensation received by such licensee in buying, selling, exchanging, leasing, auctioning or renting any real estate except to another licensee through the licensee's responsible broker.**

No licensee shall knowingly pay a commission, or other compensation to a licensed person knowing that licensee will in turn pay a portion or all of that which is received to a person who does not hold a real estate license.

A licensee who has changed to inactive status or who has transferred to another responsible broker may receive compensation from the previous responsible broker if the commission was generated from activity during the time that the licensee was under the supervision of that responsible broker.

F. Any licensee who fails in a timely manner to respond to official Mississippi Real Estate Commission written communication or who fails or neglects to abide by Mississippi Real Estate Commission's Rules and Regulations **shall be deemed, prima facie, to be guilty of improper dealing.**

G. A real estate broker or salesperson in the ordinary course of business may give an opinion as to the sales price of real estate for the purpose of a prospective listing or sale; however, this opinion as to the listing price or the sale price shall not be referred to as an appraisal and must be completed in compliance with the Real Estate Broker's License Act and must conform to the Standards established by the National Association of Broker Price Opinion Professionals (NABPOP).

H. When an offer is made on property owned by a party with whom a broker has entered into a listing agreement, such broker shall document and date the seller's personal acceptance or rejection of the offer and upon written request, shall provide a copy of such document to the person making the offer.

I. A real estate licensee shall not be exempt from disciplinary actions by the commission when selling property owned by the licensee.

Documents

A. A real estate licensee shall immediately (at the time of signing) deliver a true and correct copy of any instrument to any party or parties executing the same.

B. All exclusive listing agreements shall be in writing, properly identify the property to be sold, and contain all of the terms and conditions under which the transaction is to be consummated; including the sales price, the considerations to be paid, the signatures of all parties to the agreement, and a definite date of expiration.

No listing agreement shall contain any provision requiring the listing party to notify the broker of their intention to cancel the listing **after such definite expiration date**. An "Exclusive Agency" listing or "Exclusive Right to Sell" listing **shall clearly indicate in the listing agreement that it is such an agreement.**

C. All exclusive buyer representation agreements shall be in writing and properly identify the terms and conditions under which the buyer will rely on the broker for the purchase of real estate; including the sales price, the considerations to be paid, the signatures of all parties to the agreement, and **a definite date of expiration.** The buyer may terminate the agreement **upon fifteen (15) calendar** days written notice to the buyer's exclusive agent. An Exclusive Buyer Representation agreement **shall clearly indicate in the body of the document that it is such an agreement.**

D. In the event that more than one written offer is made before the owner has accepted an offer, any other written offer received by the listing broker, whether from a prospective purchaser or from another licensee cooperating in a sale, **shall be presented to the owner unless the listing broker has specific, written instructions from the owner to postpone the presentation of other offers.**

Broker should caution the seller against countering on more than one offer at the same time.

E. Every real estate contact must reflect whom the broker represents by a statement **over** the signatures of the parties to the contract.

F. No licensee shall represent to a lender or any other interested party, either verbally or through the preparation of a false sales contract, **an amount in excess of the true and actual selling price.**

G. A real estate broker must keep on file for **three years** following its consummation, complete records relating to any real estate transaction. This includes, but is not limited to: listings, options, leases, offers to purchase, contracts of sale, escrow records, agency agreements and copies of all closing statements.

Advertising

A. The use of any copyrighted term or insignia on stationery, office signs, or in advertising by any licensee not authorized to do so, will be considered as **"substantial misrepresentation"** and cause for refusal, suspension, or revocation of the license.

A licensee shall not advertise to sell, buy, exchange, auction, rent or lease property in a manner indicating that the offer to sell, buy, exchange, auction, rent, or lease such property is being made by a private party not engaged in the real estate business.

No advertisement shall be inserted by a licensee in any publication where only a post office box number, telephone number, or street address appears. Every licensee, when advertising real estate in any publication, shall indicate that the party advertising is licensed in real estate. All advertising must be under the direct supervision and in the name of the responsible broker or in the name of the real estate firm.

B. When a licensee is advertising their own property for sale, purchase or exchange which is not listed with a broker, the licensee must indicate that he or she is licensed. The disclosure of licensee's status must be made in all forms of advertising, including the "for sale" sign. ***No Blind Ads**

C. In addition to disclosing their licensed status in advertisements, licensees are required to disclose their licensed status on all contracts for real estate in which they have an ownership interest.

A broker shall advertise in the name in which the license is issued. A broker may use a descriptive term after the broker's name to indicate the occupation in which engaged, for example, "realty", "real estate", "property management". If advertising in any other form, a partnership, trade name, association, company or corporation license must be obtained prior to advertising in that manner.

Earnest Money

A. **The responsible broker is responsible at all times for earnest money deposits.**

Earnest money accepted by the broker or any licensee for which the broker is responsible and upon acceptance of a mutually agreeable contract is required to deposit the money into a trust account prior to the close of business of the next banking day.

The responsible broker is required to promptly account for and remit the full amount of the deposit or earnest money at the consummation or termination of transaction.

A licensee is required to pay over to the responsible broker all deposits and earnest money **immediately** upon receipt thereof.

Earnest money must be returned promptly when the purchaser is rightfully entitled to same allowing **reasonable time for clearance** of the earnest money check. In the event of uncertainty as to the proper disposition of earnest money, the broker may turn earnest money over to a court of law for disposition. Failure to comply with this regulation shall constitute grounds for revocation or suspension of license.

B. When the broker is the agent for the seller and for any reason the seller fails or is unable to consummate the transaction, the broker has no right to any portion of the earnest money deposited by the purchaser, **even if a commission has been earned.**

The entire amount of the earnest money deposit must be returned to the purchaser and the broker should **look to the seller for compensation**.

C. **Accurate records** shall be kept on escrow accounts of all monies received, disbursed, or on hand. All monies shall be individually identified as to a particular transaction. Escrow records shall be kept in accordance with standard accounting practices and shall be subject to inspection at all times by the Commission.

Monies received in a trust account on behalf of clients or customers **are not assets of the broker**;

however, **a broker may deposit and keep in each escrow account or rental account some personal funds for the express purpose of covering service charges and other bank debits related to each account. * A broker can deposit funds into a trust account.**

D. If a broker, as escrow agent, accepts a check and later finds that such check has not been honored by the bank on which it was drawn, the broker shall **immediately notify** all parties involved in the transaction.

Real Estate Training Institute – Pre Exam Workbook

Agency Relationship Disclosure

Purpose

Consumers shall be fully informed of the agency relationships in real estate transactions.

This rule places specific requirements on Brokers to disclose their agency relationship. This does not abrogate the laws of agency as recognized under common law and compliance with the prescribed disclosures will not always guarantee that a Broker has fulfilled all of his responsibilities under the common law of agency.

Compliance will be necessary in order to protect licensees from impositions of sanctions against their license by the Mississippi Real Estate Commission.

Special situations, where unusual facts exist or where one or more parties involved are especially vulnerable, could require additional disclosures not contemplated by this rule. In such cases, Brokers should seek legal advice prior to entering into an agency relationship.

Definitions

A. "Agency" shall mean the relationship created when one person, the Principal (client), delegates to another, the agent, the right to act on his behalf in a real estate transaction and to exercise some degree of discretion while so acting.   *The Principal delegates authority and the agent consents to act.

Agency may be entered into by expressed agreement, implied through the actions of the agent and or ratified after the fact by the principal accepting the benefits of an agent's previously unauthorized act.

An agency gives rise to a fiduciary relationship and imposes on the agent, as the fiduciary of the principal, certain duties, obligations, and high standards of good faith and loyalty

B. "Agent" shall mean one who is authorized to act on behalf of and represent another.

A real estate broker is the agent of the principal (client) to whom a fiduciary obligation is owed.

Salespersons licensed under the broker are subagents of the Broker, regardless of the location of the office in which the salesperson works.

C. **"Client"** shall mean the person to whom the agent owes a **fiduciary duty**. It can be a seller, buyer, landlord, tenant or both.

D. "Compensation" is that fee paid to a broker for the rendering of services. Compensation, when considered alone, is not the determining factor in an agency relationship. The relationship can be

Real Estate Training Institute – Pre Exam Workbook

created regardless of whether the seller pays the fee, the buyer pays the fee, both pay the fee or neither pays a fee.

E. "Customer" shall mean that person not represented in a real estate transaction. ***It may be the buyer, seller, landlord or tenant.**

F. "Disclosed Dual Agent" shall mean that agent representing both parties to a real estate transaction with the informed consent of both parties, with written understanding of specific duties and representation to be afforded each party.

There may be situations where disclosed dual agency presents conflicts of interest that cannot be resolved without breach of duty to one party or another. * The reason why some brokers will not do a dual agency.

Brokers who practice disclosed dual agency should do so with the utmost caution to protect consumers and themselves from inadvertent violation of demanding common law standards of disclosed dual agency. *What brokers who practice dual agency should do.

G. "Fiduciary Responsibilities" are those duties due the principal (client) in a real estate transaction are:

(1) **'Loyalty'** - the agent must put the interests of the principal above the interests of the agent or any third party.

(2) **'Obedience'** - the agent agrees to obey any lawful instruction from the principal in the execution of the transaction that is the subject of the agency.

(3) **'Disclosure'** - the agent must disclose to the principal any information the agent becomes aware of in connection with the agency.

(4) **'Confidentiality'** - the agent must keep private information provided by the principal and information which would give a customer an advantage over the principal strictly confidential, unless the agent has the principal's permission to disclose the information. This duty lives on after the agency relationship is terminated.

(5) **'Reasonable skill, care and diligence'** - the agent must perform all duties with the care and diligence which may be reasonably expected of someone undertaking such duties.

(6) **'Full accounting'** - the agent must provide a full accounting of any money or 10goods coming into the agent's possession which belong to the principal or other parties.

H. "First Substantive Meeting" shall be: **WHAT'S IMPORTANT**

Real Estate Training Institute – Pre Exam Workbook

(1) In a real estate transaction in which the Broker is the agent for the seller, first substantive meeting shall be before or just immediately prior to the first of any of the following:

(a) Showing the property to a prospective buyer.

(b) **<u>Eliciting confidential information</u>** from a buyer concerning the buyers' real estate **<u>needs, motivation, or financial qualifications.</u>**

(c) **<u>The execution of any agreements</u>**

(2) For the seller's agent, the definition <u>shall not include</u>: **WHAT'S NOT IMPORTANT**

(a) A bona fide "open house" or model home showing which encompasses

(b) Preliminary conversations or **"small talk"** concerning **price range, location and property styles**.

(c) Responding to **general factual questions** from a prospective buyer concerning properties that have been advertised for sale or lease.

(3) When the Broker is the agent for the buyer, first substantive meeting shall <u>be at the initial contact with a seller or a seller's agent</u> or before or just immediately prior to the first of any of the following: **WHAT'S IMPORTANT**

(a) Showing the property of a seller to a represented buyer.

(b) Eliciting any **confidential information** from a seller concerning their real estate **needs, motivation, or financial qualifications.**

(c) The **execution of any agreements**

(4) For the buyer's agent, the definition shall not include: **WHAT'S NOT IMPORTANT**

(a) A bona fide "open House" or model home showing which encompasses

(b) Preliminary conversations **or "small talk"** concerning **price range, location and property styles**.

(c) Responding to **general factual questions** from a prospective buyer concerning properties that have been advertised for sale or lease.

I. "Single Agency" shall mean a broker who has chosen to represent only one party to a real estate transaction. It may be either the buyer, seller, lessor or lessee or any party in a transaction.

Disclosure Requirements

A. In a single agency, a broker is required to disclose, in writing, to the party for whom the broker is an agent in a real estate transaction that the broker is the agent of the party.

The written disclosure must be made before the time an agreement for representation is entered into between the broker and the party. This shall be on an MREC Agency Disclosure Form.

B. In a single agency, a real estate broker is required to disclose, in writing, to the party for whom the broker is not an agent, that the broker is an agent of another party in the transaction.

The written disclosure shall be made at the time of the first substantive meeting with the party for whom the broker is not an agent. This shall be on an MREC Agency Disclosure Form.

C. Brokers operating in the capacity of disclosed dual agents must obtain the informed written consent of all parties prior to or at the time of formalization of the dual agency.

Informed written consent to disclosed dual agency shall be deemed to have been timely obtained if all of the following occur:

(1) The seller, at the time an agreement for representation is entered into between the broker and seller, gives written consent to dual agency by signing the Consent To Dual Agency portion of MREC Form A.

(2) The buyer, at the time an agreement for representation is entered into between the broker and buyer, gives written consent to dual agency by signing the Consent To Dual Agency portion of MREC Form A.

(3) The Broker must confirm that the buyer(s) understands and consents to the consensual dual agency relationship prior to the signing of an offer to purchase.

The buyer shall give his/her consent by signing the MREC Dual Agency Confirmation Form which shall be **attached to the offer to purchase.**

The Broker must confirm that the seller(s) also understands and consents to the consensual dual agency relationship prior to presenting the offer to purchase.

The seller shall give his/her consent by signing the MREC Dual Agency Confirmation Form attached to the buyer's offer.

Real Estate Training Institute – Pre Exam Workbook

The form shall remain attached to the offer to purchase regardless of the outcome of the offer to purchase.

D. In the event the agency relationship changes between the parties to a real estate transaction, new disclosure forms will be acknowledged by all parties involved.

E. In the event one or more parties are not available to sign one or more of the Disclosure Forms, the disclosure will be accomplished orally. The applicable form will be so noted by the Broker and said forms will be forwarded for signature(s) as soon as possible. Written electronic transmission will fulfill this requirement.

F. In the event any party receiving a disclosure form requests not to sign that form acknowledging receipt, the Broker shall annotate the form with the following statement:

"A COPY OF THIS FORM WAS DELIVERED TO

_____ DATE_____. RECIPIENT

DECLINED TO ACKNOWLEDGE RECEIPT OF THIS FORM."

G. The terms of the agency relationship shall be ratified on all contracts pertaining to real estate transactions.

H. The Commission mandated disclosure form may be duplicated in content and size but not altered.

*An agent is allowed to make the print on MREC forms larger because of the ADA. American with Disabilities Act.

I. Completed Agency Disclosure Forms shall be maintained in accordance with MS Real Estate Law.

Disclosure Exception

A licensee shall not be required to comply with the provisions of Disclosure Law when engaged in transactions with any

corporation,

non-profit corporation,

professional corporation,

Real Estate Training Institute – Pre Exam Workbook

professional association,

limited liability company,

partnership,

real estate investment trust,

business trust,

charitable trust,

family trust,

or any governmental entity in transactions involving real estate.

Operating under this exception in no way circumvents the common law of agency.

Complaint Procedure

Notifications of Complaints to the Commission

A. All complaints submitted to the Commission shall be properly certified on forms furnished by the Commission.

B. Every licensee shall, **within ten days,** notify the Real Estate Commission of any adverse court decisions in which the licensee appeared as a defendant. *Includes Civil Suits

C. It shall be mandatory for a responsible broker to notify the Commission if the responsible broker has reason to believe that a licensee for whom the broker is responsible has violated the Real Estate License Law or Rules and Regulations of the Commission.

D. If a broker finds that a licensee licensed under that broker has been operating independently or through some other broker, the broker shall notify the Commission immediately and forward said individual's license to the Commission.

E. A Real Estate Commissioner shall avoid private interviews, arguments, briefs or communication that may influence said Commissioner's decision on any pending complaints or hearings.

F. The expiration, suspension or revocation of a responsible broker's license shall automatically suspend the license of every real estate licensee currently under the supervision of that broker. In such cases, a licensee may transfer to another responsible broker.

Real Estate Training Institute – Pre Exam Workbook

Continuing Education

Approved Courses

A. Any course that meets the educational requirements as set forth in the Mississippi Real Estate Broker's License Act of 1954, as Amended.

B. Any course sponsored or provided by the Mississippi Real Estate Commission.

C. Any course which has been individually approved by the Commission pursuant to the provisions of this rule and which must be approved prior to presentation of the course, except that, in the Commission's discretion, courses which have not received such prior approval but which meet the proper criteria may be approved for credit for licensees who have completed such course.

D. Any course which has been approved for real estate continuing education by any state or country which is a member of the Association of Real Estate License Law Officials (ARELLO) and which course satisfies the requirements set forth in Rule VI (B) (3) with the exception of instruction in license law which pertains solely to a state other than Mississippi.

INSPECTION OF OFFERINGS FROM OUT OF STATE

Out-of-state Developers

Out-of-state land developers who desire to advertise out-of-state property in Mississippi (except in national publications) shall first contact the Mississippi Real Estate Commission to have the property approved for advertising. The Mississippi Real Estate Commission may in its discretion conduct an on-site inspection of the property at the cost of the developer. The developer shall, upon request from the Mississippi Real Estate Commission, provide such documentation which will establish the truth and accuracy of the proposed advertisements. A Mississippi broker who becomes the agent or representative of the out-of-state developer, shall be responsible for the truth and accuracy of representation, offerings and advertising of such properties in the State of Mississippi.

Time Shares

Licensing

Any seller, other than the developer and its regular employees, of a timeshare plan within the State of Mississippi must be a licensed Real Estate Broker or Real Estate Salesperson

Real Estate Training Institute – Pre Exam Workbook

pursuant to and subject to Mississippi Law and the Rules and Regulations of the Mississippi Real Estate Commission.

Definitions

A. "Accommodations" means any structure, service improvement, facility, apartment, condominium or cooperative unit, cabin, lodge, hotel or motel room, or any other private or commercial structure, which is situated on real property and designed for occupancy by one or more individuals.

B. "Advertising" or "Advertisement" means any written, oral, or electronic communication which contains a promotion, inducement, or offer to sell a timeshare plan, including, but not limited to, brochures, pamphlets, radio and television scripts, electronic media, telephone and direct mail solicitations, and other means of promotion.

C. "Assessment" means the share of funds required for the payment of common expenses that are assessed from time to time against each timeshare interest owner by the managing entity.

D. "Association" means the organized body consisting of the owners of timeshare interests in a timeshare plan.

E. "Common Expenses" means taxes, casualty and liability insurance, and those expenses properly incurred for the maintenance, operation, and repair of all accommodation constituting the timeshare plan and any other expenses designated as common expenses by the timeshare instrument.

F. "Developer" means and includes any person who creates a timeshare plan or is in the business of selling timeshare interests, or employs agents to do the same, or any person who succeeds to the interest of a developer by sale, lease, assignment, mortgage, or other transfer, but the term includes only those persons who offer timeshare interests for disposition in the ordinary course of business and does not include those sellers who sell timeshare interests on the developer's behalf.

G. "Managing entity" means the natural person or other entity that undertakes the duties, responsibilities, and obligations of the management of a timeshare plan.

H. "Exchange program" means any method, arrangement, or procedure for the voluntary exchange of timeshare interests or other property interests. The term does not include the assignment of the right to use and occupy accommodations to owners of timeshare interests within a timeshare plan. Any method, arrangement, or procedure that otherwise meets this definition in which the purchaser's total contractual financial obligation exceeds three thousand dollars ($3,000) per any individual, recurring timeshare period, shall be regulated as a timeshare plan in accordance with these rules. For purposes of determining the purchaser's total contractual financial obligation, amounts to be paid as a result of renewals and options to renew shall be included except for the following:

Real Estate Training Institute – Pre Exam Workbook

(1) the amounts to be paid as a result of any optional renewal that a purchaser, in his or her sole discretion may elect to exercise or

(2) the amounts to be paid as a result of any automatic renewal in which the purchaser has a right to terminate during the renewal period at any time and receive a pro rata refund for the remaining unexpired renewal term or

(3) amounts to be paid as a result of an automatic renewal wherein the purchaser receives a written notice no less than 30 nor more than 90 days prior to the date of renewal informing the purchaser of the right to terminate prior to the date of renewal.

Notwithstanding these exceptions, if the contractual financial obligation exceeds three thousand dollars ($3,000) for any three-year period of any renewal term, amounts to be paid as a result of that renewal shall be included in determining the purchaser's total contractual financial obligation.

I. "Offer to sell", "offer for sale," "offered for sale," or "offer" means solicitation of purchasers, the taking of reservations, or any other method whereby a purchaser is offered the opportunity to participate in a timeshare plan.

J. "Purchaser" means any person, other than a developer, who by means of a voluntary transfer for consideration acquires a legal or equitable interest in a timeshare plan other 19than as security for an obligation.

K. "Reservation system" means the method or arrangement which purchasers are required to utilize in order to reserve the use and occupancy of accommodations in a timeshare plan.

L. "Seller" means any developer or any other person, or agent or employee thereof: who offers timeshare periods for sale to the public in the ordinary course of business, except a person who has acquired a timeshare period for the person's own use and occupancy and who later offers it for resale.

M. "Timeshare instrument" means one or more documents, by whatever name denominated, creating or governing the operation of a timeshare plan and includes the declaration or other legal instrument dedicating the accommodations to the timeshare plan.

N. "Timeshare interest" means and includes either of the following:

(1) A "timeshare estate," which is the right to occupy a timeshare property, coupled with a freehold estate or an estate for years with a future interest in a timeshare property or a specified portion thereof.

(2) A "timeshare plan" which is the right to occupy a timeshare property, which right is neither coupled with a freehold interest, nor coupled with an estate for years with a future interest, in a timeshare property.

Real Estate Training Institute – Pre Exam Workbook

O. "Timeshare plan" means any arrangement, plan, scheme, or similar device, other than an exchange program, whether by membership agreement, sale, lease, deed, license, right to use agreement, or by any other means, whereby a purchaser, in exchange for consideration, receives ownership rights in or the right to use accommodations for a period of time less than a full year during any given year, on a recurring basis for more than one year, but not necessarily for consecutive years. A timeshare plan may be either of the following:

(1) A "single-site timeshare plan" which is the right to use accommodations at a single timeshare property; or

(2) A "multi-site timeshare plan" that includes either of the following:

(a) A "specific timeshare interest" which is the right to use accommodations at a specific timeshare property, together with use rights in accommodations at one or more other component sites created by or acquired through the timeshare plan's reservation system; or

(b) A "non-specific timeshare interest" which is the right to use accommodations at more than one component site created by or acquired through the timeshare plan's reservation system, but including no right to use any specific accommodation.

P. "Timeshare property" means one or more accommodations subject to the same timeshare instrument, together with any other property or rights to property appurtenant to those accommodations.

Q. "Mississippi Real Estate Commission," or "Commission" means the agency of the State of Mississippi created by §73-35-1, et seq. To regulate the licensing of real estate brokers and salespersons and by §73-35-35 directed to regulate the sale of timeshare and condominium properties.

Registration

A. Developer registration; offer or disposal of interest. - A developer, or any of its agents, shall not sell, offer or dispose of a timeshare interest in the state unless all necessary registration requirements are completed and approved by the Mississippi Real Estate Commission, or the sale, offer, or disposition is otherwise permitted by or exempt from these rules. A developer, or any of its agents, shall not sell, offer or dispose of a timeshare interest in the state while an order revoking or suspending a registration is in effect.

B. Exemptions from developer registration

(1) A person is **exempt** from the registration requirements under the following circumstances.

(a) An owner of a timeshare interest who has acquired the timeshare interest from another for the owner's own use and occupancy and who later offers it for resale; or

(b) A managing entity or an association that is offering to sell one or more timeshare interests acquired through foreclosure, deed in lieu of foreclosure or gratuitous transfer, if such acts are performed in the regular course of or as incident to the management of the association for its own account in the timeshare plan; or

(c) The person offers a timeshare plan located outside of Mississippi in a national publication or by electronic media, which is not directed to or targeted to any individual located in Mississippi and contains appropriate disclaimers; or

(d) The person is conveyed, assigned, or transferred more than seven timeshare interests from a developer in a single voluntary or involuntary transaction arid subsequently conveys, assigns, or transfers all of thtimeshare interests received from the developer to a single purchaser in a single transaction.

(e) The developer is offering a timeshare interest to a purchaser who has previously acquired a timeshare interest from the same developer if the developer has a timeshare plan registered with the Commission, which was originally approved by the Commission within the preceding seven (7) years and, further, provides the purchaser:

(A) a cancellation period of at least seven (7) calendar days;

(B) all the timeshare disclosure documents that are required to be provided to purchasers as if the sale occurred in the state or jurisdiction where the timeshare property is located; and

(ii) By making such an offering or disposition, the person is deemed to consent to the jurisdiction of the Commission in the event of a dispute with the purchaser in connection with the offering or disposition.

(f) An offering of any plan in which the purchaser's total financial obligation is $3,000 or less during the term of the plan; for purposes of determining the purchaser's total financial obligation, all amounts to be paid during any renewal or periods of optional renewal shall be included.

(g) Hotels including any hotel, inn, motel, tourist court, apartment house, rooming house, or other place where sleeping accommodations are furnished or offered for pay if four (4) or more rooms are available therein for transient guests as defined in Miss. Code Ann. §41-49-3.

(h) Campground, which is located on real property, made available to persons for camping, whether by tent, trailer, camper, cabin, recreational vehicle or similar device and shall include the outdoor recreational facilities located on the real property;

(i) Hunting camp which means land or facilities located on real property which is established for the principal purpose of hunting or fishing activities which are subject to licensing by the State of Mississippi pursuant to Miss. Code Ann. §49-7-1, et seq.

(j) Owner referrals as described in Section N of these rules

C. Developer Registration Requirements

(1) Any person who, to any individual in Mississippi, sells, offers to sell, or attempts to solicit prospective purchasers to purchase a timeshare interest, or any person who creates a timeshare plan with an accommodation in Mississippi must register the timeshare plan with the Commission unless the timeshare plan is otherwise exempt from this Chapter.

(2) The developer shall have the duty to supervise and control all aspects of the offering of a timeshare plan including, but not limited to the promotion, advertising, contracting and closing.

(3) The developer must provide proof as part of the registration that he will comply with escrow, bonding, or other financial assurance requirements for purchaser funds, including escrow during the rescission period, escrow funds until substantial completion, or bonding, letter of credit or other financial assurances acceptable to the Commission.

(4) <u>All timeshare plans shall maintain a one-to-one purchaser to accommodation ratio</u>, which is the ratio of the number of purchasers eligible to use the accommodations of a timeshare plan on a given day to the number of accommodations available for use within the plan on that day, such that the total number of purchasers eligible to use the accommodations of the timeshare plan during a given calendar year never exceeds the total number of accommodations available for use in the timeshare plan during that year. For purposes of calculation under this subsection, each purchaser must be counted at least once, and no individual timeshare unit may be counted more than 365 times per calendar year (or more than 366 times per leap year). A purchaser who is delinquent in the payment of timeshare plan assessments shall continue to be considered eligible to use the accommodations of the timeshare plan.

D. Comprehensive registration

(1) In registering a timeshare plan, the developer shall provide all of the following information:

(a) The developer's legal name, any assumed names used by the developer, principal office, street address, mailing address, primary contact person, telephone, electronic mail and facsimile numbers;

(b) The name of the developer's authorized or registered agent in Mississippi upon whom claims may be served or service of process be had, the agent's street address in Mississippi and telephone number;

(c) The name, street address, mailing address, primary contact person and telephone, electronic mail and facsimile numbers of any timeshare plans being registered;

(d) The name, street address, mailing address and telephone, electronic mail and facsimile numbers of any managing entity of the timeshare plan if other than the developer;

(e) Current status of title by a title insurance company qualified and registered to do business in Mississippi, or in the jurisdiction where the timeshare plan is located;

(f) A copy of the proposed or existing covenants, conditions and restrictions applicable to the timeshare plan;

(g) Exemplars of all contracts, deeds, fact sheets and other instruments to be used in marketing, financing and conveying the timeshare interests;

(h) A copy of the management agreement for the timeshare plan;

(i) A detailed description of the furnishing(s) and other personal property to be included in the timeshare plans;

(j) Agreement of the developer to subsidize maintenance and operation of the timeshare plan, if any;

(k) Description of other services and amenities advertised with the timesharing plan;

(l) Evidence of financial assurances, if any;

(m) Evidence of compliance with escrow or other financial assurance requirements for protection of purchaser funds pursuant to these rules.

(n) Where the timeshare plan uses a reservation system, the developer shall provide evidence that provisions are in place to assure that, in the event of termination of the operator of the reservation system, an adequate period of continued operation exists to assure a transition to a substitute operator or mechanism for the operation of the reservation system. In addition, there shall be a requirements to transfer all relevant data contained in the reservation system to the successor operator of the system.

(o) A description of the inventory control system that will ensure compliance with subsection 3.c. of this section.

(p) A public offering statement which complies with the requirements set forth below; and

(q) Any other information regarding the developer, timeshare plan, or managing entities, as reasonably required by the Commission for the protection of the purchasers.

E. Abbreviated Registration

(1) The Commission may accept an abbreviated application from a developer of a timeshare plan in which all accommodations are located outside of the state. A developer of a timeshare plan with any accommodation located in Mississippi may not file an abbreviated filing, with the exception of a succeeding developer after a merger or acquisition when the developer's timeshare plan was registered in the state immediately preceding the merger or acquisition.

(2) As a part of any application for an abbreviated registration, the developer must provide a certificate of registration or other evidence of registration from the appropriate regulatory agency in the jurisdiction in which the accommodations offered in Mississippi are located, or other evidence of compliance by the timeshare plan with the laws of the jurisdiction where the accommodations are located. Such other jurisdiction must have disclosure requirements that are substantially equivalent or greater than the information required to be disclosed to purchasers by these rules. A developer filing an abbreviated registration application must also provide the following:

(a) The developer's name, any assumed names used by the developer, the developer's principal office location, mailing address, primary contact person and telephone, electronic mail and facsimile numbers;

(b) The name, location, mailing address, primary contact person and the telephone, electronic mail and facsimile numbers of the timeshare plan, if different from the developer;

(c) The name of the authorized agent or registered agent in Mississippi upon whom claims can be served or service of process can be had, and the address in Mississippi of the authorized agent or registered agent;

(d) The names of any sales entity if other than the developer and the managing' entity and their principal office locations, mailing address and telephone, electronic mail and facsimile numbers;

(e) A statement as to whether the timeshare plan is a single-site timeshare plan or a multi-site timeshare plan and, if a multi-site timeshare plan, whether it consists of specific timeshare interests or non-specific timeshare interests;

Real Estate Training Institute – Pre Exam Workbook

(f) Disclosure of each jurisdiction in which the developer has applied for registration of the timeshare plan and whether the timeshare plan, its developer or any of its sales agents or managing entities utilized were denied registration or were the subject of any disciplinary proceedings;

(g) Copies of any disclosure documents required to be given to purchasers or required to be filed with the jurisdiction in which the timeshare plan is approved or accepted as may be requested by the Commission;

(h) The appropriate fees, if any, and

(i) Other information reasonably required by the Commission or established by rule.

F. Preliminary Permits

(1) The state may grant a preliminary permit allowing the developer to begin offering and selling timeshare interests while the registration is in process. To obtain a preliminary permit, the developer must do all of the following:

(a) Submit a formal written request to the Mississippi Real Estate Commission for a preliminary permit;

(b) Submit a substantially complete application for registration to the Commission, including any appropriate fees and exhibits;

(c) Provide evidence acceptable to the state agency that all funds received by the developer will be placed into an independent escrow account in accordance with the escrow requirements until a final registration has been granted;

(d) Give to each purchaser a copy of the proposed public offering statement that the developer has submitted to the Commission with the initial application; and

(e) Give to each purchaser the opportunity to cancel the purchase contract during the applicable recission period. The purchaser shall have an additional opportunity to cancel upon the issuance of an approved registration if the Commission determines that there is a material and adverse difference in the disclosures contained in the final public offering statement and those given to the purchaser in the proposed public offering statement.

Public Offering Statement

A. Public Offering Statement Requirements

(1) A developer must prepare a public offering statement that shall fully and accurately disclose the facts concerning the timeshare developer and timeshare plan as required by these rules. The developer shall provide the public offering statement to each purchaser of a timeshare interest in any timeshare plan prior to execution of the purchase contract. The public offering statement shall be dated and shall require the purchaser to certify in writing the receipt thereof. Upon approval by the Commission, the developer may also deliver the public offering statement on CD ROM or other electronic media.

(2) With regard to timeshare interests offered in a single-site timeshare plan or in the specific interest of a multi-site timeshare plan, the public offering statement should fully and accurately disclose the following:

(a) The name of the developer and the principal address of the developer;

(b) Information regarding the developer's business and property management experience;

(c) A description of the type of timeshare interests being offered;

(d) The number of accommodations and timeshare interests, expressed in periods of seven-days use availability or other time increments applicable to the multi-site timeshare plan for each component site committed to the multi-site timeshare plan and available for use by purchasers, purchasers and a representation about the percentage of useable time authorized for sale, and if that percentage is 100 percent, then a statement describing how adequate periods of time for maintenance and repair will be provided. A general description of the existing and proposed accommodations and amenities of the timeshare plan, including their type and number personal property furnishing the accommodation, any use restrictions, and any required fees for use;

(e) A description of any accommodations and amenities that are committed to be built, including, without limitation:

(i) the developer's schedule of commencement and completion of all accommodations and amenities;

(ii) the estimated number of accommodations per site that may become subject to the timeshare plan;

(iii) a brief description of the duration, phases, and operation of the timeshare plan; and

(iv) the extent to which financial arrangements have been provided for completion of all promised improvements.

(f) If the timeshare plan requires the use of a reservation system, include a description of the reservation system which shall include the following:

(i) The entity responsible for operating the reservation system, its relationship to the developer, and the duration of any agreement for operation of the reservation system.

(ii) A summary of the rules and regulations governing access to and use of the reservation system.

(iii) The existence of and an explanation regarding any priority reservation features that affect a purchaser's ability to make reservations for the use of a given accommodation on a first-come, first-serve basis.

(iv) An explanation of any demand-balancing standard utilized to assure equitable use of the accommodations among participants.

(g) The current annual budget, if available, or the projected annual budget for the timeshare plan. The budget must include, without limitations:

(i) a statement of the amount included in the budget as a reserve for repairs and replacement;

(ii) the projected common expense liability, if any, by category of expenditures for the timeshare plan; and

(iii) a statement of any services or expenses not reflected in the budget that the developer provides or pays.

(h) Information regarding all fees that the purchaser is required to pay in conjunction with the purchase and ownership including, but not limited to, closing cost and annual assessments;

(i) A description of any liens, defects or encumbrances on or affecting the title to the timeshare interests;

(j) A description of any financing offered by or available through the developer;

(k) **A statement that within seven (7) calendar days after receipt of the public offering statement or after execution of the purchase contract, whichever is later, a purchaser may cancel any purchase contract for a timeshare interest from a developer together with a statement providing the name and street address to which the purchaser shall mail any notice of cancellation. If by agreement of the parties by and through the purchase contract, the purchase contract allows for cancellation of the purchase contract for a period of time exceeding seven (7) calendar days, then the public offering statement shall include a statement that the cancellation of 28the purchase contract is allowing for that period of time exceeding seven (7) calendar days**

(l) A description of any bankruptcies, pending civil or criminal suits, adjudications, or disciplinary actions of which the developer has knowledge, which would have a material effect on the developer's ability to perform its obligations.

(m) Any restrictions on alienation of any number or portion of any timeshare interests;

(n) A statement describing liability and casualty insurance for the timeshare property;

(o) Any current or expected fees or charges to be paid by timeshare

purchasers for the use of any amenities related to the timeshare plan;

(p) A statement disclosing any right of first refusal or other restraint on the

transfer of all or any portion of a timeshare interest.

(q) A statement of disclosing that any deposit made in connection which the purchase of a timeshare interest shall be held by an escrow agent until expiration of any right to cancel the contract and that any deposit shall be returned to the purchaser if he or she elects to exercise his or her right of cancellation. Alternatively, if the Commission has accepted from the developer a surety bond, irrevocable letter of credit, or other financial assurance in lieu of placing deposits in an escrow account, account:

(i) a statement disclosing that the developer has provided a surety bond, irrevocable letter of credit, or other financial assurance in an amount equal to or in excess of the funds that would otherwise be placed in an escrow account and,

(ii) a description of the type of financial assurance that has been arranged,

(iii) a statement that if the purchaser elects to exercise his or her right of cancellation as provided in the contract, the developer shall return the deposit, and

(iv) a description of the person or entity to whom the purchaser shall apply for payment.

(r) If the timeshare plan provides purchasers with the opportunity to participate in an exchange program, a description of the name and address of the exchange company and the method by which a purchaser accesses the exchange program;

(s) Such other information reasonable required by the state agency and established by administrative rule necessary for the protection of purchasers of timeshare interests in timeshare plans; and

(t) Any other information that the developer, with the approval of the Commission, desires to include in the public offering statement.

(3) Public offering statements for specific timeshare interest and multi-site timeshare plans shall include the following disclosures in addition to those required in (b) above:

(a) A description of each component site, including the name and address of each Component site.

(b) The number of accommodations and timeshare interest, expressed in periods of seven-day use availability or other time increments applicable to each component site of the timeshare plan, committed to the multi-site timeshare plan and available for use by purchasers, and a representation about the percentage of useable time authorized for sale, and if that percentage is 100 percent, then a statement describing how adequate periods of time for maintenance and repair will be provided.

(c) Each type of accommodation in terms of the number of bedrooms, bathrooms, and sleeping capacity, and a statement of whether or not the accommodation contains a full kitchen. For purposes of this description, a "full kitchen" means a kitchen having a minimum of a dishwasher, range, sink, oven, and refrigerator.

(d) A description of amenities available for use by the purchaser at each component site

(e) A description of the reservation system, which shall include the following:

(i) The entity responsible for operating the reservation systems, its relationship to the developer, and the duration of any agreement for operation of the reservation system.

(ii) A summary of the rules and regulations governing access to and use of the reservation system.

(iii) The existence of and an explanation regarding any priority reservations for the use of a given accommodation on a first-come, first-served basis.

(iv) An explanation of any demand-balancing standard utilized to assure equitable use of the accommodations among participants.

(v) A description of any method utilized to permit additions, substitutions, or deletions of accommodations.

(vi) A description of any criteria utilized in the use and operation of the reservation system (such as historical occupancy levels by season, location, demand, etc.)

(f) The name and principal address of the managing entity of the multi-site timeshare plan and description of the procedures, if any, for altering the powers and responsibilities of the managing entity and for removing or replacing it.

(g) A description of any right to make any addition, substitutions, or deletion of accommodations, amenities, or component sites, and a description of the basis upon which accommodations, amenities, or component sites may be added to, substituted in, or deleted from the multi-site timeshare plan.

(h) A description of the purchaser's liability for any fees associated with the multi-site timeshare plan.

(i) The location of each component site of the multi-site timeshare plan, the historical occupancy of each component site for the prior 12-month period, if the component site was part of the multi-site timeshare plan during the 12-month time period, as well as any periodic adjustment or amendment to the reservation system that may be needed in order to respond to actual purchaser use patterns and changes in purchaser use demand for the accommodations existing at that time within the multi-site timeshare plan.

(j) Any other information that the developer, with the approval of the Commission, desires to include in the timeshare disclosure statement.

(4) Public offering statements for nonspecific timeshare multi-site timeshare plans shall include the following:

(a) The name and address of the developer.

(b) A description of the type of interest and usage rights the purchaser will receive.

(c) A description of the duration and operation of the timeshare plan.

(d) A description of the type of insurance coverage provided for each component site.

(e) An explanation of who holds title to the accommodations of each component site.

(f) The name and principal address of the managing entity of the multi-site timeshare plan and description of the procedures, if any, for altering the powers and responsibilities of the managing entity and for removing or replacing it.

(g) A description of any right to make any addition, substitutions, or deletion of accommodations, amenities, or component sites, and a description of the basis upon which accommodations, amenities, or component sites may be added to, substituted in, or deleted from the multi-site timeshare plan.

(h) A description of the purchaser's liability for any fees associated with the multi-site timeshare plan.

(i) The location of each component site of the multi-site timeshare plan, the historical occupancy of each component site for the prior 12-month period, if the component site was part of the multi-site timeshare plan during the 12-month time period, as well as any periodic adjustment or amendment to the reservation system that may be needed in order to respond to actual purchaser use patterns and changes in purchaser usedemand for the accommodations existing at that time within the multi-site timeshare plan.

(j) Any other information that the developer, with the approval of the Commission, desires to include in the timeshare disclosure statement.

Real Estate Training Institute – Pre Exam Workbook

(k) The location of each component site of the multi-site timeshare plan, the historical occupancy of each component site for the prior 12-month period, if the component site was part of the multi-site timeshare plan during such 12-month time period, as well as any periodic adjustment or amendments to the reservation system that may be needed in order to respond to actual purchaser use patterns and changes in purchaser use demand for the accommodations existing at that time within the multi-site timeshare plan.

(l) A description of any rights to make any additions, substitutions, or deletions of accommodations, amenities, or component sites, and a description of the basis upon which accommodations, amenities, or component sites may be added to, substituted in, or deleted form the multi- site timeshare plan.

(m) A description of the reservation system that shall included all of the following:

(i) The entity responsible for operating the reservation system, its relationship to the developer, and the duration of any agreement for operation of the reservation system.

(ii) A summary of the rules and regulations governing access to and use of the reservation system.

(iii) The existence of and an explanation regarding any priority reservation features that affect a purchaser's ability to make reservations for the use of a given accommodation on a first-come, first-served basis.

(n) The name and principal address of the managing entity for the multi-site timeshare plan and a description of the procedures, if any, for altering the powers and responsibilities of the managing entity and for removing or replacing it, and a description of the relationship between a multi-site timeshare plan managing entity and the managing entity of the component sites of a multi-site timeshare plan, if different from the multi-site timeshare plan managing entity.

(o) The current annual budget as provided in Section L. of these rules, along with the projected assessments and a description of the method of calculation and apportioning the assessments among purchasers, all of which shall be attached as an exhibit to the public offering statement.

(p) Any current fees or charges to be paid by timeshare purchasers for the use of any amenities related to the timeshare plan and statement that the fees or charges are subject to change.

(q) Any initial or special fee due from the purchaser at closing, together with a description of the purpose and method of calculating the fee.

(r) A description of any financing offered by or available through the developer.

(s) A description of any bankruptcies, pending civil or criminal suits, adjudications, or disciplinary actions of which the developer has knowledge, which would have a material effect on the developer's ability to perform its obligations.

(t) A statement disclosing any right of first refusal or other restraint on the transfer of all or any portion of a timeshare interest.

(u) A statement disclosing that any deposit made in connection with the purchase of a timeshare interest shall be held by an escrow agent until expiration of any right to cancel the contract and that any deposit shall be returned to the purchaser if he or she elects to exercise his or her right of cancellation. Alternatively, if the Commission has accepted from the developer a surety bond, irrevocable letter of credit, or other financial assurance in lieu of placing deposits in an escrow account, account: (i) a statement disclosing that the developer has provided a surety bond, irrevocable letter of credit, or other financial assurance in an amount equal to or in excess of the funds that would otherwise be placed in an escrow account and, (ii) a description of the type of financial assurance that has been arranged, (iii) a statement that if the purchaser elects to exercise his or her right of cancellation as provided in the contract, the developer shall return the deposit, and (iv) a description of the person or entity to whom the purchaser should apply for payment.

(v) If the timeshare plan provides purchasers with the opportunity to participate in an exchange program, a description of the name and address of the exchange company and the method by which a purchaser accesses the exchange program.

(w) Any other information that the developer, with the approval of the Commission, desires to include in the **timeshare disclosure statement.**

Amendment to Registration Information and Public Offering Statement:

The developer shall amend or supplement its Public Offering Statement and registration information to reflect any material change in any information contained therein. All such amendments, supplements and changes shall be filed with and approved by the Commission.

Each approved amendment to the Public Offering Statement, other than an amendment made only for the purpose of the addition of a phase or phases to the timeshare plan in the manner described in the timeshare instrument or any amendment that does not materially alter or modify the offering in a manner that is adverse to a purchaser, shall be delivered to a purchaser no later than 10 days prior to closing.

Registration Review Time Frames

Every registration required to be filed with the Commission must be reviewed and issued a certificate of registration in accordance with the following schedule:

Real Estate Training Institute – Pre Exam Workbook

A. Comprehensive registration. Registration shall be effective only upon the issuance of a certificate of registration issued by the Commission, which, in the ordinary course of business, should occur no more than sixty (60) calendar days after actual receipt by the state agency of the properly completed application. The Commission must provide a list of deficiencies in the application, if any, and the time for issuance of the certificate of registration by the Commission will be sixty (60) calendar days from receipt by the Commission of the information listed in the deficiencies in the application.

B. Abbreviated registration. Registration shall be effective only upon the issuance of a certificate of registration issued by the Commission, which, in the ordinary course of business, should occur no more than thirty (30) calendar days after receipt by the

Commission of the properly completed application. The Commission must provide a list of deficiencies in the application, if any, and the time for issuance of the certificate of registration by the Commission will occur no more than thirty (30) calendar days from receipt by the Commission of the information listed in the deficiencies in the application.

C. Preliminary permit. A preliminary permit shall be issued within twenty (20) calendar days after receipt of a properly completed application, unless the Commission provides to the applicant a list of deficiencies in the application. A preliminary permit shall be issued within fifteen (15) calendar days after receipt by the Commission of the information listed in the deficiencies in the application.

D. The applicant nor a presumption of approval of the application. The Commission may, for cause, extend the approval periods.

Purchase Contracts

A. Each developer shall furnish each purchaser with a fully completed and executed copy of a contract, which contract shall include the following information:

(1) The actual date the contract is executed by all parties;

(2) The names and addresses of the seller, the developer and the timeshare plan;

(3) The total financial obligation of the purchaser, including the purchase price and any additional charges to which the purchaser may be subject, such as any recurring assessment;

(4) The estimated date of availability of each accommodation, which is not completed;

(5) A description of the nature and duration of the timeshare interest being sold, including whether any interests in real property is being conveyed and the specific number of years or months constituting the term of contract;

(6) Immediately above the signature line of the purchaser(s), the following statement shall be printed in conspicuous type:

<u>You may cancel this contract without any penalty or obligation within seven (7) calendar days from the date you sign this contract and seven (7) calendar days after you receive the public offering statement, whichever is later. If you decide to cancel this contract, you must notify the developer in writing of your intent to cancel. Your notice of cancellation shall be effective upon the date sent and shall be sent to (name of developer) at (address of developer). If you cancel the contract during a the seven-day cancellation period, the developer shall refund to you all payments made under the contract within thirty (30) days after receipt of your cancellation notice.</u>

No purchaser should rely upon

(7) These statements in Paragraph f. may not be waived and failure to include them in a timeshare contract shall render the contract void.

(8) Seller shall refund all payments made by the purchaser under the contract and return all negotiable instruments, other than checks, executed by the purchaser in connection with the contract within 30 days from the receipt of the notice of cancellation transmitted to the developer from the purchaser or if the purchaser has received benefits under the contract, refund all payments made less actual cost of benefits actually received by the purchaser before the date of cancellation, with an accounting of the actual costs of the benefits deducted from payments refunded.

Exchange Program

A. If a purchaser is offered the opportunity to subscribe to an exchange program, the purchaser should receive written information concerning the exchange program prior to or concurrently with the execution of the contract with the exchange company. Such information should include, without limitation, the following information.

(1) The name and address of the exchange company;

(2) The names of all officers, directors and shareholders of greater that 10% interests of the exchange company;

(3) A description of the purchaser's contractual relationship with the exchange program and the procedure by which changes may be made;

(4) A description of the procedure to qualify for and effectuate changes;

(5) A description of the limitations, restrictions or priority employed in the operation of the exchange program;

(6) The fees or range of fees for participation in the exchange program and the circumstances under which the fees may be changed;

(7) The name and address of each timeshare plan participating in the exchange program;

(8) The number of timeshare interests reported in seven (7) day usage periods in each timeshare plan participating in the exchange program; and

(9) The number of purchasers for each timeshare plan participating in the exchange program.

B The exchange program should report on an annual basis following an audit by an independent certified public accountant the following:

(1) The number of purchasers enrolled in the exchange program;

(2) The number of accommodations that have current affiliation agreements with the exchange program;

(3) The percentage of confirmed reservations;

(4) The number of timeshare periods for which the exchange program has an outstanding obligation to provide an exchange to a purchaser who relinquished a timeshare period during the year; and

(5) The number of exchanges confirmed by the exchange program during the year.

C. No developer shall have any liability with respect to any violation of these rules arising out of the publication by the developer of information provided to it by an exchange company pursuant to this section. No exchange company shall have any liability with respect to any violation of these rules arising out of the use by a developer of information relating to an exchange program other than that provided to the developer by the exchange company.

D. An exchange company may elect to deny exchange privileges to any purchaser whose use of the accommodations of the purchaser's timeshare plan is denied, and no exchange program or exchange company shall be liable to any of its members or any third parties on account of any such denial of exchange privileges.

In order to protect the purchaser's right to refund during the rescission period and during any period in which construction of the timeshare property is not complete and available for occupancy by purchasers, the developer shall provide financial assurances as required by this section.

A. A developer of a timeshare plan shall deposit into an escrow account in an acceptable escrow depository all funds that are received in Mississippi during the purchaser's rescission period. An acceptable escrow depository includes banks, trust companies, saving and loans associations, real estate broker trust accounts at such an institution, title insurers, and underwritten title companies.

The handling of these funds shall be in accordance with an executed escrow agreement between an escrow agreement between an escrow agent and the developer. Funds will be handled to assure the following:

(1) Funds may be disbursed to the developer by the escrow agent from the escrow account or from the broker trust account only after expiration of the purchaser's rescission period and in accordance with the purchase contract, subject to paragraph 2.

(2) If a prospective purchaser properly cancels the purchase contract following expiration of the cancellation period pursuant to its terms, the funds shall be paid to the prospective purchaser or paid to the developer if the prospective purchaser's funds have been previously refunded by the developer.

B. If a developer contracts to sell a timeshare interest and the construction of the accommodation in which the timeshare interest being conveyed is located has not been completed, the developer, upon expiration of the rescission period, shall continue to maintain in an escrow account all funds received by or on behalf of the developer from the prospective purchaser under his or her purchase contract. The Commission shall determine the types of documentation which shall be required for evidence of completion, including, but not limited to, a certificate of occupancy, a certificate of substantial completion, or an inspection by the State Fire Marshal or designee or an equivalent public safety inspection by the appropriate agency in the applicable jurisdiction. Unless the developer submits an alternative financial assurance in accordance with paragraph 3., funds shall not be released from escrow until a certificate of occupancy, or its equivalent, has been obtained and the rescission period has passed, and the timeshare interest can be transferred free and clear of blanket encumbrances, including mechanics' liens. Funds to be released from escrow shall be released as follows:

(1) If a prospective purchaser properly cancels the purchase contract pursuant to its terms, the funds shall be paid to the prospective purchaser or paid to the developer if the developer has previously refunded the prospective purchaser's funds. (See "1 above)

(2) If a prospective purchaser defaults in the performance of the prospective purchaser's obligations under the purchase contract, the funds shall be paid to the developer.

(3) If the funds of a prospective purchaser have not been previously disbursed in accordance with the provisions of this paragraph 2., they may be disbursed to the developer by the escrow agent upon the issuance of acceptable evidence of completion of construction and closing.

C In lieu of the provisions in paragraphs 1 and 2, the Commission may accept from the developer a surety bond, escrow bond, irrevocable letter of credit, or other financial assurance or arrangement acceptable to the Commission. Any acceptable financial assurances shall be in an amount equal to or in excess of the lesser of

Real Estate Training Institute – Pre Exam Workbook

(1) the funds that would otherwise be place in escrow, or

(2) in an amount equal to the cost to complete the incomplete property in which the timeshare interest is located. However, in no event shall the amount be less that the amount of funds that would otherwise be placed in escrow pursuant to subparagraph a. of paragraph 1.

D. The developer shall provide escrow account or broker trust account information to the Commission and shall execute in writing an authorization consenting to an audit or examination of the account by the Commission. The developer shall make documents related to the escrow or trust account or escrow obligation available to the Commission upon request. The escrow agent or broker shall maintain any disputed funds in the escrow account until either of the following occurs:

(1) Receipt of written direction agreed to by signature of all parties.

(2) Deposit of the funds with a court of competent jurisdiction in which a civil action regarding the funds has been filed

E. Excluding any encumbrance placed against the purchaser's timeshare interest securing the purchaser's payment of purchase money financing for the purchase, the developer shall not be entitled to the release of any funds escrowed under this section J. with respect to each timeshare interest and any other property or rights to property appurtenant to the timeshare interest, including any amenities represented to the purchaser as being part of the timeshare plan, until the developer has provided satisfactory evidence to the Commission of one of the following:

(1) The timeshare Interest together with any other property or rights to property appurtenant to the timeshare interest, including any amenities represented to the purchaser as being part of the timeshare plan, are free and clear of any of the claims of the developer, any owner of the underlying fee, a mortgagee, judgment creditor, or other lien holder, or any other person having an interest in or lien or encumbrance against the timeshare interest or appurtenant property or property rights.

(2) The developer, any owner of the underlying fee, a mortgagee, judgment creditor, or other lien holder, or any other person having an interest in or lien or encumbrance against the timeshare interest or appurtenant property or property rights, including any amenities represented to the purchaser as being part of the timeshare plan, has recorded a subordination and notice to creditors document in the appropriate public records of the jurisdiction in which the timeshare interest is located. The subordination document shall expressly and effectively provide that the interest holder's right, lien or encumbrance shall not adversely affect, and shall be subordinate to, the rights of the owners of the timeshare interests in the timeshare plan regardless of the date of purchase.

(3) The developer, any owner of the underlying fee, a mortgagee, judgment creditor, or other lien holder, or any other person having an interest in or lien or encumbrance against the timeshare interest or appurtenant property or property rights, including any amenities represented to the purchaser as being part of the timeshare plan, has transferred the subject accommodations,

amenities, or all use rights in the amenities to a nonprofit organization or owners' association to be held for the use and benefit of the owners of the timeshare plan, which organization or owners association shall act as a fiduciary to the purchasers, and the developer has transferred control of the entity to the owners or does not exercise its voting rights in the entity with respect to the subject accommodations or amenities: Prior to the transfer, any lien or other encumbrance against the accommodation or facility shall be made subject to a subordination and notice to creditors, instrument pursuant to subparagraph b. or be free and clear of all liens and encumbrances.

(4) Alternative arrangements have been made which are adequate to protect the rights of the purchasers of the timeshare interests and approved by the Commission.

F. Nothing in this section shall prevent a developer from accessing any escrow funds if the developer has complied with paragraph 3 of this section.

G. The developer shall notify the Commission of the extent to which an accommodation may become subject to a tax or other lien arising out of claims against other purchasers in the same timeshare plan.

H. Developers, sellers, escrow agents, brokers and their employees and agents have a fiduciary duty to purchasers with respect to funds required to be deposited under these rules. Any Mississippi broker or salesperson who fails to comply with rules concerning the establishment of an escrow or broker trust account, deposits of funds, and property into escrow or withdrawal there from, shall be in violation of the Mississippi Real Estate Brokers Act of 1954, as amended, and the Rules and Regulations of the Commission. The failure to establish an escrow or trust account or to place funds therein as required under these rules is prima facie evidence of an intentional and purposeful violation.40

Insurance

A. For single site timeshare plans and component sites of multi-site timeshare plans located in this state, the timeshare instrument shall require that the following insurance be at all times maintained in force to protect timeshare interest owners in the timeshare plan:

(1) Insurance against property damage as a result of fire and other hazards commonly insured against, covering all real and personal property comprising the timeshare plan in an amount not less than 80 percent of the full replacement value of the timeshare property.

(2) Liability insurance against death, bodily injury, and property damage arising out of or in connection with the use, ownership, or maintenance for the accommodations of the timeshare plan. The amounts of the insurance shall be determined by the association, but shall not be less than five hundred thousand dollars ($500,000) to One Million Dollars ($1,000,000) for personal injury and One Hundred Thousand Dollars ($100,000) for property damage.

B. In a timeshare use offering, the trustee, if one exists, shall be a named coinsured, and if for any reason, title to the accommodation is not held in trust, the association shall be named as a coinsured as the agent for each of the timeshare interest owners.

C. In a timeshare estate offering, the association shall be named as a coinsured if it has title to the property or as a coinsured as agent for each of the timeshare interests owners if title is held by the owners as tenants in common.

Advertising and Marketing:

A. No advertising shall:

(1) Misrepresent a fact or create a false or misleading impression regarding the timeshare plan.

(2) Make a prediction of increases in the price or value of timeshare periods.

(3) Contain any contradictory statements.

(4) Describe any improvements to the timeshare plan that will not be built or that are described as completed when not completed.

B. No promotional device, sweepstakes, lodging certificate, gift award, premium, discount, drawing, prize or display in connection with an offer to sell a timeshare interest may be utilized without the applicable disclosure as follows:

(1) That the promotional device is being used for the purposes of soliciting sales of timeshare periods;

(2) Of the name and address of each timeshare plan or business entity participating in the program;

(3) Of the date and year when all prizes are to be awarded;

(4) Of the method by which all prizes are to be awarded;

(5) If applicable, a statement that it is a national program with multiple sponsors and the gifts offered are not limited solely to customers of said development, but apply also to other developments.

C. The following are not considered to be advertising materials:

(1) Any stockholder communication, financial report, prospectus or other material required to be delivered to owners, prospective purchasers or other persons by an agency of any state or the federal government;

(2) Any communication addressed to and relating to the account of any person who has previously executed a contract for the purchase of a timeshare interest in a timeshare plan to which the communication relates;

(3) Any oral or written statement disseminated to the broadcast, print or other news media, other than paid advertising, regarding plans for the acquisition or development of timeshare property. However, any redistribution of such oral or written statements to a prospective purchaser in any manner would constitute an advertisement;

(4) Any publication or material relating to the promotion of accommodations for transient rental, so long as a mandatory tour of a timeshare plan or attendance at a mandatory sales presentation is not a term or condition of the availability of such accommodations, so long as the failure of the transient renter to take a tour of a timeshare plan or attend a sales presentation does not result in the transient renter receiving less than what was promised in such materials;

(5) Any audio, written or visual publication or material relating to an exchange company or exchange program providing to an existing member of that exchange company or exchange program.

Management

A. Before the first sale of a timeshare period, the developer shall create or provide for a managing entity, which may be the developer, a separate management firm, or an owner's association, or some combination thereof.

B. The management entity shall act in the capacity of fiduciary to the purchasers of the timeshare plans.

C. The duties of the management entity shall include, but are not limited to:

(1) Management and maintenance of all accommodations constituting the timeshare plan.

(2) Preparing an itemized annual operating and reserve budget.

(3) The assessment and collection of funds for common expenses.

(4) The assessment and collection of property taxes and casualty insurance and liability insurance against the owners, for which managing entity shall he primarily liable.

(5) Maintenance of all books and records concerning the timeshare plan, and making all of them reasonably available for inspection by any purchaser, or the authorized agent of such purchaser.

Real Estate Training Institute – Pre Exam Workbook

(6) Arranging for an annual independent audit to be conducted of all the books and financial records of the timeshare plan by a certified public accountant. A copy of the audit shall be forwarded to the officers of the owner's association; or, if no association exists, the owner of each timeshare period shall be notified in writing that such audit is available upon request.

(7) Scheduling occupancy of the timeshare units so that all purchasers will be provided the use and possession of the accommodations for which they have contracted.

(8) Notifying purchasers of common assessments and the identity of the managing entity.

(9) Performing any other functions and duties that are necessary and proper to maintain the accommodations and operate the owners association as provided in the contract or the timeshare instruments.

(10) Maintaining appropriate insurance as required by Rule 8.9 of these rules.

D. The managing entity shall not be required to provide a reserve budget for any timeshare plan or accommodation for which a timeshare instrument has been approved prior to adoption of these rules.

Liens

A. The management entity has a lien on a timeshare period from the date an assessment becomes due.

B. The management entity may bring an action in its name to foreclose a lien for assessments in the manner a mortgage of real property is foreclosed, and may bring an action to recover a money judgment for the unpaid assessments, or, when no interest in real property is conveyed, an action under the Uniform Commercial Code.

C. The lien is effective from the date of recording in the public records of the county or counties in which the accommodations are located, or as otherwise provided by the laws of the jurisdiction in which the accommodations are located.

D. A judgment in any action or suit brought under this section may include costs and reasonable attorney's fees for the prevailing party.

E. Labor or materials furnished to a unit shall not be the basis for the filing of a lien against the timeshare unit of any timeshare interest owner not expressly consenting to or requesting the labor or materials.

Owner Referrals

A. Referrals of prospective customers to the developer by any existing timeshare owner shall be permitted, without the owner holding a real estate license and compensation may be paid to the referring owner, only under the following circumstances:

(1) The existing timeshare owner refers no more than twenty (20) prospective customers in any twelve (12) month period; and

(2) The existing timeshare owner limits his or her activities to referring customers to the developer or the developer's employees or agents and does not show, discuss terms or conditions of purchase or otherwise participate in any negotiations with the purchase of a timeshare interest.

Administration

A. Invitations to bid on the Errors and Omissions coverage shall be by advertisement published in the appropriate newspaper having state-wide coverage.

B. Selection and approval of the Errors and Omissions Insurance carrier shall be by Commissioners utilizing consultants or committees as deemed appropriate by the Commission.

C. Upon approval of the carrier, invoices shall be sent via First Class Mail to all licensees; including companies and corporations; along with the necessary information describing the various available coverages, the period of coverage and the minimum requirements for independent coverage if desired by a licensee.

D. Coverage shall be a twelve month period beginning October 1, 1994, and continuing thereafter on twelve month basis.

E. Premiums shall be collected by the carrier or the Commission, at the Commission's discretion.

F. The Commission may maintain computer or written records as required for accurate documentation and administration of this program.

Licensee Status

A. Active licensees not submitting the required premium or providing the required proof of acceptable independent coverage within 30 days after the due date of the premium shall be placed automatically on inactive status at the end of the 30 day period.

B. Inactive licensees will not be required to pay the premium until changing to active status and the premium will be assessed on a pro rata basis. However, inactive licensees will be invoiced at the beginning of the policy period. They may pay the full premium at that time if they desire.

C. New licensees will be given notice when their license is issued to provide proof of coverage within 30 days of the issuance of license or pay the premium specified on a pro rata basis. Failure to do so will result in their license being changed to inactive status.

Independent Coverage ***Same as for Agents and Brokers

A. Licensees having independent coverage shall submit proof of coverage by the beginning of the policy period as set forth above. Any deficiency in supplying proof of coverage must be corrected within no more than 30 days after the beginning of the policy period. Proof of coverage shall be by a "Certificate of Insurance" provided by the independent insurance carrier.

B. Minimum requirements of independent coverage shall be:

(1) Coverage must be for all activities for which a real estate license is required.

(2) A per claim limit is not less than $100,000.00.

(3) The deductible is not more than $2,500.00 per licensee, per claim, for any damages and the deductible is not more than $1,000.00 per licensee, per claim, for defense costs.

(4) The independent insurance carrier shall agree to a non-cancelable policy or provide a letter of commitment to notify the Commission 30 days prior to intention to cancel.

Real Estate Training Institute – Pre Exam Workbook

CHAPTER 7

Professions and Occupations

Oral Proceedings & Declaratory Opinions

Oral Proceedings

Scope.

These rules apply to all oral proceedings held for the purpose of providing the public with an opportunity to make oral presentations on proposed new rules and amendments to rules before the Mississippi Real Estate Commission.

Source: Miss. Code Ann. § 25-43-3.104 (Rev. 2010).

When Oral Proceedings will be scheduled on Proposed Rules.

The Commission will conduct an oral proceeding on a proposed rule or amendment if requested by a political subdivision, an agency or ten (10) persons in writing within twenty (20) days after the filing of the notice of the proposed rule.

Source: Miss. Code Ann. § 25-43-3.104 (Rev. 2010).

Request Format.

Each request must be printed or typewritten, or must be in legible handwriting. Each request must be submitted on standard business letter-size paper (81/2 inches by 11 inches). Requests may be in the form of a letter addressed to the Commission and signed by the requestor(s).

Source: Miss. Code Ann. § 25-43-3.104 (Rev. 2010).

Notification of Oral Proceeding.

The date, time and place of all oral proceedings shall be filed with the Secretary of State's office and mailed to each requestor. The oral proceedings will be scheduled no earlier than twenty (20) days from the filing of this information with the Secretary of State.

Source: Miss. Code Ann. § 25-43-3.104 (Rev. 2010).

Presiding Officer.

The Commission Administrator or his designee, who is familiar with the substance of the proposed rule, shall preside at the oral proceeding on a proposed rule.

Real Estate Training Institute – Pre Exam Workbook

Source: Miss. Code Ann. § 25-43-3.104 (Rev. 2010).

Public Presentation and Participation.

A. At an oral proceeding on a proposed rule, persons may make oral statements and make documentary and physical submissions, which may include data, views, comments or arguments concerning the proposed rule.

B. Persons wishing to make oral presentations at such a proceeding shall notify the Board at least one business day prior to the proceeding and indicate the general subject of their presentations. The presiding officer in his or her discretion may allow individuals to participate that have not previously contacted the Commission.

C. At the proceeding, those who participate shall indicate their names and addresses, identify any persons or organizations they may represent, and provide any other information relating to their participation deemed appropriate by the presiding officer.

D. The presiding officer may place time limitations on individual oral presentations when necessary to assure the orderly and expeditious conduct of the oral proceeding. To encourage joint oral presentations and to avoid repetition, additional time may be provided for persons whose presentations represent the views of other individuals as well as their own views.

E. Persons making oral presentations are encouraged to avoid restating matters that have already been submitted in writing.

F. There shall be no interruption of a participant who has been given the floor by the presiding officer, except that the presiding officer may in his or her discretion interrupt or end the participant's time where the orderly conduct of the proceeding so requires.

Source: Miss. Code Ann. § 25-43-3.104 (Rev. 2010).

Conduct of Oral Proceeding.

A. Presiding Officer - The presiding officer shall have authority to conduct the proceeding in his or her discretion for the orderly conduct of the proceeding. The presiding officer shall:

(1) call proceeding to order;

(2) give a brief synopsis of the proposed rule, a statement of the statutory authority for the proposed rule, and the reasons provided by the Board for the proposed rule;

(3) call on those individuals who have contacted the Commission about speaking on or against the proposed rule;

(4) allow for rebuttal statements following all participant's comments; and

(5) adjourn the proceeding.

B. Questions. - The presiding officer, where time permits and to facilitate the exchange of information, may open the floor to questions or general discussion. The presiding officer may question participants and permit the questioning of participants by other participants about any matter relating to that rule-making proceeding, including any prior written submissions made by those participants in that proceeding; but no participant shall be required to answer any question.

C. Physical and Documentary Submissions. - Submissions presented by participants in an oral proceeding shall be submitted to the presiding officer. Such submissions become the property of the Commission and are subject to the Commission's public records request procedure.

D. Recording. - The Commission may record oral proceedings by stenographic or electronic means.

Source: Miss. Code Ann. § 25-43-3.104 (Rev. 2010).

Scope.

These rules set forth the Mississippi Real Estate Commission's rules governing the form, content and filing of requests for declaratory opinions, and the Commission's procedures regarding the requests. These rules are intended to supplement and be read in conjunction with the provisions of the Mississippi Administrative Procedures Law, which may contain additional information regarding the issuance of declaratory opinions. In the event of any conflict between these rules and the Mississippi Administrative Procedures Law, the latter shall govern.

Source: Miss. Code Ann. § 25-43-2-103 (Rev. 2010).

Persons Who May Request Declaratory Opinions.

Any person with a substantial interest in the subject matter may request a declaratory opinion from the Commission by following the specified procedures. A substantial interest in the subject matter means: an individual, business, group or other entity that is directly affected by the Commission's administration of the laws within its primary jurisdiction. Primary jurisdiction of the agency means the agency has a constitutional or statutory grant of authority in the subject matter at issue.

Source: Miss. Code Ann. § 25-43-2-103 (Rev. 2010).

Subjects Which May Be Addressed in Declaratory Opinions.

The Commission will issue declaratory opinions regarding the applicability to specified facts of:

A. a statute administered or enforced by the Commission or

B. a rule promulgated by the Commission.

Real Estate Training Institute – Pre Exam Workbook

The Commission will not issue a declaratory opinion a statute or rule which is outside the primary jurisdiction of the Commission.

Source: Miss. Code Ann. § 25-43-2-103 (Rev. 2010).

Circumstances In Which Declaratory Opinions Will Not Be Issued.

The Commission may, for good cause, refuse to issue, a declaratory opinion. The circumstances in which declaratory opinions will not be issued include, but are not necessarily limited to:

A. Lack of clarity concerning the question presented;

B. There is pending or anticipated litigation, administrative action, or other adjudication which may either answer the question presented by the request or otherwise make an answer unnecessary;

C. The statute or rule on which a declaratory opinion is sought is clear and not in need of interpretation to answer the question presented by the request;

D. The facts presented in the request are not sufficient to answer the question presented;

E. The request fails to contain information required by these rules or the requestor failed to follow the procedure set forth in these rules;

F. The request seeks to resolve issues which have become moot, or are abstract or hypothetical such that the requestor is not substantially affected by the statute or rule on which a declaratory opinion is sought;

G. No controversy exists concerning the issue as the requestor is not faced with existing facts or those certain to arise which raise a question concerning the application of the statute or rule;

H. The question presented by the request concerns the legal validity of a statute or rule;

I. The request is not based upon facts calculated to aid in the planning of future conduct but is, instead, based on past conduct in an effort to establish the effect of that conduct,

J. No clear answer is determinable;

K. The question presented by the request involves the application of a criminal statute or a set of facts which may constitute a crime;

L. The answer to the question presented would require the disclosure of information which is privileged or otherwise protected by law from disclosure;

M. The question is currently the subject of an Attorney General's opinion request or has been answered by an Attorney General's Opinion;

N. A similar request is pending before this agency or any other agency or a proceeding is pending on the same subject matter before any agency, administrative or judicial tribunal, or where such an opinion would constitute the unauthorized practice of law;

O. Where issuance of a declaratory opinion may adversely affect the interests of the State, the Commission or any of their officers or employees in any litigation which is pending or may reasonably be expected to arise;

P. The question involves eligibility for a license, permit, certificate or other approval by the Commission or some other agency, and there is a statutory or regulatory application process by which eligibility for said license, permit, certificate or other approval would be determined.

Source: Miss. Code Ann. § 25-43-2-103 (Rev. 2010).

Written Request Required.

Each request must be printed or typewritten, or must be in legible handwriting. Each request must be submitted on standard business letter-size paper (81/2 inches by 11 inches). Requests may be in the form of a letter addressed to the Board.

Source: Miss. Code Ann. § 25-43-2-103 (Rev. 2010).

Where to Send Requests.

All requests must be sent to the Commission Administrator, The Mississippi Real Estate Commission: (1) by mail at P.O. Box 12685, Jackson, MS 39236; or (2) delivered to 2506 Lakeland Drive, Suite 300, Flowood, MS 39232; or (3) sent via facsimile to (601 932-2990. All requests must be sent to the attention of Declaratory Opinion Request as follows: ATTN: DECLARATORY OPINION REQUEST

Source: Miss. Code Ann. § 25-43-2-103 (Rev. 2010).

Name, Address, and Signature of Requestor.

Each request must include the full name, telephone number and mailing address of the requestor. All requests shall be signed by the person filing the request, who shall attest that the request complies with the requirements set forth in these rules, including but not limited to a full, complete and accurate statement of relevant facts and that there are no related proceedings pending before any other administrative or judicial tribunal.51

Source: Miss. Code Ann. § 25-43-2-103 (Rev. 2010).

Question Presented.

Each request shall contain the following:

A. A clear and concise statement of all facts on which the opinion is requested;

B. A citation to the statute or rule at issue;

C. The question(s) sought to be answered in the opinion, stated clearly;

D. A suggested proposed opinion from the requestor, stating the answers desired by petitioner and a summary of the reasons in support of those answers;

E. The identity of all other known persons involved in or impacted by the described factual situation, including their relationship to the facts, name, mailing address and telephone number; and

F. A statement to show that the person seeking the opinion has a substantial interest in the

subject matter.

Source: Miss. Code Ann. § 25-43-2-103 (Rev. 2010).

Time for Board Response.

Within forty-five (45) days after the receipt of a request for a declaratory opinion which complies with the requirements of these rules, the Commission shall, in writing:

A. Issue a declaratory opinion regarding the specified statute or rule as applied to the /specified circumstances;

B. Decline to issue a declaratory opinion, stating the reasons for its action; or

C. Agree to issue a declaratory opinion by a specified time but not later than ninety (90) days after receipt of the written request.

D. The forty-five (45) day period shall begin running on the first State of Mississippi business day on or after the request is received the Board, whichever is sooner.

Source: Miss. Code Ann. § 25-43-2-103 (Rev. 2010).

Opinion Not Final for Sixty Days.

A declaratory opinion shall not become final until the expiration of sixty (60) days after the issuance of the opinion. Prior to the expiration of sixty (60) days, the Commission may, in its 52discretion, withdraw or amend the declaratory opinion for any reason which is not arbitrary or capricious. Reasons for withdrawing or amending an opinion include, but are not limited to, a determination that the request failed to meet the requirements of these rules or that the opinion issued contains a legal or factual error.

Source: Miss. Code Ann. § 25-43-2-103 (Rev. 2010).

Notice by Board to third parties.

The Commission may give notice to any person, agency or entity that a declaratory opinion has been requested, and may receive and consider data, facts arguments and opinions from other persons, agencies or other entities other than the requestor.

Source: Miss. Code Ann. § 25-43-2-103 (Rev. 2010).

Public Availability of Requests and Declaratory Opinions.

Declaratory opinions and requests for declaratory opinions shall be available for public inspection and copying in accordance with the Public Records Act and the Commission public records request procedure. All declaratory opinions and requests shall be indexed by name and subject. Declaratory opinions and requests which contain information which is confidential or exempt from disclosure under the Mississippi Public Records Act or other laws shall be exempt from this requirement and shall remain confidential.

Source: Miss. Code Ann. § 25-43-2-103 (Rev. 2010).

Effect of a Declaratory Opinion.

The Commission will not pursue any civil, criminal or administrative action against a person who is issued a declaratory opinion from the Commission and who, in good faith, follows the direction of the opinion and acts in accordance therewith unless a court of competent jurisdiction holds that the opinion is manifestly wrong. Any declaratory opinion rendered by the Commission shall be binding only on the Mississippi Real Estate Commission and the person to whom the opinion is issued. No declaratory opinion will be used as precedent for any other transaction or occurrence beyond that set forth by the requesting person.

Source: Miss. Code Ann. § 25-43-2-103 (Rev. 2010).

Real Estate Training Institute – Pre Exam Workbook

Professions and Occupations

Board Organization

Members.

The Mississippi Real Estate Commission consists of five (5) persons who are appointed by the Governor with the advice and consent of the Senate. Each appointee shall have been a resident and citizen of Mississippi for at least six (6) years prior to their appointment and shall have been a real estate broker for at least five (5) years. There shall be at least one (1) Commissioner from each Congressional District, as such Districts are constituted as of July 1, 2002, and one (1) additional Commissioner shall be appointed without regard to residence in any particular Congressional District. Any member of the Commission may be reappointed by the Governor. The Commission shall organize by selecting from its members a Chairman and may do all things necessary and convenient to promulgate rules and regulations.

Real Estate Training Institute – Leslie Clauson

CHAPTER 8

PSI CONTENT OUTLINE
for the MS State Portion of the Real Estate Exam

SALESPERSON/BROKER STATE PORTION

Powers and Duties of the Real Estate Commission (Salesperson 4 Items, Broker 4 Items)

The Mississippi Real Estate Commission consists of **five (5) persons** who are **appointed by the Governor** with the advice and consent of the Senate. Each appointee shall have **been a resident and citizen of Mississippi for at least six (6) years prior to their appointment and shall have been a real estate broker for at least five (5) years. There shall be at least one (1) Commissioner from each Congressional District**, as such Districts are constituted as of July 1, 2002, and **one (1) additional Commissioner shall be appointed without regard to residence in any particular Congressional District**. Any member of the Commission may be reappointed by the Governor. The Commission shall organize by selecting from its members a Chairman and may do all things necessary and convenient to promulgate rules and regulations.

1. Hearings, including subpoena power

Any licensee who fails in a timely manner to respond to official Mississippi Real Estate Commission written communication or who fails or neglects to abide by Mississippi Real Estate Commission's Rules and Regulations shall be deemed, prima facie, to be guilty of improper dealing

The commission is authorized and directed to take legal action against any violator.

Upon complaint initiated by the commission or filed with it, the licensee or any other person charged with a violation shall be given fifteen (15) days' notice of the hearing upon the charges filed, together with a copy of the complaint.

The applicant or licensee or other violator shall have an opportunity to be heard in person or by counsel, to offer testimony, and to examine witnesses appearing in connection with the complaint.

Hearings shall be held at the offices of the Mississippi Real Estate Commission, or at the commission's sole discretion, at a place determined by the commission.

At such hearings, all witnesses shall be sworn and stenographic notes of the proceedings shall be taken and filed as a part of the record in the case.

Real Estate Training Institute – Pre Exam Workbook

Any party to the proceedings shall be furnished with a copy of such stenographic notes upon payment to the commission of such fees as it shall prescribe, not exceeding, however, the actual cost to the commission.

The commission shall render a decision on any complaint and shall immediately notify the parties to the proceedings in writing of its ruling, order or decision.

The commission has the authority to bring injunctive proceedings in any appropriate forum against any violator or violators. Judges or courts have the power to grant injunctions and are specifically granted the power and jurisdiction to hear and dispose of such proceedings.

<u>The commission is hereby authorized and empowered to issue subpoenas for the attendance of witnesses and the production of books and papers.</u>

<u>The process issued by the commission shall extend to all parts of the state</u>, and such process shall be served by any person designated by the commission for such service.

The person serving such process receive such compensation as may be allowed by the commission, not to exceed the fee prescribed by law for similar services.

All witnesses who are subpoenaed and who appear in any proceedings before the commission receive the same fees and mileage as allowed by law, and all such fees shall be taxed as part of the costs in the case.

If any witness fails or refuses to attend after the subpoena is issued by the commission or refuse to testify or refuses to produce any books and papers which is called for by the subpoena, the attendance of such witness and the giving of his testimony and the production of the books and papers shall be enforced by any court of competent jurisdiction of this state.

The commission may obtain legal counsel privately to represent it in proceedings when legal counsel is required.

Any applicant or licensee or person aggrieved shall have the right of appeal from any adverse ruling or order or decision of the commission to the circuit court of the county of residence of the applicant, licensee or person, or of the First Judicial District of Hinds County, <u>within thirty (30) days</u> from the service of notice of the action of the commission upon the parties in interest.

Notice of appeals shall be filed in the office of the clerk of the court who shall issue a writ of certiorari directed to the commission commanding it, within thirty (30) days after service thereof, to certify to such court its entire record in the matter in which the appeal has been taken.

The appeal will be heard in due course by said court, without a jury, which shall review the record and make its determination of the cause between the parties.

Any order, rule or decision of the commission shall not take effect until after the time for appeal to the court has expired.

Real Estate Training Institute – Pre Exam Workbook

In the event an appeal is taken by a defendant, in the discretion of the court, the court may dispose of the appeal and enter its decision promptly.

Any person taking an appeal shall post a satisfactory bond in the amount of Five Hundred Dollars ($ 500.00) for the payment of any costs which may be adjudged against him.

Actions taken by the commission in suspending a license are not actions from which an appeal may be taken.

2. Purpose* and jurisdiction

To safeguard the interests of the public.

The Mississippi Real Estate Commission (MREC) administers control over the commercial real estate industry in the State of Mississippi, licensing all real estate brokers and salespersons.

MREC works to assure that all real estate transactions are performed in a professional and ethical manner. Potential licensees undergo comprehensive testing and are subjected to continuing education requirements.

MREC protects the consumer by setting forth a set of rules for its licensed members, and is responsible for investigating reports of rule violations and unethical practices.

The Mississippi Real Estate Commission also monitors real estate commerce taking place between brokers licensed in Mississippi and those in other states.

The process issued by the commission shall extend to all parts of the state, and such process shall be served by any person designated by the commission for such service.

The commission may act by a majority of the members thereof, and authority is hereby given to the commission to adopt, fix and establish all rules and regulations in its opinion necessary for the conduct of its business, the holdings of hearings before it, and otherwise generally for the enforcement and administration of the provisions of this chapter.

The commission is empowered with the authority to adopt such rules and regulations as it deems appropriate to regulate the sale of timesharing and condominium properties within the state of Mississippi and the sale of timesharing and condominium properties in other states to residents of Mississippi.

The commission is authorized to assist in conducting or holding real estate courses or institutes, and to incur and pay the necessary expenses in connection, which courses or institutes shall be open to any licensee or other interested parties.

The commission is authorized to assist libraries, real estate institutes, and foundations with financial aid, or otherwise, in providing texts, sponsoring studies, surveys and educational programs for the benefit of real estate and the elevation of the real estate business.

Real Estate Training Institute – Pre Exam Workbook

3. Violations

A real estate licensee shall not be exempt from disciplinary actions by the commission when selling property owned by the licensee.

Any licensee who fails in a timely manner to respond to official Mississippi Real Estate Commission written communication or who fails or neglects to abide by Mississippi Real Estate Commission's Rules and Regulations shall be deemed, prima facie, to be guilty of improper dealing.

Grounds for refusing to issue or suspending or revoking license; hearing

The commission may, upon its own motion and shall upon the verified complaint in writing of any person, hold a hearing for the refusal of license or for the suspension or revocation of a license previously issued, or for such other action as the commission deems appropriate. The commission shall have full power to refuse a license for cause or to revoke or suspend a license where it has been obtained by false or fraudulent representation, or where the licensee in performing or attempting to perform any of the acts mentioned herein, is deemed to be guilty of:

Making any substantial misrepresentation in connection with a real estate transaction;

Making any false promises of a character likely to influence, persuade or induce;

Pursuing a continued and flagrant course of misrepresentation or making false promises through agents or salespersons or any medium of advertising or otherwise;

Any misleading or untruthful advertising;

Acting for more than one (1) party in a transaction or receiving compensation from more than one (1) party in a transaction, or both, without the knowledge of all parties for whom he acts;

Failing, within a reasonable time, to account for or to remit any monies coming into his possession which belong to others, or commingling of monies belonging to others with his own funds. Every responsible broker procuring the execution of an earnest money contract or option or other contract who shall take or receive any cash or checks shall deposit, within a reasonable period of time, the sum or sums so received in a trust or escrow account in a bank or trust company pending the consummation or termination of the transaction. "Reasonable time" in this context means by the close of business of the next banking day;

Entering a guilty plea or conviction in a court of competent jurisdiction of this state, or any other state or the United States of any felony;

Displaying a "for sale" or "for rent" sign on any property without the owner's consent;

Failing to furnish voluntarily, at the time of signing, copies of all listings, contracts and agreements to all parties executing the same;

Paying any rebate, profit or commission to any person other than a real estate broker or salesperson licensed under the provisions of this chapter;

Inducing any party to a contract, sale or lease to break such contract for the purpose of substituting in lieu thereof a new contract, where such substitution is motivated by the personal gain of the licensee;

Accepting a commission or valuable consideration as a real estate salesperson for the performance of any of the acts specified in this chapter from any person, except his employer who must be a licensed real estate broker; or

Any act or conduct, whether of the same or a different character than hereinabove specified, which constitutes or demonstrates bad faith, incompetency or untrustworthiness, or dishonest, fraudulent or improper dealing.

No real estate broker shall practice law or give legal advice directly or indirectly unless said broker be a duly licensed attorney under the laws of this state. He shall not act as a public conveyancer nor give advice or opinions as to the legal effect of instruments nor give opinions concerning the validity of title to real estate; nor shall he prevent or discourage any party to a real estate transaction from employing the services of an attorney; nor shall a broker undertake to prepare documents fixing and defining the legal rights of parties to a transaction. However, when acting as a broker, he may use an earnest money contract form. A real estate broker shall not participate in attorney's fees, unless the broker is a duly licensed attorney under the laws of this state and performs legal services in addition to brokerage services.

The commission is authorized to suspend the license of any licensee for being out of compliance with an order for support. The procedure for suspension of a license for being out of compliance with an order for support.

4. Penalties MREC can impose

Any person violating a provision of MS Real Estate License Law, upon conviction of a first violation thereof, if a person, be punished by a fine or not less than Five Hundred Dollars ($500.00) nor more than One Thousand Dollars ($1,000.00), or by imprisonment for a term not to exceed ninety (90) days, or both;

and if a corporation, be punished by a fine of not more than Two Thousand Dollars ($2,000.00).

Upon conviction of a second or subsequent violation, if a person, shall be punished by a fine of not less than One Thousand Dollars ($1,000.00) nor more than Two Thousand Dollars ($2,000.00), or by imprisonment for a term not to exceed six (6) months, or both;

and if a corporation, be punished by a fine of not less than Two Thousand Dollars ($2,000.00) nor more than Five Thousand Dollars ($5,000.00).

Real Estate Training Institute – Pre Exam Workbook

Any officer or agent of a corporation, or any member or agent of a partnership or association, who shall personally participate in or be accessory to any violation of this chapter by such corporation, partnership or association, shall be subject to the penalties herein prescribed for individuals.

In case any person, partnership, association or corporation shall have received any sum of money, or the equivalent thereto, as commission, compensation or profit by or in consequence of his violation of any provision of MS Real Estate License Law, such person, partnership, association or corporation shall also be liable to a penalty of not less than the amount of the sum of money so received and not more than four (4) times the sum so received, as may be determined by the court, which penalty may be sued for and recovered by any person aggrieved and for his use and benefit, in any court of competent jurisdiction.

No fee, commission or other valuable consideration may be paid to a person for real estate brokerage activities unless the person provides evidence of licensure or provides evidence of a cooperative agreement.

Licensing Requirements and License Maintenance (Salesperson 4 Items, Broker 4 Items)

1. General licensing requirements

Qualifications for license

Licenses shall be granted only to persons who present, and to corporations, partnerships, companies or associations whose officers, associates or partners present satisfactory proof to the commission that they are trustworthy and competent to transact the business of a real estate broker or real estate salesperson in such manner as to safeguard the interests of the public.

Every person who applies for a resident license as a real estate broker:
(a) shall be age twenty-one (21) years or over, and have his legal domicile in the State of Mississippi at the time he applies;
(b) shall be subject to the jurisdiction of this state, subject to the income tax laws and other excise laws thereof, subject to the road and bridge privilege tax laws thereof;
(c) shall not be an elector in any other state;
(d) shall have held a license as an active real estate salesperson for twelve (12) months immediately prior to making application for the broker's examination hereafter specified;
(e) shall have successfully completed a minimum of one hundred twenty (120) hours of courses in real estate as hereafter specified; and
(f) shall have successfully completed the real estate broker's examination as hereafter specified.

An applicant who has not held an active real estate salesperson's license for a period of at least twelve (12) months immediately prior to submitting an application shall have successfully completed a minimum of one hundred fifty (150) classroom hours in real estate courses, which courses are acceptable for credit toward a degree at a college or university as approved by the Southern Association of Colleges and Schools.

Every applicant for a resident license as a real estate salesperson shall be
age eighteen (18) years or over,
shall be a bona fide resident of the State of Mississippi prior to filing his application,
and shall have successfully completed a minimum of sixty (60) hours in courses in real estate
and shall have successfully completed the real estate salesperson's examination as hereafter specified.

The residency requirements do not apply to those licensees of other states who qualify and obtain nonresident licenses in this state.

The commission is authorized to exempt from such pre-licensing educational requirements, in whole or in part, a real estate licensee of another state who desires to obtain a license under this chapter; provided, however, that the pre-licensing educational requirements in the other state are determined by the commission to be equivalent to pre-licensing educational requirements in this state and provided that such state extends this same privilege or exemption to Mississippi real estate licensees.

Licenses for business entities

A corporation, partnership, company or association shall be granted a license when individual broker's licenses have been issued to every member, owner, partner or officer of such partnership, company, association or corporation who actively participates in its brokerage business and when any required fee is paid.

Licenses shall be granted only to persons who present, and to corporations, partnerships, companies or associations whose officers, associates or partners present satisfactory proof to the commission that they are trustworthy and competent to transact the business of a real estate broker or real estate salesperson in such manner as to safeguard the interests of the public.

2. Continuing and Post-licensing ed req

Temporary licenses; post-license education

Upon passing the Mississippi broker's or salesperson's examination and complying with all other conditions for licensure, a temporary license shall be issued to the applicant.

A temporary license shall be valid for a period of one (1) year following the first day of the month after its issuance.

The holder of a temporary license shall not be issued a permanent license until he has satisfactorily completed a thirty-hour post-license course.

The holder of a temporary license shall complete the entire thirty-hour course within twelve (12) months of issuance of his temporary license; otherwise this temporary license shall automatically be placed on inactive status by the Mississippi Real Estate Commission. If the holder of the temporary license does not complete the course and have his permanent license issued within one (1) year following the first day of the month after its issuance, the temporary license shall automatically expire and lapse. A temporary license is not subject to renewal procedures and may not be renewed.

The thirty-hour post-license course shall be offered by providers certified and approved by the commission, and an annual certification fee of One Thousand Dollars ($ 1,000.00) shall be charged to providers. The thirty-hour post-license coursework shall be offered in no less than fifteen-hour increments of classroom instruction. No more than eight (8) hours may be earned in a single day.

The holder of an active license who has satisfactorily completed the post-license course and whose permanent license has been issued shall not be subject to the sixteen-hour continuing education requirement in this chapter for the first renewal of his permanent license.

License renewal; continuing education requirements; exemptions; rules and regulations; reinstatement of expired license.

Each individual applicant for renewal of a license issued by the Mississippi Real Estate Commission shall, on or before the expiration date of his license, or at a time directed by the commission, submit proof of completion of not less than sixteen (16) clock hours of approved course work to the commission, in addition to any other requirements for renewal. The sixteen (16) clock hours' course work requirement shall apply to each two-year license renewal, and hours in excess thereof shall not be cumulated or credited for the purposes of subsequent license renewals except as provided in this subsection (1).

This section shall not apply to persons who have held a broker's or salesperson's license in this state for at least twenty-five (25) years and who are older than seventy (70) years of age.

Inactive licensees are not required to meet the real estate continuing education requirements specified in this section; however, such inactive licensees, before activating their license to active status, must cumulatively meet requirements missed during the period their license was inactive.

3. E & O insurance

Real estate licensees required to obtain errors and omissions insurance coverage; persons required to submit proof of errors and omissions insurance; minimum requirements of group policy issued to commission; public bid for group insurance contract; requirements for independent coverage; rules and regulations

The following persons shall submit proof of insurance:

(a) Any active individual broker, active broker-salesperson or active salesperson;

(b) Any partnership (optional); or

(c) Any corporation (optional).

Individuals whose licenses are on inactive status are not required to carry errors and omissions insurance.

All Mississippi licensees shall be covered for activities contemplated under this chapter.

Licensees may obtain errors and omissions coverage through the insurance carrier approved by the Mississippi Real Estate Commission and provided on a group policy basis.

The following are minimum requirements of the group policy to be issued to the commission,
(a) All activities contemplated under this chapter are included as covered activities

(b) A per-claim limit is not less than One Hundred Thousand Dollars ($100,000.00);

(c) An annual aggregate limit is not less than One Hundred Thousand Dollars ($100,000.00);

(d) Limits apply per licensee per claim;

(e) Maximum deductible is Two Thousand Five Hundred Dollars ($2,500.00) per licensee per claim for damages;

(f) Maximum deductible is One Thousand Dollars ($1,000.00) per licensee per claim for defense costs; and

The policy period shall be a twelve-month policy term.

Each licensee shall be notified of the required terms and conditions of coverage for the policy at least thirty (30) days before the renewal date of the policy. A certificate of coverage, showing compliance with the required terms and conditions of coverage, shall be filed with the commission by the renewal date of the policy by each licensee who elects not to participate in the insurance program administered by the commission.

If the commission is unable to obtain errors and omissions insurance coverage to insure all licensees who choose to participate in the insurance program at a premium of no more than Two Hundred Fifty Dollars ($250.00) per twelve (12) months' policy period, the requirement of insurance coverage under this section shall be void during the applicable contract period.

Licensees may obtain errors and omissions coverage independently.

The commission shall require receipt of proof of errors and omissions insurance from new licensees within thirty (30) days of licensure. Any licenses issued at any time other than policy renewal time shall be subject to a pro rata premium.

(b) For licensees not submitting proof of insurance necessary to continue active licensure, the commission shall be responsible for sending notice of deficiency to those licensees. <u>Licensees who do not correct the deficiency within thirty (30) days shall have their licenses placed on inactive status.</u>

<u>Individuals whose licenses are on inactive status are not required to carry errors and omissions insurance.</u>

OUT OF STATE DEVELOPERS

E and O Insurance is the same as for MS Licensees.

Licensees having independent coverage (E and O) shall submit proof of coverage by the beginning of the policy period as set forth above.

Any deficiency in supplying proof of coverage must be corrected within no more than 30 days after the beginning of the policy period. Proof of coverage shall be by a "Certificate of Insurance" provided by the independent insurance carrier.

Minimum requirements of independent coverage shall be:
(1) Coverage must be for all activities for which a real estate license is required under this Chapter.
(2) A per claim limit is not less than $100,000.00.
(3) The deductible is not more than $2,500.00 per licensee, per claim, for any damages and the deductible is not more than $1,000.00 per licensee, per claim, for defense costs.
(4) The independent insurance carrier shall agree to a non-cancelable policy or provide a letter of commitment to notify the Commission 30 days prior to intention to cancel.

4. Disqualifying issues

Grounds for refusing to issue or suspending or revoking license; hearing

The commission may, upon its own motion and shall upon the verified complaint in writing of any person, hold a hearing for the refusal of license or for the suspension or revocation of a license previously issued, or for such other action as the commission deems appropriate. The commission shall have full power to refuse a license for cause or to revoke or suspend a license where it has been obtained by false or fraudulent representation, or where the licensee in performing or attempting to perform any of the acts mentioned herein, is deemed to be guilty of:

Making any substantial misrepresentation in connection with a real estate transaction;

Making any false promises of a character likely to influence, persuade or induce;

Pursuing a continued and flagrant course of misrepresentation or making false promises through agents or salespersons or any medium of advertising or otherwise;

Real Estate Training Institute – Pre Exam Workbook

Any misleading or untruthful advertising;

Acting for more than one (1) party in a transaction or receiving compensation from more than one (1) party in a transaction, or both, without the knowledge of all parties for whom he acts;

Failing, within a reasonable time, to account for or to remit any monies coming into his possession which belong to others, or commingling of monies belonging to others with his own funds. Every responsible broker procuring the execution of an earnest money contract or option or other contract who shall take or receive any cash or checks shall deposit, within a reasonable period of time, the sum or sums so received in a trust or escrow account in a bank or trust company pending the consummation or termination of the transaction. "Reasonable time" in this context means by the close of business of the next banking day; (g) Entering a guilty plea or conviction in a court of competent jurisdiction of this state, or any other state or the United States of any felony;

Displaying a "for sale" or "for rent" sign on any property without the owner's consent;

Failing to furnish voluntarily, at the time of signing, copies of all listings, contracts and agreements to all parties executing the same;

Paying any rebate, profit or commission to any person other than a real estate broker or salesperson licensed under the provisions of this chapter;

Inducing any party to a contract, sale or lease to break such contract for the purpose of substituting in lieu thereof a new contract, where such substitution is motivated by the personal gain of the licensee;
Accepting a commission or valuable consideration as a real estate salesperson for the performance of any of the acts specified in this chapter from any person, except his employer who must be a licensed real estate broker; or

Any act or conduct, whether of the same or a different character than hereinabove specified, which constitutes or demonstrates bad faith, incompetency or untrustworthiness, or dishonest, fraudulent or improper dealing.

No real estate broker shall practice law or give legal advice directly or indirectly unless said broker be a duly licensed attorney under the laws of this state. He shall not act as a public conveyancer nor give advice or opinions as to the legal effect of instruments nor give opinions concerning the validity of title to real estate; nor shall he prevent or discourage any party to a real estate transaction from employing the services of an attorney; nor shall a broker undertake to prepare documents fixing and defining the legal rights of parties to a transaction. However, when acting as a broker, he may use an earnest money contract form. A real estate broker shall not participate in attorney's fees, unless the broker is a duly licensed attorney under the laws of this state and performs legal services in addition to brokerage services.
qualified under this chapter.

In addition to the reasons specified in subsection (1) of this section, the commission shall be authorized to suspend the license of any licensee for being out of compliance with an order for support, as defined in The procedure for suspension of a license for being out of compliance with an order for support.

Nothing in this chapter shall prevent an associate broker or salesperson from owning any lawfully constituted business organization, including, but not limited to, a corporation, limited liability company or limited liability partnership, for the purpose of receiving payments contemplated in this chapter. The business organization shall not be required to be licensed under this chapter and shall not engage in any other activity requiring a real estate license.

It is expressly provided that it is not the intent and purpose of the Mississippi Legislature to prevent a license from being issued to any person who is found to be of good reputation, is able to give bond, and who has lived in the State of Mississippi for the required period or is otherwise

Appeals

Any applicant or licensee or person aggrieved shall have the right of appeal from any adverse ruling or order or decision of the commission to the circuit court of the county of residence of the applicant, licensee or person, or of the First Judicial District of Hinds County, within thirty (30) days from the service of notice of the action of the commission upon the parties in interest.

Notice of appeals shall be filed in the office of the clerk of the court who shall issue a writ of certiorari directed to the commission commanding it, within thirty (30) days after service thereof, to certify to such court its entire record in the matter in which the appeal has been taken. The appeal shall thereupon be heard in due course by said court, without a jury, which shall review the record and make its determination of the cause between the parties.

Any order, rule or decision of the commission shall not take effect until after the time for appeal to said court shall have expired. In the event an appeal is taken by a defendant, such appeal may act, in the discretion of the court, as a supersedes and the court shall dispose of said appeal and enter its decision promptly.

Any person taking an appeal shall post a satisfactory bond in the amount of Five Hundred Dollars ($500.00) for the payment of any costs which may be adjudged against him.

5. Activities Requiring License (incl. time shares, auctions, prop mgmnt)

It shall be unlawful for any person, partnership, association or corporation to engage in or carry on, directly or indirectly, or to advertise or to hold himself, itself or themselves out as engaging in or carrying on the business, or act in the capacity of, a real estate broker, or a real estate salesperson, within this state, without first obtaining a license as a real estate broker or real estate salesperson as provided for in this chapter.

Time Shares

Any seller, other than the developer and its regular employees, of a timeshare plan within the State of Mississippi must be a licensed Real Estate Broker or Real Estate Salesperson pursuant to and subject to Mississippi Law and the Rules and Regulations of the Mississippi Real Estate Commission.

6. Exemptions from licensure

Exempt from the licensing requirements of this chapter shall be any person, partnership, association or corporation, who, as a bona fide owner, shall perform any aforesaid act with reference to property owned by them, or to the regular employees thereof who are on a stated salary, where such acts are performed in the regular course of business.

Attorneys at law in the performance of primary or incidental duties as such attorneys at law.

Any person holding in good faith a duly executed power of attorney from the owner, authorizing the final consummation and execution for the sale, purchase, leasing or exchange of real estate.

The acts of any person while acting as a receiver, trustee, administrator, executor, guardian or under court order, or while acting under authority of a deed of trust or will.

Public officers while performing their duties as such.

Anyone dealing exclusively in oil and gas leases and mineral rights.

Nothing in this chapter shall be construed to prohibit life insurance companies and their representatives from negotiating or attempting to negotiate loans secured by mortgages on real estate, nor shall these companies or their representatives be required to qualify as real estate brokers or agents under this chapter.

The provisions of this chapter shall not apply to the activities of mortgagees approved by the Federal Housing Administration or the United States Department of Veterans Affairs, banks chartered under the laws of the State of Mississippi or the United States, savings and loan associations chartered under the laws of the State of Mississippi or the United States, licensees under the Small Loan Regulatory Law, and under the Small Loan Privilege Tax Law, small business investment companies licensed by the Small Business Administration and chartered under the laws of the State of Mississippi, or any of their affiliates and subsidiaries, related to the making of a loan secured by a lien on real estate or to the disposing of real estate acquired by foreclosure or in lieu of foreclosure or otherwise held as security. No director, officer or employee of any such financial institution shall be required to qualify as a real estate broker or agent under this chapter when engaged in the aforesaid activities for and on behalf of such financial institution.

7. Inactive license

<u>Individuals whose licenses are on inactive status are not required to carry errors and omissions insurance.</u>

To change a license from active to inactive status, licensee shall notify the Commission in writing, shall insure that the license is returned to the Commission and shall pay the appropriate fee. A licensee who is on inactive status at time of renewal may renew the license on inactive status by filing a renewal application and paying the renewal fee. A broker who terminates a real estate business may place the business license on inactive status. To return to active status, a salesperson or broker/salesperson must file a transfer application. A broker and/or a business license may be activated by notifying the Commission by letter or transfer application including required fee.

    (4) Status change from active to inactive status.................. $ 25.00

    (5) Status change from inactive to active status.................. $ 50.00

8. Rules about receiving and Sharing Commissions.

No fee, commission or other valuable consideration may be paid to a person for real estate brokerage activities unless the person provides evidence of licensure under the provisions of this chapter or provides evidence of a cooperative agreement..

No licensee shall pay any part of a fee, commission, or other compensation received by such licensee in buying, selling, exchanging, leasing, auctioning or renting any real estate except to another licensee through the licensee's responsible broker.

No licensee shall knowingly pay a commission, or other compensation to a licensed person knowing that licensee will in turn pay a portion or all of that which is received to a person who does not hold a real estate license.

A licensee who has changed to inactive status or who has transferred to another responsible broker may receive compensation from the previous responsible broker if the commission was generated from activity during the time that the licensee was under the supervision of that responsible broker.

"Compensation" is that fee paid to a broker for the rendering of services. Compensation, when considered alone, is not the determining factor in an agency relationship. The relationship can be created regardless of whether the seller pays the fee, the buyer pays the fee, both pay the fee or neither pays a fee.

Real Estate Training Institute – Pre Exam Workbook

1. Disclosure form (delivery, who completes)

Property Condition Disclosures (Salesperson 4 Items, Broker 6 Items)

PROPERTY CONDITION DISCLOSURE STATEMENT
(EFFECTIVE JULY 1, 2008)

INFORMATIONAL STATEMENT FOR MISSISSIPPI PROPERTY CONDITION DISCLOSURE STATEMENT (EFFECTIVE JULY 1, 2008)

In accordance with Sections 89-1-501 through 89-1-527 of the Mississippi Code of 1954, as amended, effective July 1, 2005, a **TRANSFEROR** of real property consisting of not less than one (1) nor more than four (4) dwelling units shall provide a Property Condition Disclosure Statement when the transfer is by, or with the aid of, a duly licensed real estate broker or salesperson. The required Property Condition Disclosure Statement shall be in the form promulgated by the Mississippi Real Estate Commission (MREC) or on another form that contains the identical information. The MREC Form may be found at www.mrec.ms.gov.

RIGHTS OF PURCHASER AND CONSEQUENCES FOR FAILURE TO DISCLOSE

If the Property Condition Disclosure Statement is delivered **after** the Transferee has made an offer, the transferee may terminate any resulting real estate contract or withdraw any offer for a time period of three (3) days after the delivery in person or five (5) days after the delivery by deposit in mail. This termination or withdrawal will always be without penalty to the Transferee and any deposit or earnest money must be promptly returned to the prospective purchaser (despite any agreement to the contrary).

DUTY OF LICENSEE AND CONSEQUENCES OF FAILURE TO FULFILL SUCH DUTIES

The Mississippi Statute requires real estate licensees to inform their clients of those clients' duties and rights in connection with the Property Condition

Disclosure Statement. The failure of any licensee to inform their client of the clients' responsibilities could subject the licensee (salesperson and broker) to censure, suspension, or revocation of their respective real estate licenses. The licensee is not liable for any error, inaccuracy or omission in a Property Condition Disclosure Statement **unless** the licensee has actual knowledge of the error, inaccuracy or omission by the Transferor.

IMPORTANT PROVISIONS OF THE LAW

The Property Condition Disclosure Statement should not be considered a warranty by the Transferor. **The Property Condition Disclosure Statement is **NOT intended to become a part of any contract between the Transferor(s) and the Transferee(s) and it is for "disclosure" purposes only. **The Property Condition Disclosure Statement may not be used as a substitute for an inspection by a licensed home inspector or for other home warranties that the Transferor or Transferee may obtain. **Any **Appliances or Items deemed to be Personal Property** should be negotiated by the Seller and the Buyer in the Contract for the Purchase and Sale of Real Estate and all ownership rights should be transferred by a Bill of Sale or other appropriate contractual instrument. This Property Condition Disclosure Statement is not part of the Contract of Sale. **Nothing in this law precludes the rights and duties of the Transferee to inspect the property.

EXEMPTIONS

Section 89-1-501 (2) <a through i> stipulates specific exemptions from the requirement of providing a Property Condition Disclosure Statement by the Transferor of residential property. They include:

**Transfers pursuant to a court order, a writ of execution, a foreclosure sale, a bankruptcy, an eminent domain proceeding, transfers from a decree for specific performance, transfers by a mortgagor who is in default, any sale pursuant to a decree of foreclosure or by means of a deed in lieu of foreclosure, transfer by the administration of a decedent's estate, a guardianship, a conservatorship or a trust.

**Transfers from one co-owner to another, transfers from one spouse to another, transfers to a person in the lineal line of consanguinity, transfers to or from governmental entities or transfers on which no dwelling is located.

If the Transferor has NOT OCCUPIED the dwelling but, during the period of ownership, the Transferor has requested or authorized any repairs, replaced any of the mechanical equipment, has initiated any action or activity which could be documented on the Disclosure Statement or has actual knowledge of information which might impact a transferee's decision to purchase the residence, Transferors are obligated to complete those specific portions of the Disclosure Statement which are applicable to that information.

The Transferor is **REQUIRED** to sign the Disclosure Statement when the transaction is finalized to **confirm that there have been no material changes to the property.**

CONFIRMATION OF UNDERSTANDING

_____
SELLER (UPON LISTING) DATE

_____
SELLER (UPON LISTING) DATE

_____
REPRESENTING THE SELLER(S)

_____
BUYER (BEFORE OFFER)   DATE

_____
BUYER (BEFORE OFFER)   DATE

_____
REPRESENTING THE BUYER(S)

Page 1 of 3

PROPERTY CONDITION DISCLOSURE STATEMENT
To be completed by the seller with the listing of any residence.

PROPERTY CONDITION DISCLOSURE STATEMENT

THE FOLLOWING IS A PROPERTY CONDITION DISCLOSURE REQUIRED BY SECTIONS 89-1-507 THROUGH 89-1-527 OF THE MISSISSIPPI REAL ESTATE BROKERS ACT OF 1954, AS AMENDED, AND MADE BY THE **SELLER(S)** CONCERNING THE CONDITION OF THE **RESIDENTIAL PROPERTY** LOCATED AT:

_____

SELLER(S):_____

    APPROXIMATE AGE OF THE RESIDENCE_____

THIS DISCLOSURE IS NOT A WARRANTY OF ANY KIND BY THE SELLER OR ANY REAL ESTATE AGENT OF THE SELLER IN THIS TRANSACTION AND IS NOT A SUBSTITUTE FOR ANY INSPECTIONS OR WARRANTIES THE PURCHASER MAY WISH TO OBTAIN. THIS STATEMENT MAY BE MADE AVAILABLE TO OTHER PARTIES AND **IS TO BE ATTACHED TO THE LISTING AGREEMENT AND SIGNED BY THE SELLER(S).**

TO THE SELLER(S): PLEASE COMPLETE THE FOLLOWING FORM, INCLUDING ANY PAST HISTORY OF PROBLEMS, IF KNOWN. IF THE CONDITION OR QUESTION DOES NOT APPLY TO YOUR PROPERTY, MARK WITH "N/A".

IF THE RESIDENCE IS NEW/PROPOSED RESIDENTIAL CONSTRUCTION, THE **BUILDER** SHOULD COMPLETE THE PROPERTY CONDITION DISCLOSURE STATEMENT AND REFERENCE SPECIFIC PLANS/SPECIFICATIONS, MATERIALS LISTS AND/OR CHANGE ORDERS.

DO NOT LEAVE ANY BLANK SPACES. ATTACH ADDITIONAL PAGES IF NECESSARY. THIS FORM MAY BE DUPLICATED BUT NOT ALTERED
STRUCTURAL ITEMS:

A. BUILDING CODE:

WAS THE RESIDENCE BUILT IN CONFORMITY WITH AN APPROVED BUILDING CODE? YES ____ NO ____ UNKNOWN _____ IF YES,

WAS IT INSPECTED BY A CITY/COUNTY CODE ENFORCEMENT INSPECTOR? YES ____ NO ____ UNKNOWN _____

HAS A MISSISSIPPI LICENSED HOME INSPECTOR COMPLETED A HOME INSPECTION REPORT? YES ____ NO ____

B. STRUCTURAL ITEMS:

ARE YOU AWARE OF ANY FOUNDATION REPAIRS MADE IN THE PAST? YES ____ NO ____
EXPLAIN _____

ARE ANY FOUNDATION REPAIRS CURRENTLY NEEDED? YES ____ NO ____ EXPLAIN
_____

C. HISTORY OF INFESTATION, IF ANY: TERMITES, CARPENTER ANTS, ETC:

ANY EVIDENCE OF ROT, MILDEW, VERMIN, RODENTS, TERMITES, CARPENTER ANTS, OR OTHER INFESTATION? YES ____ NO ____

HAVE YOU REQUESTED TREATMENTS FOR ANY TYPE OF INFESTATIONS? YES ____ NO ____ EXPLAIN_____

ARE YOU AWARE OF ANY REPAIRED DAMAGE? YES ____ NO____ ; IF YES, PLEASE DESCRIBE_____

IS THERE CURRENTLY AN OUTSTANDING TERMITE CONTRACT? YES ____ NO ____

WHO IS THE CONTRACTOR? _____

D. ROOF:

HAS THE ROOF BEEN REPLACED OR REPAIRED DURING YOUR OWNERSHIP? YES ____ NO ____; IF YES, WHEN? _____

DURING YOUR OWNERSHIP HAVE THERE BEEN ANY LEAKS, WATER BACK UPS, OR PROBLEMS WITH THE ROOF? YES ____ NO____

THE ROOF IS ____ YEARS OLD.

E. LAND AND SITE DATA:

IS THERE AN ENGINEER'S SURVEY AVAILABLE? YES ____ NO ____

DATE THE SURVEY WAS COMPLETED_____

ARE YOU AWARE OF THE EXISTENCE OF ANY OF THE FOLLOWING, TO WIT:

ENCROACHMENTS: YES __ NO __ UNKNOWN __

Real Estate Training Institute – Pre Exam Workbook

FLOOD ZONE: YES ___ NO ___ UNKNOWN ___

EASEMENTS: YES ___ NO ___ UNKNOWN ___

SOIL/EROSION: YES ___ NO ___ UNKNOWN ___

SOIL PROBLEMS: YES ___ NO ___ UNKNOWN ___

SUBSOIL PROBLEM: YES___ NO___ UNKNOWN___

STANDING WATER: YES ___ NO ___ UNKNOWN ___

LAND FILL: YES___ NO___ UNKNOWN___

ARE YOU AWARE OF ANY CURRENT ZONING REGULATIONS WHICH WILL CAUSE THE RESIDENCE TO BE CONSIDERED A NONCONFORMING USAGE (LOT SIZE, SET BACKS, ETC) YES ___ NO ___

IF YES, PLEASE EXPLAIN _____

ARE THERE ANY RIGHTS-OF-WAY, EASEMENTS, EMINENT DOMAIN PROCEEDINGS OR SIMILAR MATTERS WHICH MAY NEGATIVELY IMPACT YOUR OWNERSHIP INTEREST IN THE RESIDENCE? YES ___ NO ___

IF YES, PLEASE EXPLAIN _____

FOR ANY REASON, HAS ANY PORTION OF THE RESIDENCE EVER SUFFERED WATER DAMAGE? YES ___ NO ___

IF YES, PLEASE EXPLAIN IN DETAIL _____

IS THE RESIDENCE CURRENTLY LOCATED IN A FEMA DESIGNATED FLOOD HAZARD ZONE? YES ___ NO ___ UNKNOWN ___

IS FLOOD INSURANCE REQUIRED? YES ___ NO ___ UNKNOWN ___

IS ANY PORTION OF THE PROPERTY DESIGNATED AS A **WETLANDS AREA?**   YES ___ NO ___ UNKNOWN ___

F. ADDITIONS/REMODELS:

Real Estate Training Institute – Pre Exam Workbook

DURING YOUR PERIOD OF OWNERSHIP, HAVE THERE BEEN ANY ADDITIONS, REMODELING, STRUCTURAL CHANGES OR ALTERATIONS TO THE RESIDENCE? YES ___ NO ___

IF YES, PLEASE EXPLAIN _____

NAME OF THE LICENSED CONTRACTOR_____

WERE ALL WORK PERMITS AND APPROVALS IN COMPLIANCE WITH THE LOCAL BUILDING CODES? YES ___ NO ___

PLEASE EXPLAIN _____

G. STRUCTURE/WALLS/WINDOWS:

HAS THERE BEEN ANY DAMAGE TO THE STRUCTURE AS A RESULT OF FIRE, WINDSTORM, TORNADOS, HURRICANE OR ANY OTHER NATURAL DISASTER? YES ___ NO ___ IF YES, PLEASE EXPLAIN _____

HAVE YOU EVER EXPERIENCED ANY PROBLEMS WITH WALLS, SIDING OR WINDOWS? YES ___ NO ___ EXPLAIN _____

H. OTHER:

ARE YOU AWARE OF ANY PROBLEMS WHICH MAY EXIST WITH THE PROPERTY BY VIRTUE OF PRIOR USAGES SUCH AS, BUT NOT LIMITED TO, **METHAMPHETAMINE LABS**, HAZARDOUS/TOXIC WASTE DISPOSAL, THE PRESENCE OF ASBESTOS COMPONENTS, LEAD-BASED PAINT, UREA-FORMALDEHYDE INSULATION, MOLD, RADON GAS, UNDERGROUND TANKS OR ANY PAST INDUSTRIAL USES OF THE PREMISES? YES ___ NO ___ IF "YES, PLEASE EXPLAIN _____

SELLER'S INITIALS _____   PAGE 2 OF 3
PURCHASER'S INITIALS _____

MECHANICAL ITEMS:

ELECTRICAL SYSTEM/PLUMBING SYSTEM:

ARE YOU AWARE OF ANY PROBLEMS OR CONDITIONS THAT AFFECT THE DESIRABILITY OR FUNCTIONALITY OF THE HEATING, COOLING, ELECTRICAL, PLUMBING, OR MECHANICAL SYSTEMS? YES ___ NO ___

Real Estate Training Institute – Pre Exam Workbook

IF YES, PLEASE EXPLAIN ALL KNOWN PROBLEMS IN COMPLETE DETAIL
_____

WATER, SEWER, & SEPTIC ITEMS:

WATER:

THE WATER SUPPLY IS: PUBLIC ____ PRIVATE ____ ON-SITE WELL ____ NEIGHBOR'S WELL ____ COMMUNITY ____

IF YOUR DRINKING WATER IS FROM A WELL, WHEN WAS THE WATER QUALITY LAST CHECKED FOR SAFETY, WHAT WERE THE RESULTS OF THE TEST AND WHO CONDUCTED THE TEST? _____

IS THE WATER SUPPLY EQUIPPED WITH A WATER SOFTENER? YES ____ NO ____ UNKNOWN ____

THE SEWAGE SYSTEM IS: PUBLIC ____ PRIVATE ____ SEPTIC ____ CESSPOOL ____ TREATMENT PLANT ____ OTHER ____

IS THERE A SEWAGE PUMP INSTALLED? YES ____ NO ____

DATE OF THE LAST SEPTIC INSPECTION _____

ARE YOU AWARE OF ANY LEAKS, BACK-UPS, OR OTHER PROBLEMS RELATING TO ANY OF THE PLUMBING, WATER, SEWAGE, OR RELATED ITEMS DURING YOUR OWNERSHIP? YES ____ NO ____

IF YES, PLEASE EXPLAIN _____

OTHER MATTERS/ITEMS:

MISCELLANEOUS:

IS THE RESIDENCE SITUATED ON LEASEHOLD OR SIXTEENTH SECTION LAND? YES ____ NO ____ EXPLAIN _____

IS THERE ANY EXISTING OR THREATENING LEGAL ACTION AFFECTING THE PROPERTY? YES ____ NO ____ EXPLAIN _____

ARE YOU AWARE OF ANY VIOLATIONS OF LOCAL/STATE/FEDERAL LAWS/REGULATIONS RELATING TO THE PROPERTY? YES ____ NO ____

Real Estate Training Institute – Pre Exam Workbook

ARE YOU AWARE OF ANY HIDDEN DEFECTS OR NEEDED REPAIRS ABOUT WHICH THE PURCHASER SHOULD BE INFORMED **PRIOR** TO THEIR PURCHASE? YES ___ NO ___

IF YES, PLEASE EXPLAIN IN DETAIL _____

WHAT IS THE **APPROXIMATE SQUARE FOOTAGE** OF THE HEATED AND COOLED LIVING AREA _____

HOW WAS THIS APPROXIMATION OF SQUARE FOOTAGE DETERMINED? _____

ARE THERE ANY FINISHED WOOD FLOORS BENEATH THE FLOOR COVERINGS? YES ___ NO ___ WHERE _____

ARE THERE ANY HOMEOWNER'S ASSOCIATION FEES ASSOCIATED WITH OWNERSHIP? YES ___ NO ___ AMOUNT _____

IF THE PROPERTY IS A CONDOMINIUM, HOW MUCH IS THE **YEARLY** MAINTENANCE FEES $_____

WHAT IS THE **YEARLY** REAL ESTATE TAX BILL? $_____

HOMESTEAD EXEMPTION HAS BEEN FILED FOR _____

IS THE PROPERTY SUBJECT TO **ANY** SPECIAL REAL PROPERTY TAX ASSESSMENTS YES ___ NO ___ EXPLAIN _____

IS THE PROPERTY LOCATED IN A **PUBLIC IMPROVEMENT (TAX) DISTRICT (PID)** YES ___ NO ___ UNKNOWN _____

WHAT IS THE AVERAGE **YEARLY** ELECTRIC BILL? $_____

WHAT IS THE AVERAGE **YEARLY** GAS BILL? $_____

IF THE RESIDENCE IS SERVICED BY PROPANE (LP) GAS, WHAT IS THE AVERAGE **YEARLY** PROPANE BILL? $_____

THE PROPANE TANK IS: OWNED _____ LEASED _____ I

F LEASED, HOW MUCH IS THE LEASE PAYMENT? $_____

IS CABLE TELEVISION SERVICE AVAILABLE AT THE SITE? YES ___ NO ___ SERVICE PROVIDER _____

Real Estate Training Institute – Pre Exam Workbook

ARE ANY ITEMS REMAINING WITH THE RESIDENCE FINANCED SEPARATELY FROM THE MORTGAGES? YES ___ NO ___

APPLIANCES/SYSTEMS REMAINING WITH RESIDENCE:
YES NO GAS/ELECTRIC AGE   LIST REPAIRS COMPETED IN LAST TWO (2) YEARS

ITEM

COOK-TOP
DISHWASHER
GARBAGE DISPOSAL
ICE-MAKER
MICROWAVE
OVEN(S)
TRASH COMPACTOR
VENT-FAN
OTHER ITEMS

MECHANICAL EQUIPMENT CONSIDERED PERSONAL PROPERTY SHOULD BE NEGOTIATED IN THE CONTRACT OF SALE OR OTHER SUCH INSTRUMENT IF THE ITEMS REMAIN WITH THE RESIDENCE.

TO THE EXTENT OF THE SELLER'S KNOWLEDGE AS A PROPERTY OWNER, THE SELLER(S) ACKNOWLEDGES THAT THE INFORMATION CONTAINED ABOVE IS TRUE AND ACCURATE FOR THOSE AREAS OF THE PROPERTY LISTED. THE OWNER(S) AGREE TO SAVE AND HOLD THE BROKER HARMLESS FROM ALL CLAIMS, DISPUTES, LITIGATION AND/OR JUDGMENTS ARISING FROM ANY INCORRECT INFORMATION SUPPLIED BY THE OWNER(S) OR FROM ANY MATERIAL FACT KNOWN BY THE OWNER(S) WHICH OWNER(S) FAIL TO DISCLOSE EXCEPT THE BROKER IS NOT HELD HARMLESS TO THE OWNER(S) IN CLAIMS, DISPUTES, LITIGATION, OR JUDGMENTS ARISING FROM CONDITIONS OF WHICH THE BROKER HAD ACTUAL KNOWLEDGE.

_____
SELLER (UPON LISTING) DATE

_____
SELLER (AT CLOSING)   DATE

_____
SELLER (UPON LISTING) DATE

Real Estate Training Institute – Pre Exam Workbook

_____
SELLER (AT CLOSING)   DATE

_____
PROSPECTIVE PURCHASER'S SIGNATURE

_____
PURCHASER(S) ACKNOWLEDGE RECEIPT OF REPORT DATE

MREC FORM #0100   PAGE 3 OF 3 EFFECTIVE DATE: JULY 1, 2008

1. Disclosure form (delivery, who completes)

The disclosures pertaining to the property proposed to be transferred shall be set forth in, and shall be made on a copy of a disclosure form, the structure and composition of which shall be determined by the Mississippi Real Estate Commission.

Each disclosure required and each act which may be performed in making the disclosure, shall be made in <u>good faith</u>.

<u>"good faith" means honesty</u>

Any disclosure made may be amended in writing by the transferor or his agent, but the amendment shall be subject to MS Real Estate License Law.

<u>A real estate licensee shall immediately (at the time of signing) deliver a true and correct copy of any instrument to any party or parties executing the same.</u>

Delivery of disclosure shall be by personal delivery to the transferee or by mail to the prospective transferee.

<u>Delivery to the spouse of a transferee shall be deemed delivery to the transferee, unless provided otherwise by contract.</u>

The transferor of any real property shall deliver to the prospective transferee the written property condition disclosure statement required as follows:

(a) In the case of a sale, <u>as soon as practicable</u> before transfer of title.

(b) In the case of transfer by a real property sales contract, or by a lease together with an option to purchase, or a ground lease coupled with improvements, <u>as soon as practicable before execution of the contract.</u> For the purpose of this paragraph, execution means the making or acceptance of an offer.

The transferor shall indicate compliance either on the receipt for deposit, the real property sales contract, the lease, or any addendum attached thereto or on a separate document.

Disclosure of information concerning size or area of property involved in real estate transaction; liability; remedy for violation of section

(1) (a) In connection with any real estate transaction, the size or area, in square footage or otherwise, of the subject property, if provided by any real estate licensee in accordance with paragraph (b)(i) and (ii), shall not be considered any warranty or guarantee of the size or area information, in square footage or otherwise, of the subject property.

(b) (i) If a real estate licensee provides any party to a real estate transaction with third-party information concerning the size or area, in square footage or otherwise, of the subject property involved in the transaction, the licensee shall identify the source of the information.

(ii) For the purposes of this section, "third-party information" means:

1. An appraisal or any measurement information prepared by a licensed appraiser;

2. A surveyor developer's plan prepared by a licensed surveyor;

3. A tax assessor's public record; or

4. A builder's plan used to construct or market the property.

(c) A real estate licensee has no duty to the seller or purchaser of real property to conduct an independent investigation of the size or area, in square footage or otherwise, of a subject property, or to independently verify the accuracy of any third-party information.

(d) A real estate licensee who has complied with the requirements of this section, as applicable, shall have no further duties to the seller or purchaser of real property regarding disclosed or undisclosed property size or area information, and shall not be subject to liability to any party for any damages sustained with regard to any conflicting measurements or opinions of size or area, including exemplary or punitive damages.

(2) (a) If a real estate licensee has provided third-party information to any party to a real estate transaction concerning size or area of the subject real property, a party to the real estate transaction may recover damages from the licensee in a civil action only when a licensee knowingly violates the duty to disclose the source of the information as required in this section.

However, nothing in this section shall provide immunity from civil liability to any licensee who knowingly misrepresents the size or area of the subject real property.

(b) The sole and exclusive civil remedy at common law or otherwise for a violation of this section by a real estate licensee shall be an action for actual damages suffered by the party as a result of such violation and shall not include exemplary or punitive damages.

(c) For any real estate transaction commenced after July 1, 2013, any civil action brought pursuant to this section shall be commenced within two (2) years after the date of transfer of the subject real property.

(d) In any civil action brought pursuant to this section, the prevailing party shall be allowed court costs and reasonable attorney fees to be set by the court and collected as costs of the action.

(e) A transfer of a possessory interest in real property subject to the provisions of this section may not be invalidated solely because of the failure of any person to comply with the provisions of this section.

(f) The provisions of this section shall apply to, regulate and determine the rights, duties, obligations and remedies, at common law or otherwise, of the seller marketing the seller's real property for sale through a real estate licensee, and of the purchaser of real property offered for sale through a real estate licensee, with respect to disclosure of third-party information concerning the subject real property's size or area, in square footage or otherwise, and this section hereby supplants and abrogates all common-law liability, rights, duties, obligations and remedies of all parties therefor

2. Stigmatizing factors

Failure to disclose nonmaterial fact regarding property <u>as site of death or felony crime, as site of act or occurrence having no effect on physical condition of property, or as being owned or occupied by persons affected or exposed to certain diseases</u>; failure to disclose information provided or maintained on registration of sex offenders

1) The fact or suspicion that real property is or was:

(a) The site of a natural death, suicide, homicide or felony crime (except for illegal drug activity that affects the physical condition of the property, its physical environment or the improvements located thereon);

(b) The site of an act or occurrence that had no effect on the physical condition of the property, its physical environment or the improvements located thereon;

(c) Owned or occupied by a person affected or exposed to any disease not known to be transmitted through common occupancy of real estate including, but not limited to, the human immunodeficiency virus (HIV) and the acquired immune deficiency syndrome (AIDS);

does not constitute a material fact that must be disclosed in a real estate transaction. A failure to disclose such nonmaterial facts or suspicions shall not give rise to a criminal, civil or administrative action against the owner of such real property, a licensed real estate broker or any affiliated licensee of the broker.

(2) A failure to disclose in any real estate transaction any information that is provided or maintained, or is required to be provided or maintained, shall not give rise to a cause of action

against an owner of real property, a licensed real estate broker or any affiliated licensee of the broker. Likewise, no cause of action shall arise against any licensed real estate broker or affiliated licensee of the broker for revealing information to a seller or buyer of real estate. Any factors, if known to a property owner or licensee shall be disclosed <u>if requested by a consumer.</u>

(3) Failure to disclose any of the facts or suspicions of facts described in subsections (1) and (2) shall not be grounds for the termination or rescission of any transaction in which real property has been or will be transferred or leased. This provision does not preclude an action against an owner of real estate who makes intentional or fraudulent misrepresentations in response to a direct inquiry from a purchaser or prospective purchaser regarding facts or suspicions that are not material to the physical condition of the property including, but not limited to, those factors listed in subsections (1) and (2).

3. Licensee responsibility to advise client, ensure completeness?

Consumers shall be fully informed of the agency relationships in real estate transactions.

This rule places specific requirements on Brokers to disclose their agency relationship. This does not abrogate the laws of agency as recognized under common law and compliance with the prescribed disclosures will not always guarantee that a Broker has fulfilled all of his responsibilities under the common law of agency. Compliance will be necessary in order to protect licensees from impositions of sanctions against their license by the Mississippi Real Estate Commission. Special situations, where unusual facts exist or where one or more parties involved are especially vulnerable, could require additional disclosures not contemplated by this rule. In such cases, Brokers should seek legal advice prior to entering into an agency relationship.

All exclusive listing agreements shall be in writing, properly identify the property to be sold, and contain all of the terms and conditions under which the transaction is to consummated; including the sales price, the considerations to be paid, the signatures of all parties to the agreement, and a definite date of expiration. No listing agreement shall contain any provision requiring the listing party to notify the broker of their intention to cancel the listing after such definite expiration date. An "Exclusive Agency" listing or "Exclusive Right to Sell" listing shall clearly indicate in the listing agreement that it is such an agreement

A real estate licensee shall immediately (at the time of signing) deliver a true and correct copy of any instrument to any party or parties executing the same.

In the event that more than one written offer is made before the owner has accepted an offer, any other written offer received by the listing broker, whether from a prospective purchaser or from another licensee cooperating in a sale, shall be presented to the owner unless the listing broker has specific, written instructions from the owner to postpone the presentation of other offers. Broker should caution the seller against countering on more than one offer at the same time.

In the event that more than one written offer is made before the owner has accepted an offer, any other written offer received by the listing broker, whether from a prospective purchaser or from another licensee cooperating in a sale, shall be presented to the owner unless the listing broker has specific, written instructions from the owner to postpone the presentation of other offers. Broker should caution the seller against countering on more than one offer at the same time.

Every real estate contact must reflect whom the broker represents by a statement over the signatures of the parties to the contract.

No licensee shall represent to a lender or any other interested party, either verbally or through the preparation of a false sales contract, an amount in excess of the true and actual selling price.

Delivery of disclosure where more than one agent; inability of delivering broker to obtain disclosure document; notification to transferee of right to disclosure

A real estate licensee shall **immediately (at the time of signing)** deliver a true and correct copy of any instrument to any party or parties executing the same.

(1) If more than one (1) licensed real estate broker is acting as an agent in a transaction, the broker who has obtained the offer made by the transferee shall deliver the disclosure required to the transferee, unless the transferor has given other written instructions for delivery.

(2) If a licensed real estate broker responsible for delivering the disclosures under this section cannot obtain the disclosure document required and does not have written assurance from the transferee that the disclosure has been received, the broker shall advise the transferee in writing of his rights to the disclosure. A licensed real estate broker responsible for delivering disclosures under this section shall maintain a record of the action taken to effect compliance.

If any disclosure, or any material amendment of any disclosure, is delivered after the execution of an offer to purchase, the transferee shall have three **(3) days after delivery in person or five (5) days after delivery by deposit in the mail,** to terminate his or her offer by delivery of a written notice of termination to the transferor or the transferor's agent.

Limit on duties and liabilities with respect to information required or delivered

(1) Neither the transferor nor any listing or selling agent shall be liable for any error, inaccuracy or omission of any information delivered if the error, inaccuracy or omission was not within the personal knowledge of the transferor or that listing or selling agent, was based on information timely provided by public agencies or by other persons providing information that is required to be disclosed, and ordinary care was exercised in obtaining and transmitting it.

(2) The delivery of any information required to be disclosed by to a prospective transferee by a public agency or other person providing information required to be shall be deemed to comply with the requirements of disclosure law and shall relieve the transferor or any listing or selling agent of any further duty with respect to that item of information.

(3) The delivery of a report or opinion prepared by a licensed engineer, land surveyor, geologist, structural pest control operator, contractor or other expert, dealing with matters within the scope

of the professional's license or expertise, shall be sufficient compliance for application of the exemption provided by subsection (1) if the information is provided to the prospective transferee pursuant to a request therefor, whether written or oral. In responding to such a request, an expert may indicate, in writing, an understanding that the information provided will be used in fulfilling the requirements of disclosure law, if so, shall indicate the required disclosures, or parts thereof, to which the information being furnished is applicable. Where such a statement is furnished, the expert shall not be responsible for any items of information, or parts thereof, other than those expressly set forth in the statement.

4. Exemptions from Disclosure - no exemption for new construction

Transfers pursuant to court order, including, but not limited to, transfers ordered by a probate court in administration of an estate, transfers pursuant to a writ of execution, transfers by any foreclosure sale, transfers by a trustee in bankruptcy, transfers by eminent domain, and transfers resulting from a decree for specific performance.

Transfers to a mortgagee by a mortgagor or successor in interest who is in default, transfers to a beneficiary of a deed of trust by a trustor or successor in interest who is in default, transfers by any foreclosure sale after default, in an obligation secured by a mortgage, transfers by a sale under a power of sale or any foreclosure sale under a decree of foreclosure after default in an obligation secured by a deed of trust or secured by any other instrument containing a power of sale, or transfers by a mortgagee or a beneficiary under a deed of trust who has acquired the real property at a sale conducted pursuant to a power of sale under a mortgage or deed of trust or a sale pursuant to a decree of foreclosure or has acquired the real property by a deed in lieu of foreclosure

Transfers by a fiduciary in the course of the administration of a decedent's estate, guardianship, conservatorship or trust.

Transfers from one co-owner to one or more other co-owners.

Transfers made to a spouse, or to a person or persons in the lineal line of consanguinity of one or more of the transferors.

Transfers between spouses resulting from a decree of dissolution of marriage or a decree of legal separation or from a property settlement agreement incidental to such a decree.

Transfers or exchanges to or from any governmental entity.

Transfers of real property on which no dwelling is located.

5. <u>Disclosure form is not part of contract</u> (see form) but is attached to listing

6. Material changes allow buyer to void contract

Agency Disclosure and Duties to Parties (Salesperson 8 Items, Broker 8 Items)

A real estate licensee shall immediately (at the time of signing) deliver a true and correct copy of any instrument to any party or parties executing the same.

"Agency" shall mean the relationship created when one person, the Principal (client), delegates to another, the agent, the right to act on his behalf in a real estate transaction and to exercise some degree of discretion while so acting. Agency may be entered into by expressed agreement, implied through the actions of the agent and or ratified after the fact by the principal accepting the benefits of an agent's previously unauthorized act. An agency gives rise to a fiduciary relationship and imposes on the agent, as the fiduciary of the principal, certain duties, obligations, and high standards of good faith and loyalty.

1. Dual Agency Disclosure

"Disclosed Dual Agent" shall mean that agent representing both parties to a real estate transaction with the informed consent of both parties, with written understanding of specific duties and representation to be afforded each party. There may be situations where disclosed dual agency presents conflicts of interest that cannot be resolved without breach of duty to one party or another. Brokers who practice disclosed dual agency should do so with the utmost caution to protect consumers and themselves from inadvertent violation of demanding common law standards of disclosed dual agency.

Real Estate Training Institute – Pre Exam Workbook

DUAL AGENCY CONFIRMATION
To be attached to all offers and contracts in dual agency situations.

DUAL AGENCY CONFIRMATION
Adopted Form of
The Mississippi Real Estate Commission Jackson, MS

Seller: _____

Buyer: _____

Property: _____

This Dual Agency Confirmation is an addendum to and made part of the Offer to Purchase dated _____, 20____, between the above-captioned Seller and Buyer for the purchase of the specifically identified property.

The undersigned acknowledges that the licensee has explained dual agency representation to them and they have received the following information regarding disclosed dual agency:

1. A disclosed dual agent is a licensee who, with the informed written consent of Seller and Buyer, is engaged as an agent for both Seller and buyer.

2. As a disclosed dual agent the licensee shall not represent the interests of one party to the exclusion or detriment of the interests of the other party. A disclosed dual agent has all the fiduciary duties to the Seller and Buyer that a Seller's or Buyer's agent has except the duties of full disclosure and undivided loyalty.

3. A disclosed dual agent may NOT disclose:
(a) To the Buyer that the Seller will accept less than the asking or listed price, unless otherwise instructed in writing by the Seller;
(b) To the Seller that the Buyer will pay a price greater than the price submitted in a written offer to the Seller, unless otherwise instructed in writing by the Buyer;
(c) The motivation of the Seller or Buyer for selling, buying or leasing a property, unless otherwise instructed in writing by the respective party or
(d) That a Seller or Buyer will agree to financing terms other than those offered unless instructed in writing by the respective party.

Real Estate Training Institute – Pre Exam Workbook

Seller and Buyer hereby confirm that they give their informed consent to the disclosed dual agency of:

Name of Brokerage Firm   **Name of Licensee**

Name of Licensee
who represent both Seller and Buyer in this transaction.

Date:_____ Seller: _____ Seller (print name):_____

Date:_____ Buyer: _____ Buyer (print name):_____

This Dual Agency Confirmation form is Seller, Buyer and Property specific. It has been adopted by the Mississippi Real Estate Commission and is required to be used by real estate licensees pursuant to Rule IV. E. of the Rules and Regulations. MREC-AD2 [Feb. 2001

> Dual Agency Agreements are not notarized.

Real Estate Training Institute – Pre Exam Workbook

2. Working with a Real Estate Broker

WORKING WITH A REAL ESTATE BROKER
   To be completed by every client or customer at first contact with a real estate licensee.

WORKING WITH A
REAL ESTATE BROKER
THIS IS NOT A LEGALLY BINDING CONTRACT
Approved 01/2003 By MS Real Estate Commission P. O. Box 12685 Jackson, MS 39232

GENERAL

Before you begin working with any real estate agent, you should know whom the agent represents in the transaction. Mississippi real estate licensees are required to disclose which party they represent in a transaction and to allow a party the right to choose or refuse among the various agency relationships.

There are several types of relationships that are possible and you should understand these at the time a broker or salesperson provides specific assistance to you in a real estate transaction,

The purpose of the Agency Disclosure is to document an acknowledgement that the consumer has been informed of various agency relationships, which are available in a real estate transaction.

For the purpose of this disclosure, the term seller and/or buyer will also include those other acts specified in Section 73-35-3 (1), of the Miss. Code, "...list, sell, purchase, exchange, rent, lease, manage, or auction any real estate, or the improvements thereon including options."

SELLER'S AGENT

A seller can enter into a "listing agreement" with a real estate firm authorizing the firm and its agent(s) to represent the seller in finding a buyer for his property. A licensee who is engaged by and acts as the agent of the Seller only is known as a Seller's Agent. A Seller's agent has the following duties and obligations:

To the Seller:
*The fiduciary duties of loyalty, confidentiality, obedience, disclosure, full accounting and the duty to use skill, care and diligence.

To the Buyer and Seller:

*A duty of honesty and fair dealing. *A duty to disclose all facts known to the Seller's agent materially affecting the value of the property, which are not known to, or readily observable by, the parties in a transaction.

BUYER'S AGENT

A buyer may contract with an agent or firm to represent him/her. A licensee who is engaged by and acts as the agent of the Buyer only is known as the Buyer's Agent.

If a Buyer wants an agent to represent him in purchasing a property, the buyer can enter into a Buyer's Agency Agreement with the agent. A Buyer's Agent has the following duties and obligations:

To the Buyer:
The fiduciary duties of loyalty, confidentiality, obedience, disclosure, full accounting and the duty to use skill, care and diligence.

To the Seller and Buyer:
*A duty of honesty and fair dealing.

DISCLOSED DUAL AGENT

A real estate agent or firm may represent more than one party in the same transaction. A Disclosed Dual Agent is a licensee who, with the informed written consent of the Seller and Buyer, is engaged as an agent for both Seller and Buyer.

As a disclosed dual agent, the licensee shall not represent the interests of one party to the exclusion or detriment of the interests of the other party. A disclosed dual agent has all the fiduciary duties to the Seller and Buyer that a Seller's or Buyer's agent has except the duties of full disclosure and undivided loyalty.

A Disclosed Dual Agent may not disclose:

(a) To the Buyer that the Seller will accept less than the asking or listed price, unless otherwise instructed in writing by the Seller.

(b) To the Seller that the Buyer will pay a price greater than the price submitted in a written offer to the Seller, unless otherwise instructed
in writing by the Buyer.

(e) The motivation of any party for selling, buying, or leasing a property, unless otherwise instructed in writing by the respective party, or

(d) That a Seller or Buyer will agree to financing terms other than those offered, unless otherwise instructed in writing by the respective
party.

Real Estate Training Institute – Pre Exam Workbook

IMPORTANT NOTICE!

"Customer" shall mean that person not represented in a real estate transaction. It may be the buyer, seller, landlord or tenant.

A Buyer may decide to work with a firm that is acting as agent for the Seller (a Seller's Agent or subagent). If a Buyer does not enter into a Buyer Agency Agreement with the firm that shows him properties, that firm and its agents may show the buyer properties as an agent or subagent working on the seller's behalf. Such a firm represents the Seller (not the Buyer) and must disclose that fact to the Buyer.

When it comes to the price and terms of an offer, the Seller's Agent will ask you to decide how much to offer for any property and upon what terms and conditions. They can explain your options to you, but the final decision is yours, as they cannot give you legal or financial advice. They will attempt to show you property in the price range and category you desire so that you will have information on which to base your decision.

The Seller's Agent will present to the Seller any written offer that you ask them to present.

You should keep to yourself any information that you do not want the Seller to know (i.e. the price you are willing to pay, other terms you are willing to accept, and your motivation for buying). The Seller's agent is required to tell all such information to the Seller.

You should not furnish the Seller's agent anything you do not want the Seller to know. If you desire, you may obtain the representation of an attorney or another real estate agent, or both.

LICENSEE -Provide a copy of disclosure acknowledgement to all parties and retain signed original for your files. SPC 01/2003   MREC Rev 01/2003

THIS IS NOT A CONTRACT. THIS IS AN ACKNOWLEDGEMENT OF DISCLOSURE

The below named Licensee has informed me that brokerage services are being provided me as a:
Client ☐☐
Client ☐☐
Client

(Seller's or Landlords Agent)

(Buyer's or Tenants Agent)
☐☐
Customer
(Not as my Agent)

(Disclosed Dual Agent)

Real Estate Training Institute – Pre Exam Workbook

By signing below, I acknowledge that I received this informative document and explanation prior to the exchange of confidential information which might affect the bargaining position in a real estate transaction involving me.
END FORM*************

3. Disclosure of licensed status if a principal

"Fiduciary Responsibilities" are those duties due the principal (client) in a real estate transaction are:

(1) 'Loyalty' - the agent must put the interests of the principal above the interests of the agent or any third party.

(2) 'Obedience' - the agent agrees to obey any lawful instruction from the principal in the execution of the transaction that is the subject of the agency.

(3) 'Disclosure' - the agent must disclose to the principal any information the agent becomes aware of in connection with the agency.

(4) 'Confidentiality' - the agent must keep private information provided by the principal and information which would give a customer an advantage over the principal strictly confidential, unless the agent has the principal's permission to disclose the information. This duty lives on after the agency relationship is terminated.

(5) 'Reasonable skill, care and diligence' - the agent must perform all duties with the care and diligence which may be reasonably expected of someone undertaking such duties.

(6) 'Full accounting' - the agent must provide a full accounting of any money or goods coming into the agent's possession which belong to the principal or other parties.

4. Timing of disclosure, Rules about parties to whom disclosure must be made

A real estate licensee shall immediately (at the time of signing) deliver a true and correct copy of any instrument to any party or parties executing the same.

Consumers shall be fully informed of the agency relationships in real estate transactions.

This rule places specific requirements on Brokers to disclose their agency relationship. This does not abrogate the laws of agency as recognized under common law and compliance with the prescribed disclosures will not always guarantee that a Broker has fulfilled all of his responsibilities under the common law of agency. Compliance will be necessary in order to protect licensees from impositions of sanctions against their license by the Mississippi Real Estate Commission. Special situations, where unusual facts exist or where one or more parties involved are especially vulnerable, could require additional disclosures not contemplated by this rule. In such cases, Brokers should seek legal advice prior to entering into an agency relationship

"First Substantive Meeting" shall be:

(1) In a real estate transaction in which the Broker is the agent for the seller, first substantive meeting shall be before or just immediately prior to the first of any of the following:

(a) Showing the property to a prospective buyer.

(b) Eliciting confidential information from a buyer concerning the buyers' real estate needs, motivation, or financial qualifications.

(c) The execution of any agreements

(2) For the seller's agent, the definition shall not include:

(a) A bona fide "open house" or model home showing which encompasses

(1) (a) above only; however, whenever an event described in (1) (b) or (1)

(c) occurs, disclosure must be made.

(b) Preliminary conversations or "small talk" concerning price range, location and property styles.

(c) Responding to general factual questions from a prospective buyer concerning properties that have been advertised for sale or lease.

(3) In a real estate transaction in which the Broker is the agent for the buyer, first substantive meeting shall be at the initial contact with a seller or a seller's agent or before or just immediately prior to the first of any of the following:

(a) Showing the property of a seller to a represented buyer.

(b) Eliciting any confidential information from a seller concerning their real estate needs, motivation, or financial qualifications.

(c) The execution of any agreements.

(4) For the buyer's agent, the definition shall not include:

(a) A bona fide "open House" or model home showing which encompasses

(3) (a) above only; however, whenever an event described in (3)

(b) or (3)

(c) occurs, disclosure must be made.

(b) Preliminary conversations or "small talk" concerning price range, location and property styles.

(c) Responding to general factual questions from a prospective buyer concerning properties that have been advertised for sale or lease.

Disclosure Requirements

A. In a single agency, a broker is required to disclose, in writing, to the party for whom the broker is an agent in a real estate transaction that the broker is the agent of the party. The written disclosure must be made before the time an agreement for representation is entered into between the broker and the party. This shall be on an MREC Agency Disclosure Form.

B. In a single agency, a real estate broker is required to disclose, in writing, to the party for whom the broker is not an agent, that the broker is an agent of another party in the transaction. The written disclosure shall be made at the time of the first substantive meeting with the party for whom the broker is not an agent. This shall be on an MREC Agency Disclosure Form.

C. Brokers operating in the capacity of disclosed dual agents must obtain the informed written consent of all parties prior to or at the time of formalization of the dual agency. Informed written consent to disclosed dual agency shall be deemed to have been timely obtained if all of the following occur:

(1) The seller, at the time an agreement for representation is entered into between the broker and seller, gives written consent to dual agency by signing the Consent To Dual Agency portion of MREC Form A.

(2) The buyer, at the time an agreement for representation is entered into between the broker and buyer, gives written consent to dual agency by signing the Consent To Dual Agency portion of MREC Form A.

(3) The Broker must confirm that the buyer(s) understands and consents to the consensual dual agency relationship prior to the signing of an offer to purchase. The buyer shall give his/her consent by signing the MREC Dual Agency Confirmation Form which shall be attached to the offer to purchase. The Broker must confirm that the seller(s) also understands and consents to the consensual dual agency relationship prior to presenting the offer to purchase. The seller shall give his/her consent by signing the MREC Dual Agency Confirmation Form attached to the buyer's offer. The form shall remain attached to the offer to purchase regardless of the outcome of the offer to purchase.

D. In the event the agency relationship changes between the parties to a real estate transaction, new disclosure forms will be acknowledged by all parties involved.

Real Estate Training Institute – Pre Exam Workbook

E. In the event one or more parties are not available to sign one or more of the Disclosure Forms, the disclosure will be accomplished orally. The applicable form will be so noted by the Broker and said forms will be forwarded for signature(s) as soon as possible. Written electronic transmission will fulfill this requirement.

F. In the event any party receiving a disclosure form requests not to sign that form acknowledging receipt, the Broker shall annotate the form with the following statement:

"A COPY OF THIS FORM WAS DELIVERED TO

_____ DATE_____. RECIPIENT

DECLINED TO ACKNOWLEDGE RECEIPT OF THIS FORM."

G. The terms of the agency relationship shall be ratified on all contracts pertaining to real estate transactions.

H. The Commission mandated disclosure form may be duplicated in content and size but not altered.

I. Completed Agency Disclosure Forms shall be maintained in accordance with MS license law (3 years)

5. Buyer may withdraw from Buyer-Broker agreement w 15 days' notice

All exclusive buyer representation agreements shall be in writing and properly identify the terms and conditions under which the buyer will rely on the broker for the purchase of real estate; including the sales price, the considerations to be paid, the signatures of all parties to the agreement, and a definite date of expiration. The buyer may terminate the agreement <u>upon fifteen (15) calendar days</u> written notice to the buyer's exclusive agent.

An Exclusive Buyer Representation agreement shall clearly indicate in the body of the document that it is such an agreement.

6. General Duties to all Parties

*See Working with a Real Estate Broker Form Above

Out-of-State Brokers and Developers (Salesperson 4 Items, Broker 3 Items)

Any seller, other than the developer and its regular employees, of a timeshare plan within the State of Mississippi must be a licensed Real Estate Broker or Real Estate Salesperson pursuant to and subject to Mississippi Law and the Rules and Regulations of the Mississippi Real Estate

Commission.

Out-of-state Developers
Out-of-state land developers who desire to advertise out-of-state property in Mississippi (except in national publications) shall first contact the Mississippi Real Estate Commission to have the property approved for advertising. The Mississippi Real Estate Commission may in its discretion conduct an on-site inspection of the property at the cost of the developer. The developer shall, upon request from the Mississippi Real Estate Commission, provide such documentation which will establish the truth and accuracy of the proposed advertisements. A Mississippi broker who becomes the agent or representative of the out-of-state developer, shall be responsible for the truth and accuracy of representation, offerings and advertising of such properties in the State of Mississippi.

A. Developer registration; offer or disposal of interest. - A developer, or any of its agents, shall not sell, offer or dispose of a timeshare interest in the state unless all necessary registration requirements are completed and approved by the Mississippi Real Estate Commission, or the sale, offer, or disposition is otherwise permitted by or exempt from these rules. A developer, or any of its agents, shall not sell, offer or dispose of a timeshare interest in the state while an order revoking or suspending a registration is in effect.

Exemptions from developer registration
(1) A person is exempt from the registration requirements under the following circumstances.

(a) An owner of a timeshare interest who has acquired the timeshare interest from another for the owner's own use and occupancy and who later offers it for resale; or

(b) A managing entity or an association that is offering to sell one or more timeshare interests acquired through foreclosure, deed in lieu of foreclosure or gratuitous transfer, if such acts are performed in the regular course of or as incident to the management of the association for its own account in the timeshare plan; or

(c) The person offers a timeshare plan located outside of Mississippi in a national publication or by electronic media, which is not directed to or targeted to any individual located in Mississippi and contains appropriate disclaimers; or

(d) The person is conveyed, assigned, or transferred more than seven timeshare interests from a developer in a single voluntary or involuntary transaction arid subsequently conveys, assigns, or transfers all of the timeshare interests received from the developer to a single purchaser in a single transaction.

(e) (i) The developer is offering a timeshare interest to a purchaser who has previously acquired a timeshare interest from the same developer if the developer has a timeshare plan registered with the Commission, which was originally approved by the Commission within the preceding seven (7) years and, further, provides the purchaser:

(A) a cancellation period of at least **seven (7) calendar days;**

Real Estate Training Institute – Pre Exam Workbook

(B) all the timeshare disclosure documents that are required to be provided to purchasers as if the sale occurred in the state or jurisdiction where the timeshare property is located; and

(ii) By making such an offering or disposition, the person is deemed to consent to the jurisdiction of the Commission in the event of a dispute with the purchaser in connection with the offering or disposition.

(f) An offering of any plan in which the purchaser's total financial obligation is $3,000 or less during the term of the plan; for purposes of determining the purchaser's total financial obligation, all amounts to be paid during any renewal or periods of optional renewal shall be included.

(g) Hotels including any hotel, inn, motel, tourist court, apartment house, rooming house, or other place where sleeping accommodations are furnished or offered for pay if four (4) or more rooms are available therein for transient guests.

(h) Campground, which is located on real property, made available to persons for camping, whether by tent, trailer, camper, cabin, recreational vehicle or similar device and shall include the outdoor recreational facilities located on the real property;

(i) Hunting camp which means land or facilities located on real property which is established for the principal purpose of hunting or fishing activities which are subject to licensing by the State of Misissippi.

(j) Owner referrals as described in Section N of these rules.

C. Developer Registration Requirements

(1) Any person who, to any individual in Mississippi, sells, offers to sell, or attempts to solicit prospective purchasers to purchase a timeshare interest, or any person 22who creates a timeshare plan with an accommodation in Mississippi must register the timeshare plan with the Commission unless the timeshare plan is otherwise exempt from this Chapter.

(2) The developer shall have the duty to supervise and control all aspects of the offering of a timeshare plan including, but not limited to the promotion, advertising, contracting and closing.

(3) The developer must provide proof as part of the registration that he will comply with escrow, bonding, or other financial assurance requirements for purchaser funds, including escrow during the rescission period, escrow funds until substantial completion, or bonding, letter of credit or other financial assurances acceptable to the Commission.

(4) All timeshare plans shall maintain a one-to-one purchaser to accommodation ratio, which is the ratio of the number of purchasers eligible to use the accommodations of a timeshare plan on a given day to the number of accommodations available for use within the plan on that day, such that the total number of purchasers eligible to use the accommodations of the timeshare plan during a given calendar year never exceeds the total number of accommodations available for use in the timeshare plan during that year. For purposes of calculation under this subsection, each purchaser must be counted at least once, and no individual timeshare unit may be counted more than 365 times per

calendar year (or more than 366 times per leap year). A purchaser who is delinquent in the payment of timeshare plan assessments shall continue to be considered eligible to use the accommodations of the timeshare plan.

Comprehensive registration

(1) In registering a timeshare plan, the developer shall provide all of the following information:

(a) The developer's legal name, any assumed names used by the developer, principal office, street address, mailing address, primary contact person, telephone, electronic mail and facsimile numbers;

(b) The name of the developer's authorized or registered agent in Mississippi upon whom claims may be served or service of process be had, the agent's street address in Mississippi and telephone number;

(c) The name, street address, mailing address, primary contact person and telephone, electronic mail and facsimile numbers of any timeshare plans being registered;

(d) The name, street address, mailing address and telephone, electronic mail and facsimile numbers of any managing entity of the timeshare plan if other than the developer;

(e) Current status of title by a title insurance company qualified and registered to do business in Mississippi, or in the jurisdiction where the timeshare plan is located;

(f) A copy of the proposed or existing covenants, conditions and restrictions applicable to the timeshare plan;

(g) Exemplars of all contracts, deeds, fact sheets and other instruments to be used in marketing, financing and conveying the timeshare interests;

(h) A copy of the management agreement for the timeshare plan;

(i) A detailed description of the furnishing(s) and other personal property to be included in the timeshare plans;

(j) Agreement of the developer to subsidize maintenance and operation of the timeshare plan, if any;

(k) Description of other services and amenities advertised with the timesharing plan;

(l) Evidence of financial assurances, if any;

(m) Evidence of compliance with escrow or other financial assurance requirements for protection of purchaser funds pursuant to these rules.

Real Estate Training Institute – Pre Exam Workbook

(n) Where the timeshare plan uses a reservation system, the developer shall provide evidence that provisions are in place to assure that, in the event of termination of the operator of the reservation system, an adequate period of continued operation exists to assure a transition to a substitute operator or mechanism for the operation of the reservation system. In addition, there shall be a requirements to transfer all relevant data contained in the reservation system to the successor operator of the system.

(o) A description of the inventory control system that will ensure compliance with subsection 3.c. of this section.

(p) A public offering statement which complies with the requirements set forth below; and

(q) Any other information regarding the developer, timeshare plan, or managing entities, as reasonably required by the Commission for the protection of the purchasers.

F. Preliminary Permits

(1) The state may grant a preliminary permit allowing the developer to begin offering and selling timeshare interests while the registration is in process. To obtain a preliminary permit, the developer must do all of the following:

(a) Submit a formal written request to the Mississippi Real Estate Commission for a preliminary permit;

(b) Submit a substantially complete application for registration to the Commission, including any appropriate fees and exhibits;

(c) Provide evidence acceptable to the state agency that all funds received by the developer will be placed into an independent escrow account in accordance with the escrow requirements until a final registration has been granted;

(d) Give to each purchaser a copy of the proposed public offering statement that the developer has submitted to the Commission with the initial application; and

(e) Give to each purchaser the opportunity to cancel the purchase contract during the applicable rescission period. The purchaser shall have an additional opportunity to cancel upon the issuance of an approved registration if the Commission determines that there is a material and adverse difference in the disclosures contained in the final public offering statement and those given to the purchaser in the proposed public offering

A statement that within seven (7) calendar days after receipt of the public offering statement or after execution of the purchase contract, whichever is later, a purchaser may cancel any purchase contract for a timeshare interest from a developer together with a statement providing the name and street address to which the purchaser shall mail any notice of cancellation. If by agreement of the parties by and through the purchase contract, the purchase contract allows for cancellation of the purchase contract for a period of time exceeding seven (7) calendar days, then the public offering statement shall include a statement that the cancellation of the purchase contract is allowing for that period of time exceeding seven (7) calendar days;

Real Estate Training Institute – Pre Exam Workbook

Preliminary permit. A preliminary permit shall be issued within twenty (20) calendar days after receipt of a properly completed application, unless the Commission provides to the applicant a list of deficiencies in the application. A preliminary permit shall be issued within fifteen (15) calendar days after receipt. You may cancel this contract without any penalty or obligation within seven (7) calendar days from the date you sign this contract and seven (7) calendar days after you receive the public offering statement, whichever is later. If you decide to cancel this contract, you must notify the developer in writing of your intent to cancel. Your notice of cancellation shall be effective upon the date sent and shall be sent to (name of developer) at (address of developer). If you cancel the contract during a the seven-day cancellation period, the developer shall refund to you all payments made under the contract within thirty (30) days after receipt of your cancellation notice.

No purchaser should rely upon representations other than those included in this contract. Seller shall refund all payments made by the purchaser under the contract and return all negotiable instruments, other than checks, executed by the purchaser in connection with the contract within 30 days from the receipt of the notice of cancellation transmitted to the developer from the purchaser or if the purchaser has received benefits under the contract, refund all payments made less actual cost of benefits actually received by the purchaser before the date of cancellation, with an accounting of the actual costs of the benefits deducted from payments refunded.

Advertising and Marketing:

A. No advertising shall:

(1) Misrepresent a fact or create a false or misleading impression regarding the timeshare plan.

(2) Make a prediction of increases in the price or value of timeshare periods.

(3) Contain any contradictory statements.

(4) Describe any improvements to the timeshare plan that will not be built or that are described as completed when not completed.

B. No promotional device, sweepstakes, lodging certificate, gift award, premium, discount, drawing, prize or display in connection with an offer to sell a timeshare interest may be utilized without the applicable disclosure as follows:

(1) That the promotional device is being used for the purposes of soliciting sales of timeshare periods;

(2) Of the name and address of each timeshare plan or business entity participating in the program;

(3) Of the date and year when all prizes are to be awarded;

(4) Of the method by which all prizes are to be awarded;

(5) If applicable, a statement that it is a national program with multiple sponsors and the gifts offered are not limited solely to customers of said development, but apply also to other developments.

C. The following are not considered to be advertising materials:

(1) Any stockholder communication, financial report, prospectus or other material required to be delivered to owners, prospective purchasers or other persons by an agency of any state or the federal government;

(2) Any communication addressed to and relating to the account of any person who has previously executed a contract for the purchase of a timeshare interest in a timeshare plan to which the communication relates;

(3) Any oral or written statement disseminated to the broadcast, print or other news media, other than paid advertising, regarding plans for the acquisition or development of timeshare property. However, any redistribution of such oral or written statements to a prospective purchaser in any manner would constitute an advertisement;

(4) Any publication or material relating to the promotion of accommodations for transient rental, so long as a mandatory tour of a timeshare plan or attendance at a mandatory sales presentation is not a term or condition of the availability of such accommodations, so long as the failure of the transient renter to take a tour of a timeshare plan or attend a sales presentation does not result in the transient renter receiving less than what was promised in such materials;

(5) Any audio, written or visual publication or material relating to an exchange company or exchange program providing to an existing member of that exchange company or exchange program.

Before the first sale of a timeshare period, the developer shall create or provide for a managing entity, which may be the developer, a separate management firm, or an owner's association, or some combination thereof.

B. The management entity shall act in the capacity of fiduciary to the purchasers of the timeshare plans.

1. *Cooperative agreements*

A licensed Mississippi broker may cooperate with a broker licensed in another state who does not hold a Mississippi license through the use of a cooperative agreement. A separate cooperative agreement must be filed for each property, prospective user or transaction with said writing reflecting the compensation to be paid to the Mississippi licensed broker. The listing or property management agreement for the Mississippi real property shall in such cases remain in the name of the Mississippi licensed broker.

The commissions or other compensation resulting from the sale/rent/lease/property management or auction of the Mississippi real property and which are earned during the period the cooperative agreement is in force shall be divided on a negotiable basis between the Mississippi broker and the nonresident broker.

A responsible (principal) nonresident broker described herein is defined as an active, licensed responsible real estate broker of another state who does not possess an active responsible nonresident real estate broker's license issued by the Mississippi Real Estate Commission (MREC). A Mississippi broker described herein is a responsible (principal) real estate broker whose license is on active status and whose license was issued by MREC either as a responsible resident Mississippi broker or as a responsible nonresident Mississippi broker.

The responsible nonresident broker cannot place any sign on real property located in the state of Mississippi without the written consent of the cooperating responsible Mississippi broker. When the consent is obtained, the sign of the responsible Mississippi broker must be placed in a prominent place and in close proximity to the responsible nonresident broker's sign. Any licensed responsible Mississippi broker assisting or cooperating in the sale, lease, property management, rental or auction of real property within the state of Mississippi with a responsible nonresident broker who fails or refuses to list his or her name in such advertisement, or fails or refuses to cross-list such property with him or her, in writing, shall be deemed in violation of Section 73-35-11 of the Real Estate Broker's License Act, and shall be subject to a revocation or suspension of his or her license. In such instance herein where a responsible Mississippi broker enters into a cooperative agreement with a responsible nonresident broker pertaining to the sale of real property within the state of Mississippi, the responsible Mississippi broker must file two copies of the cooperating agreement with the Mississippi Real Estate Commission.

Nonresident may not act except in cooperation with licensed broker of state

It shall be unlawful for any licensed broker, salesperson or other person who is not licensed as a Mississippi resident or nonresident broker or salesperson and a licensed broker or licensed salesperson in this state to perform any of the acts regulated by this chapter, except that a licensed broker of another state who does not hold a Mississippi real estate license may cooperate with a licensed broker of this state provided that any commission or fee resulting from such cooperative negotiation shall be stated on a form filed with the commission reflecting the compensation to be paid to the Mississippi broker.

Whenever a Mississippi broker enters into a cooperative agreement under this section, the Mississippi broker shall file within ten (10) days with the commission a copy of each such written agreement. By signing the agreement, the nonresident broker who is not licensed in this state agrees to abide by Mississippi law, and the rules and regulations of the commission; and further agrees that civil actions may be commenced against him in any court of competent jurisdiction in any county of this state in which a claim may arise.

The Mississippi broker shall require a listing or joint listing of the property involved. The written cooperative agreements shall specify all material terms of each agreement, including but not limited to its financial terms.

Real Estate Training Institute – Pre Exam Workbook

The showing of property located in Mississippi and negotiations pertaining thereto shall be supervised by the Mississippi broker. In all advertising of real estate located in Mississippi, the name and telephone number of the Mississippi broker shall appear and shall be given equal prominence with the name of the nonresident broker who is not licensed in this state.

The Mississippi broker shall be liable for all acts of the above cooperating broker, as well as for his own acts, arising from the execution of any cooperative agreement.

The Mississippi broker shall determine that the cooperating broker is licensed as a broker in another state.

All earnest money pertaining to a cooperative agreement must be held in escrow by the Mississippi broker unless both the buyer and seller agree in writing to relieve the Mississippi broker of this responsibility.

Real Estate Training Institute – Pre Exam Workbook

CO-OPERATIVE AGREEMENT

Revised co-op agreement with non-resident principal broker.

COOPERATING AGREEMENT WITH NON-RESIDENT PRINCIPAL BROKER   (EFFECTIVE- JULY 1, 2004)

Date Agreement Executed: _____

Agreement Expiration Date: _____

Owner/Client/Customer's Name _____

Telephone # _____

Owner/Client/Customer's Address_____

Location/Legal Description of Listed Property (if applicable) _____

_____

AGREEMENT TO BE FINALIZED "PRIOR" TO ANY LICENSABLE REAL ESTATE ACTIVITY: It is understood and agreed that this Agreement covers: **(Please check ONLY one <1> box)**

[ ] 1. A Joint or Cross Listing with participation by a Non-resident Principal Broker
[ ] 2. A Listing Referral from a Non-resident Principal Broker
[ ] 3. A Client or Customer Referral from a Non-resident Principal Broker
[ ] 4. A Purchase or Sales Contract procured by a Non-resident Principal Broker
[ ] 5. An Auction Agreement with a Non-resident Principal Broker
[ ] 6. Any Other activity for which a real estate license is required

In order to comply with the Mississippi Real Estate Brokers License Act of 1954, as Amended, and the Rules and Regulations of the Mississippi Real Estate Commission (MREC), the Mississippi Principal Broker and the Non-resident Principal Broker agree to the following:

All negotiations, including the showing, listing, and advertising of real property located within the state of Mississippi shall be handled under the direct supervision of the Mississippi Principal Broker, with the Mississippi Principal Broker taking full responsibility. **The Non-resident Principal Broker MUST be present at all times if one of his/her real estate agents, who is NOT licensed by the state of Mississippi, has a physical presence in Mississippi in connection with any real property transaction.** The Non-resident Principal Broker agrees to abide by Mississippi Law and the Rules and Regulations of the MREC and further agrees that civil actions may be commenced against him/her in any court of competent jurisdiction in any county of this state in which a claim may arise.

The Mississippi Principal Broker **MUST** confirm that the Non-resident Principal Broker is licensed as an **"ACTIVE PRINCIPAL BROKER"** in another state. This may be accomplished by direct contact with the Real Estate Licensing authority or by receiving a copy of a current real estate broker license. The Mississippi Principal Broker further agrees to notify the MREC immediately if the Non-resident Principal Broker violates any part of this Cooperative Agreement.

The Non-resident Principal Broker agrees not to place any sign on real property located within the state of Mississippi without the express written permission of the cooperating Mississippi Principal Broker. If such authority is granted, both Principal Brokers agree their signs will be placed in close proximity to one another and in a prominent place on the property. All listing or property management agreements shall be in the name of the Mississippi Principal Broker or they shall require a cross listing or joint listing of such property with the Non-resident Principal Broker.

The Non-resident Principal Broker agrees to not advertise the property in any manner unless the Mississippi Principal Broker is included in the advertising and such advertising shall be with the full knowledge of and under the direct supervision of the Mississippi Principal Broker. The name and phone number of the Mississippi Principal Broker shall be given equal prominence with the Non-resident Principal Broker. If this cooperative agreement involves a listing agreement concerning real property, the Non-resident Principal Broker affirms that the solicitation of the listing of the Mississippi property was conducted in the presence of the Mississippi Principal Broker.

The commissions, fees, or other compensations (considerations) earned during the period this Cooperative Agreement is in force shall be divided between the Mississippi Principal Broker and the Non-resident Principal Broker on a negotiable basis that is agreeable to the two brokers. The Mississippi Principal Broker shall either receive $_____ or ____% of the compensation and the Non-resident Principal Broker shall either receive $_____ or ____% of the compensation. All earnest monies or deposits shall be placed in the escrow account of the Mississippi Principal Broker unless both the buyer and the seller agree in writing to relieve the Mississippi Principal Broker of this responsibility.

No licensee shall knowingly pay a commission or a fee to a licensed person knowing that licensee will, in turn, pay any portion of the fee to an individual who does not hold a real estate license.

_____
Mississippi Broker's Name (Print)

_____
Mississippi Broker's Signature

_____
Mailing Address

_____
City, State & Zip Code

_____
Business Telephone #

_____
Non-resident Principal Broker's Name (Print)

_____
Non-resident Principal Broker's Signature

_____
Mailing Address

_____
City, State & Zip Code

_____
Business Telephone #

For a **JOINT LISTING:** I hereby agree to allow the Non-resident Principal Broker to place their sign in close proximity to my sign on the above-referenced listed property during the term of this contract.

_____
Mississippi Principal Broker's Signature

Four copies of the Agreement have been executed.

The Non-resident Principal Broker and the Mississippi Principal Broker have each received one copy.

It is the duty of the Mississippi Principal Broker to **confirm that the other two copies are filed with the Mississippi Real Estate Commission** at Post Office Box 12685, Jackson, MS 39236-2685, within 10 days after entering into the agreement.

> 2 copies within 10 days

2. Reciprocal licenses

A real estate licensee of another state who desires to obtain a license under this chapter shall be exempt from the examination provided the examination administered in the other state is determined by the Commission to be equivalent to such examination given in this state and provided that such other state extends this same privilege or exemption to Mississippi real estate licensees.

Real estate education courses obtained through sources (providers) other than those set forth in Section 73-35-7 of the statute but which are accepted in the state where the applicant is licensed, may be accepted by the Commission provided the state where the applicant is licensed has entered into a reciprocal agreement with this state.

Trust Accounts (Salesperson 4 Items, Broker 3 Items)

1. Handling of earnest money

The responsible broker is responsible at all times for earnest money deposits. Earnest money accepted by the broker or any licensee for which the broker is responsible and upon acceptance of a mutually agreeable contract is required to deposit the money into a trust account prior to the close of business of the next banking day. The responsible broker is required to promptly account for and remit the full amount of the deposit or earnest money at the consummation or termination of transaction. A licensee is required to pay over to the responsible broker all deposits and earnest money immediately upon receipt thereof. Earnest money must be returned promptly when the purchaser is rightfully entitled to same allowing reasonable time for clearance of the earnest money check. In the event of uncertainty as to the proper disposition of earnest money, the broker may turn earnest money over to a court of law for disposition. Failure to comply with this regulation shall constitute grounds for revocation or suspension of license.

When the broker is the agent for the seller and for any reason the seller fails or is unable to consummate the transaction, the broker has no right to any portion of the earnest money deposited by the purchaser, even if a commission has been earned. The entire amount of the earnest money deposit must be returned to the purchaser and the broker should look to the seller for compensation.

2. General acctg practices; no commingling

Accurate records shall be kept on escrow accounts of all monies received, disbursed, or on hand. All monies shall be individually identified as to a particular transaction. Escrow records shall be kept in accordance with standard accounting practices and shall be subject to inspection at all times by the Commission.

Monies received in a trust account on behalf of clients or customers are not assets of the broker; however, a broker may deposit and keep in each escrow account or rental account some personal funds for the express purpose of covering service charges and other bank debits related to each account.

If a broker, as escrow agent, accepts a check and later finds that such check has not been honored by the bank on which it was drawn, the broker shall immediately notify all parties involved in the transaction.

3. Broker is account holder; Salesperson may not establish prop mgt escrow acct independent of broker

The responsible broker is responsible at all times for earnest money deposits. Earnest money accepted by the broker or any licensee for which the broker is responsible and upon acceptance of a mutually agreeable contract is required to deposit the money into a trust account prior to the close of business of the next banking day. The responsible broker is required to promptly account for and remit the full amount of the deposit or earnest money at the consummation or termination of transaction. A licensee is required to pay over to the responsible broker all deposits and earnest money immediately upon receipt thereof. Earnest money must be returned promptly when the purchaser is rightfully entitled to same allowing reasonable time for clearance of the earnest money check. In the event of uncertainty as to the proper disposition of earnest money, the broker may turn earnest money over to a court of law for disposition. Failure to comply with this regulation shall constitute grounds for revocation or suspension of license.

4. Disbursement issues (interpleader)
Broker Responsibilities, Including Supervision of Sales Associates
(Salesperson 6 Items, Broker 5 Items)

1. Supervision of associated licensees

It shall be the duty of the responsible broker to instruct the licensees licensed under that broker in the fundamentals of real estate practice, ethics of the profession and the
Mississippi Real Estate License Law and to exercise supervision of their real estate activities for which a license is required.

A real estate broker who operates under the supervision of a responsible broker must not at any time act independently as a broker. The responsible broker shall at all times be responsible for the action of the affiliated broker to the same extent as though that licensee were a salesperson and that affiliated broker shall not perform any real estate service without the full consent and knowledge of his employing or supervising broker.

However, should the responsible broker agree that a broker under his supervision may perform certain real estate services outside the responsible broker's supervision or direction, the responsible broker shall notify the Commission in writing as to the exact nature of such relationship and the names of the broker or brokers involved. The responsible broker shall immediately notify the Commission in writing upon the termination of such relationship.

2. Inform MREC of change in associate status/termination

To change a license from active to inactive status, licensee shall notify the Commission in writing, shall insure that the license is returned to the Commission and shall pay the appropriate fee. A licensee who is on inactive status at time of renewal may renew the license on inactive status by filing a renewal application and paying the renewal fee. A broker who terminates a real estate business may place the business license on inactive status. To return to active status, a salesperson or broker/salesperson must file a transfer application. A broker and/or a business license may be activated by notifying the Commission by letter or transfer application including required fee.

When a licensee wishes to transfer from one broker to another, the transferring licensee must file a transfer application signed by the new broker accompanied by the transfer fee and must furnish a statement that the licensee is not carrying any listing

(2) All licenses issued to a real estate salesperson or broker-salesperson shall designate the responsible broker of such salesperson or broker-salesperson. Prompt notice in writing, within three (3) days, shall be given to the commission by any real estate salesperson of a change of responsible broker, and of the name of the principal broker into whose agency the salesperson is about to enter; and a new license shall thereupon be issued by the commission to such salesperson for the unexpired term of the original license upon the return to the commission of the license previously issued. The change of responsible broker or employment by any licensed real estate salesperson without notice to the commission as required shall automatically cancel his license. Upon termination of a salesperson's agency, the responsible broker shall within three (3) days return the salesperson's license to the commission for cancellation. It shall be unlawful for any real estate salesperson to perform any of the acts contemplated by this chapter either directly or indirectly after his agency has been terminated and his license has been returned for cancellation until his license has been reissued by the commission.

Status change from active to inactive status.................................. $ 25.00

Status change from inactive to active status.................................. $ 50.00

3. Responsibility for acts of associates

4. License display; place of business

A responsible broker must maintain an office and display the license therein. If the broker has more than one office, the broker shall display a branch office license in each branch office. The broker is responsible for the real estate practices of those licensees.

(1) Every person, partnership, association or corporation licensed as a real estate broker shall be required to have and maintain a definite place of business, which shall be a room either in his home or an office elsewhere, to be used for the transaction of real estate business, or such business and any allied business. The certificate of registration as broker and the certificate of each real estate salesperson employed by such broker shall be prominently displayed in said office. The said place of business shall be designated in the license. In case of removal from the designated address, the licensee shall make application to the commission before removal, or within ten (10) days after removal, designating the new location of such office, whereupon the commission shall forthwith issue a new license for the new location for the unexpired period.

5. Broker Price Opinion

A real estate broker or salesperson in the ordinary course of business may give an opinion as to the sales price of real estate for the purpose of a prospective listing or sale; however, this opinion as to the listing price or the sale price shall not be referred to as an appraisal and must be completed in compliance with Section 73-35-4 of the Real Estate Broker's License Act and must conform to the Standards established by the National Association of Broker Price Opinion Professionals (NABPOP).

6) The term "broker price opinion" means an estimate prepared by a real estate broker, agent, or salesperson that details the probable selling price of a particular piece of real estate property and provides a varying level of detail about the property's condition, market, and neighborhood, and information on comparable sales, but does not include an automated valuation model.

Broker's price opinion; preparation, contents and use of opinion

(1) A person licensed under this chapter may prepare a broker's price opinion and charge and collect a fee for such opinion if:

(a) The license of that licensee is active and in good standing; and

(b) The broker's price opinion meets the requirements of subsections (3) and (4) of this section.

(2) Notwithstanding any provision to the contrary, a person licensed under this chapter may prepare a broker's price opinion for:

(a) An existing or potential seller for the purposes of listing and selling a parcel of real property;

(b) An existing or potential buyer of a parcel of real property;

(c) A third party making decisions or performing due diligence related to the potential listing, offering, sale, exchange, option, lease or acquisition price of a parcel of real property; or

(d) An existing or potential lienholder or other third party for any purpose other than as the basis to determine the value of a parcel of real property, for a mortgage loan origination, including first and second mortgages, refinances, or equity lines of credit.

(e) The provisions of this subsection do not preclude the preparation of a broker's price opinion to be used in conjunction with or in addition to an appraisal.

(3) A broker's price opinion prepared under the authority granted in this section shall be in writing and shall conform to the standards and guidelines published by a nationally recognized association of providers of broker price opinions. The Mississippi Real Estate Commission shall promulgate regulations that are consistent with, but not limited to, the standards and guidelines of a nationally recognized association of providers of broker price opinions.

(4) A broker's price opinion shall be in writing and contain the following:

(a) A statement of the intended purpose of the price opinion;

(b) A brief description of the subject property and property interest to be priced;

(c) The basis of reasoning used to reach the conclusion of the price, including **the** applicable market data and/or capitalization computation;

d) Any assumptions or limiting conditions;

(e) A disclosure of any existing or contemplated interest of the broker or salesperson issuing the opinion;

(f) The effective date of the price opinion;

(g) The name and signature of the broker or salesperson issuing the price opinion;

(h) The name of the real estate brokerage firm for which the broker or salesperson is acting;

(i) The signature date;

(j) A disclaimer stating that, "This opinion is not an appraisal of the market value of the property, and may not be used in lieu of an appraisal. If an appraisal is desired, the services of a licensed or certified appraiser must be obtained. This opinion may not be used by any party as the primary basis to determine the value of a parcel of real property for a mortgage loan origination, including first and second mortgages, refinances or equity lines of credit.";

(k) A certification that the licensee is covered by errors and omissions insurance, to the extent required by state law, for all liability associated with the preparation of the broker's price opinion.

(5) If a broker's price opinion is submitted electronically or on a form supplied by the requesting party:

(a) A signature required by paragraph (g) of subsection (4) may be an electronic signature, as defined in Section 75-12-3.

(b) A signature required by paragraph (g) of subsection (4) and the disclaimer required by paragraph (j) of subsection (4) may be transmitted in a separate attachment if the electronic format or form supplied by the requesting party does not allow additional comments to be written by the licensee. The electronic format or the form supplied by the requesting party must:

(i) Reference the existence of a separate attachment; and

(ii) Include a statement that the broker's price opinion is not complete without the attachment.

(6) Notwithstanding any provisions to the contrary, a person licensed pursuant to this chapter may not prepare a broker's price opinion for any purpose in lieu of an appraisal when an appraisal is required by federal or state statute. A broker's price opinion which estimates value or worth of a parcel of real estate rather than sales price shall be deemed to be an appraisal and may not be prepared by a licensed broker or sales agent under the authority of their licensee but may only be prepared by a duly licensed appraiser and must meet the regulations promulgated by the Mississippi Real Estate Appraiser Licensing and Certification Board. A broker's price opinion may not under any circumstances be referred to as a valuation or appraisal.

6. Associates' Compensation

No licensee shall pay any part of a fee, commission, or other compensation received by such licensee in buying, selling, exchanging, leasing, auctioning or renting any real estate except to another licensee through the licensee's responsible broker.

No licensee shall knowingly pay a commission, or other compensation to a licensed person knowing that licensee will in turn pay a portion or all of that which is received to a person who does not hold a real estate license.

A licensee who has changed to inactive status or who has transferred to another responsible broker may receive compensation from the previous responsible broker if the commission was generated from activity during the time that the licensee was under the supervision of that responsible broker

Records and Documents (Salesperson 3 Items, Broker 4 Items)

Real Estate Training Institute – Pre Exam Workbook

1. Length of time to keep (Routine, if litigation)

A real estate broker must keep on file for three years following its consummation, complete records relating to any real estate transaction. This includes, but is not limited to: listings, options, leases, offers to purchase, contracts of sale, escrow records, agency agreements and copies of all closing statements.

2. Records that are included in this requirement

When an offer is made on property owned by a party with whom a broker has entered into a listing agreement, such broker shall document and date the seller's personal acceptance or rejection of the offer and upon written request, shall provide a copy of such document to the person making the offer.

3. Disposition of records after close of a business

4. Electronic records OK

Advertising/Marketing/Internet (Salesperson 3 Items, Broker 3 Items)

The use of any copyrighted term or insignia on stationery, office signs, or in advertising by any licensee not authorized to do so, will be considered as "substantial misrepresentation" and cause for refusal, suspension, or revocation of the license.

A licensee shall not advertise to sell, buy, exchange, auction, rent or lease property in a manner indicating that the offer to sell, buy, exchange, auction, rent, or lease such property is being made by a private party not engaged in the real estate business. No advertisement shall be inserted by a licensee in any publication where only a post office box number, telephone number, or street address appears. Every licensee, when advertising real estate in any publication, shall indicate that the party advertising is licensed in real estate. All advertising must be under the direct supervision and in the name of the responsible broker or in the name of the real estate firm.
When a licensee is advertising their own property for sale, purchase or exchange which is not listed with a broker, the licensee must indicate that he or she is licensed. The disclosure of licensee's status must be made in all forms of advertising, including the "for sale" sign.

C. In addition to disclosing their licensed status in advertisements, licensees are required to disclose their licensed status on all contracts for real estate in which they have an ownership interest. A broker shall advertise in the name in which the license is issued. A broker may use a descriptive term after the broker's name to indicate the occupation in which engaged, for example, "realty", "real estate", "property management". If advertising in any other form, a partnership, trade name, association, company or corporation license must be obtained prior to advertising in that manner.

OUT OF STATE DEVELOPER or TIMESHARE
Advertising and Marketing:

No advertising shall:

Misrepresent a fact or create a false or misleading impression regarding the timeshare plan.

Make a prediction of increases in the price or value of timeshare periods.

Contain any contradictory statements.

Describe any improvements to the timeshare plan that will not be built or that are described as completed when not completed.

No promotional device, sweepstakes, lodging certificate, gift award, premium, discount, drawing, prize or display in connection with an offer to sell a timeshare interest may be utilized without the applicable disclosure as follows:

(1) That the promotional device is being used for the purposes of soliciting sales of timeshare periods;

(2) Of the name and address of each timeshare plan or business entity participating in the program;

(3) Of the date and year when all prizes are to be awarded;

(4) Of the method by which all prizes are to be awarded;

(5) If applicable, a statement that it is a national program with multiple sponsors and the gifts offered are not limited solely to customers of said development, but apply also to other developments.

C. The following are not considered to be advertising materials:

(1) Any stockholder communication, financial report, prospectus or other material required to be delivered to owners, prospective purchasers or other persons by an agency of any state or the federal government;

(2) Any communication addressed to and relating to the account of any person who has previously executed a contract for the purchase of a timeshare interest in a timeshare plan to which the communication relates;

(3) Any oral or written statement disseminated to the broadcast, print or other news media, other than paid advertising, regarding plans for the acquisition or development of timeshare property.

Real Estate Training Institute – Pre Exam Workbook

However, any redistribution of such oral or written statements to a prospective purchaser in any manner would constitute an advertisement;

(4) Any publication or material relating to the promotion of accommodations for transient rental, so long as a mandatory tour of a timeshare plan or attendance at a mandatory sales presentation is not a term or condition of the availability of such accommodations, so long as the failure of the transient renter to take a tour of a timeshare plan or attend a sales presentation does not result in the transient renter receiving less than what was promised in such materials;

(5) Any audio, written or visual publication or material relating to an exchange company or exchange program providing to an existing member of that exchange company or exchange program.

1. Social media and internet are advertising (part of "ALL advertising")

All advertising must be under the direct supervision and in the name of the responsible broker or in the name of the real estate firm

2. Must advertise in broker's name

A broker shall advertise in the name in which the license is issued. A broker may use a descriptive term after the broker's name to indicate the occupation in which engaged, for example, "realty", "real estate", "property management". If advertising in any other form, a partnership, trade name, association, company or corporation license must be obtained prior to advertising in that manner.

A licensee shall not advertise to sell, buy, exchange, auction, rent or lease property in a manner indicating that the offer to sell, buy, exchange, auction, rent, or lease such property is being made by a private party not engaged in the real estate business. No advertisement shall be inserted by a licensee in any publication where only a post office box number, telephone number, or street address appears. Every licensee, when advertising real estate in any publication, shall indicate that the party advertising is licensed in real estate. All advertising must be under the direct supervision and in the name of the responsible broker or in the name of the real estate firm.

3. Broker must permit/approve advertising

All advertising must be under the direct supervision and in the name of the responsible broker or in the name of the real estate firm.

4. Private controls

When a licensee is advertising their own property for sale, purchase or exchange which is not listed with a broker, the licensee must indicate that he or she is licensed. The disclosure of licensee's status must be made in all forms of advertising, including the "for sale" sign.

In addition to disclosing their licensed status in advertisements, licensees are required to disclose their licensed status on all contracts for real estate in which they have an ownership interest.

Real Estate Training Institute – Pre Exam Workbook

CHAPTER 9

FORMS

*The MREC Forms below have been altered to fit the demands of publishing. None of the wording has been changed to the best of our knowledge. This is not a complete list of MREC Forms. All forms can be found at: http://www.mrec.state.ms.us/

The answers to several questions on the exam can be found in the following forms:

RESIDENT BROKER APPLICATION
 This application is for a Mississippi resident wishing to apply for a real estate Brokers license.

Mississippi Real Estate Commission
2506 Lakeland Drive, Suite 300
Flowood, MS 39232 OR Post Office Box 12685 Jackson, MS 39236-2685
(601) 932-6770 – Telephone * (601) 932-2990 – Fax

www.mrec.ms.gov

APPLICATION FOR RESIDENT BROKER'S LICENSE

Application Fee $135.00

Please attach Certificates of Licensure from state or states where held.

1. Legal name of Applicant _____ Age _____ Sex _____

 Name as you want to appear on your license _____

 Marital Status _____ Spouse's Name _____

2. Residence Address of Applicant
 _____
 (Number/Street)   (City)   (State)

 _____
 (County)   (Zip)   (Home Phone)   (Other Phone)

3. Physical Business Address of Applicant
 _____
 (Street/Bldg/Suite Number)   (City)   (County)

 _____
 (PO Boxy)   (City)   (State)   (Zip)   (Office Phone)   (Office Fax)

Real Estate Training Institute – Pre Exam Workbook

4. Do you understand the requirements of the real estate license laws as to maintaining a definite place of business within Mississippi and prominent display of your Mississippi Real Estate license?
_____

5. Do you certify that if granted a license, you will comply with the requirements in item # 4?
 ____Yes _____ No

6. Have you ever held a real estate license as a:

BROKER _____ Where? _____
                              (Street/Bldg/Suite Number)   *(City)*   *(County)*   *(State)*   *(From)*   *(To)*

SALESPERSON _____ Where? _____
                              (Street/Bldg/Suite Number)   *(City)*   *(County)*   *(State)*

Rev. 01/01/07

7. Have you ever applied for a real estate license in the state of Mississippi? _____ Yes ____No

8. Have you ever been denied a real estate license in this or any other state? _____ Yes_____No
(If Yes, furnish a statement of details)

9. Has ANY license ever held by you been revoked or suspended in this or any other state? ____Yes__No

_____
(From)   *(To)*

(This refers to any license for any business or profession regulated by law in this or any other state, district or possession of the United States. If YES, furnish a statement of details)

10.a. What has been your business or occupation for the past five (5) years? Give places where employed for sixty (60) days or more and account for entire time. If self-employed, list nature of your business and address.

_____
(Employer) (Street & Number) (City) (State)

_____
(Employer) (Street & Number) (City) (State)

_____
(Employer) (Street & Number) (City) (State)

From _____ To _____
(Month/Year)   (Month/Year)

From _____ To _____
(Month/Year)   (Month/Year)

From _____ To _____
(Month/Year)   (Month/Year)

10.b. Give complete summary of real estate experience, advise whether or not you have operated under a City or County Real Estate Privilege Licensure, where obtained and the date or dates of purchase. Disclose all

Real Estate Training Institute – Pre Exam Workbook

states in which you have held or currently hold a real estate license and furnish a Certification of Licensure from the state or states.
_____
_____
_____

11. What business, other than real estate, do you expect to engage in and what is the address thereof? _____

12. State if you have ever been convicted of any criminal offense. ____ Yes ____ No *(If Yes, furnish details)*

13.a. Has anyone ever obtained a judgment against you in any court involving real estate? ____ Yes ____ No *(If Yes, furnish details)*

13.b. Taken bankruptcy? _____ Yes _____ No *(If Yes, furnish petition for voluntary bankruptcy, schedules and discharge)*

14. Are you an American Citizen? _____ Yes _____ No

If not, how long have you lived in the United States? _____ Where were you born_____

15. When were you born? _____
   (Mo.Day   Yr.)

16. How long, immediately prior to date of execution of this application, have you been a resident of Mississippi? _____

17. Give the name of the city, county and state where you are registered to vote._____
   (City)   (State)   (County)

18. Social Security Number   _____

19. Do you have a Mississippi Driver's license? ____ Yes _____ No   If Yes, furnish number _____

If No, please explain _____

20. Have you ever purchases a Mississippi Car Tag? _____ Yes _____ No   I

f Yes, furnish number _____

21. Did you file a Mississippi Income Tax Return last year? _____ Yes _____ No

If No, please explain _____

22. Give the name and addresses of the banks you have accounts with.

_____
(Bank)   *(Street & Number)*   *(City)*   *(State)*   *(Zip)*

(   ) Checking   (   ) Savings   (   ) Loans   (   ) Credit Cards

_____
(Bank)   *(Street & Number)*   *(City)*   *(State)*   *(Zip)*

Real Estate Training Institute – Pre Exam Workbook

(   ) Checking   (   ) Savings   (   ) Loans   (   ) Credit Cards

_____
(Bank)   (Street & Number)   (City)   (State)   (Zip)

(   ) Checking   (   ) Savings   (   ) Loans   (   ) Credit Cards

AFFIDA VIT (READ CAREFULLY)

The undersigned, in making this application to the Mississippi Real Estate Commission for license to carry on the business of real estate Broker under the provisions of the Mississippi Real Estate Broker's License Act of 1954, as Amended, swears (or affirms) that he/she has read and is thoroughly familiar with the provisions of the aforementioned Act, and Rules and Regulations issued by the Commission, and agrees to comply fully with them. The undersigned further swears (or affirms) that all of the information given in this application is true and correct to the best of his/her knowledge and belief. Under Section 73- 35-5 (3) his/her application and other information submitted to this Commission may be reviewed by members of the general public under reasonable rule and regulations shall be prescribed by the Commission. I hereby authorize any financial institution, educational institution, or any other agency, public or private, federal or state, to release any information contained in their files to the Mississippi Real Estate Commission.

Signature of Applicant _____ **Subscribed and sworn** to before me, this

_____ day of 20 _____. My Commission expires _____

_____
Rev. 01/01/07

Notary Public CountyState

RECOMMENDATION OF THREE REAL ESTATE OWNERS

The following recommendations must be signed by three (3) citizens who have been property owners for at least three (3)years and who have known the applicant for at least three (3) years.

"I certify that I am a citizen of Mississippi, have been a property owner for at least three (3) years, and I am not related to the applicant. The applicant bears a good reputation for honesty and trustworthiness, therefore, I recommend that a real estate license be granted to the applicant."

Signature _____

Address _____
(Street & Number)   (City) (State)   (Zip)

Print Name _____

Signature _____

Address _____
(Street & Number)   (City) (State)   (Zip)

Print Name _____

Signature _____

Real Estate Training Institute – Pre Exam Workbook

Address _____
(Street & Number) (City) (State)   (Zip)

Print Name _____

REAL ESTATE EDUCATION

List below courses you have completed to satisfy the education requirements. The original certificate, grade form or transcript, certified copy thereof, must be attached.

COURSE

PROVIDER/INSTITUTION

NUMBER OF HOURS

Rev. 01/01/07

ATTACH PHOTOS BELOW

Full Face View

Profile Face View

Application **MUST** be accompanied by the following items:

1.　College transcripts or Certificates of Completion from Mississippi Approved Pre-Licensing Education Provider

2.　Proper Fee of $135.00

3.　Photos – Full Face and Profile Views

4.　Make sure signatures are **NOTARIZED** with seal where required.

5.　**ALL** questions must be answered to ensure prompt processing.

6.　If you have held or hold a Real Estate License in any other state, you **MUST** enclose a *Certification of Licensure* **(NOT A COPY OF ANY REAL ESTATE LICENSE).**

7.　Letter from Broker (if presently employed as a salesperson)

8.　Letter from bank regarding your handling of financial obligations with that institution.

Real Estate Training Institute – Pre Exam Workbook

Rev. 01/01/07

RESIDENT SALESPERSON APPLICATION *NOT EXACT COPY
Application to apply for a Resident Salesperson real estate license.

Mississippi Real Estate Commission
2506 Lakeland Drive, Suite 300
Flowood, MS 39232 OR
Post Office Box 12685 Jackson, MS 39236-2685
(601) 932-6770 – Telephone * (601) 932-2990 – Fax

www.mrec.ms.gov

APPLICATION FOR RESIDENT SALESPERSON LICENSE

Application Fee $110.00

1. Legal name of Applicant _____ Age_____ Sex_____

   Name as you want to appear on your license: _____

2. Residence Address of Applicant_____
                                             (Number/Street)   (City)

   _____
   (County)   (State)   (Zip)   (Home Phone)   (Other Phone)

3. Marital Status _____Spouse's Name _____

4. Name Of Employer to be designated on license_____
                                                     (Broker, Company, etc.)

4A. Physical address of Employer_____
                         (Street and Number)

   _____
   (P.O. Box)

   _____
   (City)   (County)   (State)   (Zip Code)   (Telephone Number)

5. Have you ever held a real estate License in Mississippi or any other state? Yes_____ No_____ (If answer is yes, please attach certification of licensure.)

A Broker_____ Where_____
              (Street and No.)   (City)   (County)   (State)   (From)   (To)

A Salesperson_____ Where_____
              (Street and No.)   (City)   (County)   (State)   (From)   (To)

Real Estate Training Institute – Pre Exam Workbook

6. Have you ever before applied for a real estate License in the State of Mississippi? Yes_____ No_____

7. Have you ever been denied a real estate license in this or any other state? Yes___ No___ (If answer is "Yes" furnish statement of details)

8. Has ANY license ever held by you been revoked or suspended, in this or any other state? Yes___ No___ (If answer is "Yes" furnish statement of details)   (This refers on any license for any business or profession regulated by law in this or any other state, or district or possession of the United States.)

9. What has been your business or occupation for past five years? Give places where employed for sixty days or more, and account for entire time. If self-employed, list nature of business and address.

_____ From_____ To_____ (Employer)   (Street &
(Number)   (City)   (State)   (Mo. & Yr.)   (Mo. & Yr.)

_____ From_____ To_____ (Employer)   (Street &
(Number)   (City)   (State)   (Mo. & Yr.)   (Mo. & Yr.)

_____ From_____ To_____ (Employer)   (Street &
(Number)   (City)   (State)   (Mo. & Yr.)   (Mo. & Yr.)

_____ From_____ To_____ (Employer)   (Street &
(Number)   (City)   (State)   (Mo. & Yr.)   (Mo. & Yr.)

10. Years Education (Circle highest school year completed) 1 2 3 4 5 6 7 8 9 10 11 12 13 14 15 16 17 18 19 20

11. What business other than real estate, do you expect to engage in, and what is the address of such business? ___ _____

12. Give the **names and address of three** business person who have known you for the last five years. Relatives should not be listed.
_____
_____
_____

13. Have you ever been convicted of any criminal offense or entered a plea of guilty/nolo contend ere? Yes_____ No_____
(if answer is "**Yes**" furnish a detail statement of all facts)

14. Has anyone every obtained a judgment against you? Yes____ No____
(if answer is "**Yes**" furnish a detail statement of all facts)

15. Are you an American Citizen? Yes_____ No_____

16. Have you ever declared bankruptcy? Yes_____ No_____
(If answer is "**Yes**" furnish petition for voluntary bankruptcy schedules and discharge)

17. When were you born? _____ Where? _____
           (Mo. Day   Yr.)   (City)   (County)   (State)

18. How long, immediately prior to date of the execution of this application, have you been a resident of Mississippi?
_____

19. Social Security Number: _____

20. Did you file a Mississippi Income Tax return last year? Yes_____ No_____ If answer is "No" please explain:

Real Estate Training Institute – Pre Exam Workbook

_____

21. Do you have a Mississippi Driver's license? Yes_____ No_____   If **"Yes"** furnish number_____

22. Give the name and addresses of the banks you have accounts with.

_____
(Bank)   (Street & Number)   (City)   (Zip Code)

( ) Checking   ( ) Savings   ( ) Loans   ( ) Credit Cards

_____
(Bank)   (Street & Number)   (City)   (Zip Code)

( ) Checking   ( ) Savings   ( ) Loans   ( ) Credit Cards

RECOMMENDATION OF THREE REAL ESTATE OWNERS
(Must be in addition to references listed on preceding page)

The following recommendation must be signed by three citizens, real estate owners, not related to the applicant, who own real estate.

(DO NOT USE THE SAME INDIVIDUALS AS USED IN ITEM 12.)

I certify that I own real estate and I have known the applicant for at least 1 month, and that the applicant named herein, is a resident of Mississippi, bears a good reputation for honesty, competency, and fair dealings. I recommend that a license be granted to applicant to engage in the business of real estate as stated in the business of real estate as stated in the foregoing application.

Signature_____ Address_____
                                                (Street and Number)   (City)   (State)
Print Name _____

Signature_____ Address_____
                                                (Street and Number)   (City)   (State)
Print Name _____

Signature_____ Address_____
                                                (Street and Number)   (City)   (State)
Print Name _____

TO BE COMPLETED BY RESPIONSIBLE (SPONSORING) BROKER

Responsible Broker's comments regarding applicant's qualifications, integrity and character: _____

_____

_____

_____

_____

AFFIDAVIT OF SPONSORING BROKER (Read Carefully)

The undersigned hereby swears (or affirms) that I am the sponsoring broker of the applicant, that , in my opinion, the applicant is honest and trustworthy, that I have thoroughly discussed with the applicant the conditions under which the applicant's license may be revoked or suspended under the provisions of Section 73-35-21, Mississippi Code of 1972, as amended, as well as the Rules and Regulations of the Mississippi Real

Real Estate Training Institute – Pre Exam Workbook

Estate Commission and am convinced that the applicant understands said provisions and Rules and Regulations, and hereby recommend that a license be granted to the applicant.

_____ Signature of Sponsoring Broker

Subscribed and sworn to before me, this _____ day of _____ 20_____

My Commission expires_____

_____
Notary Public   County   State

REAL ESTATE EDUCATION

List below courses you have completed to satisfy the educational requirements. The original certificate, grade form or transcript, certified copy thereof, must be attached (Copies unless certified cannot be accepted.

Course _____ _____

Provider/Institution _____ _____

No. of Hours _____ _____

ATTACH PHOTOS BELOW

Full Face View

Profile Face View

Application **MUST** be accompanied by the following items:

1. College transcripts or Certificates of Completion from Mississippi Approved Pre-Licensing Education Provider

2. Proper Fee of $110.00

3. Photos – Full Face and Profile Views

4. Make sure signatures are **NOTARIZED** with seal where required.

5. **ALL** questions must be answered to ensure prompt processing.

6. If you have held or hold a Real Estate License in any other state, you **MUST** enclose a *Certification of Licensure* **(NOT A COPY OF ANY REAL ESTATE LICENSE).**

AFFIDAVIT

(Read Carefully) The undersigned, in making this application to the Mississippi Real Estate Commission for license to carry on the business of real estate Salesperson under the provisions of the Mississippi Real Estate Broker's License Act of 1954, as Amended, swears (or affirms) that he or she has read and is thoroughly familiar with the provisions of the aforementioned Act, and Rules and Regulations issued by the Commission, and agrees to comply fully with them. The

Real Estate Training Institute – Pre Exam Workbook

undersigned further swears (or affirms) that all of the information given in this application is true and correct to the best of his or her knowledge and belief. Under Section 73-35-5 (3) all records kept in the office of the Commission are a matter of Public Record. Therefore, this application and other information submitted to this Commission may be reviewed by members of the general public under reasonable rules and regulations as shall be prescribed the Commission. I hereby authorize financial institutions, educational institutions, or other agencies, public or private, federal or state, to release any information contained in their files to the Mississippi Real Estate Commission.

Signature of Applicant _____ Subscribed and sworn to before me, this _____ day of _____ 20 _____

My commission expires:_____

_____
Notary Public
County State

Real Estate Training Institute – Leslie Clauson

WORKING WITH A REAL ESTATE BROKER
To be completed by every client or customer at first contact with a real estate licensee.

WORKING WITH A
REAL ESTATE BROKER
THIS IS NOT A LEGALLY BINDING CONTRACT

Approved 01/2003 by MS Real Estate Commission P. O. Box 12685 Jackson, MS 39232

GENERAL

Before you begin working with any real estate agent, you should know whom the agent represents in the transaction. Mississippi real estate licensees are required to disclose which party they represent in a transaction and to allow a party the right to choose or refuse among the various agency relationships.

There are several types of relationships that are possible and you should understand these at the time a broker or salesperson provides specific assistance to you in a real estate transaction,

The purpose of the Agency Disclosure is to document an acknowledgement that the consumer has been informed of various agency relationships, which are available in a real estate transaction.

For the purpose of this disclosure, the term seller and/or buyer will also include those other acts specified in Section 73-35-3 (1), of the Miss. Code, "...list, sell, purchase, exchange, rent, lease, manage, or auction any real estate, or the improvements thereon including options."

SELLER'S AGENT

A seller can enter into a "listing agreement" with a real estate firm authorizing the firm and its agent(s) to represent the seller in finding a buyer for his property. A licensee who is engaged by and acts as the agent of the Seller only is known as a Seller's Agent. A Seller's agent has the following duties and obligations:

To the Seller:
*The fiduciary duties of loyalty, confidentiality, obedience, disclosure, full accounting and the duty to use skill, care and diligence.

To the Buyer and Seller:
*A duty of honesty and fair dealing. *A duty to disclose all facts known to the Seller's agent materially affecting the value of the property, which are not known to, or readily observable by, the parties in a transaction.

Real Estate Training Institute – Pre Exam Workbook

BUYER'S AGENT

A buyer may contract with an agent or firm to represent him/her. A licensee who is engaged by and acts as the agent of the Buyer only is known as the Buyer's Agent.

If a Buyer wants an agent to represent him in purchasing a property, the buyer can enter into a Buyer's Agency Agreement with the agent. A Buyer's Agent has the following duties and obligations:

To the Buyer:
The fiduciary duties of loyalty, confidentiality, obedience, disclosure, full accounting and the duty to use skill, care and diligence.

To the Seller and Buyer:
*A duty of honesty and fair dealing.

DISCLOSED DUAL AGENT

A real estate agent or firm may represent more than one party in the same transaction. A Disclosed Dual Agent is a licensee who, with the informed written consent of the Seller and Buyer, is engaged as an agent for both Seller and Buyer.

As a disclosed dual agent, the licensee shall not represent the interests of one party to the exclusion or detriment of the interests of the other party. A disclosed dual agent has all the fiduciary duties to the Seller and Buyer that a Seller's or Buyer's agent has except the duties of full disclosure and undivided loyalty.

A Disclosed Dual Agent may not disclose:

(a) To the Buyer that the Seller will accept less than the asking or listed price, unless otherwise instructed in writing by the Seller.

(b) To the Seller that the Buyer will pay a price greater than the price submitted in a written offer to the Seller, unless otherwise instructed in writing by the Buyer.

(e) The motivation of any party for selling, buying, or leasing a property, unless otherwise instructed in writing by the respective party, or

(d) That a Seller or Buyer will agree to financing terms other than those offered, unless otherwise instructed in writing by the respective Party.

IMPORTANT NOTICE!

"Customer" shall mean that person not represented in a real estate transaction. It may be the buyer, seller, landlord or tenant.

A Buyer may decide to work with a firm that is acting as agent for the Seller (a Seller's Agent or subagent). If a Buyer does not enter into a Buyer Agency Agreement with the firm that shows him properties, that firm and its agents may show the buyer properties as an agent or subagent working on the seller's behalf. Such a firm represents the Seller (not the Buyer) and must disclose that fact to the Buyer.

When it comes to the price and terms of an offer, the Seller's Agent will ask you to decide how much to offer for any property and upon what terms and conditions. They can explain your options to you, but the final decision is yours, as they cannot give you legal or financial advice. They will attempt to show you property in the price range and category you desire so that you will have information on which to base your decision.

The Seller's Agent will present to the Seller any written offer that you ask them to present.

You should keep to yourself any information that you do not want the Seller to know (i.e. the price you are willing to pay, other terms you are willing to accept, and your motivation for buying). The Seller's agent is required to tell all such information to the Seller.

You should not furnish the Seller's agent anything you do not want the Seller to know. If you desire, you may obtain the representation of an attorney or another real estate agent, or both.

LICENSEE -Provide a copy of disclosure acknowledgement to all parties and retain signed original for your files. SPC 01/2003   MREC Rev 01/2003

THIS IS NOT A CONTRACT. THIS IS AN ACKNOWLEDGEMENT OF DISCLOSURE

The below named Licensee has informed me that brokerage services are being provided me as a:
Client ☐☐
Client ☐☐
Client

(Seller's or Landlords Agent)

(Buyer's or Tenants Agent)
☐☐
Customer
(Not as my Agent)

(Disclosed Dual Agent)

By signing below, I acknowledge that I received this informative document and explanation prior to the exchange of confidential information which might affect the bargaining position in a real estate transaction involving me.

Real Estate Training Institute – Pre Exam Workbook

DUAL AGENCY CONFIRMATION
To be attached to all offers and contracts in dual agency situations.

DUAL AGENCY CONFIRMATION
Adopted Form of
The Mississippi Real Estate Commission Jackson, MS

Seller: _____

Buyer: _____

Property: _____

This Dual Agency Confirmation is an addendum to and made part of the Offer to Purchase dated
_____, 20____, between the above-captioned Seller and Buyer for the purchase of the specifically identified property.

The undersigned acknowledges that the licensee has explained dual agency representation to them and they have received the following information regarding disclosed dual agency:

1. A disclosed dual agent is a licensee who, with the informed written consent of Seller and Buyer, is engaged as an agent for both Seller and buyer.

2. As a disclosed dual agent the licensee shall not represent the interests of one party to the exclusion or detriment of the interests of the other party. A disclosed dual agent has all the fiduciary duties to the Seller and Buyer that a Seller's or Buyer's agent has except the duties of full disclosure and undivided loyalty.

3. A disclosed dual agent may NOT disclose:
(a) To the Buyer that the Seller will accept less than the asking or listed price, unless otherwise instructed in writing by the Seller;
(b) To the Seller that the Buyer will pay a price greater than the price submitted in a written offer to the Seller, unless otherwise instructed in writing by the Buyer;
(c) The motivation of the Seller or Buyer for selling, buying or leasing a property, unless otherwise instructed in writing by the respective party or
(d) That a Seller or Buyer will agree to financing terms other than those offered unless instructed in writing by the respective party.

Real Estate Training Institute – Pre Exam Workbook

Seller and Buyer hereby confirm that they give their informed consent to the disclosed dual agency of:

Name of Brokerage Firm   **Name of Licensee**

Name of Licensee
who represent both Seller and Buyer in this transaction.

Date:_____ Seller: _____ Seller (print name):_____

Date:_____ Buyer: _____ Buyer (print name):_____

This Dual Agency Confirmation form is Seller, Buyer and Property specific. It has been adopted by the Mississippi Real Estate Commission and is required to be used by real estate licensees pursuant to Rule IV. E. of the Rules and Regulations. MREC-AD2 [Feb. 2001

Real Estate Training Institute – Pre Exam Workbook

PROPERTY CONDITION DISCLOSURE STATEMENT
(EFFECTIVE JULY 1, 2008)

INFORMATIONAL STATEMENT FOR MISSISSIPPI PROPERTY CONDITION DISCLOSURE STATEMENT (EFFECTIVE JULY 1, 2008)

In accordance with Sections 89-1-501 through 89-1-527 of the Mississippi Code of 1954, as amended, effective July 1, 2005, a **TRANSFEROR** of real property consisting of not less than one (1) nor more than four (4) dwelling units shall provide a Property Condition Disclosure Statement when the transfer is by, or with the aid of, a duly licensed real estate broker or salesperson. The required Property Condition Disclosure Statement shall be in the form promulgated by the Mississippi Real Estate Commission (MREC) or on another form that contains the identical information. The MREC Form may be found at www.mrec.ms.gov.

RIGHTS OF PURCHASER AND CONSEQUENCES FOR FAILURE TO DISCLOSE

If the Property Condition Disclosure Statement is delivered **after** the Transferee has made an offer, the transferee may terminate any resulting real estate contract or withdraw any offer for a time period of three (3) days after the delivery in person or five (5) days after the delivery by deposit in mail. This termination or withdrawal will always be without penalty to the Transferee and any deposit or earnest money must be promptly returned to the prospective purchaser (despite any agreement to the contrary).

DUTY OF LICENSEE AND CONSEQUENCES OF FAILURE TO FULFILL SUCH DUTIES

The Mississippi Statute requires real estate licensees to inform their clients of those clients' duties and rights in connection with the Property Condition Disclosure Statement. The failure of any licensee to inform their client of the clients' responsibilities could subject the licensee (salesperson and broker) to censure, suspension, or revocation of their respective real estate licenses. The licensee is not liable for any error, inaccuracy or omission in a Property Condition Disclosure Statement **unless** the licensee has actual knowledge of the error, inaccuracy or omission by the Transferor.

IMPORTANT PROVISIONS OF THE LAW

The Property Condition Disclosure Statement should not be considered a warranty by the Transferor. **The Property Condition Disclosure Statement is **NOT intended to become a part of any contract between the Transferor(s) and the Transferee(s) and it is for "disclosure" purposes only. **The Property Condition Disclosure Statement may not be used as a substitute for an inspection by a licensed home inspector or for other home warranties that the Transferor or Transferee may obtain. **Any **Appliances or Items deemed to be Personal Property** should be negotiated by the Seller and the Buyer in the Contract for the Purchase and Sale of Real Estate and all ownership rights should be transferred by a Bill of Sale or other appropriate contractual instrument. This Property Condition Disclosure Statement is not part of the Contract of Sale. **Nothing in this law precludes the rights and duties of the Transferee to inspect the property.

EXEMPTIONS

Section 89-1-501 (2) <a through i> stipulates specific exemptions from the requirement of providing a Property Condition Disclosure Statement by the Transferor of residential property. They include:

**Transfers pursuant to a court order, a writ of execution, a foreclosure sale, a bankruptcy, an eminent domain proceeding, transfers from a decree for specific performance, transfers by a mortgagor who is in default, any sale pursuant to a decree of foreclosure or by means of a deed in lieu of foreclosure, transfer by the administration of a decedent's estate, a guardianship, a conservatorship or a trust.

**Transfers from one co-owner to another, transfers from one spouse to another, transfers to a person in the lineal line of consanguinity, transfers to or from governmental entities or transfers on which no dwelling is located.

If the Transferor has NOT OCCUPIED the dwelling but, during the period of ownership, the Transferor has requested or authorized any repairs, replaced any of the mechanical equipment, has initiated any action or activity which could be documented on the Disclosure Statement or has actual knowledge of information which might impact a transferee's decision to purchase the residence, Transferors are obligated to complete those specific portions of the Disclosure Statement which are applicable to that information.

The Transferor is **REQUIRED** to sign the Disclosure Statement when the transaction is finalized to **confirm that there have been no material changes to the property.**

CONFIRMATION OF UNDERSTANDING

_____
SELLER (UPON LISTING) DATE

_____
SELLER (UPON LISTING) DATE

_____
REPRESENTING THE SELLER(S)

_____
BUYER(BEFORE OFFER)   DATE

_____
BUYER(BEFORE OFFER)   DATE

_____
REPRESENTING THE BUYER(S)

Page 1 of 3

Real Estate Training Institute – Pre Exam Workbook

PROPERTY CONDITION DISCLOSURE STATEMENT
To be completed by the seller with the listing of any residence.

PROPERTY CONDITION DISCLOSURE STATEMENT

THE FOLLOWING IS A PROPERTY CONDITION DISCLOSURE REQUIRED BY SECTIONS 89-1-507 THROUGH 89-1-527 OF THE MISSISSIPPI REAL ESTATE BROKERS ACT OF 1954, AS AMENDED, AND MADE BY THE **SELLER(S)** CONCERNING THE CONDITION OF THE **RESIDENTIAL PROPERTY** LOCATED AT:

_____

SELLER(S):_____ APPROXIMATE AGE OF THE RESIDENCE_____

THIS DISCLOSURE IS NOT A WARRANTY OF ANY KIND BY THE SELLER OR ANY REAL ESTATE AGENT OF THE SELLER IN THIS TRANSACTION AND IS NOT A SUBSTITUTE FOR ANY INSPECTIONS OR WARRANTIES THE PURCHASER MAY WISH TO OBTAIN. THIS STATEMENT MAY BE MADE AVAILABLE TO OTHER PARTIES AND **IS TO BE ATTACHED TO THE LISTING AGREEMENT AND SIGNED BY THE SELLER(S).**

TO THE SELLER(S): PLEASE COMPLETE THE FOLLOWING FORM, INCLUDING ANY PAST HISTORY OF PROBLEMS, IF KNOWN. IF THE CONDITION OR QUESTION DOES NOT APPLY TO YOUR PROPERTY, MARK WITH "N/A".

IF THE RESIDENCE IS NEW/PROPOSED RESIDENTIAL CONSTRUCTION, THE **BUILDER** SHOULD COMPLETE THE PROPERTY CONDITION DISCLOSURE STATEMENT AND REFERENCE SPECIFIC PLANS/SPECIFICATIONS, MATERIALS LISTS AND/OR CHANGE ORDERS.

DO NOT LEAVE ANY BLANK SPACES. ATTACH ADDITIONAL PAGES IF NECESSARY. THIS FORM MAY BE DUPLICATED BUT NOT ALTERED
STRUCTURAL ITEMS:

A. BUILDING CODE:

WAS THE RESIDENCE BUILT IN CONFORMITY WITH AN APPROVED BUILDING CODE? YES ____ NO ____ UNKNOWN _____ IF YES,

WAS IT INSPECTED BY A CITY/COUNTY CODE ENFORCEMENT INSPECTOR? YES ____ NO ____ UNKNOWN _____

Real Estate Training Institute – Pre Exam Workbook

Has a Mississippi Licensed Home Inspector completed a Home Inspection

REPORT? YES ____ NO ____

B. STRUCTURAL ITEMS:

ARE YOU AWARE OF ANY FOUNDATION REPAIRS MADE IN THE PAST? YES ____ NO ____
EXPLAIN _____

ARE ANY FOUNDATION REPAIRS CURRENTLY NEEDED? YES ____ NO ____ EXPLAIN
_____

C. HISTORY OF INFESTATION, IF ANY: TERMITES, CARPENTER ANTS, ETC:

ANY EVIDENCE OF ROT, MILDEW, VERMIN, RODENTS, TERMITES, CARPENTER ANTS, OR OTHER INFESTATION? YES ____ NO ____

HAVE YOU REQUESTED TREATMENTS FOR ANY TYPE OF INFESTATIONS? YES ____ NO ____ EXPLAIN_____

ARE YOU AWARE OF ANY REPAIRED DAMAGE? YES ____ NO____; IF YES, PLEASE DESCRIBE_____

IS THERE CURRENTLY AN OUTSTANDING TERMITE CONTRACT? YES ____ NO ____

WHO IS THE CONTRACTOR? _____

D. ROOF:

HAS THE ROOF BEEN REPLACED OR REPAIRED DURING YOUR OWNERSHIP? YES ____ NO ____; IF YES, WHEN? _____

DURING YOUR OWNERSHIP HAVE THERE BEEN ANY LEAKS, WATER BACK UPS, OR PROBLEMS WITH THE ROOF? YES ____ NO ____

THE ROOF IS ____ YEARS OLD.

E. LAND AND SITE DATA:

IS THERE AN ENGINEER'S SURVEY AVAILABLE? YES ____ NO ____

DATE THE SURVEY WAS COMPLETED_____

Real Estate Training Institute – Pre Exam Workbook

ARE YOU AWARE OF THE EXISTENCE OF ANY OF THE FOLLOWING, TO WIT:

ENCROACHMENTS: YES __ NO __ UNKNOWN __

FLOOD ZONE: YES __ NO __ UNKNOWN __

EASEMENTS: YES __ NO __ UNKNOWN __

SOIL/EROSION: YES __ NO __ UNKNOWN __

SOIL PROBLEMS: YES __ NO __ UNKNOWN __

SUBSOIL PROBLEM: YES__ NO__ UNKNOWN___

STANDING WATER: YES __ NO __ UNKNOWN __

LAND FILL: YES__ NO__ UNKNOWN___

ARE YOU AWARE OF ANY CURRENT ZONING REGULATIONS WHICH WILL CAUSE THE RESIDENCE TO BE CONSIDERED A NONCONFORMING USAGE (LOT SIZE, SET BACKS, ETC) YES ___ NO ___

IF YES, PLEASE EXPLAIN _____

ARE THERE ANY RIGHTS-OF-WAY, EASEMENTS, EMINENT DOMAIN PROCEEDINGS OR SIMILAR MATTERS WHICH MAY NEGATIVELY IMPACT YOUR OWNERSHIP INTEREST IN THE RESIDENCE? YES ___ NO ___

IF YES, PLEASE EXPLAIN _____

FOR ANY REASON, HAS ANY PORTION OF THE RESIDENCE EVER SUFFERED WATER DAMAGE? YES ___ NO ___

IF YES, PLEASE EXPLAIN IN DETAIL _____

IS THE RESIDENCE CURRENTLY LOCATED IN A FEMA DESIGNATED FLOOD HAZARD ZONE? YES __ NO __ UNKNOWN ___;

IS FLOOD INSURANCE REQUIRED? YES ___ NO ___ UNKNOWN _____

IS ANY PORTION OF THE PROPERTY DESIGNATED AS A **WETLANDS AREA?** YES ___ NO ___ UNKNOWN _____

F. ADDITIONS/REMODELS:

DURING YOUR PERIOD OF OWNERSHIP, HAVE THERE BEEN ANY ADDITIONS, REMODELING, STRUCTURAL CHANGES OR ALTERATIONS TO THE RESIDENCE? YES ___ NO ___

IF YES, PLEASE EXPLAIN _____

NAME OF THE LICENSED CONTRACTOR_____

WERE ALL WORK PERMITS AND APPROVALS IN COMPLIANCE WITH THE LOCAL BUILDING CODES? YES ___ NO ___

PLEASE EXPLAIN _____

G. STRUCTURE/WALLS/WINDOWS:

HAS THERE BEEN ANY DAMAGE TO THE STRUCTURE AS A RESULT OF FIRE, WINDSTORM, TORNADOS, HURRICANE OR ANY OTHER NATURAL DISASTER? YES ___ NO ___ IF YES, PLEASE EXPLAIN _____

HAVE YOU EVER EXPERIENCED ANY PROBLEMS WITH WALLS, SIDING OR WINDOWS? YES ___ NO ___ EXPLAIN _____

H. OTHER:

ARE YOU AWARE OF ANY PROBLEMS WHICH MAY EXIST WITH THE PROPERTY BY VIRTUE OF PRIOR USAGES SUCH AS, BUT NOT LIMITED TO, **METHAMPHETAMINE LABS**, HAZARDOUS/TOXIC WASTE DISPOSAL, THE PRESENCE OF ASBESTOS COMPONENTS, LEAD-BASED PAINT, UREA-FORMALDEHYDE INSULATION, MOLD, RADON GAS, UNDERGROUND TANKS OR ANY PAST INDUSTRIAL USES OF THE PREMISES? YES ___ NO ___

IF "YES, PLEASE EXPLAIN _____

SELLER'S INITIALS _____ PAGE 2 OF 3 PURCHASER'S INITIALS _____

MECHANICAL ITEMS:

ELECTRICAL SYSTEM/PLUMBING SYSTEM:

Real Estate Training Institute – Pre Exam Workbook

ARE YOU AWARE OF ANY PROBLEMS OR CONDITIONS THAT AFFECT THE DESIRABILITY OR FUNCTIONALITY OF THE HEATING, COOLING, ELECTRICAL, PLUMBING, OR MECHANICAL SYSTEMS? YES ___ NO ___

IF YES, PLEASE EXPLAIN ALL KNOWN PROBLEMS IN COMPLETE DETAIL
_____

WATER, SEWER, & SEPTIC ITEMS:

WATER:

THE WATER SUPPLY IS: PUBLIC ____ PRIVATE ___ ON-SITE WELL ___ NEIGHBOR'S WELL ___ COMMUNITY ____

IF YOUR DRINKING WATER IS FROM A WELL, WHEN WAS THE WATER QUALITY LAST CHECKED FOR SAFETY, WHAT WERE THE RESULTS OF THE TEST AND WHO CONDUCTED THE TEST? _____

IS THE WATER SUPPLY EQUIPPED WITH A WATER SOFTENER? YES ____ NO ____ UNKNOWN ____

THE SEWAGE SYSTEM IS: PUBLIC ___ PRIVATE ___ SEPTIC ___ CESSPOOL ___ TREATMENT PLANT ___ OTHER ____

IS THERE A SEWAGE PUMP INSTALLED? YES ___ NO ___

DATE OF THE LAST SEPTIC INSPECTION _____

ARE YOU AWARE OF ANY LEAKS, BACK-UPS, OR OTHER PROBLEMS RELATING TO ANY OF THE PLUMBING, WATER, SEWAGE, OR RELATED ITEMS DURING YOUR OWNERSHIP? YES ___ NO ___.

IF YES, PLEASE EXPLAIN _____

OTHER MATTERS/ITEMS:

MISCELLANEOUS:

IS THE RESIDENCE SITUATED ON LEASEHOLD OR SIXTEENTH SECTION LAND? YES ___ NO ___ EXPLAIN _____

IS THERE ANY EXISTING OR THREATENING LEGAL ACTION AFFECTING THE PROPERTY?
YES ___ NO ___ EXPLAIN_____

ARE YOU AWARE OF ANY VIOLATIONS OF LOCAL/STATE/FEDERAL LAWS/REGULATIONS RELATING TO THE PROPERTY? YES ___ NO ___

ARE YOU AWARE OF ANY HIDDEN DEFECTS OR NEEDED REPAIRS ABOUT WHICH THE PURCHASER SHOULD BE INFORMED **PRIOR** TO THEIR PURCHASE? YES ___ NO ___

IF YES, PLEASE EXPLAIN IN DETAIL _____

WHAT IS THE **APPROXIMATE SQUARE FOOTAGE** OF THE HEATED AND COOLED LIVING AREA _____

HOW WAS THIS APPROXIMATION OF SQUARE FOOTAGE DETERMINED?
_____

ARE THERE ANY FINISHED WOOD FLOORS BENEATH THE FLOOR COVERINGS? YES ___ NO ___ WHERE _____

ARE THERE ANY HOMEOWNER'S ASSOCIATION FEES ASSOCIATED WITH OWNERSHIP?
YES ___ NO ___ AMOUNT _____

IF THE PROPERTY IS A CONDOMINIUM, HOW MUCH IS THE **YEARLY** MAINTENANCE FEES
$_____

WHAT IS THE **YEARLY** REAL ESTATE TAX BILL? $_____

HOMESTEAD EXEMPTION HAS BEEN FILED FOR _____

IS THE PROPERTY SUBJECT TO **ANY** SPECIAL REAL PROPERTY TAX ASSESSMENTS YES ___ NO ___ EXPLAIN _____

IS THE PROPERTY LOCATED IN A **PUBLIC IMPROVEMENT (TAX) DISTRICT (PID)** YES ___ NO ___ UNKNOWN _____

WHAT IS THE AVERAGE **YEARLY** ELECTRIC BILL? $_____

WHAT IS THE AVERAGE **YEARLY** GAS BILL? $_____

IF THE RESIDENCE IS SERVICED BY PROPANE (LP) GAS, WHAT IS THE AVERAGE **YEARLY** PROPANE BILL? $_____

Real Estate Training Institute – Pre Exam Workbook

THE PROPANE TANK IS: OWNED _____ LEASED _____
IF LEASED, HOW MUCH IS THE LEASE PAYMENT? $_____

IS CABLE TELEVISION SERVICE AVAILABLE AT THE SITE? YES ___ NO ___ SERVICE PROVIDER _____

ARE ANY ITEMS REMAINING WITH THE RESIDENCE FINANCED SEPARATELY FROM THE MORTGAGES? YES ___ NO ___

APPLIANCES/SYSTEMS REMAINING WITH RESIDENCE:

YES NO
GAS/ELECTRIC AGE

LIST REPAIRS COMPETED IN LAST TWO (2) YEARS

ITEM

COOK-TOP
DISHWASHER
GARBAGE DISPOSAL
ICE-MAKER
MICROWAVE
OVEN(S)
TRASH COMPACTOR
VENT-FAN
OTHER ITEMS

MECHANICAL EQUIPMENT CONSIDERED PERSONAL PROPERTY SHOULD BE NEGOTIATED IN THE CONTRACT OF SALE OR OTHER SUCH INSTRUMENT IF THE ITEMS REMAIN WITH THE RESIDENCE.

TO THE EXTENT OF THE SELLER'S KNOWLEDGE AS A PROPERTY OWNER, THE SELLER(S) ACKNOWLEDGES THAT THE INFORMATION CONTAINED ABOVE IS TRUE AND ACCURATE FOR THOSE AREAS OF THE PROPERTY LISTED. THE OWNER(S) AGREE TO SAVE AND HOLD THE BROKER HARMLESS FROM ALL CLAIMS, DISPUTES, LITIGATION AND/OR JUDGMENTS ARISING FROM ANY INCORRECT INFORMATION SUPPLIED BY THE OWNER(S) OR FROM ANY MATERIAL FACT KNOWN BY THE OWNER(S) WHICH OWNER(S) FAIL TO DISCLOSE EXCEPT THE BROKER IS NOT HELD HARMLESS TO THE OWNER(S) IN CLAIMS, DISPUTES, LITIGATION, OR JUDGMENTS ARISING FROM CONDITIONS OF WHICH THE BROKER HAD ACTUAL KNOWLEDGE.

Real Estate Training Institute – Pre Exam Workbook

_____
SELLER (UPON LISTING) DATE

_____
SELLER (AT CLOSING)   DATE

_____
SELLER (UPON LISTING) DATE

_____
SELLER (AT CLOSING)   DATE

_____
PROSPECTIVE PURCHASER'S SIGNATURE
_____
PURCHASER(S) ACKNOWLEDGE RECEIPT OF REPORT DATE

MREC FORM #0100   PAGE 3 OF 3 EFFECTIVE DATE: JULY 1, 2008

Real Estate Training Institute – Pre Exam Workbook

CO-OPERATIVE AGREEMENT
Revised co-op agreement with non-resident principal broker.

COOPERATING AGREEMENT WITH NON-RESIDENT PRINCIPAL BROKER   (EFFECTIVE- JULY 1, 2004)

Date Agreement Executed: _____

Agreement Expiration Date: _____

Owner/Client/Customer's Name _____

Telephone # _____

Owner/Client/Customer's Address_____

Location/Legal Description of Listed Property (if applicable) _____

_____

AGREEMENT TO BE FINALIZED "PRIOR" TO ANY LICENSABLE REAL ESTATE ACTIVITY: It is understood and agreed that this Agreement covers: **(Please check ONLY one <1> box)**

[ ] 1. A Joint or Cross Listing with participation by a Non-resident Principal Broker
[ ] 2. A Listing Referral from a Non-resident Principal Broker
[ ] 3. A Client or Customer Referral from a Non-resident Principal Broker
[ ] 4. A Purchase or Sales Contract procured by a Non-resident Principal Broker
[ ] 5. An Auction Agreement with a Non-resident Principal Broker
[ ] 6. Any Other activity for which a real estate license is required

In order to comply with the Mississippi Real Estate Brokers License Act of 1954, as Amended, and the Rules and Regulations of the Mississippi Real Estate Commission (MREC), the Mississippi Principal Broker and the Non-resident Principal Broker agree to the following:

All negotiations, including the showing, listing, and advertising of real property located within the state of Mississippi shall be handled under the direct supervision of the Mississippi Principal Broker, with the Mississippi Principal Broker taking full responsibility. **The Non-resident Principal Broker MUST be present at all times if one of his/her real estate agents, who is NOT licensed by the state of Mississippi, has a physical presence in Mississippi in connection with any real property transaction.** The Non-resident Principal Broker agrees to abide by Mississippi Law and the Rules and Regulations of the MREC and further agrees that civil actions may be commenced against him/her in any court of competent jurisdiction in any county of this state in which a claim may arise.

The Mississippi Principal Broker **MUST** confirm that the Non-resident Principal Broker is licensed as an **"ACTIVE PRINCIPAL BROKER"** in another state. This may be accomplished by direct contact with the Real Estate Licensing authority or by receiving a copy of a current real estate broker license. The Mississippi Principal Broker further agrees to notify the MREC immediately if the Non-resident Principal Broker violates any part of this Cooperative Agreement.

The Non-resident Principal Broker agrees not to place any sign on real property located within the state of Mississippi without the express written permission of the cooperating Mississippi Principal Broker. If such authority is granted, both Principal Brokers agree their signs will be placed in close proximity to one another and in a prominent place on the property. All listing or property management agreements shall be in the name of the Mississippi Principal Broker or they shall require a cross listing or joint listing of such property with the Non-resident Principal Broker.

The Non-resident Principal Broker agrees to not advertise the property in any manner unless the Mississippi Principal Broker is included in the advertising and such advertising shall be with the full knowledge of and under the direct supervision of the Mississippi Principal Broker. The name and phone number of the Mississippi Principal Broker shall be given equal prominence with the Non-resident Principal Broker. If this cooperative agreement involves a listing agreement concerning real property, the Non-resident Principal Broker affirms that the solicitation of the listing of the Mississippi property was conducted in the presence of the Mississippi Principal Broker.

The commissions, fees, or other compensations (considerations) earned during the period this Cooperative Agreement is in force shall be divided between the Mississippi Principal Broker and the Non-resident Principal Broker on a negotiable basis that is agreeable to the two brokers. The Mississippi Principal Broker shall either receive $_____ or ____% of the compensation and the Non-resident Principal Broker shall either receive $_____ or ____% of the compensation. All earnest monies or deposits shall be placed in the escrow account of the Mississippi Principal Broker unless both the buyer and the seller agree in writing to relieve the Mississippi Principal Broker of this responsibility.

No licensee shall knowingly pay a commission or a fee to a licensed person knowing that licensee will, in turn, pay any portion of the fee to an individual who does not hold a real estate license.

_____
Mississippi Broker's Name (Print)

_____
Mississippi Broker's Signature

_____
Mailing Address

_____
City, State & Zip Code

Real Estate Training Institute – Pre Exam Workbook

_____
Business Telephone #

_____
Non-resident Principal Broker's Name (Print)

_____
Non-resident Principal Broker's Signature

_____
Mailing Address

_____
City, State & Zip Code

_____
Business Telephone #

For a **JOINT LISTING:** I hereby agree to allow the Non-resident Principal Broker to place their sign in close proximity to my sign on the above-referenced listed property during the term of this contract.

_____
Mississippi Principal Broker's Signature

Four copies of the Agreement have been executed.

The Non-resident Principal Broker and the Mississippi Principal Broker have each received one copy.

It is the duty of the Mississippi Principal Broker to **confirm that the other two copies are filed with the Mississippi Real Estate Commission** at Post Office Box 12685, Jackson, MS 39236-2685, within 10 days after entering into the agreement.

Rev. 01/01/07

Real Estate Training Institute – Pre Exam Workbook

INACTIVE STATUS ADDRESS FORM
To be used when any licensee is placing their license on "inactive" status.

Mississippi Real Estate Commission
2506 Lakeland Drive, Suite 300
Flowood, MS 39232 Post Office Box 12685 Jackson, MS 39236-2685
(601) 932-6770 – Telephone * (601) 932-2990 – Fax

www.mrec.ms.gov

INACTIVE STATUS ADDRESS FORM

$25.00 – Fee

Please maintain my real estate license on inactive status. Renewal information and other correspondence should be sent to me at the following address:

NAME: _____   LICENSE NUMBER:_____

ADDRESS: _____

_____

_____

HOME PHONE: _____ OTHER PHONE: _____

E-MAIL   _____

I understand that my license MUST be renewed when due as if I were on active status and that the Mississippi Real Estate Commission (MREC) must be notified within ten (10) days of a change of address. There is NO charge for a change of address while on inactive status. If you do not notify the MREC of changes, we have no way of contacting you and your licensing file may be CLOSED.

_____   _____
Signature   Date

Real Estate Training Institute – Leslie Clauson

CHAPTER 10

STATE EXAMS

State Final Exam One

1. Special situations, where unusual facts exist or where one or more parties involved are especially vulnerable, could require additional disclosures not contemplated. In such cases, brokers
1. should not accept to represent any party.
2. should be extra careful.
3. should seek legal advice prior to entering into an agency relationship.
4. should make sure that a notary public verifies the identity of all parties.

2. If a broker, as escrow agent, accepts a check and later finds that such check has not been honored by the bank on which it was drawn, the broker shall
1. immediately notify all parties involved in the transaction.
2. call the check writer and ask for a cashier's check.
3. immediately close the books on that transaction.
4. sue the bad check writer for specific performance.

3. Monies received in a trust account on behalf of clients or customers are not assets of the broker; however, a broker may deposit and keep in each escrow account or rental account some personal funds for the express purpose
1. of paying his office bills.
2. of paying commission
3. of covering service charges and other bank debits related to each account.
4. None of the above.

4. When the broker is agent for the seller and for any reason the seller fails or is unable to consummate the transaction, the broker has no right to any portion of the money deposited by the purchaser, even if the commission has been earned. The money must be returned to the purchaser and the broker
1. under no circumstance receive payment for his actions.
2. must sue the seller for specific performance.
3. must sue the buyer's agent for specific performance.
4. should look to the seller for compensation.

Real Estate Training Institute – Pre Exam Workbook

5. Earnest money accepted by the broker or any licensee for which the broker is responsible and upon acceptance of a mutually agreeable contract is required to deposit the money
1. into his personal account.
2. into a trust account within three business days.
3. into a safe deposit box in his office.
4. into a trust account prior to the close of business of the next banking day.

6. An agent made real estate signs to put in the front yard of his client's home. He did not put the name of his responsible broker or name of his real estate firm on the sign.
1. It's OK to have signs called "Blind Ads".
2. This is a "Blind Ad" and is in violation.
3. The agent can't put up signs.
4. None of the above.

7. When a licensee is advertising their own property for sale, purchase or exchange which is not listed with a broker, the licensee must;
1. The licensee is not allowed to sell his own property without his broker listing it.
2. The licensee does not have to state he or she is an agent.
3. The licensee must indicate he or she is licensed.
4. The licensee must not tell his broker.

8. The use of any copyrighted term or insignia on stationary, office signs, or in advertisement by any licensee not authorized to do so, will be considered
1. as "substantial misrepresentation" and cause for refusal, suspension, or revocation of the license.
2. as a "substantial material fact" and cause for refusal, suspension, or revocation of the license.
3. as a "substantial misrepresentation" and cause for a penalty of up to $2,000.
4. as a "substantial misrepresentation" and cause for a penalty of no more than $10,000.

9. A real estate broker must keep on file following its consummation complete records relating to any real estate transaction for
1. one year.
2. two years.
3. three years.
4. five years

10. Every contract must reflect whom the broker represents by statement
1. under the signatures of the parties to the contract.
2. over the signatures of the parties to the contract.
3. on the side in a hand written statement.
4. All of the above.

Real Estate Training Institute – Pre Exam Workbook

11. Broker Bob received an offer this morning for a property he has listed. Bob promptly called his client and then faxed the offer to his client. Later that day Bob received a second offer that was lower and had bad credit terms for financing. What should Broker Bob do?
1. Not present the second offer because the first offer is higher.
2. Present the second offer because the seller has not accepted the first offer and any other written offer received by the broker in a sale shall be presented to the owner.
3. Hold off on presenting the second offer until his client accepts the first offer.
4. Both 1 and 3

12. All exclusive buyer representation agreements shall be in writing and properly identify the terms and conditions under which the buyer will rely on the broker for the purchase of real estate including the sales price, the considerations to be paid, and the nature of all parties to the agreement and a definite date of expiration.
1. The exclusive buyer agreement does not have to indicate in the document that it is such an agreement.
2. Copies of the exclusive buyer's agreement do not have to be given to the buyer after signing.
3. The buyer may terminate the agreement upon fifteen (15) calendar day's written notice to the buyer's exclusive agent.
4. The exclusive buyer agreement must not clearly state that the agreement is such.

13. A real estate licensee shall deliver a true and correct copy of any instrument to any party or parties executing the same
1. within five days.
2. within 3 days.
3. immediately (at the time of signing).
4. No copies need to be given to any party.

14. When an offer is made on a property owned by a party with whom the broker has entered into a listing agreement, such broker shall document and date an acceptance or rejection of the offer and
1. make five copies.
2. then show his salespeople how he documented the information.
3. upon written request, shall provide a copy of such document to the person making the offer.
4. upon verbal request, shall provide a copy of such document to the person refusing the offer.

15. A real estate broker or salesperson in the ordinary course of his business may give an opinion as to the price of real estate for the purpose of a prospective listing or sale, however this opinion as to the listing price or sale price
1. must not refer to this as an appraisal.
2. must not take compensation.
3. Both 1 and 2
4. Neither 1 nor 2

Real Estate Training Institute – Pre Exam Workbook

16. Any licensee who fails in a timely manner to respond to official Mississippi Real Estate Commission written communication or who fails or neglects to abide by Mississippi Real Estate Commission Rules and Regulations shall be deemed
1. to irresponsible to sell real estate.
2. prima facie, to be guilty of improper dealing.
3. to be harboring a criminal.
4. on vacation.

17. Peggy, a salesperson for broker Bob listed and sold a property. Before being paid for that executed transaction, Peggy changed responsible brokers. Broker Bob
1. owes Peggy nothing.
2. must only pay Peggy's new responsible broker.
3. can pay Peggy her commission directly.
4. owes Peggy interest.

18. No licensee shall pay any part of a fee, commission or other compensation received by such licensee in buying, selling, exchanging, leasing, auctioning or renting any real estate
1. except to a licensee through the licensee's responsible broker.
2. to the customer directly as a referral fee.
3. to your neighbor for getting his brother to list with you.
4. All of the above.

19. When advertising a property shared by an out of state broker
1. the name of the Mississippi broker must be listed.
2. the name of the seller must be listed.
3. the Mississippi broker must contact the Real Estate Commission.
4. the Mississippi broker has to pay the full amount of the ad.

20. When there is a cooperative agreement with a nonresident broker, the listing or property management agreement for the Mississippi property
1. must remain in the name of the Mississippi broker.
2. must remain in the name of both brokers.
3. must remain in the name of the out of state broker.
4. must remain with no name.

21. When an agent transfers to a new broker and within 3 days gives written notice to the Commission the name of the principal broker into whose agency he is about to enter, he
1. The agent makes a notation on his license and gives it to the new broker.
2. mails his license to the Commission and a new license will be issued for the unexpired term of the original license.
3. needs to attend more ethics classes.
4. mails his license to his new broker.

Real Estate Training Institute – Pre Exam Workbook

22. Applicants for a real estate license
1. must have a responsible broker before applying for their license.
2. may take the exam but has ten days to find a responsible broker.
3. may not take the exam without a responsible broker.
4. may not send in the license fee.

23. It is not the duty of the responsible broker
1. to instruct the licensees licensed under that broker in the fundamentals of real estate practice.
2. to instruct the licensees licensed under that broker in ethics of the profession and the Mississippi Real Estate Law.
3. to exercise supervision of his licensees of their real estate activities.
4. to make sure each agent has completed their post licensing education and kept their license current.

24. A salesperson has a listing with his responsible broker, Broker A. The salesperson decided to transfer to a new broker before the listing expires. When the agent moves to the new broker, who owns the listing?
1. The agent.
2. The listing automatically gets cancelled.
3. The listing moves to the salesperson's new broker.
4. Broker A.

25. Any person who willfully and negligently does not deliver the needed disclosures shall be liable
1. and the seller has to take his property back uncontested.
2. in the amount of actual damages suffered by a transferee.
3. for up to $100,000.
4. for no more than $100,000.

26. Who are exempt from having a real estate license?
1. Brokers
2. A Public Official holding an auction.
3. A Licensee selling her own home.
4. None of the above.

27. The five Commissioners appointed by the Governor with advise and consent from the Senate have the power to do all of the following except
1. appoint a Commissioner.
2. given 15 days' notice of a hearing to a licensee when the licensee has a violation charged against him.
3. issue subpoenas for the attendance of witnesses and the production of books and papers.
4. Both 1 and 3.

Real Estate Training Institute – Pre Exam Workbook

28. Can the Real Estate Commissioners issue subpoenas?
1. No because it is a legal matter.
2. Yes because it is within the authority of the Commission's power.
3. No because they need to contact the appropriate local public official to issue such subpoenas.
4. Yes but only if there is proof of a crime being committed.

29. Licensee following notification of action resulting from a Commissioner hearing
1. has 30 days to appeal any ruling and post a required $500 bond for any costs which may be adjudged against him.
2. has 60 days to appeal any ruling and post a required $1000 bond for any expenses that may be incurred.
3. has 15 days to appeal and no bond is required.
4. has 30 days to appeal and no bond is required.

30. An earnest money deposit pertaining to a cooperative agreement must be held in escrow
1. by the nonresident broker unless both buyer and seller agree otherwise.
2. can be held by either of the brokers depending on who has a more secure trust account.
3. by the Mississippi broker unless both the buyer and seller agree in writing to relieve the Mississippi broker of this responsibility.
4. the Seller holds the earnest money deposit.

31. Notice in writing shall be given to the Commission by any real estate salesperson with a change of responsible broker within
1. 5 days
2. 3 days
3. two weeks
4. No notice is required.

32. When changing responsible brokers
1. the Commission shall issue a new license for a period of one year and when the agent completes the mandatory hours of continuing education will issue a license for 4 more years.
2. the Commission has no more than 30 days to issue a new license.
3. a new license shall thereupon be issued by the Commission to such salesperson for the unexpired term of the original license upon the return to the Commission of the license previously issued.
4. the Commission doesn't care if a salesperson changes responsible broker and no notice needs be submitted.

33. Brokers may give legal advice
1. when a client asks how to take title.
2. when a client is getting a divorce.
3. when the client is under 18.
4. never.

34. Licensees may obtain errors and omissions coverage independently if the coverage contained in the policy follows the minimum requirement of
1. a per claim limit is not less than $1,000.
2. a per claim limit is not less than $10,000.
3. a per claim limit is not less than $100,000.
4. There is no minimum limit.

35. Commissioners are vested with power of court to issue and enforce subpoenas, levy fines and
1. appoint other commissioners.
2. set commission fee limits brokers can charge a client.
3. levy jail terms.
4. None of the above.

36. All license fee funds must be submitted to the State Treasury with detailed explanation
1. on a monthly basis.
2. on a quarterly basis.
3. on a daily basis.
4. on a weekly basis.

37. Any person charged with a violation shall be given_____days notice of the hearing upon the charges filed, together with a copy of the complaint.
1. Three days
2. Five days
3. Fifteen days
4. Thirty days

38. Any person taking appeal shall post a satisfactory bond in the amount of _____ dollars for the payment of any costs which may be adjudged against him.
1. $100
2. $200
3. $400
4. $500

39. Funds received by the Commission are used to
1. fund Mississippi Real Estate Commission operations.
2. fund highway projects.
3. fund referral fees.
4. fund kickbacks.

40. Licensees who do not show proof of E and O Insurance have 30 days to correct the deficiency. If the deficiency is not corrected within the 30 days
1. the Commission will fine the responsible broker.
2. the licensee's licenses will be placed on inactive status.
3. the Commission will close the office of the licensee.
4. the Commission will do nothing.

Real Estate Training Institute – Pre Exam Workbook

State Final Exam One
1-3
2-1
3-3
4-4
5-4
6-2
7-3
8-1
9-3
10-2
11-2
12-3
13-3
14-3
15-1
16-2
17-3
18-1
19-1
20-1
21-2
22-2
23-4
24-4
25-2
26-2
27-1
28-2
29-1
30-3
31-2
32-3
33-4
34-3
35-3
36-4
37-3
38-4
39-1
40-2

Real Estate Training Institute – Pre Exam Workbook

State Final Exam Two

1. Failure to renew your license on time will result in a penalty of double fee. 30 days late, will result
1. in triple penalty.
2. in having to retake the real estate exam.
3. in having to participate with an extra 30 hours of post licensing.
4. in the license being cancelled.

2. The extent of cooperation of reciprocity with other states.
1. Vary.
2. All states are the same.
3. Neither one nor two are correct.
4. All of the above.

3. Legal action by the Commission for a violation may take the form of a fine of not more than $1,000 and or up to 90 days in jail, or both. The second violation can be
1. up to 2 years in jail.
2. a fine of $5,000.
3. up to a $2,000 fine and up to 6 months in jail or both.
4. None of the above.

4. Every applicant for a resident license as a real estate salesperson shall be
1. 21 years of age and a resident of Mississippi for 5 years.
2. 18 years of age or older and be a bona fide resident of the state of Mississippi prior to filing his application.
3. 16 years of age and a resident of Mississippi.
4. None of the above.

5. A licensee shall not be required to comply with disclosure requirements when engaged in transactions with
1. a corporation, non-profit corporation, Professional Corporation.
2. professional association, limited liability company, partnership, real estate investment trust, business trust, charitable trust, family trust.
3. any governmental entity in transactions involving real estate.
4. All of the above.

6. The responsible broker must report any licensee for whom that broker is responsible to the commission if
1. he/she believes the agent scored low on the real estate exam.
2. he/she believes that a licensee has let his/her license expire.
3. he/she believes that a licensee is slacking.
4. he/she believes that a licensee has violated laws rules or regulations.

Real Estate Training Institute – Pre Exam Workbook

7. Developers of timeshares and any of his agents cannot practice timeshare
1. without meeting registration requirements of the MREC.
2. without the developer and his employees pass a Mississippi real estate license exam.
3. unless the developer becomes a responsible broker.
4. within the state of Mississippi.

8. The MREC will issue a (timeshare) preliminary permit in 20 days
1. if the developer resides within the state of Mississippi.
2. unless deficiencies are found on the application.
3. unless the developer has over 15 employees.
4. unless the Commission is overworked.

9. A developer with a timeshare must return all payments made under the contract within
1. within 7 days of written cancellation from the purchaser.
2. as soon as the check clears the bank.
3. within 30 days of a cancellation notice.
4. within 24 hours of a cancellation notice.

10. A real estate broker must keep on file following its consummation complete records relating to any real estate transaction for
1. one year.
2. two years.
3. three years.
4. five years.

11. In addition to disclosing their licensed status on all advertisements, licensees are required to disclose their license status
1. on all contracts for real estate in which they have an ownership interest.
2. on all contracts regardless.
3. on all receipts they receive.
4. never.

12. When a licensee is advertising their own property for sale, purchase or exchange which is not listed with a broker, the licensee must
1. The licensee is not allowed to sell his own property without his broker listing it.
2. The licensee does not have to state he or she is an agent.
3. The licensee must indicate he or she is licensed.
4. The licensee must not tell his broker.

Real Estate Training Institute – Pre Exam Workbook

13. The expiration, suspension or revocation of a responsible broker's license shall automatically suspend the license of every real estate licensee currently under the supervision of that broker. In such cases
1. all licensees will automatically lose their licenses.
2. a licensee may transfer to another responsible broker.
3. a licensee cannot transfer to another broker until the original responsible broker acquires a new license.
4. a licensee must avoid the responsible broker whose license has been suspended at all costs.

14. Every licensee shall notify the Real Estate Commission of any adverse court decisions in which the licensee appeared as a defendant
1. within 10 days.
2. within 30 days.
3. within 24 hours.
4. Never.

15. The Commission mandated disclosure form
1. may be altered to fit the terms of the transaction.
2. may be altered and duplicated before presenting copies to all parties involved in the transaction.
3. may be duplicated in content and size but not altered.
4. may be duplicated in content and altered, but not in size.

16. In the event one or more parties are not available to sign one or more disclosures forms, the disclosure will be accomplished orally. The applicable form will be so noted by the broker and said forms will be forwarded for signatures as soon as possible.
1. Written electronic transmission will not fulfill the legal requirement.
2. Both 1 and 4.
3. Written electronic transmission will fulfill this requirement.
4. Written electronic transmission will not fulfill this requirement.

17. In the event the agency relationship changes between the parties to a real estate transaction
1. The original disclosure shall be modified to document the changes.
2. Addendums to the original disclosures forms must be acknowledged by all parties to the transaction.
3. New disclosure forms will be acknowledged by all parties involved.
4. The original disclosures are legal.

18. In dual agency
1. the buyer shall give his/her consent by modifying the MREC Single Agency Agreement to reflect the dual agency.
2. the buyer shall give his/her consent by signing the MREC Dual Agency Confirmation Form which shall be attached to the offer to purchase.
3. the buyer shall give his/her consent by meeting the seller to pass papers.
4. None of the above.

19. For the buyer's agent, the first substantial meeting shall not include
1. a bona fide open house or model home.
2. preliminary conversations or small talk concerning price range, location and property styles.
3. responding to general factual questions from a prospective buyer concerning properties that have been advertised for sale or lease.
4. All of the above.

20. When the broker is the agent for the buyer, first substantive meeting is
1. showing the property of a seller to a represented buyer.
2. eliciting any confidential information from a seller concerning their real estate needs, motivation, or financial qualifications.
3. the execution of any agreements.
4. All of the above.

21. For the seller's agent, the first substantive meeting does not include
1. a bona fide open house where the customer asks specific questions about finance terms or down payment assistance programs.
2. eliciting confidential information.
3. a bona fide open house or model home showing, small talk concerning price range, location and property styles and responding to general factual questions.
4. None of the above.

22. When an offer is made on a property owned by a party with whom the broker has entered into a listing agreement, such broker shall document and date an acceptance or rejection of the offer and
1. make five copies.
2. then show his salespeople how he documented the information.
3. upon written request, shall provide a copy of such document to the person making the offer.
4. upon verbal request, shall provide a copy of such document to the person refusing the offer.

23. "Fiduciary Responsibility" are those duties due the principal (client) in a real estate transaction are
1. Care, Honesty and Due Diligence.
2. Honest and Fair Dealing.
3. Full Accounting, Disclosure, Honest Dealings and Care.
4. Loyalty, Obedience, Disclosure, Confidentiality, Reasonable Skill, Care and Diligence and Full Accounting.

24. Brokers who practice disclosed dual agency
1. should do so with the utmost care to protect consumers from other brokers who may violate common law standards.
2. are in violation of Mississippi Real Estate Law and their license may be suspended or revoked.
3. should do so with the utmost caution to protect consumers and themselves from inadvertent violation of demanding common law standards of disclosed dual agency.
4. are in violation of National Real Estate Law and may be fined of no more than $500,000.

Real Estate Training Institute – Pre Exam Workbook

25. Special situations, where unusual facts exist or where one or more parties involved are especially vulnerable, could require additional disclosures not contemplated. In such cases, brokers
1. should not accept to represent any party.
2. should be extra careful.
3. should seek legal advice prior to entering into an agency relationship.
4. should make sure that a notary public verifies the identity of all parties.

26. Who are exempt from having a real estate license?
1. Brokers
2. A Public Official holding an auction.
3. A Licensee selling her own home.
4. None of the above.

27. The five Commissioners appointed by the Governor with advise and consent from the Senate have the power to do all of the following except
1. appoint a Commissioner.
2. give 15 days' notice of a hearing to a licensee when the licensee has a violation charged against him.
3. issue subpoenas for the attendance of witnesses and the production of books and papers.
4. Both 1 and 3.

28. Can the Real Estate Commissioners issue subpoenas?
1. No because it is a legal matter.
2. Yes because it is within the authority of the Commission's power.
3. No because they need to contact the appropriate local public official to issue such subpoenas.
4. Yes but only if there is proof of a crime being committed.

29. A broker applicant who has not held a salesperson license for a period of 12 months immediately prior to submitting an application, must
1. have a master's degree from a college or university as approved by the Southern Association of Colleges and Schools.
2. have successfully completed 120 class room hours in real estate courses, which courses are acceptable by the Commissioners.
3. have successfully completed 150 classroom hours in real estate courses, which courses are acceptable for credit toward a degree at a college or university as approved by the Southern Association of Colleges and Schools.
4. have attended a college that is approved by the Southern Association of Colleges and Schools.

30. It is unlawful to carry out the business of a broker or salesperson without
1. a high school diploma.
2. the approval of your county's supervisors.
3. a license.
4. Both 1 and 3.

31. A Licensee following notification of action resulting from a Commissioner hearing
1. has 30 days to appeal any ruling and post a required $500 bond for any costs which may be adjudged against him.
2. has 60 days to appeal any ruling and post a required $1000 bond for any expenses that may be incurred.
3. has 15 days to appeal and no bond is required.
4. has 30 days to appeal and no bond is required.

32. Whenever a Mississippi broker enters into a cooperating agreement with a nonresident broker, the Mississippi broker
1. must file two copies of the cooperating agreement within 10 days with the Mississippi Real Estate Commission.
2. no need to file anything with the Commission since the broker has his own business license.
3. must file a copy of the agreement with the Department of Real Estate.
4. must contact the Commission in the state where the nonresident broker resides.

33. When changing responsible brokers
1. the Commission shall issue a new license for a period of one year and when the agent completes the mandatory hours of continuing education will issue a license for 4 more years.
2. the Commission has no more than 30 days to issue a new license.
3. a new license shall thereupon be issued by the Commission to such salesperson for the unexpired term of the original license upon the return to the Commission of the license previously issued.
4. the Commission doesn't care if a salesperson changes responsible broker and no notice needs be submitted.

34. Brokers may give legal advice
1. when a client asks how to take title.
2. when a client is getting a divorce.
3. when the client is under 18.
4. never.

35. Licensees may obtain errors and omissions coverage independently if the coverage contained in the policy follows the minimum requirement of
1. a per claim limit is not less than $1,000.
2. a per claim limit is not less than $10,000.
3. a per claim limit is not less than $100,000.
4. There is no minimum limit.

36. Commissioners are vested with power of court to issue and enforce subpoenas, levy fines and
1. appoint other commissioners.
2. set commission fee limits brokers can charge a client.
3. levy jail terms.
4. None of the above.

37. Any applicant or licensee or person aggrieved shall have the right of appeal from any adverse or order or decision the Commission to the circuit court of the county of the residence of the applicant, licensee or person or of the First Judicial District of Hinds County within _____ days from the service of notice of the action of the Commission.
1. five
2. ten
3. twenty
4. thirty

38. Funds received by the Commission are used to
1. fund Mississippi Real Estate Commission operations.
2. fund highway projects.
3. fund referral fees.
4. fund kickbacks

39. All monies which shall be paid into the state treasury are credited
1. to the "real estate license fund".
2. to the state general fund.
3. are not credited anywhere.
4. None of the above.

40. No fee, commission or other valuable consideration may be paid to a person for real estate brokerage activities unless the person provides evidence of
1. a social security number and ID.
2. a license or a cooperating agreement.
3. a personal bank account or a trust account.
4. None of the above.

Real Estate Training Institute – Pre Exam Workbook

Answers

State Final Exam Two

1-4
2-1
3-3
4-2
5-4
6-4
7-1
8-2
9-3
10-3
11-1
12-3
13-2
14-1
15-3
16-3
17-3
18-2
19-4
20-4
21-3
22-3
23-4
24-3
25-3
26-2
27-1
28-2
29-3
30-3
31-1
32-1
33-3
34-4
35-3
36-3
37-4
38-1
39-1
40-2

Real Estate Training Institute – Pre Exam Workbook

State Final Exam Three
This is Your MS License Law State Final
Use answer sheets. Do not write on this exam.

1. Who are exempt from having a real estate license?
1. Brokers
2. A Public Official holding an auction.
3. A Licensee selling her own home.
4. None of the above.

2. The following people may be excluded from holding a real estate license except
1. attorneys and Public officers performing their duties as such.
2. a person holding a duly executed power of attorney from the owner and a receiver, trustee, administrator, executor, guardian or under court order or while acting under authority of a deed of trust or will.
3. anyone dealing in oil and gas leases and mineral rights.
4. a person who places an ad on the internet under their responsible broker.

3. The five Commissioners appointed by the Governor with advise and consent from the Senate have the power to do all of the following except
1. appoint a Commissioner.
2. give 15 days notice of a hearing to a licensee when the licensee has a violation charged against him.
3. issue subpoenas for the attendance of witnesses and the production of books and papers.
4. Both 1 and 3

4. Can the Real Estate Commissioners issue subpoenas?
1. No, because it is a legal matter.
2. Yes, because it is within the authority of the Commission's power.
3. No, because they need to contact the appropriate local public official to issue such subpoenas.
4. Yes, but only if there is proof of a crime being committed.

5. A broker applicant who has not held a salesperson license for a period of 12 months immediately prior to submitting an application, must
1. have a master's degree from a college or university as approved by the Southern Association of Colleges and Schools.
2. have successfully completed 120 class room hours in real estate courses, which courses are acceptable by the Commissioners.
3. have successfully completed 150 classroom hours in real estate courses, which courses are acceptable for credit toward a degree at a college or university as approved by the Southern Association of Colleges and Schools.
4. have attended a college that is approved by the Southern Association of Colleges and Schools.

Real Estate Training Institute – Pre Exam Workbook

6. A non-resident may apply for a nonresident's license in Mississippi
1. provided the individual is a licensed broker or is a broker salesperson or salesperson affiliated with a resident or nonresident Mississippi broker.
2. provided a non-resident who applies for a broker's license and who will maintain an office in Mississippi.
3. provided the non-resident not maintain a place of business within Mississippi provided he is regularly actively engaged in the real estate business and maintains a place of business in the other state.
4. All of the above.

7. It is unlawful to carry out the business of a broker or salesperson without
1. a high school diploma.
2. the approval of your county's supervisors.
3. a license.
4. Both 1 and 3.

8. The following may be exempt from having a license
1. attorneys and executed power of attorney.
2. receiver, trustee, administrator and public Officers.
3. those dealing in oil/gas leases and mineral rights.
4. All of the above.

9. Licensee following notification of action resulting from a Commissioner hearing
1. has 30 days to appeal any ruling and post a required $500 bond for any costs which may be adjudged against him.
2. has 60 days to appeal any ruling and post a required $1000 bond for any expenses that may be incurred.
3. has 15 days to appeal and no bond is required.
4. has 30 days to appeal and no bond is required.

10. Whenever a Mississippi broker enters into a cooperating agreement with a non-resident broker, the Mississippi broker, he
1. must file two copies of the cooperating agreement within 10 days with the Mississippi Real Estate Commission.
2. No need to file anything with the Commission since the broker has his own business license.
3. must file a copy of the agreement with the Department of Real Estate.
4. must contact the Commission in the state where the non-resident broker resides.

11. When a broker has an agreement with a non-resident broker, involving a property located in Mississippi all advertising must have the name and telephone number of the Mississippi broker
1. and the address of the non-resident broker
2. and the Mississippi broker shall be given equal prominence.
3. and the non-resident broker's signs are the only signs allowed on the property for sale.
4. None of the above.

Real Estate Training Institute – Pre Exam Workbook

12. When both the non-resident broker and the Mississippi broker have their company signs on a property listed together, the signs
1. should be placed with the non-resident broker sign in front of the Mississippi broker's signs as a courtesy.
2. of the non-resident broker should be at least 10 times the size of the Mississippi Broker.
3. should have equal prominence and be placed side by side.
4. It doesn't matter where the signs are placed.

13. The Mississippi broker in a non-resident cooperating broker agreement
1. shall be liable for all acts of the cooperating broker
2. shall be liable for his own acts.
3. shall be liable for his own acts only.
4. Both 1 and 2.

14. An earnest money deposit pertaining to a cooperative agreement must be held in escrow
1. by the non-resident broker unless both buyer and seller agree otherwise.
2. It can be held by either of the brokers depending on who has a more secure trust account.
3. by the Mississippi broker unless both the buyer and seller agree in writing to relieve the Mississippi broker of this responsibility.
4. The Seller holds the earnest money deposit.

15. All licenses issued to a real estate salesperson or broker salesperson
1. shall designate the responsible broker of such salesperson or broker salesperson.
2. shall designate the home phone number and home address of each person.
3. Both 1 and 2.
4. Neither 1 nor 2.

16. Notice in writing shall be given to the Commission by any real estate salesperson with a change of responsible broker within
1. 5 days
2. 3 days
3. two weeks
4. No notice is required.

17. When within 3 days a salesperson notifies the Commission of a change of broker,
1. the salesperson must give the name of his responsible broker and the name of the principal broker into whose agency the salesperson is about to enter.
2. the salesperson does not need to name the broker the salesperson is transferring to until the first of the year.
3. the salesperson is not allowed to change brokers more than three times a year.
4. the salesperson must include the names of his bank in case a suit is brought against him.

Real Estate Training Institute – Pre Exam Workbook

18. When changing responsible brokers
1. the Commission shall issue a new license for a period of one year and when the agent completes the mandatory hours of continuing education will issue a license for 4 more years.
2. the Commission has no more than 30 days to issue a new license.
3. a new license shall thereupon be issued by the Commission to such salesperson for the unexpired term of the original license upon the return to the Commission of the license previously issued.
4. The Commission doesn't care if a salesperson changes responsible broker and no notice needs be submitted.

19. Brokers may give legal advice
1. when a client asks how to take title.
2. when a client is getting a divorce.
3. when the client is under 18.
4. Never.

20. Licensees may obtain errors and omissions coverage independently if the coverage contained in the policy follows the minimum requirement of
1. a per claim limit is not less than $1,000.
2. a per claim limit is not less than $10,000.
3. a per claim limit is not less than $100,000.
4. There is no minimum limit.

21. All (5) five commissioners appointed by the Governor with advice and consent of the Senate
1. must be a resident of Mississippi for at least 6 years prior to his appointment and his vocation for at least 5 years shall be that of real estate broker.
2. must be a resident for 6 years and a salesperson/broker for 5 years.
3. must be a college graduate and scored over 89% on the broker's exam.
4. can be a non-resident if he has been a managing broker for 5 years.

22. Commissioners are vested with power of court to issue and enforce subpoenas, levy fines and
1. appoint other commissioners.
2. set commission fee limits brokers can charge a client.
3. levy jail terms.
4. None of the above.

23. All license fee funds must be submitted to the State Treasury with detailed explanation
1. on a monthly basis.
2. on a quarterly basis.
3. on a daily basis.
4. on a weekly basis.

24. Real Estate Commissioners
1. are from each congressional district and one at large.
2. are from North, South, East and West Mississippi with one at large.
3. are two democrats and two republicans and one independent.
4. All of the above.

25. Any applicant or licensee or person aggrieved shall have the right of appeal from any adverse or order or decision the Commission to the circuit court of the county of the residence of the applicant, licensee or person or of the First Judicial District of Hinds County within _____ days from the service of notice of the action of the Commission.
1. five days
2. ten days
3. twenty days
4. thirty days

26. Any person charged with a violation shall be given_____ days notice of the hearing upon the charges filed, together with a copy of the complaint.
1. three days
2. five days
3. fifteen days
4. thirty days

27. Any person taking appeal shall post a satisfactory bond in the amount of _____ dollars for the payment of any costs which may be adjudged against him.
1. $100
2. $200
3. $400
4. $500

28. Funds received by the Commission are used to
1. fund Mississippi Real Estate Commission operations.
2. fund highway projects.
3. fund referral fees.
4. fund kickbacks.

29. Licensees who do not show proof of E and O Insurance have 30 days to correct the deficiency. If the deficiency is not corrected within the 30 days
1. the Commission will fine the responsible broker.
2. the licensee's licenses will be placed on inactive status.
3. the Commission will close the office of the licensee.
4. the Commission will do nothing.

30. All monies which shall be paid into the state treasury are credited
1. to the "real estate license fund".
2. to the state general fund.
3. It is not credited anywhere.
4. None of the above.

31. Monies from the "real estate license fund" are used for
1. salaries and expenses.
2. printing an annual directory of licensees.
3. educational purposes and maintenance of a searchable internet based web site which shall satisfy the requirement for publication of a directory of licensees.
4. All of the above.

32. No fee, commission or other valuable consideration may be paid to a person for real estate brokerage activities unless the person provides evidence of
1. a social security number and ID.
2. a license or a cooperating agreement.
3. a personal bank account or a trust account.
4. None of the above.

33. A broker wants to pay his neighbor a referral fee for sending the broker the neighbor's sister who purchased a home through that broker.
1. The broker cannot pay his neighbor a fee unless the neighbor is a licensed real estate agent and then the broker would need to pay his broker.
2. The broker can pay his neighbor a referral fee because no one will find out.
3. The broker can pay his neighbor by automatic deposit.
4. None of the above.

34. IREBEA (Interest on Real Estate Broker's Escrow Accounts) is
1. mandatory
2. voluntary
3. based on the amount of deposits on hand
4. dependent on how long a broker has been in business.

35. The determination of whether a client's funds are nominal in amount or to be held for a short period of time
1. rest in the judgment of the client.
2. rest in the sound judgment of each broker, and no charge of ethical impropriety or other breach of professional conduct shall attend a broker's exercise of judgment in that regard.
3. is regulated by the Senate.
4. Both 1 and 3.

Real Estate Training Institute – Pre Exam Workbook

36. The interest in a IREBEA account for nominal or short term deposits shall be made quarterly to
1. the Real Estate Commission.
2. the State Treasury.
3. the Mississippi Housing Opportunity Fund.
4. the Mississippi Legal Help Foundation.

37. Participation in IREBEA is accomplished by
1. Broker written notice to an authorized financial institute.
2. Broker verbal notice to an authorized financial institute.
3. The broker opening a company account.
4. All of the above is sufficient.

38. Transfer Disclosures are mandatory for all of the following except
1. transfer of a Duplex.
2. transfer of a four unit apartment building.
3. a transfer from one co-owner to one or more other co-owners.
4. All of the above.

39. The transferor of a duplex shall deliver to the prospective transferee the written property disclosure statement
1. within 3 days
2. within 5 days after the close of escrow.
3. when the transferor meets with the transferee.
4. as soon as practicable before the transfer of title.

40. In the case of transfer by a real property sales contract, or by a lease together with an option to purchase, or a ground lease coupled with improvements, delivery of the Transfer Disclosure Statement is delivered
1. as soon as practicable after the execution of the contract.
2. as soon as practicable before the execution of the contract.
3. after the contract has been voided.
4. None of the above.

41. The transferor shall indicate delivery of the Property Disclosure Statement on
1. the receipt for deposit or the real property sales contract or the lease.
2. any addendum attached thereto or on a separate document.
3. Either 1 and 2.
4. Neither 1 nor 2.

42. Delivery of the Real Estate Transfer Disclosure is mandatory in all of the following cases except
1. a transfer of a one to four unit dwelling.
2. a transfer between neighbors.
3. a transfer to a government entity.
4. a transfer of a single family home.

43. If any disclosure, or any material amendment of any disclosure, required to be made is delivered after the execution of an offer to purchase
1. the transferee shall have three (3) days after delivery in person or five (5) days after delivery by deposit in mail to terminate his or her offer by delivery of a written notice of termination to the transferor or the transferor's agent.
2. the transferee shall have three (3) days after delivery in person or five (5) days after delivery by mail to terminate his or her offer by making verbal cancellations.
3. Both 1 and 2 are acceptable.
4. Neither 1 nor 2 is acceptable.

44. Neither the transferor nor any listing or selling agent shall be liable for an error, inaccuracy or omission of information delivered
1. if the seller lives on the property.
2. if the error, inaccuracy or omission was not within their personal knowledge.
3. if the buyer doesn't seem to care.
4. All of the above.

45. An agent without personal knowledge will not be held responsible for an error when the error was by a
1. licensed engineer, land surveyor or geologist.
2. structural pest operator or contractor
3. experts dealing in matters within the scope of the professional's license or expertise.
4. All of the above.

46. Delivery to a spouse of a transferee
1. shall not be deemed delivery to the transferee.
2. shall be deemed delivery to the transferee unless provided otherwise in the contracts.
3. shall only be deemed a delivery to the transferee if they were married within the state of Mississippi before 1981.
4. shall never be deemed delivery to the transferee under any circumstances.

47. Any person who willfully and negligently does not deliver the needed disclosures shall be liable
1. and if the seller has to take his property back uncontested.
2. in the amount of actual damages suffered by a transferee.
3. for up to $100,000.
4. for no more than $100,000.

48. Real Estate Transfer Disclosures are needed for
1. office buildings when a real estate professional is involved.
2. shopping centers.
3. residential stock cooperatives of one to four units when a real estate professional is involved.
4. None of the above.

Real Estate Training Institute – Pre Exam Workbook

49. A nonmaterial fact which need not be disclosed is
1. illegal drug activity that affects the physical condition of the property.
2. the seller or any resident of the property died or is sick from AIDS.
3. the foundation of the house has shifted and it is built on a hill that's sliding.
4. the property is located below a runway path for the local airport and the house shakes so bad the buyer will have to replace several windows a year from noise vibration breakage.

50. A salesperson has a listing with his responsible broker, Broker A. The salesperson decided to transfer to a new broker before the listing expires. When the agent moves to the new broker, who owns the listing?
1. The agent.
2. The listing automatically gets cancelled.
3. The listing moves to the salesperson's new broker.
4. Broker A

51. It is not the duty of the responsible broker
1. to instruct the licensees licensed under that broker in the fundamentals of real estate practice.
2. to instruct the licensees licensed under that broker in ethics of the profession and the Mississippi Real Estate Law.
3. to exercise supervision of his licensees of their real estate activities.
4. to make sure each agent has completed their post licensing education and kept their license current.

52. An affiliated broker cannot act independently of his employing broker
1. without the full consent and knowledge of his employing broker.
2. without full disclosure of his client.
3. without full consent and knowledge of both the buyer and seller.
4. ever, once employed by his responsible broker.

53. Applicants for a real estate license
1. must have a responsible broker before applying for their license.
2. may take the exam but has ten days to find a responsible broker.
3. may not take the exam without a responsible broker.
4. may not send in the license fee.

54. A change of responsible broker requires the salesperson
1. to within 3 days give written notice to the Commission
2. call the commission and tell them.
3. to take all of his listings with him.
4. All of the above.

55. When an agent transfers to a new broker and within 3 days gives written notice to the Commission the name of the principal broker into whose agency he is about to enter
1. the agent makes a notation on his license and gives it to the new broker.
2. he mails his license to the Commission and a new license will be issued for the unexpired term of the original license.
3. he needs to attend more ethics classes.
4. he mails his license to his new broker.

56. A licensed Mississippi broker may cooperate with a broker licensed in another state who does not hold a Mississippi license
1. as long as it's agreed upon by both brokers.
2. as long as the buyer and seller know.
3. through the use of a cooperative agreement.
4. Never.

57. A separate cooperating agreement must be filed for each property, prospective user or transaction with said writing
1. reflecting the relationship of the brokers.
2. reflecting the compensation to be paid to the Mississippi licensed broker.
3. reflecting the price of the property.
4. reflecting the client(s).

58. When there is a cooperative agreement with a non-resident broker, the listing or property management agreement for the Mississippi property
1. must remain in the name of the Mississippi broker.
2. must remain in the name of both brokers.
3. must remain in the name of the out of state broker.
4. must remain with no name.

59. How many copies of a cooperative agreement must a Mississippi broker file with the Mississippi Real Estate Commission?
1. One
2. Two
3. Three
4. Four

60. The non-resident broker cannot place any sign on real property located in Mississippi without the written consent of the cooperating Mississippi broker. When both brokers place signs on the property.
1. The Mississippi broker's sign must be larger.
2. The out of state broker can only use vinyl signs.
3. They should be placed side by side in a prominent place and in close proximity.
4. Only one broker's sign can be placed.

61. When advertising a property shared by an out of state broker
1. the name of the Mississippi broker must be listed.
2. the name of the seller must be listed.
3. the Mississippi broker must contact the Real Estate Commission.
4. None of the above.

62. A responsible broker must maintain an office and display the license therein. If the broker has more than one office
1. the broker need not display licenses in branch offices.
2. the broker shall display a branch office license in each branch office.
3. there are no branch offices allowed.
4. None of the above.

63. No licensee shall pay any part of a fee, commission or other compensation received by such licensee in buying, selling, exchanging, leasing, auctioning or renting any real estate
1. except to a licensee through the licensee's responsible broker.
2. to the customer directly as a referral fee.
3. to your neighbor for getting his brother to list with you.
4. All of the above

64. The responsible broker must
1. hold meetings every Tuesday.
2. tell agents the hours they have to make phone calls.
3. hang in the office all licenses of the licensees he is responsible for.
4. take Fridays off.

65. Peggy, a salesperson for broker Bob listed and sold a property. Before being paid for that executed transaction, Peggy changed responsible brokers. Broker Bob
1. owes Peggy nothing.
2. must only pay Peggy's new responsible broker.
3. can pay Peggy her commission directly.
4. owes Peggy interest.

66. Any licensee who fails in a timely manner to respond to official Mississippi Real Estate Commission written communication or who fails or neglects to abide by Mississippi Real Estate Commission Rules and Regulations shall be deemed
1. to irresponsible to sell real estate.
2. prima facie, to be guilty of improper dealing.
3. to be harboring a criminal.
4. on vacation.

67. A real estate broker or salesperson in the ordinary course of his business may give an opinion as to the price of real estate for the purpose of a prospective listing or sale, however this opinion as to the listing price or sale price
1. must not refer to this as an appraisal.
2. must not take compensation.
3. Both 1 and 2
4. Neither 1 nor 2

68. When an offer is made on a property owned by a party with whom the broker has entered into a listing agreement, such broker shall document and date an acceptance or rejection of the offer and
1. make five copies.
2. then show his salespeople how he documented the information.
3. upon written request, shall provide a copy of such document to the person making the offer.
4. upon verbal request, shall provide a copy of such document to the person refusing the offer.

69. A real estate licensee shall deliver a true and correct copy of any instrument to any party or parties executing the same
1. within five days.
2. within 3 days.
3. immediately (at the time of signing).
4. No copies need to be given to any party.

70. All exclusive listing agreements shall be in writing, properly identify the property to be sold and contain all of the terms and conditions under which the transaction is to be consummated including the sales price, the considerations to be paid, the signatures of all parties to the agreement and
1. a provision requiring the listing party to notify the broker of their intention to cancel the listing.
2. a definite date of expiration.
3. Both 1 and 2.
4. Neither 1 nor 2.

71. All exclusive buyer representation agreements shall be in writing and properly identify the terms and conditions under which the buyer will rely on the broker for the purchase of real estate including the sales price, the considerations to be paid, and the nature of all parties to the agreement and a definite date of expiration.
1. The exclusive buyer agreement does not have to indicate in the document that it is such an agreement.
2. Copies of the exclusive buyer's agreement do not have to be given to the buyer after signing.
3. The buyer may terminate the agreement upon fifteen (15) calendar days written notice to the buyer's exclusive agent.
4. The exclusive buyer agreement must not clearly state that the agreement is such.

72. Broker Bob received an offer this morning for a property he has listed. Bob promptly called his client and then faxed the offer to his client. Later that day, Bob received a second offer that was lower and had bad credit terms for financing. What should Broker Bob do?
1. Not present the second offer because the first offer is higher.
2. Present the second offer because the seller has not accepted the first offer and any other written offer received by the broker in a sale shall be presented to the owner.
3. Hold off on presenting the second offer until his client accepts the first offer.
4. Both 1 and 3.

73. Every contract must reflect whom the broker represents by statement
1. under the signatures of the parties to the contract.
2. over the signatures of the parties to the contract.
3. on the side in a hand written statement.
4. All of the above.

74. A real estate broker must keep on file following it's consummation complete records relating to any real estate transaction for
1. one year.
2. two years.
3. three years.
4. five years.

75. The use of any copyrighted term or insignia on stationary, office signs, or in advertisement by any licensee not authorized to do so, will be considered
1. as "substantial misrepresentation" and cause for refusal, suspension, or revocation of the license.
2. as a "substantial material fact" and cause for refusal, suspension, or revocation of the license.
3. as a "substantial misrepresentation" and cause for a penalty of up to $2,000.
4. as a "substantial misrepresentation" and cause for a penalty of no more than $10,000.

76. A salesperson wants to advertise on an internet web page.
1. He may do so without checking with his broker first.
2. He does not need to specify that he is an agent.
3. All advertising must be under the direct supervision and in the name of the responsible broker or in the name of the real estate firm.
4. The internet doesn't fall under the terms of advertising.

77. When a licensee is advertising their own property for sale, purchase or exchange which is not listed with a broker, the licensee must;
1. the licensee is not allowed to sell his own property without his broker listing it.
2. the licensee does not have to state he or she is an agent.
3. the licensee must indicate he or she is licensed.
4. the licensee must not tell his broker.

78. In addition to disclosing their licensed status on all advertisements, licensees are required to disclose their license status
1. on all contracts for real estate in which they have an ownership interest.
2. on all contracts regardless.
3. on all receipts they receive.
4. Never.

79. An agent made real estate signs to put in the front yard of his client's home. He did not put the name of his responsible broker or name of his real estate firm on the sign.
1. It's OK to have signs called "Blind Ads".
2. This is a "Blind Ad" and is in violation.
3. The agent can't put up signs.
4. None of the above.

80. Earnest money accepted by the broker or any licensee for which the broker is responsible and upon acceptance of a mutually agreeable contract is required to deposit the money
1. into his personal account.
2. into a trust account within three business days.
3. into a safe deposit box in his office.
4. into a trust account prior to the close of business of the next banking day.

81. When a broker is agent for the seller and for any reason the seller fails or is unable to consummate the transaction, the broker has no right to any portion of the money deposited by the purchaser
1. is a false statement because the commission was earned.
2. even if the commission was earned.
3. is just plain wrong.
4. 1 and 3 are correct.

82. When the broker is agent for the seller and for any reason the seller fails or is unable to consummate the transaction, the broker has no right to any portion of the money deposited by the purchaser, even if the commission has been earned. The money must be returned to the purchaser and the broker
1. under no circumstance receive payment for his actions.
2. must sue the seller for specific performance.
3. must sue the buyer's agent for specific performance.
4. should look to the seller for compensation.

83. Monies received in a trust account on behalf of clients or customers are not assets of the broker; however, a broker may deposit and keep in each escrow account or rental account some personal funds for the express purpose
1. of paying his office bills.
2. of paying commission
3. of covering service charges and other bank debits related to each account.
4. None of the above.

84. If a broker, as escrow agent, accepts a check and later finds that such check has not been honored by the bank on which it was drawn, the broker shall
1. immediately notify all parties involved in the transaction.
2. call the check writer and ask for a cashier's check.
3. immediately close the books on that transaction.
4. sue the bad check writer for specific performance

85. Special situations, where unusual facts exist or where one or more parties involved are especially vulnerable, could require additional disclosures not contemplated. In such cases, brokers
1. should not accept to represent any party.
2. should be extra careful.
3. should seek legal advice prior to entering into an agency relationship.
4. should make sure that a notary public verifies the identity of all parties.

86. "Disclosed Dual Agent" is when
1. an agent representing both parties to a real estate transaction with the verbal commitment to do one's best.
2. an agent representing both parties to a real estate transaction with the informed consent of both parties, with written understanding of specific duties and representation to be afforded each party.
3. an agent representing the seller and two parties making offers on the same property on the same day.
4. an agent representing two sellers at the same time with written informed consent of both parties and the understanding of specific duties to both.

87. Dual Agency is not practiced by some brokers because
1. there may be situations where disclosed dual agency presents situations where the agent may have to conceal nonmaterial facts.
2. there may be situations where disclosed dual agency presents conflicts with the buyer when the agent knows the seller will take less than the asking price.
3. there may be situations where dual agency is not disclosed in writing in order to conceal latent defects.
4. there may be situations where disclosed dual agency presents conflicts of interest that cannot be resolved without breach of duty to one party or another.

88. Brokers who practice disclosed dual agency
1. should do so with the utmost care to protect consumers from other brokers who may violate common law standards.
2. are in violation of Mississippi Real Estate Law and their license may be suspended or revoked.
3. should do so with the utmost caution to protect consumers and themselves from inadvertent violation of demanding common law standards of disclosed dual agency.
4. are in violation of National Real Estate Law and may be fined of no more than $500,000.

89. "Fiduciary Responsibility" are those duties due the principal (client) in a real estate transaction are
1. Care, Honesty and Due Diligence.
2. Honest and Fair Dealing.
3. Full Accounting, Disclosure, Honest Dealings and Care.
4. Loyalty, Obedience, Disclosure, Confidentiality, Reasonable Skill, Care and Diligence and Full Accounting.

90. When the broker is the agent for the seller, "first substantive meeting" shall be before or just immediately prior to the first of any of the following
1. showing the property, eliciting confidential information and the execution of any agreements.
2. showing the property, telephone communication and first meeting in the office.
3. showing the property, before any chit chat or small talk.
4. before any small talk.

91. For the seller's agent, the first substantive meeting does not include
1. a bona fide open house where the customer asks specific questions about finance terms or down payment assistance programs.
2. eliciting confidential information.
3. a bona fide open house or model home showing, small talk concerning price range, location and property styles and responding to general factual questions.
4. None of the above.

92. When the broker is the agent for the buyer, first substantive meeting is
1. showing the property of a seller to a represented buyer.
2. eliciting any confidential information from a seller concerning their real estate needs, motivation, or financial qualifications.
3. the execution of any agreements.
4. All of the above.

93. For the buyer's agent, the first substantial meeting shall not include
1. a bona fide open house or model home.
2. preliminary conversations or small talk concerning price range, location and property styles.
3. responding to general factual questions from a prospective buyer concerning properties that have been advertised for sale or lease.
4. All of the above.

94. In dual agency
1. the buyer shall give his/her consent by modifying the MREC Single Agency Agreement to reflect the dual agency.
2. the buyer shall give his/her consent by signing the MREC Dual Agency Confirmation Form which shall be attached to the offer to purchase.
3. the buyer shall give his/her consent by meeting the seller to pass papers.
4. None of the above.

Real Estate Training Institute – Pre Exam Workbook

95. In the event the agency relationship changes between the parties to a real estate transaction
1. the original disclosure shall be modified to document the changes
2. addendums to the original disclosures forms must be acknowledged by all parties to the transaction.
3. new disclosure forms will be acknowledged by all parties involved.
4. the original disclosures are legal.

96. In the event one or more parties are not available to sign one or more disclosures forms, the disclosure will be accomplished orally. The applicable form will be so noted by the broker and said forms will be forwarded for signatures as soon as possible.
1. Written electronic transmission will not fulfill the legal requirement.
2. Both 1 and 4
3. Written electronic transmission will fulfill this requirement.
4. Written electronic transmission will not fulfill this requirement.

97. The Commission mandated disclosure form
1. may be altered to fit the terms of the transaction.
2. may be altered and duplicated before presenting copies to all parties involved in the transaction.
3. may be duplicated in content and size but not altered.
4. may be duplicated in content and altered, but not in size.

98. Every licensee shall notify the Real Estate Commission of any adverse court decisions in which the licensee appeared as a defendant
1. within 10 days.
2. within 30 days.
3. within 24 hours.
4. never.

99. The expiration, suspension or revocation of a responsible broker's license shall automatically suspend the license of every real estate licensee currently under the supervision of that broker. In such cases
1. all licensees will automatically lose their licenses.
2. a licensee may transfer to another responsible broker.
3. a licensee cannot transfer to another broker until the original responsible broker acquires a new license.
4. a licensee must avoid the responsible broker whose license has been suspended at all costs.

100. Any seller of a timeshare plan with the state of Mississippi must be a licensed Real Estate Broker or Real Estate Salesperson except
1. there are no exceptions.
2. the developer and his regular employees.
3. everyone has to be licensed.
4. Both 1 and 3

101. A person who offers a timeshare plan located outside of Mississippi in a national publication or by electronic media, which is not directed to or targeted to any individual located in Mississippi and contains appropriate disclaimers
1. must register with the state of Mississippi.
2. is exempt from licensee requirements.
3. is exempt from the registration requirements.
4. None of the above.

102. A purchaser of a time share may cancel the contract
1. within 3 months after receiving the public offering
2. within 7 calendar days of signing the contract or 7 calendar days of receiving the public offering statement.
3. after the first visit if the purchaser decides they no longer want it.
4. None of the above.

103. A developer with a timeshare must return all payments made under the contract within
1. within 5 days of written cancellation from the purchaser.
2. as soon as the check clears the bank.
3. within 30 days of a cancellation notice.
4. within 24 hours of a cancellation notice.

104. The MREC will issue a (timeshare) preliminary permit in 20 days
1. if the developer resides within the state of Mississippi.
2. unless deficiencies are found on the application.
3. unless the developer has over 15 employees.
4. unless the Commission is overworked.

105. Developers of timeshares and any of his agents cannot practice timeshare
1. without meeting registration requirements of the MREC.
2. without the developer and his employees pass a Mississippi real estate license exam.
3. unless the developer becomes a responsible broker.
4. within the state of Mississippi.

106. The responsible broker must report any licensee for whom that broker is responsible to the commission if
1. she/he believes the agent scored low on the real estate exam.
2. she/he believes that a licensee has let his/her license expire.
3. she/he believes that a licensee is slacking.
4. she/he believes that a licensee has violated laws rules or regulations.

Real Estate Training Institute – Pre Exam Workbook

107. A licensee shall not be required to comply with disclosure requirements when engaged in transactions with
1. corporation, nonprofit corporation, professional corporation
2. professional association, limited liability company, partnership, real estate investment trust, business trust, charitable trust, family trust
3. any governmental entity in transactions involving real estate.
4. All of the above.

108. Every applicant for a resident license as a real estate salesperson shall be
1. 21 years of age and a resident of Mississippi for 5 years.
2. 18 years of age or older and be a bona fide resident of the state of Mississippi prior to filing his application.
3. 16 years of age and a resident of Mississippi.
4. None of the above.

109. Legal action by the Commission for a violation may take the form of a fine of not more than $1,000 and or up to ninety (90) days in jail, or both. The second violation can be
1. up to 2 years in jail.
2. a fine of $5,000
3. up to a $2,000 fine and up to 6 months in jail or both
4. None of the above.

110. The extent of cooperation of reciprocity with other states
1. vary
2. are all the same.
3. Neither answer is correct.
4. All of the above.

111. Failure to renew your license on time will result in a penalty of double fee. 30 days late, will result
1. in triple penalty.
2. in having to retake the real estate exam.
3. in having to participate with an extra 30 hours of post licensing.
4. in the license being cancelled.

Real Estate Training Institute – Pre Exam Workbook

Answers

State Final Exam Three

1. Who are exempt from having a real estate license?
2. A Public Official holding an auction.

2. The following people may be excluded from holding a real estate license except
4. a person who places an ad on the internet under their responsible broker.

3. The five Commissioners appointed by the Governor with advise and consent from the Senate have the power to do all of the following except
1. appoint a Commissioner.

4. Can the Real Estate Commissioners issue subpoenas?
2. Yes, because it is within the authority of the Commission's power.

5. A broker applicant who has not held a salesperson license for a period of 12 months immediately prior to submitting an application, must
3. have successfully completed 150 classroom hours in real estate courses, which courses are acceptable for credit toward a degree at a college or university as approved by the Southern Association of Colleges and Schools.

6. A non-resident may apply for a nonresident's license in Mississippi
4. All of the above.

7. It is unlawful to carry out the business of a broker or salesperson without
3. A license.

8. The following may be exempt from having a license
4. All of the above.

9. Licensee following notification of action resulting from a Commissioner hearing
1. has 30 days to appeal any ruling and post a required $500 bond for any costs which may be adjudged against him.

10. Whenever a Mississippi broker enters into a cooperating agreement with a non-resident broker, the Mississippi broker he
1. must file two copies of the cooperating agreement within 10 days with the Mississippi Real Estate Commission.

11. When a broker has an agreement with a non-resident broker, involving a property located in Mississippi all advertising must have the name and telephone number of the Mississippi broker.

Real Estate Training Institute – Pre Exam Workbook

2. and the Mississippi broker shall be given equal prominence.

12. When both the non-resident broker and the Mississippi broker have their company signs on a property listed together, the signs
3. should have equal prominence and be placed side by side.

13. The Mississippi broker in a non-resident cooperating broker agreement
4. Both 1 and 2.

14. An earnest money deposit pertaining to a cooperative agreement must be held in escrow
3. by the Mississippi broker unless both the buyer and seller agree in writing to relieve the Mississippi broker of this responsibility.

15. all licenses issued to a real estate salesperson or broker salesperson
1. Shall designate the responsible broker of such salesperson or broker salesperson.

16. notice in writing shall be given to the Commission by any real estate salesperson with a change of responsible broker within
2. 3 days

17. When within 3 days a salesperson notifies the Commission of a change of broker.
1. the salesperson must give the name of his responsible broker and the name of the principal broker into whose agency the salesperson is about to enter.

18. When changing responsible brokers
3. a new license shall thereupon be issued by the Commission to such salesperson for the unexpired term of the original license upon the return to the Commission of the license previously issued.

19. Brokers may give legal advice
4. Never.

20. Licensees may obtain errors and omissions coverage independently if the coverage contained in the policy follows the minimum requirement of
3. a per claim limit is not less than $100,000.

21. all (5) five commissioners appointed by the Governor with advice and consent of the Senate
1. Must be a resident of Mississippi for at least 6 years prior to his appointment and his vocation for at least 5 years shall be that of real estate broker.

22. Commissioners are vested with power of court to issue and enforce subpoenas, levy fines and
3. levy jail terms.

23. All license fee funds must be submitted to the State Treasury with detailed explanation
4. on a weekly basis.

24. Real Estate Commissioners
1. are from each congressional district and one at large.

25. Any applicant or licensee or person aggrieved shall have the right of appeal from any adverse or order or decision the Commission to the circuit court of the county of the residence of the applicant, licensee or person or of the First Judicial District of Hinds County within _____ days from the service of notice of the action of the Commission.
4. thirty days

26. Any person charged with a violation shall be given _____ days notice of the hearing upon the charges filed, together with a copy of the complaint.
3. fifteen days

27. Any person taking appeal shall post a satisfactory bond in the amount of _____ dollars for the payment of any costs which may be adjudged against him.
4. $500

28. Funds received by the Commission are used to
1. fund Mississippi Real Estate Commission operations.

29. Licensees who do not show proof of E and O Insurance have 30 days to correct the deficiency. If the deficiency is not corrected within the 30 days
2. the licensee's licenses will be placed on inactive status.

30. All monies which shall be paid into the state treasury are credited
1. to the "real estate license fund".

31. Monies from the "real estate license fund" are used for
4. All of the above.

32. No fee, commission or other valuable consideration may be paid to a person for real estate brokerage activities unless the person provides evidence of
2. a license or a cooperating agreement.

33. A broker wants to pay his neighbor a referral fee for sending the broker the neighbor's sister who purchased a home through that broker.
1. the broker cannot pay his neighbor a fee unless the neighbor is a licensed real estate agent and then the broker would need to pay his broker.

34. IREBEA (Interest on Real Estate Broker's Escrow Accounts) is
2. voluntary

35. The determination of whether a client's funds are nominal in amount or to be held for a short period of time
2. rest in the sound judgment of each broker, and no charge of ethical impropriety or other breach of professional conduct shall attend a broker's exercise of judgment in that regard.

Real Estate Training Institute – Pre Exam Workbook

36. The interest in a IREBEA account for nominal or short term deposits shall be made quarterly to
3. the Mississippi Housing Opportunity Fund.

37. Participation in IREBEA is accomplished by
1. broker written notice to an authorized financial institute.

38. Transfer Disclosures are mandatory for all of the following except
3. a transfer from one co-owner to one or more other co-owners.

39. The transferor of a duplex shall deliver to the prospective transferee the written property disclosure statement
4. as soon as practicable before the transfer of title.

40. In the case of transfer by a real property sales contract, or by a lease together with an option to purchase, or a ground lease coupled with improvements, delivery of the Transfer Disclosure Statement is delivered
2. as soon as practicable before the execution of the contract.

41. The transferor shall indicate delivery of the Property Disclosure Statement on
3. either 1 and 2.

42. Delivery of the Real Estate Transfer Disclosure is mandatory in all of the following cases except
3. a transfer to a government entity.

43. If any disclosure, or any material amendment of any disclosure, required to be made is delivered after the execution of an offer to purchase
1. the transferee shall have three (3) days after delivery in person or five (5) days after delivery by deposit in mail to terminate his or her offer by delivery of a written notice of termination to the transferor or the transferor's agent.

44. Neither the transferor nor any listing or selling agent shall be liable for an error, inaccuracy or omission of information delivered
2. if the error, inaccuracy or omission was not within their personal knowledge.

45. An agent without personal knowledge will not be held responsible for an error when the error was by a
4. All of the above.

46. Delivery to a spouse of a transferee
2. shall be deemed delivery to the transferee unless provided otherwise in the contracts.

47. Any person who willfully and negligently does not deliver the needed disclosures shall be liable
2. in the amount of actual damages suffered by a transferee.

48. Real Estate Transfer Disclosures are needed for
3. residential stock cooperatives of one to four units when a real estate professional is involved.

49. A nonmaterial fact which need not be disclosed is
2. the seller or any resident of the property died or is sick from AIDS.

50. A salesperson has a listing with his responsible broker, Broker A. The salesperson decided to transfer to a new broker before the listing expires. When the agent moves to the new broker, who owns the listing?
4. Broker A

51. It is not the duty of the responsible broker
4. to make sure each agent has completed their post licensing education and kept their license current.

52. An affiliated broker cannot act independently of his employing broker
1. Without the full consent and knowledge of his employing broker.

53. Applicants for a real estate license
2. May take the exam but have ten days to find a responsible broker.

54. A change of responsible broker requires the salesperson
1. to within 3 days give written notice to the Commission

55. When an agent transfers to a new broker and within 3 days gives written notice to the Commission the name of the principal broker into whose agency he is about to enter, he
2. mails his license to the Commission and a new license will be issued for the unexpired term of the original license.

56. A licensed Mississippi broker may cooperate with a broker licensed in another state who does not hold a Mississippi license
3. through the use of a cooperative agreement.

57. A separate cooperating agreement must be filed for each property, prospective user or transaction with said writing
2. reflecting the compensation to be paid to the Mississippi licensed broker.

58. When there is a cooperative agreement with a non-resident broker, the listing or property management agreement for the Mississippi property
1. must remain in the name of the Mississippi broker.

59. How many copies of a cooperative agreement must a Mississippi broker file with the Mississippi Real Estate Commission?
2. Two

60. The non-resident broker cannot place any sign on real property located in Mississippi without the written consent of the cooperating Mississippi broker. When both brokers place signs on the property.
3. they should be placed side by side in a prominent place and in close proximity.

61. When advertising a property shared by an out of state broker
1. the name of the Mississippi broker must be listed.

62. A responsible broker must maintain an office and display the license therein. If the broker has more than one office
2. the broker shall display a branch office license in each branch office.

63. No licensee shall pay any part of a fee, commission or other compensation received by such licensee in buying, selling, exchanging, leasing, auctioning or renting any real estate
1. except to a licensee through the licensee's responsible broker.

64. The responsible broker must
3. hang in the office all licenses of the licensees he is responsible for.

65. Peggy, a salesperson for broker Bob listed and sold a property. Before being paid for that executed transaction, Peggy changed responsible brokers. Broker Bob
3. can pay Peggy her commission directly.

66. Any licensee who fails in a timely manner to respond to official Mississippi Real Estate Commission written communication or who fails or neglects to abide by Mississippi Real Estate Commission Rules and Regulations shall be deemed
2. prima facie, to be guilty of improper dealing.

67. A real estate broker or salesperson in the ordinary course of his business may give an opinion as to the price of real estate for the purpose of a prospective listing or sale, however this opinion as to the listing price or sale price
1. must not refer to this as an appraisal.

68. When an offer is made on a property owned by a party with whom the broker has entered into a listing agreement, such broker shall document and date an acceptance or rejection of the offer and
3. upon written request, shall provide a copy of such document to the person making the offer.

69. A real estate licensee shall deliver a true and correct copy of any instrument to any party or parties executing the same
3. immediately (at the time of signing).

70. All exclusive listing agreements shall be in writing, properly identify the property to be sold and contain all of the terms and conditions under which the transaction is to be consummated including the sales price, the considerations to be paid, the signatures of all parties to the agreement and
2. a definite date of expiration.

71. All exclusive buyer representation agreements shall be in writing and properly identify the terms and conditions under which the buyer will rely on the broker for the purchase of real estate including the sales price, the considerations to be paid, and the nature of all parties to the agreement and a definite date of expiration.
3. the buyer may terminate the agreement upon fifteen (15) calendar days written notice to the buyer's exclusive agent.

72. Broker Bob received an offer this morning for a property he has listed. Bob promptly called his client and then faxed the offer to his client. Later that day, Bob received a second offer that was lower and had bad credit terms for financing. What should Broker Bob do?
2. present the second offer because the seller has not accepted the first offer and any other written offer received by the broker in a sale shall be presented to the owner.

73. Every contract must reflect whom the broker represents by statement
2. over the signatures of the parties to the contract.

74. A real estate broker must keep on file following it's consummation complete records relating to any real estate transaction for
3. Three years.

75. The use of any copyrighted term or insignia on stationary, office signs, or in advertisement by any licensee not authorized to do so, will be considered
1. as "substantial misrepresentation" and cause for refusal, suspension, or revocation of the license.

76. A salesperson wants to advertise on an internet web page.
3. all advertising must be under the direct supervision and in the name of the responsible broker or in the name of the real estate firm.

77. When a licensee is advertising their own property for sale, purchase or exchange which is not listed with a broker, the licensee must
3. the licensee must indicate he or she is licensed.

78. In addition to disclosing their licensed status on all advertisements, licensees are required to disclose their license status
1. on all contracts for real estate in which they have an ownership interest.

79. An agent made real estate signs to put in the front yard of his client's home. He did not put the name of his responsible broker or name of his real estate firm on the sign.
2. this is a "Blind Ad" and is in violation.

80. Earnest money accepted by the broker or any licensee for which the broker is responsible and upon acceptance of a mutually agreeable contract is required to deposit the money
4. into a trust account prior to the close of business of the next banking day.

81. When a broker is agent for the seller and for any reason the seller fails or is unable to consummate the transaction, the broker has no right to any portion of the money deposited by the purchaser
2. even if the commission was earned.

82. When the broker is agent for the seller and for any reason the seller fails or is unable to consummate the transaction, the broker has no right to any portion of the money deposited by the purchaser, even if the commission has been earned. The money must be returned to the purchaser and the broker
4. should look to the seller for compensation.

83. Monies received in a trust account on behalf of clients or customers are not assets of the broker; however, a broker may deposit and keep in each escrow account or rental account some personal funds for the express purpose
3. of covering service charges and other bank debits related to each account.

84. If a broker, as escrow agent, accepts a check and later finds that such check has not been honored by the bank on which it was drawn, the broker shall
1. immediately notify all parties involved in the transaction.

85. Special situations, where unusual facts exist or where one or more parties involved are especially vulnerable, could require additional disclosures not contemplated. In such cases, brokers
3. should seek legal advice prior to entering into an agency relationship.

86. "Disclosed Dual Agent" is when
2. an agent representing both parties to a real estate transaction with the informed consent of both parties, with written understanding of specific duties and representation to be afforded each party.

87. Dual Agency is not practiced by some brokers because
4. there may be situations where disclosed dual agency presents conflicts of interest that cannot be resolved without breach of duty to one party or another.

88. Brokers who practice disclosed dual agency
3. should do so with the utmost caution to protect consumers and themselves from inadvertent violation of demanding common law standards of disclosed dual agency.

89. "Fiduciary Responsibility" are those duties due the principal (client) in a real estate transaction are
4. Loyalty, Obedience, Disclosure, Confidentiality, Reasonable Skill, Care and Diligence and Full Accounting.

90. When the broker is the agent for the seller, "first substantive meeting" shall be before or just immediately prior to the first of any of the following
1. showing the property, eliciting confidential information and the execution of any agreements.

91. For the seller's agent, the first substantive meeting does not include

3. a bona fide open house or model home showing, small talk concerning price range, location and property styles and responding to general factual questions.

92. When the broker is the agent for the buyer, first substantive meeting is
4. All of the above.

93. For the buyer's agent, the first substantial meeting shall not include
4. All of the above.

94. In dual agency
2. the buyer shall give his/her consent by signing the MREC Dual Agency Confirmation Form which shall be attached to the offer to purchase.

95. In the event the agency relationship changes between the parties to a real estate transaction
3. new disclosure forms will be acknowledged by all parties involved.

96. In the event one or more parties are not available to sign one or more disclosures forms, the disclosure will be accomplished orally. The applicable form will be so noted by the broker and said forms will be forwarded for signatures as soon as possible.
3. written electronic transmission will fulfill this requirement.

97. The Commission mandated disclosure form
3. may be duplicated in content and size but not altered.

98. Every licensee shall notify the Real Estate Commission of any adverse court decisions in which the licensee appeared as a defendant
1. within 10 days.

99. The expiration, suspension or revocation of a responsible broker's license shall automatically suspend the license of every real estate licensee currently under the supervision of that broker. In such cases
2. a licensee may transfer to another responsible broker.

100. Any seller of a timeshare plan with the state of Mississippi must be a licensed Real Estate Broker or Real Estate Salesperson except
2. the developer and his regular employees.

101. A person who offers a timeshare plan located outside of Mississippi in a national publication or by electronic media, which is not directed to or targeted to any individual located in Mississippi and contains appropriate disclaimers
3. is exempt from the registration requirements.

102. A purchaser of a time share may cancel the contract
2. within 7 calendar days of signing the contract or 7 calendar days of receiving the public offering statement.

103. A developer with a timeshare must return all payments made under the contract within
3. within 30 days of a cancellation notice.

104. The MREC will issue a (timeshare) preliminary permit in 20 days
2. unless deficiencies are found on the application.

105. Developers of timeshares and any of his agents cannot practice timeshare
1. without meeting registration requirements of the MREC.

106. The responsible broker must report any licensee for whom that broker is responsible to the commission if
4. she/he believes that a licensee has violated laws rules or regulations.

107. a licensee shall not be required to comply with disclosure requirements when engaged in transactions with
4. All of the above.

108. Every applicant for a resident license as a real estate salesperson shall be
2. 18 years of age or older and be a bona fide resident of the state of Mississippi prior to filing his application.

109. Legal action by the Commission for a violation may take the form of a fine of not more than $1,000 and or up to ninety (90) days in jail, or both. The second violation can be
3. up to a $2,000 fine and up to 6 months in jail or both

110. The extent of cooperation of reciprocity with other states.
1. vary

111. Failure to renew your license on time will result in a penalty of double fee. 30 days late, will result
4. in the license being cancelled.

Real Estate Training Institute – Pre Exam Workbook

Chapter 11
Blank Answer Sheets

1.___	24.___	47.___	70.___	93.___	116.___	139.___
2.___	25.___	48.___	71.___	94.___	117.___	140.___
3.___	26.___	49.___	72.___	95.___	118.___	141.___
4.___	27.___	50.___	73.___	96.___	119.___	142.___
5.___	28.___	51.___	74.___	97.___	120.___	143.___
6.___	29.___	52.___	75.___	98.___	121.___	144.___
7.___	30.___	53.___	76.___	99.___	122.___	145.___
8.___	31.___	54.___	77.___	100.___	123.___	146.___
9.___	32.___	55.___	78.___	101.___	124.___	147.___
10.___	33.___	56.___	79.___	102.___	125.___	148.___
11.___	34.___	57.___	80.___	103.___	126.___	149.___
12.___	35.___	58.___	81.___	104.___	127.___	150.___
13.___	36.___	59.___	82.___	105.___	128.___	151.___
14.___	37.___	60.___	83.___	106.___	129.___	152.___
15.___	38.___	61.___	84.___	107.___	130.___	153.___
16.___	39.___	62.___	85.___	108.___	131.___	154.___
17.___	40.___	63.___	86.___	109.___	132.___	155.___
18.___	41.___	64.___	87.___	110.___	133.___	156.___
19.___	42.___	65.___	88.___	111.___	134.___	157.___
20.___	43.___	66.___	89.___	112.___	135.___	158.___
21.___	44.___	67.___	90.___	113.___	136.___	159.___
22.___	45.___	68.___	91.___	114.___	137.___	160.___
23.___	46.___	69.___	92.___	115.___	138.___	161.___

Real Estate Training Institute – Leslie Clauson

1.____	24.____	47.____	70.____	93.____	116.____	139.____
2.____	25.____	48.____	71.____	94.____	117.____	140.____
3.____	26.____	49.____	72.____	95.____	118.____	141.____
4.____	27.____	50.____	73.____	96.____	119.____	142.____
5.____	28.____	51.____	74.____	97.____	120.____	143.____
6.____	29.____	52.____	75.____	98.____	121.____	144.____
7.____	30.____	53.____	76.____	99.____	122.____	145.____
8.____	31.____	54.____	77.____	100.____	123.____	146.____
9.____	32.____	55.____	78.____	101.____	124.____	147.____
10.____	33.____	56.____	79.____	102.____	125.____	148.____
11.____	34.____	57.____	80.____	103.____	126.____	149.____
12.____	35.____	58.____	81.____	104.____	127.____	150.____
13.____	36.____	59.____	82.____	105.____	128.____	151.____
14.____	37.____	60.____	83.____	106.____	129.____	152.____
15.____	38.____	61.____	84.____	107.____	130.____	153.____
16.____	39.____	62.____	85.____	108.____	131.____	154.____
17.____	40.____	63.____	86.____	109.____	132.____	155.____
18.____	41.____	64.____	87.____	110.____	133.____	156.____
19.____	42.____	65.____	88.____	111.____	134.____	157.____
20.____	43.____	66.____	89.____	112.____	135.____	158.____
21.____	44.____	67.____	90.____	113.____	136.____	159.____
22.____	45.____	68.____	91.____	114.____	137.____	160.____
23.____	46.____	69.____	92.____	115.____	138.____	161.____

Real Estate Training Institute – Leslie Clauson

1.___	24.___	47.___	70.___	93.___	116.___	139.___
2.___	25.___	48.___	71.___	94.___	117.___	140.___
3.___	26.___	49.___	72.___	95.___	118.___	141.___
4.___	27.___	50.___	73.___	96.___	119.___	142.___
5.___	28.___	51.___	74.___	97.___	120.___	143.___
6.___	29.___	52.___	75.___	98.___	121.___	144.___
7.___	30.___	53.___	76.___	99.___	122.___	145.___
8.___	31.___	54.___	77.___	100.___	123.___	146.___
9.___	32.___	55.___	78.___	101.___	124.___	147.___
10.___	33.___	56.___	79.___	102.___	125.___	148.___
11.___	34.___	57.___	80.___	103.___	126.___	149.___
12.___	35.___	58.___	81.___	104.___	127.___	150.___
13.___	36.___	59.___	82.___	105.___	128.___	151.___
14.___	37.___	60.___	83.___	106.___	129.___	152.___
15.___	38.___	61.___	84.___	107.___	130.___	153.___
16.___	39.___	62.___	85.___	108.___	131.___	154.___
17.___	40.___	63.___	86.___	109.___	132.___	155.___
18.___	41.___	64.___	87.___	110.___	133.___	156.___
19.___	42.___	65.___	88.___	111.___	134.___	157.___
20.___	43.___	66.___	89.___	112.___	135.___	158.___
21.___	44.___	67.___	90.___	113.___	136.___	159.___
22.___	45.___	68.___	91.___	114.___	137.___	160.___
23.___	46.___	69.___	92.___	115.___	138.___	161.___

Real Estate Training Institute – Leslie Clauson

1.___	24.___	47.___	70.___	93.___	116.___	139.___
2.___	25.___	48.___	71.___	94.___	117.___	140.___
3.___	26.___	49.___	72.___	95.___	118.___	141.___
4.___	27.___	50.___	73.___	96.___	119.___	142.___
5.___	28.___	51.___	74.___	97.___	120.___	143.___
6.___	29.___	52.___	75.___	98.___	121.___	144.___
7.___	30.___	53.___	76.___	99.___	122.___	145.___
8.___	31.___	54.___	77.___	100.___	123.___	146.___
9.___	32.___	55.___	78.___	101.___	124.___	147.___
10.___	33.___	56.___	79.___	102.___	125.___	148.___
11.___	34.___	57.___	80.___	103.___	126.___	149.___
12.___	35.___	58.___	81.___	104.___	127.___	150.___
13.___	36.___	59.___	82.___	105.___	128.___	151.___
14.___	37.___	60.___	83.___	106.___	129.___	152.___
15.___	38.___	61.___	84.___	107.___	130.___	153.___
16.___	39.___	62.___	85.___	108.___	131.___	154.___
17.___	40.___	63.___	86.___	109.___	132.___	155.___
18.___	41.___	64.___	87.___	110.___	133.___	156.___
19.___	42.___	65.___	88.___	111.___	134.___	157.___
20.___	43.___	66.___	89.___	112.___	135.___	158.___
21.___	44.___	67.___	90.___	113.___	136.___	159.___
22.___	45.___	68.___	91.___	114.___	137.___	160.___
23.___	46.___	69.___	92.___	115.___	138.___	161.___

Real Estate Training Institute – Leslie Clauson

1.____   24.____   47.____   70.____   93.____   116.____   139.____
2.____   25.____   48.____   71.____   94.____   117.____   140.____
3.____   26.____   49.____   72.____   95.____   118.____   141.____
4.____   27.____   50.____   73.____   96.____   119.____   142.____
5.____   28.____   51.____   74.____   97.____   120.____   143.____
6.____   29.____   52.____   75.____   98.____   121.____   144.____
7.____   30.____   53.____   76.____   99.____   122.____   145.____
8.____   31.____   54.____   77.____   100.____ 123.____   146.____
9.____   32.____   55.____   78.____   101.____ 124.____   147.____
10.____ 33.____   56.____   79.____   102.____ 125.____   148.____
11.____ 34.____   57.____   80.____   103.____ 126.____   149.____
12.____ 35.____   58.____   81.____   104.____ 127.____   150.____
13.____ 36.____   59.____   82.____   105.____ 128.____   151.____
14.____ 37.____   60.____   83.____   106.____ 129.____   152.____
15.____ 38.____   61.____   84.____   107.____ 130.____   153.____
16.____ 39.____   62.____   85.____   108.____ 131.____   154.____
17.____ 40.____   63.____   86.____   109.____ 132.____   155.____
18.____ 41.____   64.____   87.____   110.____ 133.____   156.____
19.____ 42.____   65.____   88.____   111.____ 134.____   157.____
20.____ 43.____   66.____   89.____   112.____ 135.____   158.____
21.____ 44.____   67.____   90.____   113.____ 136.____   159.____
22.____ 45.____   68.____   91.____   114.____ 137.____   160.____
23.____ 46.____   69.____   92.____   115.____ 138.____   161.____

Real Estate Training Institute – Leslie Clauson

1.____	24.____	47.____	70.____	93.____	116.____	139.____
2.____	25.____	48.____	71.____	94.____	117.____	140.____
3.____	26.____	49.____	72.____	95.____	118.____	141.____
4.____	27.____	50.____	73.____	96.____	119.____	142.____
5.____	28.____	51.____	74.____	97.____	120.____	143.____
6.____	29.____	52.____	75.____	98.____	121.____	144.____
7.____	30.____	53.____	76.____	99.____	122.____	145.____
8.____	31.____	54.____	77.____	100.____	123.____	146.____
9.____	32.____	55.____	78.____	101.____	124.____	147.____
10.____	33.____	56.____	79.____	102.____	125.____	148.____
11.____	34.____	57.____	80.____	103.____	126.____	149.____
12.____	35.____	58.____	81.____	104.____	127.____	150.____
13.____	36.____	59.____	82.____	105.____	128.____	151.____
14.____	37.____	60.____	83.____	106.____	129.____	152.____
15.____	38.____	61.____	84.____	107.____	130.____	153.____
16.____	39.____	62.____	85.____	108.____	131.____	154.____
17.____	40.____	63.____	86.____	109.____	132.____	155.____
18.____	41.____	64.____	87.____	110.____	133.____	156.____
19.____	42.____	65.____	88.____	111.____	134.____	157.____
20.____	43.____	66.____	89.____	112.____	135.____	158.____
21.____	44.____	67.____	90.____	113.____	136.____	159.____
22.____	45.____	68.____	91.____	114.____	137.____	160.____
23.____	46.____	69.____	92.____	115.____	138.____	161.____

Real Estate Training Institute – Leslie Clauson

1.____	24.____	47.____	70.____	93.____	116.____	139.____	
2.____	25.____	48.____	71.____	94.____	117.____	140.____	
3.____	26.____	49.____	72.____	95.____	118.____	141.____	
4.____	27.____	50.____	73.____	96.____	119.____	142.____	
5.____	28.____	51.____	74.____	97.____	120.____	143.____	
6.____	29.____	52.____	75.____	98.____	121.____	144.____	
7.____	30.____	53.____	76.____	99.____	122.____	145.____	
8.____	31.____	54.____	77.____	100.____	123.____	146.____	
9.____	32.____	55.____	78.____	101.____	124.____	147.____	
10.____	33.____	56.____	79.____	102.____	125.____	148.____	
11.____	34.____	57.____	80.____	103.____	126.____	149.____	
12.____	35.____	58.____	81.____	104.____	127.____	150.____	
13.____	36.____	59.____	82.____	105.____	128.____	151.____	
14.____	37.____	60.____	83.____	106.____	129.____	152.____	
15.____	38.____	61.____	84.____	107.____	130.____	153.____	
16.____	39.____	62.____	85.____	108.____	131.____	154.____	
17.____	40.____	63.____	86.____	109.____	132.____	155.____	
18.____	41.____	64.____	87.____	110.____	133.____	156.____	
19.____	42.____	65.____	88.____	111.____	134.____	157.____	
20.____	43.____	66.____	89.____	112.____	135.____	158.____	
21.____	44.____	67.____	90.____	113.____	136.____	159.____	
22.____	45.____	68.____	91.____	114.____	137.____	160.____	
23.____	46.____	69.____	92.____	115.____	138.____	161.____	

Real Estate Training Institute – Leslie Clauson

1.____	24.____	47.____	70.____	93.____	116.____	139.____
2.____	25.____	48.____	71.____	94.____	117.____	140.____
3.____	26.____	49.____	72.____	95.____	118.____	141.____
4.____	27.____	50.____	73.____	96.____	119.____	142.____
5.____	28.____	51.____	74.____	97.____	120.____	143.____
6.____	29.____	52.____	75.____	98.____	121.____	144.____
7.____	30.____	53.____	76.____	99.____	122.____	145.____
8.____	31.____	54.____	77.____	100.____	123.____	146.____
9.____	32.____	55.____	78.____	101.____	124.____	147.____
10.____	33.____	56.____	79.____	102.____	125.____	148.____
11.____	34.____	57.____	80.____	103.____	126.____	149.____
12.____	35.____	58.____	81.____	104.____	127.____	150.____
13.____	36.____	59.____	82.____	105.____	128.____	151.____
14.____	37.____	60.____	83.____	106.____	129.____	152.____
15.____	38.____	61.____	84.____	107.____	130.____	153.____
16.____	39.____	62.____	85.____	108.____	131.____	154.____
17.____	40.____	63.____	86.____	109.____	132.____	155.____
18.____	41.____	64.____	87.____	110.____	133.____	156.____
19.____	42.____	65.____	88.____	111.____	134.____	157.____
20.____	43.____	66.____	89.____	112.____	135.____	158.____
21.____	44.____	67.____	90.____	113.____	136.____	159.____
22.____	45.____	68.____	91.____	114.____	137.____	160.____
23.____	46.____	69.____	92.____	115.____	138.____	161.____

Real Estate Training Institute – Leslie Clauson

1.____ 24.____ 47.____ 70.____ 93.____ 116.____ 139.____
2.____ 25.____ 48.____ 71.____ 94.____ 117.____ 140.____
3.____ 26.____ 49.____ 72.____ 95.____ 118.____ 141.____
4.____ 27.____ 50.____ 73.____ 96.____ 119.____ 142.____
5.____ 28.____ 51.____ 74.____ 97.____ 120.____ 143.____
6.____ 29.____ 52.____ 75.____ 98.____ 121.____ 144.____
7.____ 30.____ 53.____ 76.____ 99.____ 122.____ 145.____
8.____ 31.____ 54.____ 77.____ 100.____ 123.____ 146.____
9.____ 32.____ 55.____ 78.____ 101.____ 124.____ 147.____
10.____ 33.____ 56.____ 79.____ 102.____ 125.____ 148.____
11.____ 34.____ 57.____ 80.____ 103.____ 126.____ 149.____
12.____ 35.____ 58.____ 81.____ 104.____ 127.____ 150.____
13.____ 36.____ 59.____ 82.____ 105.____ 128.____ 151.____
14.____ 37.____ 60.____ 83.____ 106.____ 129.____ 152.____
15.____ 38.____ 61.____ 84.____ 107.____ 130.____ 153.____
16.____ 39.____ 62.____ 85.____ 108.____ 131.____ 154.____
17.____ 40.____ 63.____ 86.____ 109.____ 132.____ 155.____
18.____ 41.____ 64.____ 87.____ 110.____ 133.____ 156.____
19.____ 42.____ 65.____ 88.____ 111.____ 134.____ 157.____
20.____ 43.____ 66.____ 89.____ 112.____ 135.____ 158.____
21.____ 44.____ 67.____ 90.____ 113.____ 136.____ 159.____
22.____ 45.____ 68.____ 91.____ 114.____ 137.____ 160.____
23.____ 46.____ 69.____ 92.____ 115.____ 138.____ 161.____

Real Estate Training Institute – Leslie Clauson

1.___	24.___	47.___	70.___	93.___	116.___	139.___
2.___	25.___	48.___	71.___	94.___	117.___	140.___
3.___	26.___	49.___	72.___	95.___	118.___	141.___
4.___	27.___	50.___	73.___	96.___	119.___	142.___
5.___	28.___	51.___	74.___	97.___	120.___	143.___
6.___	29.___	52.___	75.___	98.___	121.___	144.___
7.___	30.___	53.___	76.___	99.___	122.___	145.___
8.___	31.___	54.___	77.___	100.___	123.___	146.___
9.___	32.___	55.___	78.___	101.___	124.___	147.___
10.___	33.___	56.___	79.___	102.___	125.___	148.___
11.___	34.___	57.___	80.___	103.___	126.___	149.___
12.___	35.___	58.___	81.___	104.___	127.___	150.___
13.___	36.___	59.___	82.___	105.___	128.___	151.___
14.___	37.___	60.___	83.___	106.___	129.___	152.___
15.___	38.___	61.___	84.___	107.___	130.___	153.___
16.___	39.___	62.___	85.___	108.___	131.___	154.___
17.___	40.___	63.___	86.___	109.___	132.___	155.___
18.___	41.___	64.___	87.___	110.___	133.___	156.___
19.___	42.___	65.___	88.___	111.___	134.___	157.___
20.___	43.___	66.___	89.___	112.___	135.___	158.___
21.___	44.___	67.___	90.___	113.___	136.___	159.___
22.___	45.___	68.___	91.___	114.___	137.___	160.___
23.___	46.___	69.___	92.___	115.___	138.___	161.___

Real Estate Training Institute – Leslie Clauson

1.___	24.___	47.___	70.___	93.___	116.___	139.___
2.___	25.___	48.___	71.___	94.___	117.___	140.___
3.___	26.___	49.___	72.___	95.___	118.___	141.___
4.___	27.___	50.___	73.___	96.___	119.___	142.___
5.___	28.___	51.___	74.___	97.___	120.___	143.___
6.___	29.___	52.___	75.___	98.___	121.___	144.___
7.___	30.___	53.___	76.___	99.___	122.___	145.___
8.___	31.___	54.___	77.___	100.___	123.___	146.___
9.___	32.___	55.___	78.___	101.___	124.___	147.___
10.___	33.___	56.___	79.___	102.___	125.___	148.___
11.___	34.___	57.___	80.___	103.___	126.___	149.___
12.___	35.___	58.___	81.___	104.___	127.___	150.___
13.___	36.___	59.___	82.___	105.___	128.___	151.___
14.___	37.___	60.___	83.___	106.___	129.___	152.___
15.___	38.___	61.___	84.___	107.___	130.___	153.___
16.___	39.___	62.___	85.___	108.___	131.___	154.___
17.___	40.___	63.___	86.___	109.___	132.___	155.___
18.___	41.___	64.___	87.___	110.___	133.___	156.___
19.___	42.___	65.___	88.___	111.___	134.___	157.___
20.___	43.___	66.___	89.___	112.___	135.___	158.___
21.___	44.___	67.___	90.___	113.___	136.___	159.___
22.___	45.___	68.___	91.___	114.___	137.___	160.___
23.___	46.___	69.___	92.___	115.___	138.___	161.___

Real Estate Training Institute – Leslie Clauson

1.____	24.____	47.____	70.____	93.____	116.____	139.____
2.____	25.____	48.____	71.____	94.____	117.____	140.____
3.____	26.____	49.____	72.____	95.____	118.____	141.____
4.____	27.____	50.____	73.____	96.____	119.____	142.____
5.____	28.____	51.____	74.____	97.____	120.____	143.____
6.____	29.____	52.____	75.____	98.____	121.____	144.____
7.____	30.____	53.____	76.____	99.____	122.____	145.____
8.____	31.____	54.____	77.____	100.____	123.____	146.____
9.____	32.____	55.____	78.____	101.____	124.____	147.____
10.____	33.____	56.____	79.____	102.____	125.____	148.____
11.____	34.____	57.____	80.____	103.____	126.____	149.____
12.____	35.____	58.____	81.____	104.____	127.____	150.____
13.____	36.____	59.____	82.____	105.____	128.____	151.____
14.____	37.____	60.____	83.____	106.____	129.____	152.____
15.____	38.____	61.____	84.____	107.____	130.____	153.____
16.____	39.____	62.____	85.____	108.____	131.____	154.____
17.____	40.____	63.____	86.____	109.____	132.____	155.____
18.____	41.____	64.	87.____	110.____	133.____	156.____
19.____	42.____	65.____	88.____	111.____	134.____	157.____
20.____	43.____	66.____	89.____	112.____	135.____	158.____
21.____	44.____	67.____	90.____	113.____	136.____	159.____
22.____	45.____	68.____	91.____	114.____	137.____	160.____
23.____	46.____	69.____	92.____	115.____	138.____	161.____

Real Estate Training Institute – Leslie Clauson

1.____	24.____	47.____	70.____	93.____	116.____	139.____
2.____	25.____	48.____	71.____	94.____	117.____	140.____
3.____	26.____	49.____	72.____	95.____	118.____	141.____
4.____	27.____	50.____	73.____	96.____	119.____	142.____
5.____	28.____	51.____	74.____	97.____	120.____	143.____
6.____	29.____	52.____	75.____	98.____	121.____	144.____
7.____	30.____	53.____	76.____	99.____	122.____	145.____
8.____	31.____	54.____	77.____	100.____	123.____	146.____
9.____	32.____	55.____	78.____	101.____	124.____	147.____
10.____	33.____	56.____	79.____	102.____	125.____	148.____
11.____	34.____	57.____	80.____	103.____	126.____	149.____
12.____	35.____	58.____	81.____	104.____	127.____	150.____
13.____	36.____	59.____	82.____	105.____	128.____	151.____
14.____	37.____	60.____	83.____	106.____	129.____	152.____
15.____	38.____	61.____	84.____	107.____	130.____	153.____
16.____	39.____	62.____	85.____	108.____	131.____	154.____
17.____	40.____	63.____	86.____	109.____	132.____	155.____
18.____	41.____	64.____	87.____	110.____	133.____	156.____
19.____	42.____	65.____	88.____	111.____	134.____	157.____
20.____	43.____	66.____	89.____	112.____	135.____	158.____
21.____	44.____	67.____	90.____	113.____	136.____	159.____
22.____	45.____	68.____	91.____	114.____	137.____	160.____
23.____	46.____	69.____	92.____	115.____	138.____	161.____

Real Estate Training Institute – Leslie Clauson

1.___	24.___	47.___	70.___	93.___	116.___	139.___
2.___	25.___	48.___	71.___	94.___	117.___	140.___
3.___	26.___	49.___	72.___	95.___	118.___	141.___
4.___	27.___	50.___	73.___	96.___	119.___	142.___
5.___	28.___	51.___	74.___	97.___	120.___	143.___
6.___	29.___	52.___	75.___	98.___	121.___	144.___
7.___	30.___	53.___	76.___	99.___	122.___	145.___
8.___	31.___	54.___	77.___	100.___	123.___	146.___
9.___	32.___	55.___	78.___	101.___	124.___	147.___
10.___	33.___	56.___	79.___	102.___	125.___	148.___
11.___	34.___	57.___	80.___	103.___	126.___	149.___
12.___	35.___	58.___	81.___	104.___	127.___	150.___
13.___	36.___	59.___	82.___	105.___	128.___	151.___
14.___	37.___	60.___	83.___	106.___	129.___	152.___
15.___	38.___	61.___	84.___	107.___	130.___	153.___
16.___	39.___	62.___	85.___	108.___	131.___	154.___
17.___	40.___	63.___	86.___	109.___	132.___	155.___
18.___	41.___	64.___	87.	110.___	133.___	156.___
19.___	42.___	65.___	88.___	111.___	134.___	157.___
20.___	43.___	66.___	89.___	112.___	135.___	158.___
21.___	44.___	67.___	90.___	113.___	136.___	159.___
22.___	45.___	68.___	91.___	114.___	137.___	160.___
23.___	46.___	69.___	92.___	115.___	138.___	161.___

Real Estate Training Institute – Leslie Clauson

1.____ 24.____ 47.____ 70.____ 93.____ 116.____ 139.____
2.____ 25.____ 48.____ 71.____ 94.____ 117.____ 140.____
3.____ 26.____ 49.____ 72.____ 95.____ 118.____ 141.____
4.____ 27.____ 50.____ 73.____ 96.____ 119.____ 142.____
5.____ 28.____ 51.____ 74.____ 97.____ 120.____ 143.____
6.____ 29.____ 52.____ 75.____ 98.____ 121.____ 144.____
7.____ 30.____ 53.____ 76.____ 99.____ 122.____ 145.____
8.____ 31.____ 54.____ 77.____ 100.____ 123.____ 146.____
9.____ 32.____ 55.____ 78.____ 101.____ 124.____ 147.____
10.____ 33.____ 56.____ 79.____ 102.____ 125.____ 148.____
11.____ 34.____ 57.____ 80.____ 103.____ 126.____ 149.____
12.____ 35.____ 58.____ 81.____ 104.____ 127.____ 150.____
13.____ 36.____ 59.____ 82.____ 105.____ 128.____ 151.____
14.____ 37.____ 60.____ 83.____ 106.____ 129.____ 152.____
15.____ 38.____ 61.____ 84.____ 107.____ 130.____ 153.____
16.____ 39.____ 62.____ 85.____ 108.____ 131.____ 154.____
17.____ 40.____ 63.____ 86.____ 109.____ 132.____ 155.____
18.____ 41.____ 64.____ 87.____ 110.____ 133.____ 156.____
19.____ 42.____ 65.____ 88.____ 111.____ 134.____ 157.____
20.____ 43.____ 66.____ 89.____ 112.____ 135.____ 158.____
21.____ 44.____ 67.____ 90.____ 113.____ 136.____ 159.____
22.____ 45.____ 68.____ 91.____ 114.____ 137.____ 160.____
23.____ 46.____ 69.____ 92.____ 115.____ 138.____ 161.____

Real Estate Training Institute – Leslie Clauson

1.____	24.____	47.____	70.____	93.____	116.____	139.____
2.____	25.____	48.____	71.____	94.____	117.____	140.____
3.____	26.____	49.____	72.____	95.____	118.____	141.____
4.____	27.____	50.____	73.____	96.____	119.____	142.____
5.____	28.____	51.____	74.____	97.____	120.____	143.____
6.____	29.____	52.____	75.____	98.____	121.____	144.____
7.____	30.____	53.____	76.____	99.____	122.____	145.____
8.____	31.____	54.____	77.____	100.____	123.____	146.____
9.____	32.____	55.____	78.____	101.____	124.____	147.____
10.____	33.____	56.____	79.____	102.____	125.____	148.____
11.____	34.____	57.____	80.____	103.____	126.____	149.____
12.____	35.____	58.____	81.____	104.____	127.____	150.____
13.____	36.____	59.____	82.____	105.____	128.____	151.____
14.____	37.____	60.____	83.____	106.____	129.____	152.____
15.____	38.____	61.____	84.____	107.____	130.____	153.____
16.____	39.____	62.____	85.____	108.____	131.____	154.____
17.____	40.____	63.____	86.____	109.____	132.____	155.____
18.____	41.____	64.____	87.____	110.____	133.____	156.____
19.____	42.____	65.____	88.____	111.____	134.____	157.____
20.____	43.____	66.____	89.____	112.____	135.____	158.____
21.____	44.____	67.____	90.____	113.____	136.____	159.____
22.____	45.____	68.____	91.____	114.____	137.____	160.____
23.____	46.____	69.____	92.____	115.____	138.____	161.____

Real Estate Training Institute – Leslie Clauson

1.____	24.____	47.____	70.____	93.____	116.____	139.____
2.____	25.____	48.____	71.____	94.____	117.____	140.____
3.____	26.____	49.____	72.____	95.____	118.____	141.____
4.____	27.____	50.____	73.____	96.____	119.____	142.____
5.____	28.____	51.____	74.____	97.____	120.____	143.____
6.____	29.____	52.____	75.____	98.____	121.____	144.____
7.____	30.____	53.____	76.____	99.____	122.____	145.____
8.____	31.____	54.____	77.____	100.____	123.____	146.____
9.____	32.____	55.____	78.____	101.____	124.____	147.____
10.____	33.____	56.____	79.____	102.____	125.____	148.____
11.____	34.____	57.____	80.____	103.____	126.____	149.____
12.____	35.____	58.____	81.____	104.____	127.____	150.____
13.____	36.____	59.____	82.____	105.____	128.____	151.____
14.____	37.____	60.____	83.____	106.____	129.____	152.____
15.____	38.____	61.____	84.____	107.____	130.____	153.____
16.____	39.____	62.____	85.____	108.____	131.____	154.____
17.____	40.____	63.____	86.____	109.____	132.____	155.____
18.____	41.____	64.____	87.____	110.____	133.____	156.____
19.____	42.____	65.____	88.____	111.____	134.____	157.____
20.____	43.____	66.____	89.____	112.____	135.____	158.____
21.____	44.____	67.____	90.____	113.____	136.____	159.____
22.____	45.____	68.____	91.____	114.____	137.____	160.____
23.____	46.____	69.____	92.____	115.____	138.____	161.____

Real Estate Training Institute – Leslie Clauson

1.____	24.____	47.____	70.____	93.____	116.____	139.____
2.____	25.____	48.____	71.____	94.____	117.____	140.____
3.____	26.____	49.____	72.____	95.____	118.____	141.____
4.____	27.____	50.____	73.____	96.____	119.____	142.____
5.____	28.____	51.____	74.____	97.____	120.____	143.____
6.____	29.____	52.____	75.____	98.____	121.____	144.____
7.____	30.____	53.____	76.____	99.____	122.____	145.____
8.____	31.____	54.____	77.____	100.____	123.____	146.____
9.____	32.____	55.____	78.____	101.____	124.____	147.____
10.____	33.____	56.____	79.____	102.____	125.____	148.____
11.____	34.____	57.____	80.____	103.____	126.____	149.____
12.____	35.____	58.____	81.____	104.____	127.____	150.____
13.____	36.____	59.____	82.____	105.____	128.____	151.____
14.____	37.____	60.____	83.____	106.____	129.____	152.____
15.____	38.____	61.____	84.____	107.____	130.____	153.____
16.____	39.____	62.____	85.____	108.____	131.____	154.____
17.____	40.____	63.____	86.____	109.____	132.____	155.____
18.____	41.____	64.____	87.____	110.____	133.____	156.____
19.____	42.____	65.____	88.____	111.____	134.____	157.____
20.____	43.____	66.____	89.____	112.____	135.____	158.____
21.____	44.____	67.____	90.____	113.____	136.____	159.____
22.____	45.____	68.____	91.____	114.____	137.____	160.____
23.____	46.____	69.____	92.____	115.____	138.____	161.____

Real Estate Training Institute – Leslie Clauson

1.____	24.____	47.____	70.____	93.____	116.____	139.____
2.____	25.____	48.____	71.____	94.____	117.____	140.____
3.____	26.____	49.____	72.____	95.____	118.____	141.____
4.____	27.____	50.____	73.____	96.____	119.____	142.____
5.____	28.____	51.____	74.____	97.____	120.____	143.____
6.____	29.____	52.____	75.____	98.____	121.____	144.____
7.____	30.____	53.____	76.____	99.____	122.____	145.____
8.____	31.____	54.____	77.____	100.____	123.____	146.____
9.____	32.____	55.____	78.____	101.____	124.____	147.____
10.____	33.____	56.____	79.____	102.____	125.____	148.____
11.____	34.____	57.____	80.____	103.____	126.____	149.____
12.____	35.____	58.____	81.____	104.____	127.____	150.____
13.____	36.____	59.____	82.____	105.____	128.____	151.____
14.____	37.____	60.____	83.____	106.____	129.____	152.____
15.____	38.____	61.____	84.____	107.____	130.____	153.____
16.____	39.____	62.____	85.____	108.____	131.____	154.____
17.____	40.____	63.____	86.____	109.____	132.____	155.____
18.____	41.____	64.____	87.____	110.____	133.____	156.____
19.____	42.____	65.____	88.____	111.____	134.____	157.____
20.____	43.____	66.____	89.____	112.____	135.____	158.____
21.____	44.____	67.____	90.____	113.____	136.____	159.____
22.____	45.____	68.____	91.____	114.____	137.____	160.____
23.____	46.____	69.____	92.____	115.____	138.____	161.____

Real Estate Training Institute – Leslie Clauson

1.____	24.____	47.____	70.____	93.____	116.____	139.____
2.____	25.____	48.____	71.____	94.____	117.____	140.____
3.____	26.____	49.____	72.____	95.____	118.____	141.____
4.____	27.____	50.____	73.____	96.____	119.____	142.____
5.____	28.____	51.____	74.____	97.____	120.____	143.____
6.____	29.____	52.____	75.____	98.____	121.____	144.____
7.____	30.____	53.____	76.____	99.____	122.____	145.____
8.____	31.____	54.____	77.____	100.____	123.____	146.____
9.____	32.____	55.____	78.____	101.____	124.____	147.____
10.____	33.____	56.____	79.____	102.____	125.____	148.____
11.____	34.____	57.____	80.____	103.____	126.____	149.____
12.____	35.____	58.____	81.____	104.____	127.____	150.____
13.____	36.____	59.____	82.____	105.____	128.____	151.____
14.____	37.____	60.____	83.____	106.____	129.____	152.____
15.____	38.____	61.____	84.____	107.____	130.____	153.____
16.____	39.____	62.____	85.____	108.____	131.____	154.____
17.____	40.____	63.____	86.____	109.____	132.____	155.____
18.____	41.____	64.____	87.____	110.____	133.____	156.____
19.____	42.____	65.____	88.____	111.____	134.____	157.____
20.____	43.____	66.____	89.____	112.____	135.____	158.____
21.____	44.____	67.____	90.____	113.____	136.____	159.____
22.____	45.____	68.____	91.____	114.____	137.____	160.____
23.____	46.____	69.____	92.____	115.____	138.____	161.____

Real Estate Training Institute – Leslie Clauson

1.____	24.____	47.____	70.____	93.____	116.____	139.____
2.____	25.____	48.____	71.____	94.____	117.____	140.____
3.____	26.____	49.____	72.____	95.____	118.____	141.____
4.____	27.____	50.____	73.____	96.____	119.____	142.____
5.____	28.____	51.____	74.____	97.____	120.____	143.____
6.____	29.____	52.____	75.____	98.____	121.____	144.____
7.____	30.____	53.____	76.____	99.____	122.____	145.____
8.____	31.____	54.____	77.____	100.____	123.____	146.____
9.____	32.____	55.____	78.____	101.____	124.____	147.____
10.____	33.____	56.____	79.____	102.____	125.____	148.____
11.____	34.____	57.____	80.____	103.____	126.____	149.____
12.____	35.____	58.____	81.____	104.____	127.____	150.____
13.____	36.____	59.____	82.____	105.____	128.____	151.____
14.____	37.____	60.____	83.____	106.____	129.____	152.____
15.____	38.____	61.____	84.____	107.____	130.____	153.____
16.____	39.____	62.____	85.____	108.____	131.____	154.____
17.____	40.____	63.____	86.____	109.____	132.____	155.____
18.____	41.____	64.____	87.____	110.____	133.____	156.____
19.____	42.____	65.____	88.____	111.____	134.____	157.____
20.____	43.____	66.____	89.____	112.____	135.____	158.____
21.____	44.____	67.____	90.____	113.____	136.____	159.____
22.____	45.____	68.____	91.____	114.____	137.____	160.____
23.____	46.____	69.____	92.____	115.____	138.____	161.____

Real Estate Training Institute – Leslie Clauson

1.____	24.____	47.____	70.____	93.____	116.____	139.____
2.____	25.____	48.____	71.____	94.____	117.____	140.____
3.____	26.____	49.____	72.____	95.____	118.____	141.____
4.____	27.____	50.____	73.____	96.____	119.____	142.____
5.____	28.____	51.____	74.____	97.____	120.____	143.____
6.____	29.____	52.____	75.____	98.____	121.____	144.____
7.____	30.____	53.____	76.____	99.____	122.____	145.____
8.____	31.____	54.____	77.____	100.____	123.____	146.____
9.____	32.____	55.____	78.____	101.____	124.____	147.____
10.____	33.____	56.____	79.____	102.____	125.____	148.____
11.____	34.____	57.____	80.____	103.____	126.____	149.____
12.____	35.____	58.____	81.____	104.____	127.____	150.____
13.____	36.____	59.____	82.____	105.____	128.____	151.____
14.____	37.____	60.____	83.____	106.____	129.____	152.____
15.____	38.____	61.____	84.____	107.____	130.____	153.____
16.____	39.____	62.____	85.____	108.____	131.____	154.____
17.____	40.____	63.____	86.____	109.____	132.____	155.____
18.____	41.____	64.____	87.____	110.____	133.____	156.____
19.____	42.____	65.____	88.____	111.____	134.____	157.____
20.____	43.____	66.____	89.____	112.____	135.____	158.____
21.____	44.____	67.____	90.____	113.____	136.____	159.____
22.____	45.____	68.____	91.____	114.____	137.____	160.____
23.____	46.____	69.____	92.____	115.____	138.____	161.____

Real Estate Training Institute – Leslie Clauson

1._____   24._____   47._____   70._____   93._____   116._____   139._____
2._____   25._____   48._____   71._____   94._____   117._____   140._____
3._____   26._____   49._____   72._____   95._____   118._____   141._____
4._____   27._____   50._____   73._____   96._____   119._____   142._____
5._____   28._____   51._____   74._____   97._____   120._____   143._____
6._____   29._____   52._____   75._____   98._____   121._____   144._____
7._____   30._____   53._____   76._____   99._____   122._____   145._____
8._____   31._____   54._____   77._____   100._____   123._____   146._____
9._____   32._____   55._____   78._____   101._____   124._____   147._____
10._____   33._____   56._____   79._____   102._____   125._____   148._____
11._____   34._____   57._____   80._____   103._____   126._____   149._____
12._____   35._____   58._____   81._____   104._____   127._____   150._____
13._____   36._____   59._____   82._____   105._____   128._____   151._____
14._____   37._____   60._____   83._____   106._____   129._____   152._____
15._____   38._____   61._____   84._____   107._____   130._____   153._____
16._____   39._____   62._____   85._____   108._____   131._____   154._____
17._____   40._____   63._____   86._____   109._____   132._____   155._____
18._____   41._____   64._____   87._____   110._____   133._____   156._____
19._____   42._____   65._____   88._____   111._____   134._____   157._____
20._____   43._____   66._____   89._____   112._____   135._____   158._____
21._____   44._____   67._____   90._____   113._____   136._____   159._____
22._____   45._____   68._____   91._____   114._____   137._____   160._____
23._____   46._____   69._____   92._____   115._____   138._____   161._____

Real Estate Training Institute – Leslie Clauson

1.____	24.____	47.____	70.____	93.____	116.____	139.____
2.____	25.____	48.____	71.____	94.____	117.____	140.____
3.____	26.____	49.____	72.____	95.____	118.____	141.____
4.____	27.____	50.____	73.____	96.____	119.____	142.____
5.____	28.____	51.____	74.____	97.____	120.____	143.____
6.____	29.____	52.____	75.____	98.____	121.____	144.____
7.____	30.____	53.____	76.____	99.____	122.____	145.____
8.____	31.____	54.____	77.____	100.____	123.____	146.____
9.____	32.____	55.____	78.____	101.____	124.____	147.____
10.____	33.____	56.____	79.____	102.____	125.____	148.____
11.____	34.____	57.____	80.____	103.____	126.____	149.____
12.____	35.____	58.____	81.____	104.____	127.____	150.____
13.____	36.____	59.____	82.____	105.____	128.____	151.____
14.____	37.____	60.____	83.____	106.____	129.____	152.____
15.____	38.____	61.____	84.____	107.____	130.____	153.____
16.____	39.____	62.____	85.____	108.____	131.____	154.____
17.____	40.____	63.____	86.____	109.____	132.____	155.____
18.____	41.____	64.____	87.____	110.____	133.____	156.____
19.____	42.____	65.____	88.____	111.____	134.____	157.____
20.____	43.____	66.____	89.____	112.____	135.____	158.____
21.____	44.____	67.____	90.____	113.____	136.____	159.____
22.____	45.____	68.____	91.____	114.____	137.____	160.____
23.____	46.____	69.____	92.____	115.____	138.____	161.____

Real Estate Training Institute – Leslie Clauson

1.____	24.____	47.____	70.____	93.____	116.____	139.____
2.____	25.____	48.____	71.____	94.____	117.____	140.____
3.____	26.____	49.____	72.____	95.____	118.____	141.____
4.____	27.____	50.____	73.____	96.____	119.____	142.____
5.____	28.____	51.____	74.____	97.____	120.____	143.____
6.____	29.____	52.____	75.____	98.____	121.____	144.____
7.____	30.____	53.____	76.____	99.____	122.____	145.____
8.____	31.____	54.____	77.____	100.____	123.____	146.____
9.____	32.____	55.____	78.____	101.____	124.____	147.____
10.____	33.____	56.____	79.____	102.____	125.____	148.____
11.____	34.____	57.____	80.____	103.____	126.____	149.____
12.____	35.____	58.____	81.____	104.____	127.____	150.____
13.____	36.____	59.____	82.____	105.____	128.____	151.____
14.____	37.____	60.____	83.____	106.____	129.____	152.____
15.____	38.____	61.____	84.____	107.____	130.____	153.____
16.____	39.____	62.____	85.____	108.____	131.____	154.____
17.____	40.____	63.____	86.____	109.____	132.____	155.____
18.____	41.____	64.____	87.____	110.____	133.____	156.____
19.____	42.____	65.____	88.____	111.____	134.____	157.____
20.____	43.____	66.____	89.____	112.____	135.____	158.____
21.____	44.____	67.____	90.____	113.____	136.____	159.____
22.____	45.____	68.____	91.____	114.____	137.____	160.____
23.____	46.____	69.____	92.____	115.____	138.____	161.____

Real Estate Training Institute – Leslie Clauson

1.____	24.____	47.____	70.____	93.____	116.____	139.____
2.____	25.____	48.____	71.____	94.____	117.____	140.____
3.____	26.____	49.____	72.____	95.____	118.____	141.____
4.____	27.____	50.____	73.____	96.____	119.____	142.____
5.____	28.____	51.____	74.____	97.____	120.____	143.____
6.____	29.____	52.____	75.____	98.____	121.____	144.____
7.____	30.____	53.____	76.____	99.____	122.____	145.____
8.____	31.____	54.____	77.____	100.____	123.____	146.____
9.____	32.____	55.____	78.____	101.____	124.____	147.____
10.____	33.____	56.____	79.____	102.____	125.____	148.____
11.____	34.____	57.____	80.____	103.____	126.____	149.____
12.____	35.____	58.____	81.____	104.____	127.____	150.____
13.____	36.____	59.____	82.____	105.____	128.____	151.____
14.____	37.____	60.____	83.____	106.____	129.____	152.____
15.____	38.____	61.____	84.____	107.____	130.____	153.____
16.____	39.____	62.____	85.____	108.____	131.____	154.____
17.____	40.____	63.____	86.____	109.____	132.____	155.____
18.____	41.____	64.____	87.____	110.	133.____	156.____
19.____	42.____	65.____	88.____	111.____	134.____	157.____
20.____	43.____	66.____	89.____	112.____	135.____	158.____
21.____	44.____	67.____	90.____	113.____	136.____	159.____
22.____	45.____	68.____	91.____	114.____	137.____	160.____
23.____	46.____	69.____	92.____	115.____	138.____	161.____

Real Estate Training Institute – Leslie Clauson

1.____	24.____	47.____	70.____	93.____	116.____	139.____
2.____	25.____	48.____	71.____	94.____	117.____	140.____
3.____	26.____	49.____	72.____	95.____	118.____	141.____
4.____	27.____	50.____	73.____	96.____	119.____	142.____
5.____	28.____	51.____	74.____	97.____	120.____	143.____
6.____	29.____	52.____	75.____	98.____	121.____	144.____
7.____	30.____	53.____	76.____	99.____	122.____	145.____
8.____	31.____	54.____	77.____	100.____	123.____	146.____
9.____	32.____	55.____	78.____	101.____	124.____	147.____
10.____	33.____	56.____	79.____	102.____	125.____	148.____
11.____	34.____	57.____	80.____	103.____	126.____	149.____
12.____	35.____	58.____	81.____	104.____	127.____	150.____
13.____	36.____	59.____	82.____	105.____	128.____	151.____
14.____	37.____	60.____	83.____	106.____	129.____	152.____
15.____	38.____	61.____	84.____	107.____	130.____	153.____
16.____	39.____	62.____	85.____	108.____	131.____	154.____
17.____	40.____	63.____	86.____	109.____	132.____	155.____
18.____	41.____	64.____	87.____	110.____	133.____	156.____
19.____	42.____	65.____	88.____	111.____	134.____	157.____
20.____	43.____	66.____	89.____	112.____	135.____	158.____
21.____	44.____	67.____	90.____	113.____	136.____	159.____
22.____	45.____	68.____	91.____	114.____	137.____	160.____
23.____	46.____	69.____	92.____	115.____	138.____	161.____

Real Estate Training Institute – Leslie Clauson

1.___	24.___	47.___	70.___	93.___	116.___	139.___
2.___	25.___	48.___	71.___	94.___	117.___	140.___
3.___	26.___	49.___	72.___	95.___	118.___	141.___
4.___	27.___	50.___	73.___	96.___	119.___	142.___
5.___	28.___	51.___	74.___	97.___	120.___	143.___
6.___	29.___	52.___	75.___	98.___	121.___	144.___
7.___	30.___	53.___	76.___	99.___	122.___	145.___
8.___	31.___	54.___	77.___	100.___	123.___	146.___
9.___	32.___	55.___	78.___	101.___	124.___	147.___
10.___	33.___	56.___	79.___	102.___	125.___	148.___
11.___	34.___	57.___	80.___	103.___	126.___	149.___
12.___	35.___	58.___	81.___	104.___	127.___	150.___
13.___	36.___	59.___	82.___	105.___	128.___	151.___
14.___	37.___	60.___	83.___	106.___	129.___	152.___
15.___	38.___	61.___	84.___	107.___	130.___	153.___
16.___	39.___	62.___	85.___	108.___	131.___	154.___
17.___	40.___	63.___	86.___	109.___	132.___	155.___
18.___	41.___	64.___	87.___	110.___	133.___	156.___
19.___	42.___	65.___	88.___	111.___	134.___	157.___
20.___	43.___	66.___	89.___	112.___	135.___	158.___
21.___	44.___	67.___	90.___	113.___	136.___	159.___
22.___	45.___	68.___	91.___	114.___	137.___	160.___
23.___	46.___	69.___	92.___	115.___	138.___	161.___

Real Estate Training Institute – Leslie Clauson

1. ____
2. ____
3. ____
4. ____
5. ____
6. ____
7. ____
8. ____
9. ____
10. ____
11. ____
12. ____
13. ____
14. ____
15. ____
16. ____
17. ____
18. ____
19. ____
20. ____
21. ____
22. ____
23. ____
24. ____
25. ____
26. ____
27. ____
28. ____
29. ____
30. ____
31. ____
32. ____
33. ____
34. ____
35. ____
36. ____
37. ____
38. ____
39. ____
40. ____
41. ____
42. ____
43. ____
44. ____
45. ____
46. ____
47. ____
48. ____
49. ____
50. ____
51. ____
52. ____
53. ____
54. ____
55. ____
56. ____
57. ____
58. ____
59. ____
60. ____
61. ____
62. ____
63. ____
64. ____
65. ____
66. ____
67. ____
68. ____
69. ____
70. ____
71. ____
72. ____
73. ____
74. ____
75. ____
76. ____
77. ____
78. ____
79. ____
80. ____
81. ____
82. ____
83. ____
84. ____
85. ____
86. ____
87. ____
88. ____
89. ____
90. ____
91. ____
92. ____
93. ____
94. ____
95. ____
96. ____
97. ____
98. ____
99. ____
100. ____
101. ____
102. ____
103. ____
104. ____
105. ____
106. ____
107. ____
108. ____
109. ____
110. ____
111. ____
112. ____
113. ____
114. ____
115. ____
116. ____
117. ____
118. ____
119. ____
120. ____
121. ____
122. ____
123. ____
124. ____
125. ____
126. ____
127. ____
128. ____
129. ____
130. ____
131. ____
132. ____
133. ____
134. ____
135. ____
136. ____
137. ____
138. ____
139. ____
140. ____
141. ____
142. ____
143. ____
144. ____
145. ____
146. ____
147. ____
148. ____
149. ____
150. ____
151. ____
152. ____
153. ____
154. ____
155. ____
156. ____
157. ____
158. ____
159. ____
160. ____
161. ____

Real Estate Training Institute – Leslie Clauson

1.____	24.____	47.____	70.____	93.____	116.____	139.____
2.____	25.____	48.____	71.____	94.____	117.____	140.____
3.____	26.____	49.____	72.____	95.____	118.____	141.____
4.____	27.____	50.____	73.____	96.____	119.____	142.____
5.____	28.____	51.____	74.____	97.____	120.____	143.____
6.____	29.____	52.____	75.____	98.____	121.____	144.____
7.____	30.____	53.____	76.____	99.____	122.____	145.____
8.____	31.____	54.____	77.____	100.____	123.____	146.____
9.____	32.____	55.____	78.____	101.____	124.____	147.____
10.____	33.____	56.____	79.____	102.____	125.____	148.____
11.____	34.____	57.____	80.____	103.____	126.____	149.____
12.____	35.____	58.____	81.____	104.____	127.____	150.____
13.____	36.____	59.____	82.____	105.____	128.____	151.____
14.____	37.____	60.____	83.____	106.____	129.____	152.____
15.____	38.____	61.____	84.____	107.____	130.____	153.____
16.____	39.____	62.____	85.____	108.____	131.____	154.____
17.____	40.____	63.____	86.____	109.____	132.____	155.____
18.____	41.____	64.____	87.____	110.____	133.____	156.____
19.____	42.____	65.____	88.____	111.____	134.____	157.____
20.____	43.____	66.____	89.____	112.____	135.____	158.____
21.____	44.____	67.____	90.____	113.____	136.____	159.____
22.____	45.____	68.____	91.____	114.____	137.____	160.____
23.____	46.____	69.____	92.____	115.____	138.____	161.____

Real Estate Training Institute – Leslie Clauson

1.____	24.____	47.____	70.____	93.____	116.____	139.____
2.____	25.____	48.____	71.____	94.____	117.____	140.____
3.____	26.____	49.____	72.____	95.____	118.____	141.____
4.____	27.____	50.____	73.____	96.____	119.____	142.____
5.____	28.____	51.____	74.____	97.____	120.____	143.____
6.____	29.____	52.____	75.____	98.____	121.____	144.____
7.____	30.____	53.____	76.____	99.____	122.____	145.____
8.____	31.____	54.____	77.____	100.____	123.____	146.____
9.____	32.____	55.____	78.____	101.____	124.____	147.____
10.____	33.____	56.____	79.____	102.____	125.____	148.____
11.____	34.____	57.____	80.____	103.____	126.____	149.____
12.____	35.____	58.____	81.____	104.____	127.____	150.____
13.____	36.____	59.____	82.____	105.____	128.____	151.____
14.____	37.____	60.____	83.____	106.____	129.____	152.____
15.____	38.____	61.____	84.____	107.____	130.____	153.____
16.____	39.____	62.____	85.____	108.____	131.____	154.____
17.____	40.____	63.____	86.____	109.____	132.____	155.____
18.____	41.____	64.____	87.____	110.____	133.____	156.____
19.____	42.____	65.____	88.____	111.____	134.____	157.____
20.____	43.____	66.____	89.____	112.____	135.____	158.____
21.____	44.____	67.____	90.____	113.____	136.____	159.____
22.____	45.____	68.____	91.____	114.____	137.____	160.____
23.____	46.____	69.____	92.____	115.____	138.____	161.____

Real Estate Training Institute – Leslie Clauson

1.____	24.____	47.____	70.____	93.____	116.____	139.____
2.____	25.____	48.____	71.____	94.____	117.____	140.____
3.____	26.____	49.____	72.____	95.____	118.____	141.____
4.____	27.____	50.____	73.____	96.____	119.____	142.____
5.____	28.____	51.____	74.____	97.____	120.____	143.____
6.____	29.____	52.____	75.____	98.____	121.____	144.____
7.____	30.____	53.____	76.____	99.____	122.____	145.____
8.____	31.____	54.____	77.____	100.____	123.____	146.____
9.____	32.____	55.____	78.____	101.____	124.____	147.____
10.____	33.____	56.____	79.____	102.____	125.____	148.____
11.____	34.____	57.____	80.____	103.____	126.____	149.____
12.____	35.____	58.____	81.____	104.____	127.____	150.____
13.____	36.____	59.____	82.____	105.____	128.____	151.____
14.____	37.____	60.____	83.____	106.____	129.____	152.____
15.____	38.____	61.____	84.____	107.____	130.____	153.____
16.____	39.____	62.____	85.____	108.____	131.____	154.____
17.____	40.____	63.____	86.____	109.____	132.____	155.____
18.____	41.____	64.____	87.____	110.____	133.____	156.____
19.____	42.____	65.____	88.____	111.____	134.____	157.____
20.____	43.____	66.____	89.____	112.____	135.____	158.____
21.____	44.____	67.____	90.____	113.____	136.____	159.____
22.____	45.____	68.____	91.____	114.____	137.____	160.____
23.____	46.____	69.____	92.____	115.____	138.____	161.____

Real Estate Training Institute – Leslie Clauson

1._____   24._____   47._____   70._____   93._____   116._____   139._____
2._____   25._____   48._____   71._____   94._____   117._____   140._____
3._____   26._____   49._____   72._____   95._____   118._____   141._____
4._____   27._____   50._____   73._____   96._____   119._____   142._____
5._____   28._____   51._____   74._____   97._____   120._____   143._____
6._____   29._____   52._____   75._____   98._____   121._____   144._____
7._____   30._____   53._____   76._____   99._____   122._____   145._____
8._____   31._____   54._____   77._____   100._____ 123._____   146._____
9._____   32._____   55._____   78._____   101._____ 124._____   147._____
10._____ 33._____   56._____   79._____   102._____ 125._____   148._____
11._____ 34._____   57._____   80._____   103._____ 126._____   149._____
12._____ 35._____   58._____   81._____   104._____ 127._____   150._____
13._____ 36._____   59._____   82._____   105._____ 128._____   151._____
14._____ 37._____   60._____   83._____   106._____ 129._____   152._____
15._____ 38._____   61._____   84._____   107._____ 130._____   153._____
16._____ 39._____   62._____   85._____   108._____ 131._____   154._____
17._____ 40._____   63._____   86._____   109._____ 132._____   155._____
18._____ 41._____   64._____   87._____   110._____ 133._____   156._____
19._____ 42._____   65._____   88._____   111._____ 134._____   157._____
20._____ 43._____   66._____   89._____   112._____ 135._____   158._____
21._____ 44._____   67._____   90._____   113._____ 136._____   159._____
22._____ 45._____   68._____   91._____   114._____ 137._____   160._____
23._____ 46._____   69._____   92._____   115._____ 138._____   161._____

Real Estate Training Institute – Leslie Clauson

1.____	24.____	47.____	70.____	93.____	116.____	139.____
2.____	25.____	48.____	71.____	94.____	117.____	140.____
3.____	26.____	49.____	72.____	95.____	118.____	141.____
4.____	27.____	50.____	73.____	96.____	119.____	142.____
5.____	28.____	51.____	74.____	97.____	120.____	143.____
6.____	29.____	52.____	75.____	98.____	121.____	144.____
7.____	30.____	53.____	76.____	99.____	122.____	145.____
8.____	31.____	54.____	77.____	100.____	123.____	146.____
9.____	32.____	55.____	78.____	101.____	124.____	147.____
10.____	33.____	56.____	79.____	102.____	125.____	148.____
11.____	34.____	57.____	80.____	103.____	126.____	149.____
12.____	35.____	58.____	81.____	104.____	127.____	150.____
13.____	36.____	59.____	82.____	105.____	128.____	151.____
14.____	37.____	60.____	83.____	106.____	129.____	152.____
15.____	38.____	61.____	84.____	107.____	130.____	153.____
16.____	39.____	62.____	85.____	108.____	131.____	154.____
17.____	40.____	63.____	86.____	109.____	132.____	155.____
18.____	41.____	64.____	87.____	110.____	133.____	156.____
19.____	42.____	65.____	88.____	111.____	134.____	157.____
20.____	43.____	66.____	89.____	112.____	135.____	158.____
21.____	44.____	67.____	90.____	113.____	136.____	159.____
22.____	45.____	68.____	91.____	114.____	137.____	160.____
23.____	46.____	69.____	92.____	115.____	138.____	161.____

Real Estate Training Institute – Leslie Clauson

1.____	24.____	47.____	70.____	93.____	116.____	139.____
2.____	25.____	48.____	71.____	94.____	117.____	140.____
3.____	26.____	49.____	72.____	95.____	118.____	141.____
4.____	27.____	50.____	73.____	96.____	119.____	142.____
5.____	28.____	51.____	74.____	97.____	120.____	143.____
6.____	29.____	52.____	75.____	98.____	121.____	144.____
7.____	30.____	53.____	76.____	99.____	122.____	145.____
8.____	31.____	54.____	77.____	100.____	123.____	146.____
9.____	32.____	55.____	78.____	101.____	124.____	147.____
10.____	33.____	56.____	79.____	102.____	125.____	148.____
11.____	34.____	57.____	80.____	103.____	126.____	149.____
12.____	35.____	58.____	81.____	104.____	127.____	150.____
13.____	36.____	59.____	82.____	105.____	128.____	151.____
14.____	37.____	60.____	83.____	106.____	129.____	152.____
15.____	38.____	61.____	84.____	107.____	130.____	153.____
16.____	39.____	62.____	85.____	108.____	131.____	154.____
17.____	40.____	63.____	86.____	109.____	132.____	155.____
18.____	41.____	64.____	87.____	110.____	133.____	156.____
19.____	42.____	65.____	88.____	111.____	134.____	157.____
20.____	43.____	66.____	89.____	112.____	135.____	158.____
21.____	44.____	67.____	90.____	113.____	136.____	159.____
22.____	45.____	68.____	91.____	114.____	137.____	160.____
23.____	46.____	69.____	92.____	115.____	138.____	161.____

Real Estate Training Institute – Leslie Clauson

1.____	24.____	47.____	70.____	93.____	116.____	139.____
2.____	25.____	48.____	71.____	94.____	117.____	140.____
3.____	26.____	49.____	72.____	95.____	118.____	141.____
4.____	27.____	50.____	73.____	96.____	119.____	142.____
5.____	28.____	51.____	74.____	97.____	120.____	143.____
6.____	29.____	52.____	75.____	98.____	121.____	144.____
7.____	30.____	53.____	76.____	99.____	122.____	145.____
8.____	31.____	54.____	77.____	100.____	123.____	146.____
9.____	32.____	55.____	78.____	101.____	124.____	147.____
10.____	33.____	56.____	79.____	102.____	125.____	148.____
11.____	34.____	57.____	80.____	103.____	126.____	149.____
12.____	35.____	58.____	81.____	104.____	127.____	150.____
13.____	36.____	59.____	82.____	105.____	128.____	151.____
14.____	37.____	60.____	83.____	106.____	129.____	152.____
15.____	38.____	61.____	84.____	107.____	130.____	153.____
16.____	39.____	62.____	85.____	108.____	131.____	154.____
17.____	40.____	63.____	86.____	109.____	132.____	155.____
18.____	41.____	64.____	87.____	110.____	133.____	156.____
19.____	42.____	65.____	88.____	111.____	134.____	157.____
20.____	43.____	66.____	89.____	112.____	135.____	158.____
21.____	44.____	67.____	90.____	113.____	136.____	159.____
22.____	45.____	68.____	91.____	114.____	137.____	160.____
23.____	46.____	69.____	92.____	115.____	138.____	161.____

Real Estate Training Institute – Leslie Clauson

1.____	24.____	47.____	70.____	93.____	116.____	139.____
2.____	25.____	48.____	71.____	94.____	117.____	140.____
3.____	26.____	49.____	72.____	95.____	118.____	141.____
4.____	27.____	50.____	73.____	96.____	119.____	142.____
5.____	28.____	51.____	74.____	97.____	120.____	143.____
6.____	29.____	52.____	75.____	98.____	121.____	144.____
7.____	30.____	53.____	76.____	99.____	122.____	145.____
8.____	31.____	54.____	77.____	100.____	123.____	146.____
9.____	32.____	55.____	78.____	101.____	124.____	147.____
10.____	33.____	56.____	79.____	102.____	125.____	148.____
11.____	34.____	57.____	80.____	103.____	126.____	149.____
12.____	35.____	58.____	81.____	104.____	127.____	150.____
13.____	36.____	59.____	82.____	105.____	128.____	151.____
14.____	37.____	60.____	83.____	106.____	129.____	152.____
15.____	38.____	61.____	84.____	107.____	130.____	153.____
16.____	39.____	62.____	85.____	108.____	131.____	154.____
17.____	40.____	63.____	86.____	109.____	132.____	155.____
18.____	41.____	64.____	87.____	110.____	133.____	156.____
19.____	42.____	65.____	88.____	111.____	134.____	157.____
20.____	43.____	66.____	89.____	112.____	135.____	158.____
21.____	44.____	67.____	90.____	113.____	136.____	159.____
22.____	45.____	68.____	91.____	114.____	137.____	160.____
23.____	46.____	69.____	92.____	115.____	138.____	161.____

Real Estate Training Institute – Leslie Clauson

1.____	24.____	47.____	70.____	93.____	116.____	139.____
2.____	25.____	48.____	71.____	94.____	117.____	140.____
3.____	26.____	49.____	72.____	95.____	118.____	141.____
4.____	27.____	50.____	73.____	96.____	119.____	142.____
5.____	28.____	51.____	74.____	97.____	120.____	143.____
6.____	29.____	52.____	75.____	98.____	121.____	144.____
7.____	30.____	53.____	76.____	99.____	122.____	145.____
8.____	31.____	54.____	77.____	100.____	123.____	146.____
9.____	32.____	55.____	78.____	101.____	124.____	147.____
10.____	33.____	56.____	79.____	102.____	125.____	148.____
11.____	34.____	57.____	80.____	103.____	126.____	149.____
12.____	35.____	58.____	81.____	104.____	127.____	150.____
13.____	36.____	59.____	82.____	105.____	128.____	151.____
14.____	37.____	60.____	83.____	106.____	129.____	152.____
15.____	38.____	61.____	84.____	107.____	130.____	153.____
16.____	39.____	62.____	85.____	108.____	131.____	154.____
17.____	40.____	63.____	86.____	109.____	132.____	155.____
18.____	41.____	64.____	87.____	110.____	133.____	156.____
19.____	42.____	65.____	88.____	111.____	134.____	157.____
20.____	43.____	66.____	89.____	112.____	135.____	158.____
21.____	44.____	67.____	90.____	113.____	136.____	159.____
22.____	45.____	68.____	91.____	114.____	137.____	160.____
23.____	46.____	69.____	92.____	115.____	138.____	161.____

Real Estate Training Institute – Leslie Clauson

1.____   24.____   47.____   70.____   93.____   116.____   139.____
2.____   25.____   48.____   71.____   94.____   117.____   140.____
3.____   26.____   49.____   72.____   95.____   118.____   141.____
4.____   27.____   50.____   73.____   96.____   119.____   142.____
5.____   28.____   51.____   74.____   97.____   120.____   143.____
6.____   29.____   52.____   75.____   98.____   121.____   144.____
7.____   30.____   53.____   76.____   99.____   122.____   145.____
8.____   31.____   54.____   77.____   100.____ 123.____   146.____
9.____   32.____   55.____   78.____   101.____ 124.____   147.____
10.____ 33.____   56.____   79.____   102.____ 125.____   148.____
11.____ 34.____   57.____   80.____   103.____ 126.____   149.____
12.____ 35.____   58.____   81.____   104.____ 127.____   150.____
13.____ 36.____   59.____   82.____   105.____ 128.____   151.____
14.____ 37.____   60.____   83.____   106.____ 129.____   152.____
15.____ 38.____   61.____   84.____   107.____ 130.____   153.____
16.____ 39.____   62.____   85.____   108.____ 131.____   154.____
17.____ 40.____   63.____   86.____   109.____ 132.____   155.____
18.____ 41.____   64.____   87.____   110.____ 133.____   156.____
19.____ 42.____   65.____   88.____   111.____ 134.____   157.____
20.____ 43.____   66.____   89.____   112.____ 135.____   158.____
21.____ 44.____   67.____   90.____   113.____ 136.____   159.____
22.____ 45.____   68.____   91.____   114.____ 137.____   160.____
23.____ 46.____   69.____   92.____   115.____ 138.____   161.____

Real Estate Training Institute – Leslie Clauson

1.____	24.____	47.____	70.____	93.____	116.____	139.____
2.____	25.____	48.____	71.____	94.____	117.____	140.____
3.____	26.____	49.____	72.____	95.____	118.____	141.____
4.____	27.____	50.____	73.____	96.____	119.____	142.____
5.____	28.____	51.____	74.____	97.____	120.____	143.____
6.____	29.____	52.____	75.____	98.____	121.____	144.____
7.____	30.____	53.____	76.____	99.____	122.____	145.____
8.____	31.____	54.____	77.____	100.____	123.____	146.____
9.____	32.____	55.____	78.____	101.____	124.____	147.____
10.____	33.____	56.____	79.____	102.____	125.____	148.____
11.____	34.____	57.____	80.____	103.____	126.____	149.____
12.____	35.____	58.____	81.____	104.____	127.____	150.____
13.____	36.____	59.____	82.____	105.____	128.____	151.____
14.____	37.____	60.____	83.____	106.____	129.____	152.____
15.____	38.____	61.____	84.____	107.____	130.____	153.____
16.____	39.____	62.____	85.____	108.____	131.____	154.____
17.____	40.____	63.____	86.____	109.____	132.____	155.____
18.____	41.____	64.____	87.____	110.____	133.____	156.____
19.____	42.____	65.____	88.____	111.____	134.____	157.____
20.____	43.____	66.____	89.____	112.____	135.____	158.____
21.____	44.____	67.____	90.____	113.____	136.____	159.____
22.____	45.____	68.____	91.____	114.____	137.____	160.____
23.____	46.____	69.____	92.____	115.____	138.____	161.____

Real Estate Training Institute – Leslie Clauson

1.____ 24.____ 47.____ 70.____ 93.____ 116.____ 139.____
2.____ 25.____ 48.____ 71.____ 94.____ 117.____ 140.____
3.____ 26.____ 49.____ 72.____ 95.____ 118.____ 141.____
4.____ 27.____ 50.____ 73.____ 96.____ 119.____ 142.____
5.____ 28.____ 51.____ 74.____ 97.____ 120.____ 143.____
6.____ 29.____ 52.____ 75.____ 98.____ 121.____ 144.____
7.____ 30.____ 53.____ 76.____ 99.____ 122.____ 145.____
8.____ 31.____ 54.____ 77.____ 100.____ 123.____ 146.____
9.____ 32.____ 55.____ 78.____ 101.____ 124.____ 147.____
10.____ 33.____ 56.____ 79.____ 102.____ 125.____ 148.____
11.____ 34.____ 57.____ 80.____ 103.____ 126.____ 149.____
12.____ 35.____ 58.____ 81.____ 104.____ 127.____ 150.____
13.____ 36.____ 59.____ 82.____ 105.____ 128.____ 151.____
14.____ 37.____ 60.____ 83.____ 106.____ 129.____ 152.____
15.____ 38.____ 61.____ 84.____ 107.____ 130.____ 153.____
16.____ 39.____ 62.____ 85.____ 108.____ 131.____ 154.____
17.____ 40.____ 63.____ 86.____ 109.____ 132.____ 155.____
18.____ 41.____ 64.____ 87.____ 110.____ 133.____ 156.____
19.____ 42.____ 65.____ 88.____ 111.____ 134.____ 157.____
20.____ 43.____ 66.____ 89.____ 112.____ 135.____ 158.____
21.____ 44.____ 67.____ 90.____ 113.____ 136.____ 159.____
22.____ 45.____ 68.____ 91.____ 114.____ 137.____ 160.____
23.____ 46.____ 69.____ 92.____ 115.____ 138.____ 161.____

Real Estate Training Institute – Leslie Clauson

1.___	24.___	47.___	70.___	93.___	116.___	139.___
2.___	25.___	48.___	71.___	94.___	117.___	140.___
3.___	26.___	49.___	72.___	95.___	118.___	141.___
4.___	27.___	50.___	73.___	96.___	119.___	142.___
5.___	28.___	51.___	74.___	97.___	120.___	143.___
6.___	29.___	52.___	75.___	98.___	121.___	144.___
7.___	30.___	53.___	76.___	99.___	122.___	145.___
8.___	31.___	54.___	77.___	100.___	123.___	146.___
9.___	32.___	55.___	78.___	101.___	124.___	147.___
10.___	33.___	56.___	79.___	102.___	125.___	148.___
11.___	34.___	57.___	80.___	103.___	126.___	149.___
12.___	35.___	58.___	81.___	104.___	127.___	150.___
13.___	36.___	59.___	82.___	105.___	128.___	151.___
14.___	37.___	60.___	83.___	106.___	129.___	152.___
15.___	38.___	61.___	84.___	107.___	130.___	153.___
16.___	39.___	62.___	85.___	108.___	131.___	154.___
17.___	40.___	63.___	86.___	109.___	132.___	155.___
18.___	41.___	64.___	87.___	110.___	133.___	156.___
19.___	42.___	65.___	88.___	111.___	134.___	157.___
20.___	43.___	66.___	89.___	112.___	135.___	158.___
21.___	44.___	67.___	90.___	113.___	136.___	159.___
22.___	45.___	68.___	91.___	114.___	137.___	160.___
23.___	46.___	69.___	92.___	115.___	138.___	161.___

Real Estate Training Institute – Leslie Clauson

1.____	24.____	47.____	70.____	93.____	116.____	139.____
2.____	25.____	48.____	71.____	94.____	117.____	140.____
3.____	26.____	49.____	72.____	95.____	118.____	141.____
4.____	27.____	50.____	73.____	96.____	119.____	142.____
5.____	28.____	51.____	74.____	97.____	120.____	143.____
6.____	29.____	52.____	75.____	98.____	121.____	144.____
7.____	30.____	53.____	76.____	99.____	122.____	145.____
8.____	31.____	54.____	77.____	100.____	123.____	146.____
9.____	32.____	55.____	78.____	101.____	124.____	147.____
10.____	33.____	56.____	79.____	102.____	125.____	148.____
11.____	34.____	57.____	80.____	103.____	126.____	149.____
12.____	35.____	58.____	81.____	104.____	127.____	150.____
13.____	36.____	59.____	82.____	105.____	128.____	151.____
14.____	37.____	60.____	83.____	106.____	129.____	152.____
15.____	38.____	61.____	84.____	107.____	130.____	153.____
16.____	39.____	62.____	85.____	108.____	131.____	154.____
17.____	40.____	63.____	86.____	109.____	132.____	155.____
18.____	41.____	64.____	87.____	110.____	133.____	156.____
19.____	42.____	65.____	88.____	111.____	134.____	157.____
20.____	43.____	66.____	89.____	112.____	135.____	158.____
21.____	44.____	67.____	90.____	113.____	136.____	159.____
22.____	45.____	68.____	91.____	114.____	137.____	160.____
23.____	46.____	69.____	92.____	115.____	138.____	161.____

Real Estate Training Institute – Leslie Clauson

1.____	24.____	47.____	70.____	93.____	116.____	139.____
2.____	25.____	48.____	71.____	94.____	117.____	140.____
3.____	26.____	49.____	72.____	95.____	118.____	141.____
4.____	27.____	50.____	73.____	96.____	119.____	142.____
5.____	28.____	51.____	74.____	97.____	120.____	143.____
6.____	29.____	52.____	75.____	98.____	121.____	144.____
7.____	30.____	53.____	76.____	99.____	122.____	145.____
8.____	31.____	54.____	77.____	100.____	123.____	146.____
9.____	32.____	55.____	78.____	101.____	124.____	147.____
10.____	33.____	56.____	79.____	102.____	125.____	148.____
11.____	34.____	57.____	80.____	103.____	126.____	149.____
12.____	35.____	58.____	81.____	104.____	127.____	150.____
13.____	36.____	59.____	82.____	105.____	128.____	151.____
14.____	37.____	60.____	83.____	106.____	129.____	152.____
15.____	38.____	61.____	84.____	107.____	130.____	153.____
16.____	39.____	62.____	85.____	108.____	131.____	154.____
17.____	40.____	63.____	86.____	109.____	132.____	155.____
18.____	41.____	64.____	87.	110.____	133.____	156.____
19.____	42.____	65.____	88.____	111.____	134.____	157.____
20.____	43.____	66.____	89.____	112.____	135.____	158.____
21.____	44.____	67.____	90.____	113.____	136.____	159.____
22.____	45.____	68.____	91.____	114.____	137.____	160.____
23.____	46.____	69.____	92.____	115.____	138.____	161.____

Real Estate Training Institute – Leslie Clauson

1.____ 24.____ 47.____ 70.____ 93.____ 116.____ 139.____
2.____ 25.____ 48.____ 71.____ 94.____ 117.____ 140.____
3.____ 26.____ 49.____ 72.____ 95.____ 118.____ 141.____
4.____ 27.____ 50.____ 73.____ 96.____ 119.____ 142.____
5.____ 28.____ 51.____ 74.____ 97.____ 120.____ 143.____
6.____ 29.____ 52.____ 75.____ 98.____ 121.____ 144.____
7.____ 30.____ 53.____ 76.____ 99.____ 122.____ 145.____
8.____ 31.____ 54.____ 77.____ 100.____ 123.____ 146.____
9.____ 32.____ 55.____ 78.____ 101.____ 124.____ 147.____
10.____ 33.____ 56.____ 79.____ 102.____ 125.____ 148.____
11.____ 34.____ 57.____ 80.____ 103.____ 126.____ 149.____
12.____ 35.____ 58.____ 81.____ 104.____ 127.____ 150.____
13.____ 36.____ 59.____ 82.____ 105.____ 128.____ 151.____
14.____ 37.____ 60.____ 83.____ 106.____ 129.____ 152.____
15.____ 38.____ 61.____ 84.____ 107.____ 130.____ 153.____
16.____ 39.____ 62.____ 85.____ 108.____ 131.____ 154.____
17.____ 40.____ 63.____ 86.____ 109.____ 132.____ 155.____
18.____ 41.____ 64.____ 87.____ 110.____ 133.____ 156.____
19.____ 42.____ 65.____ 88.____ 111.____ 134.____ 157.____
20.____ 43.____ 66.____ 89.____ 112.____ 135.____ 158.____
21.____ 44.____ 67.____ 90.____ 113.____ 136.____ 159.____
22.____ 45.____ 68.____ 91.____ 114.____ 137.____ 160.____
23.____ 46.____ 69.____ 92.____ 115.____ 138.____ 161.____

Real Estate Training Institute – Leslie Clauson

1.____	24.____	47.____	70.____	93.____	116.____	139.____
2.____	25.____	48.____	71.____	94.____	117.____	140.____
3.____	26.____	49.____	72.____	95.____	118.____	141.____
4.____	27.____	50.____	73.____	96.____	119.____	142.____
5.____	28.____	51.____	74.____	97.____	120.____	143.____
6.____	29.____	52.____	75.____	98.____	121.____	144.____
7.____	30.____	53.____	76.____	99.____	122.____	145.____
8.____	31.____	54.____	77.____	100.____	123.____	146.____
9.____	32.____	55.____	78.____	101.____	124.____	147.____
10.____	33.____	56.____	79.____	102.____	125.____	148.____
11.____	34.____	57.____	80.____	103.____	126.____	149.____
12.____	35.____	58.____	81.____	104.____	127.____	150.____
13.____	36.____	59.____	82.____	105.____	128.____	151.____
14.____	37.____	60.____	83.____	106.____	129.____	152.____
15.____	38.____	61.____	84.____	107.____	130.____	153.____
16.____	39.____	62.____	85.____	108.____	131.____	154.____
17.____	40.____	63.____	86.____	109.____	132.____	155.____
18.____	41.____	64.____	87.____	110.____	133.____	156.____
19.____	42.____	65.____	88.____	111.____	134.____	157.____
20.____	43.____	66.____	89.____	112.____	135.____	158.____
21.____	44.____	67.____	90.____	113.____	136.____	159.____
22.____	45.____	68.____	91.____	114.____	137.____	160.____
23.____	46.____	69.____	92.____	115.____	138.____	161.____

Real Estate Training Institute – Pre Exam Workbook

1._____	24._____	47._____	70._____	93._____	116._____	139._____
2._____	25._____	48._____	71._____	94._____	117._____	140._____
3._____	26._____	49._____	72._____	95._____	118._____	141._____
4._____	27._____	50._____	73._____	96._____	119._____	142._____
5._____	28._____	51._____	74._____	97._____	120._____	143._____
6._____	29._____	52._____	75._____	98._____	121._____	144._____
7._____	30._____	53._____	76._____	99._____	122._____	145._____
8._____	31._____	54._____	77._____	100._____	123._____	146._____
9._____	32._____	55._____	78._____	101._____	124._____	147._____
10._____	33._____	56._____	79._____	102._____	125._____	148._____
11._____	34._____	57._____	80._____	103._____	126._____	149._____
12._____	35._____	58._____	81._____	104._____	127._____	150._____
13._____	36._____	59._____	82._____	105._____	128._____	151._____
14._____	37._____	60._____	83._____	106._____	129._____	152._____
15._____	38._____	61._____	84._____	107._____	130._____	153._____
16._____	39._____	62._____	85._____	108._____	131._____	154._____
17._____	40._____	63._____	86._____	109._____	132._____	155._____
18._____	41._____	64._____	87._____	110._____	133._____	156._____
19._____	42._____	65._____	88._____	111._____	134._____	157._____
20._____	43._____	66._____	89._____	112._____	135._____	158._____
21._____	44._____	67._____	90._____	113._____	136._____	159._____
22._____	45._____	68._____	91._____	114._____	137._____	160._____
23._____	46._____	69._____	92._____	115._____	138._____	161._____

Real Estate Training Institute – Leslie Clauson

1.____	24.____	47.____	70.____	93.____	116.____	139.____
2.____	25.____	48.____	71.____	94.____	117.____	140.____
3.____	26.____	49.____	72.____	95.____	118.____	141.____
4.____	27.____	50.____	73.____	96.____	119.____	142.____
5.____	28.____	51.____	74.____	97.____	120.____	143.____
6.____	29.____	52.____	75.____	98.____	121.____	144.____
7.____	30.____	53.____	76.____	99.____	122.____	145.____
8.____	31.____	54.____	77.____	100.____	123.____	146.____
9.____	32.____	55.____	78.____	101.____	124.____	147.____
10.____	33.____	56.____	79.____	102.____	125.____	148.____
11.____	34.____	57.____	80.____	103.____	126.____	149.____
12.____	35.____	58.____	81.____	104.____	127.____	150.____
13.____	36.____	59.____	82.____	105.____	128.____	151.____
14.____	37.____	60.____	83.____	106.____	129.____	152.____
15.____	38.____	61.____	84.____	107.____	130.____	153.____
16.____	39.____	62.____	85.____	108.____	131.____	154.____
17.____	40.____	63.____	86.____	109.____	132.____	155.____
18.____	41.____	64.____	87.____	110.____	133.____	156.____
19.____	42.____	65.____	88.____	111.____	134.____	157.____
20.____	43.____	66.____	89.____	112.____	135.____	158.____
21.____	44.____	67.____	90.____	113.____	136.____	159.____
22.____	45.____	68.____	91.____	114.____	137.____	160.____
23.____	46.____	69.____	92.____	115.____	138.____	161.____

Real Estate Training Institute – Leslie Clauson

1.____	24.____	47.____	70.____	93.____	116.____	139.____
2.____	25.____	48.____	71.____	94.____	117.____	140.____
3.____	26.____	49.____	72.____	95.____	118.____	141.____
4.____	27.____	50.____	73.____	96.____	119.____	142.____
5.____	28.____	51.____	74.____	97.____	120.____	143.____
6.____	29.____	52.____	75.____	98.____	121.____	144.____
7.____	30.____	53.____	76.____	99.____	122.____	145.____
8.____	31.____	54.____	77.____	100.____	123.____	146.____
9.____	32.____	55.____	78.____	101.____	124.____	147.____
10.____	33.____	56.____	79.____	102.____	125.____	148.____
11.____	34.____	57.____	80.____	103.____	126.____	149.____
12.____	35.____	58.____	81.____	104.____	127.____	150.____
13.____	36.____	59.____	82.____	105.____	128.____	151.____
14.____	37.____	60.____	83.____	106.____	129.____	152.____
15.____	38.____	61.____	84.____	107.____	130.____	153.____
16.____	39.____	62.____	85.____	108.____	131.____	154.____
17.____	40.____	63.____	86.____	109.____	132.____	155.____
18.____	41.____	64.____	87.____	110.____	133.____	156.____
19.____	42.____	65.____	88.____	111.____	134.____	157.____
20.____	43.____	66.____	89.____	112.____	135.____	158.____
21.____	44.____	67.____	90.____	113.____	136.____	159.____
22.____	45.____	68.____	91.____	114.____	137.____	160.____
23.____	46.____	69.____	92.____	115.____	138.____	161.____

Real Estate Training Institute – Leslie Clauson

1._____	24._____	47._____	70._____	93._____	116._____	139._____
2._____	25._____	48._____	71._____	94._____	117._____	140._____
3._____	26._____	49._____	72._____	95._____	118._____	141._____
4._____	27._____	50._____	73._____	96._____	119._____	142._____
5._____	28._____	51._____	74._____	97._____	120._____	143._____
6._____	29._____	52._____	75._____	98._____	121._____	144._____
7._____	30._____	53._____	76._____	99._____	122._____	145._____
8._____	31._____	54._____	77._____	100._____	123._____	146._____
9._____	32._____	55._____	78._____	101._____	124._____	147._____
10._____	33._____	56._____	79._____	102._____	125._____	148._____
11._____	34._____	57._____	80._____	103._____	126._____	149._____
12._____	35._____	58._____	81._____	104._____	127._____	150._____
13._____	36._____	59._____	82._____	105._____	128._____	151._____
14._____	37._____	60._____	83._____	106._____	129._____	152._____
15._____	38._____	61._____	84._____	107._____	130._____	153._____
16._____	39._____	62._____	85._____	108._____	131._____	154._____
17._____	40._____	63._____	86._____	109._____	132._____	155._____
18._____	41._____	64._____	87._____	110._____	133._____	156._____
19._____	42._____	65._____	88._____	111._____	134._____	157._____
20._____	43._____	66._____	89._____	112._____	135._____	158._____
21._____	44._____	67._____	90._____	113._____	136._____	159._____
22._____	45._____	68._____	91._____	114._____	137._____	160._____
23._____	46._____	69._____	92._____	115._____	138._____	161._____

Real Estate Training Institute – Leslie Clauson

1.____ 24.____ 47.____ 70.____ 93.____ 116.____ 139.____
2.____ 25.____ 48.____ 71.____ 94.____ 117.____ 140.____
3.____ 26.____ 49.____ 72.____ 95.____ 118.____ 141.____
4.____ 27.____ 50.____ 73.____ 96.____ 119.____ 142.____
5.____ 28.____ 51.____ 74.____ 97.____ 120.____ 143.____
6.____ 29.____ 52.____ 75.____ 98.____ 121.____ 144.____
7.____ 30.____ 53.____ 76.____ 99.____ 122.____ 145.____
8.____ 31.____ 54.____ 77.____ 100.____ 123.____ 146.____
9.____ 32.____ 55.____ 78.____ 101.____ 124.____ 147.____
10.____ 33.____ 56.____ 79.____ 102.____ 125.____ 148.____
11.____ 34.____ 57.____ 80.____ 103.____ 126.____ 149.____
12.____ 35.____ 58.____ 81.____ 104.____ 127.____ 150.____
13.____ 36.____ 59.____ 82.____ 105.____ 128.____ 151.____
14.____ 37.____ 60.____ 83.____ 106.____ 129.____ 152.____
15.____ 38.____ 61.____ 84.____ 107.____ 130.____ 153.____
16.____ 39.____ 62.____ 85.____ 108.____ 131.____ 154.____
17.____ 40.____ 63.____ 86.____ 109.____ 132.____ 155.____
18.____ 41.____ 64.____ 87.____ 110.____ 133.____ 156.____
19.____ 42.____ 65.____ 88.____ 111.____ 134.____ 157.____
20.____ 43.____ 66.____ 89.____ 112.____ 135.____ 158.____
21.____ 44.____ 67.____ 90.____ 113.____ 136.____ 159.____
22.____ 45.____ 68.____ 91.____ 114.____ 137.____ 160.____
23.____ 46.____ 69.____ 92.____ 115.____ 138.____ 161.____

Real Estate Training Institute – Leslie Clauson

1.___	24.___	47.___	70.___	93.___	116.___	139.___
2.___	25.___	48.___	71.___	94.___	117.___	140.___
3.___	26.___	49.___	72.___	95.___	118.___	141.___
4.___	27.___	50.___	73.___	96.___	119.___	142.___
5.___	28.___	51.___	74.___	97.___	120.___	143.___
6.___	29.___	52.___	75.___	98.___	121.___	144.___
7.___	30.___	53.___	76.___	99.___	122.___	145.___
8.___	31.___	54.___	77.___	100.___	123.___	146.___
9.___	32.___	55.___	78.___	101.___	124.___	147.___
10.___	33.___	56.___	79.___	102.___	125.___	148.___
11.___	34.___	57.___	80.___	103.___	126.___	149.___
12.___	35.___	58.___	81.___	104.___	127.___	150.___
13.___	36.___	59.___	82.___	105.___	128.___	151.___
14.___	37.___	60.___	83.___	106.___	129.___	152.___
15.___	38.___	61.___	84.___	107.___	130.___	153.___
16.___	39.___	62.___	85.___	108.___	131.___	154.___
17.___	40.___	63.___	86.___	109.___	132.___	155.___
18.___	41.___	64.___	87.___	110.___	133.___	156.___
19.___	42.___	65.___	88.___	111.___	134.___	157.___
20.___	43.___	66.___	89.___	112.___	135.___	158.___
21.___	44.___	67.___	90.___	113.___	136.___	159.___
22.___	45.___	68.___	91.___	114.___	137.___	160.___
23.___	46.___	69.___	92.___	115.___	138.___	161.___

Real Estate Training Institute – Leslie Clauson

1.____   24.____   47.____   70.____   93.____   116.____   139.____
2.____   25.____   48.____   71.____   94.____   117.____   140.____
3.____   26.____   49.____   72.____   95.____   118.____   141.____
4.____   27.____   50.____   73.____   96.____   119.____   142.____
5.____   28.____   51.____   74.____   97.____   120.____   143.____
6.____   29.____   52.____   75.____   98.____   121.____   144.____
7.____   30.____   53.____   76.____   99.____   122.____   145.____
8.____   31.____   54.____   77.____   100.____   123.____   146.____
9.____   32.____   55.____   78.____   101.____   124.____   147.____
10.____   33.____   56.____   79.____   102.____   125.____   148.____
11.____   34.____   57.____   80.____   103.____   126.____   149.____
12.____   35.____   58.____   81.____   104.____   127.____   150.____
13.____   36.____   59.____   82.____   105.____   128.____   151.____
14.____   37.____   60.____   83.____   106.____   129.____   152.____
15.____   38.____   61.____   84.____   107.____   130.____   153.____
16.____   39.____   62.____   85.____   108.____   131.____   154.____
17.____   40.____   63.____   86.____   109.____   132.____   155.____
18.____   41.____   64.____   87.____   110.____   133.____   156.____
19.____   42.____   65.____   88.____   111.____   134.____   157.____
20.____   43.____   66.____   89.____   112.____   135.____   158.____
21.____   44.____   67.____   90.____   113.____   136.____   159.____
22.____   45.____   68.____   91.____   114.____   137.____   160.____
23.____   46.____   69.____   92.____   115.____   138.____   161.____

Real Estate Training Institute – Leslie Clauson

1.____   24.____   47.____   70.____   93.____   116.____   139.____
2.____   25.____   48.____   71.____   94.____   117.____   140.____
3.____   26.____   49.____   72.____   95.____   118.____   141.____
4.____   27.____   50.____   73.____   96.____   119.____   142.____
5.____   28.____   51.____   74.____   97.____   120.____   143.____
6.____   29.____   52.____   75.____   98.____   121.____   144.____
7.____   30.____   53.____   76.____   99.____   122.____   145.____
8.____   31.____   54.____   77.____   100.____ 123.____   146.____
9.____   32.____   55.____   78.____   101.____ 124.____   147.____
10.____ 33.____   56.____   79.____   102.____ 125.____   148.____
11.____ 34.____   57.____   80.____   103.____ 126.____   149.____
12.____ 35.____   58.____   81.____   104.____ 127.____   150.____
13.____ 36.____   59.____   82.____   105.____ 128.____   151.____
14.____ 37.____   60.____   83.____   106.____ 129.____   152.____
15.____ 38.____   61.____   84.____   107.____ 130.____   153.____
16.____ 39.____   62.____   85.____   108.____ 131.____   154.____
17.____ 40.____   63.____   86.____   109.____ 132.____   155.____
18.____ 41.____   64.____   87.____   110.____ 133.____   156.____
19.____ 42.____   65.____   88.____   111.____ 134.____   157.____
20.____ 43.____   66.____   89.____   112.____ 135.____   158.____
21.____ 44.____   67.____   90.____   113.____ 136.____   159.____
22.____ 45.____   68.____   91.____   114.____ 137.____   160.____
23.____ 46.____   69.____   92.____   115.____ 138.____   161.____

Real Estate Training Institute – Leslie Clauson

1.____   24.____   47.____   70.____   93.____   116.____   139.____
2.____   25.____   48.____   71.____   94.____   117.____   140.____
3.____   26.____   49.____   72.____   95.____   118.____   141.____
4.____   27.____   50.____   73.____   96.____   119.____   142.____
5.____   28.____   51.____   74.____   97.____   120.____   143.____
6.____   29.____   52.____   75.____   98.____   121.____   144.____
7.____   30.____   53.____   76.____   99.____   122.____   145.____
8.____   31.____   54.____   77.____   100.____ 123.____   146.____
9.____   32.____   55.____   78.____   101.____ 124.____   147.____
10.____ 33.____   56.____   79.____   102.____ 125.____   148.____
11.____ 34.____   57.____   80.____   103.____ 126.____   149.____
12.____ 35.____   58.____   81.____   104.____ 127.____   150.____
13.____ 36.____   59.____   82.____   105.____ 128.____   151.____
14.____ 37.____   60.____   83.____   106.____ 129.____   152.____
15.____ 38.____   61.____   84.____   107.____ 130.____   153.____
16.____ 39.____   62.____   85.____   108.____ 131.____   154.____
17.____ 40.____   63.____   86.____   109.____ 132.____   155.____
18.____ 41.____   64.____   87.____   110.____ 133.____   156.____
19.____ 42.____   65.____   88.____   111.____ 134.____   157.____
20.____ 43.____   66.____   89.____   112.____ 135.____   158.____
21.____ 44.____   67.____   90.____   113.____ 136.____   159.____
22.____ 45.____   68.____   91.____   114.____ 137.____   160.____
23.____ 46.____   69.____   92.____   115.____ 138.____   161.____

Real Estate Training Institute – Leslie Clauson

1._____	24._____	47._____	70._____	93._____	116._____	139._____
2._____	25._____	48._____	71._____	94._____	117._____	140._____
3._____	26._____	49._____	72._____	95._____	118._____	141._____
4._____	27._____	50._____	73._____	96._____	119._____	142._____
5._____	28._____	51._____	74._____	97._____	120._____	143._____
6._____	29._____	52._____	75._____	98._____	121._____	144._____
7._____	30._____	53._____	76._____	99._____	122._____	145._____
8._____	31._____	54._____	77._____	100._____	123._____	146._____
9._____	32._____	55._____	78._____	101._____	124._____	147._____
10._____	33._____	56._____	79._____	102._____	125._____	148._____
11._____	34._____	57._____	80._____	103._____	126._____	149._____
12._____	35._____	58._____	81._____	104._____	127._____	150._____
13._____	36._____	59._____	82._____	105._____	128._____	151._____
14._____	37._____	60._____	83._____	106._____	129._____	152._____
15._____	38._____	61._____	84._____	107._____	130._____	153._____
16._____	39._____	62._____	85._____	108._____	131._____	154._____
17._____	40._____	63._____	86._____	109._____	132._____	155._____
18._____	41._____	64._____	87._____	110._____	133._____	156._____
19._____	42._____	65._____	88._____	111._____	134._____	157._____
20._____	43._____	66._____	89._____	112._____	135._____	158._____
21._____	44._____	67._____	90._____	113._____	136._____	159._____
22._____	45._____	68._____	91._____	114._____	137._____	160._____
23._____	46._____	69._____	92._____	115._____	138._____	161._____

Real Estate Training Institute – Leslie Clauson

1.____	24.____	47.____	70.____	93.____	116.____	139.____
2.____	25.____	48.____	71.____	94.____	117.____	140.____
3.____	26.____	49.____	72.____	95.____	118.____	141.____
4.____	27.____	50.____	73.____	96.____	119.____	142.____
5.____	28.____	51.____	74.____	97.____	120.____	143.____
6.____	29.____	52.____	75.____	98.____	121.____	144.____
7.____	30.____	53.____	76.____	99.____	122.____	145.____
8.____	31.____	54.____	77.____	100.____	123.____	146.____
9.____	32.____	55.____	78.____	101.____	124.____	147.____
10.____	33.____	56.____	79.____	102.____	125.____	148.____
11.____	34.____	57.____	80.____	103.____	126.____	149.____
12.____	35.____	58.____	81.____	104.____	127.____	150.____
13.____	36.____	59.____	82.____	105.____	128.____	151.____
14.____	37.____	60.____	83.____	106.____	129.____	152.____
15.____	38.____	61.____	84.____	107.____	130.____	153.____
16.____	39.____	62.____	85.____	108.____	131.____	154.____
17.____	40.____	63.____	86.____	109.____	132.____	155.____
18.____	41.____	64.____	87.____	110.____	133.____	156.____
19.____	42.____	65.____	88.____	111.____	134.____	157.____
20.____	43.____	66.____	89.____	112.____	135.____	158.____
21.____	44.____	67.____	90.____	113.____	136.____	159.____
22.____	45.____	68.____	91.____	114.____	137.____	160.____
23.____	46.____	69.____	92.____	115.____	138.____	161.____

Real Estate Training Institute – Leslie Clauson

1.____	24.____	47.____	70.____	93.____	116.____	139.____
2.____	25.____	48.____	71.____	94.____	117.____	140.____
3.____	26.____	49.____	72.____	95.____	118.____	141.____
4.____	27.____	50.____	73.____	96.____	119.____	142.____
5.____	28.____	51.____	74.____	97.____	120.____	143.____
6.____	29.____	52.____	75.____	98.____	121.____	144.____
7.____	30.____	53.____	76.____	99.____	122.____	145.____
8.____	31.____	54.____	77.____	100.____	123.____	146.____
9.____	32.____	55.____	78.____	101.____	124.____	147.____
10.____	33.____	56.____	79.____	102.____	125.____	148.____
11.____	34.____	57.____	80.____	103.____	126.____	149.____
12.____	35.____	58.____	81.____	104.____	127.____	150.____
13.____	36.____	59.____	82.____	105.____	128.____	151.____
14.____	37.____	60.____	83.____	106.____	129.____	152.____
15.____	38.____	61.____	84.____	107.____	130.____	153.____
16.____	39.____	62.____	85.____	108.____	131.____	154.____
17.____	40.____	63.____	86.____	109.____	132.____	155.____
18.____	41.____	64.____	87.____	110.____	133.____	156.____
19.____	42.____	65.____	88.____	111.____	134.____	157.____
20.____	43.____	66.____	89.____	112.____	135.____	158.____
21.____	44.____	67.____	90.____	113.____	136.____	159.____
22.____	45.____	68.____	91.____	114.____	137.____	160.____
23.____	46.____	69.____	92.____	115.____	138.____	161.____

Real Estate Training Institute – Leslie Clauson

1.____	24.____	47.____	70.____	93.____	116.____	139.____
2.____	25.____	48.____	71.____	94.____	117.____	140.____
3.____	26.____	49.____	72.____	95.____	118.____	141.____
4.____	27.____	50.____	73.____	96.____	119.____	142.____
5.____	28.____	51.____	74.____	97.____	120.____	143.____
6.____	29.____	52.____	75.____	98.____	121.____	144.____
7.____	30.____	53.____	76.____	99.____	122.____	145.____
8.____	31.____	54.____	77.____	100.____	123.____	146.____
9.____	32.____	55.____	78.____	101.____	124.____	147.____
10.____	33.____	56.____	79.____	102.____	125.____	148.____
11.____	34.____	57.____	80.____	103.____	126.____	149.____
12.____	35.____	58.____	81.____	104.____	127.____	150.____
13.____	36.____	59.____	82.____	105.____	128.____	151.____
14.____	37.____	60.____	83.____	106.____	129.____	152.____
15.____	38.____	61.____	84.____	107.____	130.____	153.____
16.____	39.____	62.____	85.____	108.____	131.____	154.____
17.____	40.____	63.____	86.____	109.____	132.____	155.____
18.____	41.____	64.____	87.____	110.____	133.____	156.____
19.____	42.____	65.____	88.____	111.____	134.____	157.____
20.____	43.____	66.____	89.____	112.____	135.____	158.____
21.____	44.____	67.____	90.____	113.____	136.____	159.____
22.____	45.____	68.____	91.____	114.____	137.____	160.____
23.____	46.____	69.____	92.____	115.____	138.____	161.____

Real Estate Training Institute – Leslie Clauson

1.____	24.____	47.____	70.____	93.____	116.____	139.____
2.____	25.____	48.____	71.____	94.____	117.____	140.____
3.____	26.____	49.____	72.____	95.____	118.____	141.____
4.____	27.____	50.____	73.____	96.____	119.____	142.____
5.____	28.____	51.____	74.____	97.____	120.____	143.____
6.____	29.____	52.____	75.____	98.____	121.____	144.____
7.____	30.____	53.____	76.____	99.____	122.____	145.____
8.____	31.____	54.____	77.____	100.____	123.____	146.____
9.____	32.____	55.____	78.____	101.____	124.____	147.____
10.____	33.____	56.____	79.____	102.____	125.____	148.____
11.____	34.____	57.____	80.____	103.____	126.____	149.____
12.____	35.____	58.____	81.____	104.____	127.____	150.____
13.____	36.____	59.____	82.____	105.____	128.____	151.____
14.____	37.____	60.____	83.____	106.____	129.____	152.____
15.____	38.____	61.____	84.____	107.____	130.____	153.____
16.____	39.____	62.____	85.____	108.____	131.____	154.____
17.____	40.____	63.____	86.____	109.____	132.____	155.____
18.____	41.____	64.____	87.____	110.____	133.____	156.____
19.____	42.____	65.____	88.____	111.____	134.____	157.____
20.____	43.____	66.____	89.____	112.____	135.____	158.____
21.____	44.____	67.____	90.____	113.____	136.____	159.____
22.____	45.____	68.____	91.____	114.____	137.____	160.____
23.____	46.____	69.____	92.____	115.____	138.____	161.____

Real Estate Training Institute – Leslie Clauson

1.____	24.____	47.____	70.____	93.____	116.____	139.____
2.____	25.____	48.____	71.____	94.____	117.____	140.____
3.____	26.____	49.____	72.____	95.____	118.____	141.____
4.____	27.____	50.____	73.____	96.____	119.____	142.____
5.____	28.____	51.____	74.____	97.____	120.____	143.____
6.____	29.____	52.____	75.____	98.____	121.____	144.____
7.____	30.____	53.____	76.____	99.____	122.____	145.____
8.____	31.____	54.____	77.____	100.____	123.____	146.____
9.____	32.____	55.____	78.____	101.____	124.____	147.____
10.____	33.____	56.____	79.____	102.____	125.____	148.____
11.____	34.____	57.____	80.____	103.____	126.____	149.____
12.____	35.____	58.____	81.____	104.____	127.____	150.____
13.____	36.____	59.____	82.____	105.____	128.____	151.____
14.____	37.____	60.____	83.____	106.____	129.____	152.____
15.____	38.____	61.____	84.____	107.____	130.____	153.____
16.____	39.____	62.____	85.____	108.____	131.____	154.____
17.____	40.____	63.____	86.____	109.____	132.____	155.____
18.____	41.____	64.____	87.____	110.____	133.____	156.____
19.____	42.____	65.____	88.____	111.____	134.____	157.____
20.____	43.____	66.____	89.____	112.____	135.____	158.____
21.____	44.____	67.____	90.____	113.____	136.____	159.____
22.____	45.____	68.____	91.____	114.____	137.____	160.____
23.____	46.____	69.____	92.____	115.____	138.____	161.____

Real Estate Training Institute – Leslie Clauson

1.____	24.____	47.____	70.____	93.____	116.____	139.____
2.____	25.____	48.____	71.____	94.____	117.____	140.____
3.____	26.____	49.____	72.____	95.____	118.____	141.____
4.____	27.____	50.____	73.____	96.____	119.____	142.____
5.____	28.____	51.____	74.____	97.____	120.____	143.____
6.____	29.____	52.____	75.____	98.____	121.____	144.____
7.____	30.____	53.____	76.____	99.____	122.____	145.____
8.____	31.____	54.____	77.____	100.____	123.____	146.____
9.____	32.____	55.____	78.____	101.____	124.____	147.____
10.____	33.____	56.____	79.____	102.____	125.____	148.____
11.____	34.____	57.____	80.____	103.____	126.____	149.____
12.____	35.____	58.____	81.____	104.____	127.____	150.____
13.____	36.____	59.____	82.____	105.____	128.____	151.____
14.____	37.____	60.____	83.____	106.____	129.____	152.____
15.____	38.____	61.____	84.____	107.____	130.____	153.____
16.____	39.____	62.____	85.____	108.____	131.____	154.____
17.____	40.____	63.____	86.____	109.____	132.____	155.____
18.____	41.____	64.____	87.____	110.____	133.____	156.____
19.____	42.____	65.____	88.____	111.____	134.____	157.____
20.____	43.____	66.____	89.____	112.____	135.____	158.____
21.____	44.____	67.____	90.____	113.____	136.____	159.____
22.____	45.____	68.____	91.____	114.____	137.____	160.____
23.____	46.____	69.____	92.____	115.____	138.____	161.____

Real Estate Training Institute – Leslie Clauson

1.____	24.____	47.____	70.____	93.____	116.____	139.____
2.____	25.____	48.____	71.____	94.____	117.____	140.____
3.____	26.____	49.____	72.____	95.____	118.____	141.____
4.____	27.____	50.____	73.____	96.____	119.____	142.____
5.____	28.____	51.____	74.____	97.____	120.____	143.____
6.____	29.____	52.____	75.____	98.____	121.____	144.____
7.____	30.____	53.____	76.____	99.____	122.____	145.____
8.____	31.____	54.____	77.____	100.____	123.____	146.____
9.____	32.____	55.____	78.____	101.____	124.____	147.____
10.____	33.____	56.____	79.____	102.____	125.____	148.____
11.____	34.____	57.____	80.____	103.____	126.____	149.____
12.____	35.____	58.____	81.____	104.____	127.____	150.____
13.____	36.____	59.____	82.____	105.____	128.____	151.____
14.____	37.____	60.____	83.____	106.____	129.____	152.____
15.____	38.____	61.____	84.____	107.____	130.____	153.____
16.____	39.____	62.____	85.____	108.____	131.____	154.____
17.____	40.____	63.____	86.____	109.____	132.____	155.____
18.____	41.____	64.____	87.____	110.____	133.____	156.____
19.____	42.____	65.____	88.____	111.____	134.____	157.____
20.____	43.____	66.____	89.____	112.____	135.____	158.____
21.____	44.____	67.____	90.____	113.____	136.____	159.____
22.____	45.____	68.____	91.____	114.____	137.____	160.____
23.____	46.____	69.____	92.____	115.____	138.____	161.____

Real Estate Training Institute – Leslie Clauson

1.____	24.____	47.____	70.____	93.____	116.____	139.____
2.____	25.____	48.____	71.____	94.____	117.____	140.____
3.____	26.____	49.____	72.____	95.____	118.____	141.____
4.____	27.____	50.____	73.____	96.____	119.____	142.____
5.____	28.____	51.____	74.____	97.____	120.____	143.____
6.____	29.____	52.____	75.____	98.____	121.____	144.____
7.____	30.____	53.____	76.____	99.____	122.____	145.____
8.____	31.____	54.____	77.____	100.____	123.____	146.____
9.____	32.____	55.____	78.____	101.____	124.____	147.____
10.____	33.____	56.____	79.____	102.____	125.____	148.____
11.____	34.____	57.____	80.____	103.____	126.____	149.____
12.____	35.____	58.____	81.____	104.____	127.____	150.____
13.____	36.____	59.____	82.____	105.____	128.____	151.____
14.____	37.____	60.____	83.____	106.____	129.____	152.____
15.____	38.____	61.____	84.____	107.____	130.____	153.____
16.____	39.____	62.____	85.____	108.____	131.____	154.____
17.____	40.____	63.____	86.____	109.____	132.____	155.____
18.____	41.____	64.____	87.____	110.____	133.____	156.____
19.____	42.____	65.____	88.____	111.____	134.____	157.____
20.____	43.____	66.____	89.____	112.____	135.____	158.____
21.____	44.____	67.____	90.____	113.____	136.____	159.____
22.____	45.____	68.____	91.____	114.____	137.____	160.____
23.____	46.____	69.____	92.____	115.____	138.____	161.____

Real Estate Training Institute – Leslie Clauson

1.____   24.____   47.____   70.____   93.____   116.____   139.____
2.____   25.____   48.____   71.____   94.____   117.____   140.____
3.____   26.____   49.____   72.____   95.____   118.____   141.____
4.____   27.____   50.____   73.____   96.____   119.____   142.____
5.____   28.____   51.____   74.____   97.____   120.____   143.____
6.____   29.____   52.____   75.____   98.____   121.____   144.____
7.____   30.____   53.____   76.____   99.____   122.____   145.____
8.____   31.____   54.____   77.____   100.____ 123.____   146.____
9.____   32.____   55.____   78.____   101.____ 124.____   147.____
10.____ 33.____   56.____   79.____   102.____ 125.____   148.____
11.____ 34.____   57.____   80.____   103.____ 126.____   149.____
12.____ 35.____   58.____   81.____   104.____ 127.____   150.____
13.____ 36.____   59.____   82.____   105.____ 128.____   151.____
14.____ 37.____   60.____   83.____   106.____ 129.____   152.____
15.____ 38.____   61.____   84.____   107.____ 130.____   153.____
16.____ 39.____   62.____   85.____   108.____ 131.____   154.____
17.____ 40.____   63.____   86.____   109.____ 132.____   155.____
18.____ 41.____   64.____   87.____   110.____ 133.____   156.____
19.____ 42.____   65.____   88.____   111.____ 134.____   157.____
20.____ 43.____   66.____   89.____   112.____ 135.____   158.____
21.____ 44.____   67.____   90.____   113.____ 136.____   159.____
22.____ 45.____   68.____   91.____   114.____ 137.____   160.____
23.____ 46.____   69.____   92.____   115.____ 138.____   161.____

Real Estate Training Institute – Leslie Clauson

1._____	24._____	47._____	70._____	93._____	116._____	139._____
2._____	25._____	48._____	71._____	94._____	117._____	140._____
3._____	26._____	49._____	72._____	95._____	118._____	141._____
4._____	27._____	50._____	73._____	96._____	119._____	142._____
5._____	28._____	51._____	74._____	97._____	120._____	143._____
6._____	29._____	52._____	75._____	98._____	121._____	144._____
7._____	30._____	53._____	76._____	99._____	122._____	145._____
8._____	31._____	54._____	77._____	100._____	123._____	146._____
9._____	32._____	55._____	78._____	101._____	124._____	147._____
10._____	33._____	56._____	79._____	102._____	125._____	148._____
11._____	34._____	57._____	80._____	103._____	126._____	149._____
12._____	35._____	58._____	81._____	104._____	127._____	150._____
13._____	36._____	59._____	82._____	105._____	128._____	151._____
14._____	37._____	60._____	83._____	106._____	129._____	152._____
15._____	38._____	61._____	84._____	107._____	130._____	153._____
16._____	39._____	62._____	85._____	108._____	131._____	154._____
17._____	40._____	63._____	86._____	109._____	132._____	155._____
18._____	41._____	64._____	87._____	110._____	133._____	156._____
19._____	42._____	65._____	88._____	111._____	134._____	157._____
20._____	43._____	66._____	89._____	112._____	135._____	158._____
21._____	44._____	67._____	90._____	113._____	136._____	159._____
22._____	45._____	68._____	91._____	114._____	137._____	160._____
23._____	46._____	69._____	92._____	115._____	138._____	161._____

Real Estate Training Institute – Leslie Clauson

1.____	24.____	47.____	70.____	93.____	116.____	139.____
2.____	25.____	48.____	71.____	94.____	117.____	140.____
3.____	26.____	49.____	72.____	95.____	118.____	141.____
4.____	27.____	50.____	73.____	96.____	119.____	142.____
5.____	28.____	51.____	74.____	97.____	120.____	143.____
6.____	29.____	52.____	75.____	98.____	121.____	144.____
7.____	30.____	53.____	76.____	99.____	122.____	145.____
8.____	31.____	54.____	77.____	100.____	123.____	146.____
9.____	32.____	55.____	78.____	101.____	124.____	147.____
10.____	33.____	56.____	79.____	102.____	125.____	148.____
11.____	34.____	57.____	80.____	103.____	126.____	149.____
12.____	35.____	58.____	81.____	104.____	127.____	150.____
13.____	36.____	59.____	82.____	105.____	128.____	151.____
14.____	37.____	60.____	83.____	106.____	129.____	152.____
15.____	38.____	61.____	84.____	107.____	130.____	153.____
16.____	39.____	62.____	85.____	108.____	131.____	154.____
17.____	40.____	63.____	86.____	109.____	132.____	155.____
18.____	41.____	64.____	87.____	110.____	133.____	156.____
19.____	42.____	65.____	88.____	111.____	134.____	157.____
20.____	43.____	66.____	89.____	112.____	135.____	158.____
21.____	44.____	67.____	90.____	113.____	136.____	159.____
22.____	45.____	68.____	91.____	114.____	137.____	160.____
23.____	46.____	69.____	92.____	115.____	138.____	161.____

Real Estate Training Institute – Leslie Clauson

1.____	24.____	47.____	70.____	93.____	116.____	139.____
2.____	25.____	48.____	71.____	94.____	117.____	140.____
3.____	26.____	49.____	72.____	95.____	118.____	141.____
4.____	27.____	50.____	73.____	96.____	119.____	142.____
5.____	28.____	51.____	74.____	97.____	120.____	143.____
6.____	29.____	52.____	75.____	98.____	121.____	144.____
7.____	30.____	53.____	76.____	99.____	122.____	145.____
8.____	31.____	54.____	77.____	100.____	123.____	146.____
9.____	32.____	55.____	78.____	101.____	124.____	147.____
10.____	33.____	56.____	79.____	102.____	125.____	148.____
11.____	34.____	57.____	80.____	103.____	126.____	149.____
12.____	35.____	58.____	81.____	104.____	127.____	150.____
13.____	36.____	59.____	82.____	105.____	128.____	151.____
14.____	37.____	60.____	83.____	106.____	129.____	152.____
15.____	38.____	61.____	84.____	107.____	130.____	153.____
16.____	39.____	62.____	85.____	108.____	131.____	154.____
17.____	40.____	63.____	86.____	109.____	132.____	155.____
18.____	41.____	64.____	87.____	110.____	133.____	156.____
19.____	42.____	65.____	88.____	111.____	134.____	157.____
20.____	43.____	66.____	89.____	112.____	135.____	158.____
21.____	44.____	67.____	90.____	113.____	136.____	159.____
22.____	45.____	68.____	91.____	114.____	137.____	160.____
23.____	46.____	69.____	92.____	115.____	138.____	161.____

Real Estate Training Institute – Leslie Clauson

1.____	24.____	47.____	70.____	93.____	116.____	139.____
2.____	25.____	48.____	71.____	94.____	117.____	140.____
3.____	26.____	49.____	72.____	95.____	118.____	141.____
4.____	27.____	50.____	73.____	96.____	119.____	142.____
5.____	28.____	51.____	74.____	97.____	120.____	143.____
6.____	29.____	52.____	75.____	98.____	121.____	144.____
7.____	30.____	53.____	76.____	99.____	122.____	145.____
8.____	31.____	54.____	77.____	100.____	123.____	146.____
9.____	32.____	55.____	78.____	101.____	124.____	147.____
10.____	33.____	56.____	79.____	102.____	125.____	148.____
11.____	34.____	57.____	80.____	103.____	126.____	149.____
12.____	35.____	58.____	81.____	104.____	127.____	150.____
13.____	36.____	59.____	82.____	105.____	128.____	151.____
14.____	37.____	60.____	83.____	106.____	129.____	152.____
15.____	38.____	61.____	84.____	107.____	130.____	153.____
16.____	39.____	62.____	85.____	108.____	131.____	154.____
17.____	40.____	63.____	86.____	109.____	132.____	155.____
18.____	41.____	64.____	87.____	110.____	133.____	156.____
19.____	42.____	65.____	88.____	111.____	134.____	157.____
20.____	43.____	66.____	89.____	112.____	135.____	158.____
21.____	44.____	67.____	90.____	113.____	136.____	159.____
22.____	45.____	68.____	91.____	114.____	137.____	160.____
23.____	46.____	69.____	92.____	115.____	138.____	161.____

Real Estate Training Institute – Leslie Clauson

1.____	24.____	47.____	70.____	93.____	116.____	139.____
2.____	25.____	48.____	71.____	94.____	117.____	140.____
3.____	26.____	49.____	72.____	95.____	118.____	141.____
4.____	27.____	50.____	73.____	96.____	119.____	142.____
5.____	28.____	51.____	74.____	97.____	120.____	143.____
6.____	29.____	52.____	75.____	98.____	121.____	144.____
7.____	30.____	53.____	76.____	99.____	122.____	145.____
8.____	31.____	54.____	77.____	100.____	123.____	146.____
9.____	32.____	55.____	78.____	101.____	124.____	147.____
10.____	33.____	56.____	79.____	102.____	125.____	148.____
11.____	34.____	57.____	80.____	103.____	126.____	149.____
12.____	35.____	58.____	81.____	104.____	127.____	150.____
13.____	36.____	59.____	82.____	105.____	128.____	151.____
14.____	37.____	60.____	83.____	106.____	129.____	152.____
15.____	38.____	61.____	84.____	107.____	130.____	153.____
16.____	39.____	62.____	85.____	108.____	131.____	154.____
17.____	40.____	63.____	86.____	109.____	132.____	155.____
18.____	41.____	64.____	87.____	110.____	133.____	156.____
19.____	42.____	65.____	88.____	111.____	134.____	157.____
20.____	43.____	66.____	89.____	112.____	135.____	158.____
21.____	44.____	67.____	90.____	113.____	136.____	159.____
22.____	45.____	68.____	91.____	114.____	137.____	160.____
23.____	46.____	69.____	92.____	115.____	138.____	161.____

Real Estate Training Institute – Leslie Clauson

1.____	24.____	47.____	70.____	93.____	116.____	139.____
2.____	25.____	48.____	71.____	94.____	117.____	140.____
3.____	26.____	49.____	72.____	95.____	118.____	141.____
4.____	27.____	50.____	73.____	96.____	119.____	142.____
5.____	28.____	51.____	74.____	97.____	120.____	143.____
6.____	29.____	52.____	75.____	98.____	121.____	144.____
7.____	30.____	53.____	76.____	99.____	122.____	145.____
8.____	31.____	54.____	77.____	100.____	123.____	146.____
9.____	32.____	55.____	78.____	101.____	124.____	147.____
10.____	33.____	56.____	79.____	102.____	125.____	148.____
11.____	34.____	57.____	80.____	103.____	126.____	149.____
12.____	35.____	58.____	81.____	104.____	127.____	150.____
13.____	36.____	59.____	82.____	105.____	128.____	151.____
14.____	37.____	60.____	83.____	106.____	129.____	152.____
15.____	38.____	61.____	84.____	107.____	130.____	153.____
16.____	39.____	62.____	85.____	108.____	131.____	154.____
17.____	40.____	63.____	86.____	109.____	132.____	155.____
18.____	41.____	64.____	87.____	110.____	133.____	156.____
19.____	42.____	65.____	88.____	111.____	134.____	157.____
20.____	43.____	66.____	89.____	112.____	135.____	158.____
21.____	44.____	67.____	90.____	113.____	136.____	159.____
22.____	45.____	68.____	91.____	114.____	137.____	160.____
23.____	46.____	69.____	92.____	115.____	138.____	161.____

Real Estate Training Institute – Leslie Clauson

1.____	24.____	47.____	70.____	93.____	116.____	139.____
2.____	25.____	48.____	71.____	94.____	117.____	140.____
3.____	26.____	49.____	72.____	95.____	118.____	141.____
4.____	27.____	50.____	73.____	96.____	119.____	142.____
5.____	28.____	51.____	74.____	97.____	120.____	143.____
6.____	29.____	52.____	75.____	98.____	121.____	144.____
7.____	30.____	53.____	76.____	99.____	122.____	145.____
8.____	31.____	54.____	77.____	100.____	123.____	146.____
9.____	32.____	55.____	78.____	101.____	124.____	147.____
10.____	33.____	56.____	79.____	102.____	125.____	148.____
11.____	34.____	57.____	80.____	103.____	126.____	149.____
12.____	35.____	58.____	81.____	104.____	127.____	150.____
13.____	36.____	59.____	82.____	105.____	128.____	151.____
14.____	37.____	60.____	83.____	106.____	129.____	152.____
15.____	38.____	61.____	84.____	107.____	130.____	153.____
16.____	39.____	62.____	85.____	108.____	131.____	154.____
17.____	40.____	63.____	86.____	109.____	132.____	155.____
18.____	41.____	64.____	87.____	110.____	133.____	156.____
19.____	42.____	65.____	88.____	111.____	134.____	157.____
20.____	43.____	66.____	89.____	112.____	135.____	158.____
21.____	44.____	67.____	90.____	113.____	136.____	159.____
22.____	45.____	68.____	91.____	114.____	137.____	160.____
23.____	46.____	69.____	92.____	115.____	138.____	161.____

Real Estate Training Institute – Pre Exam Workbook

1.____	24.____	47.____	70.____	93.____	116.____	139.____
2.____	25.____	48.____	71.____	94.____	117.____	140.____
3.____	26.____	49.____	72.____	95.____	118.____	141.____
4.____	27.____	50.____	73.____	96.____	119.____	142.____
5.____	28.____	51.____	74.____	97.____	120.____	143.____
6.____	29.____	52.____	75.____	98.____	121.____	144.____
7.____	30.____	53.____	76.____	99.____	122.____	145.____
8.____	31.____	54.____	77.____	100.____	123.____	146.____
9.____	32.____	55.____	78.____	101.____	124.____	147.____
10.____	33.____	56.____	79.____	102.____	125.____	148.____
11.____	34.____	57.____	80.____	103.____	126.____	149.____
12.____	35.____	58.____	81.____	104.____	127.____	150.____
13.____	36.____	59.____	82.____	105.____	128.____	151.____
14.____	37.____	60.____	83.____	106.____	129.____	152.____
15.____	38.____	61.____	84.____	107.____	130.____	153.____
16.____	39.____	62.____	85.____	108.____	131.____	154.____
17.____	40.____	63.____	86.____	109.____	132.____	155.____
18.____	41.____	64.____	87.____	110.____	133.____	156.____
19.____	42.____	65.____	88.____	111.____	134.____	157.____
20.____	43.____	66.____	89.____	112.____	135.____	158.____
21.____	44.____	67.____	90.____	113.____	136.____	159.____
22.____	45.____	68.____	91.____	114.____	137.____	160.____
23.____	46.____	69.____	92.____	115.____	138.____	161.____

Real Estate Training Institute – Leslie Clauson

Reciprocal States:

Alabama	Full	334-242-5544
Arkansas	Full	501-683-8010
Colorado	Full	303-894-2166
Connecticut	Full	860-713-6150
Delaware	Partial	302-744-4500
District of Columbia	Partial	202-727-7184
Florida	Full	407-481-5632
Georgia	Full	404-656-3916
Hawaii	Partial	808-586-2643
Idaho	Partial	208-334-3285
Illinois	Full	217-785-9300
Indiana	Partial	317-234-2912
Iowa	Full	515-281-7393
Kansas	Partial	785-296-3411
Kentucky	Full	502-425-4273
Louisiana	Partial	225-765-0191
Maine	Partial	207-624-8603
Massachusetts	Full	617-727-2373
Missouri	Partial	573-751-2628
Nebraska	Full	402-471-2004
New York	Full – Brokers Only	518-473-2728
North Carolina	Full	919-875-3700

Real Estate Training Institute – Pre Exam Workbook

Ohio	Full	614-466-4100
Oklahoma	Full	405-521-3387
Oregon	Partial	503-378-4170
South Dakota	Full	605-773-3600
Tennessee	Partial	615-741-2273
Utah	Full	801-530-6747
Virginia	Full	804-367-8526
Wyoming	Full	307-777-7141
NO RECIPROCITY		
Alaska	Arizona	California
Maryland	Michigan	Nevada
New Mexico	South Carolina	Texas
Washington	Wisconsin	

Real Estate Training Institute – Pre Exam Workbook

The Final Steps:

Once the three finals are marked with a "PASS" from the Real Estate Training Institute, students will be issued a diploma.

The diploma is attached to the completed application along with the MREC fee.

The application is to be mailed to MREC.

Physical Address:
Lefleur's Bluff Tower, Suite 300
4780 I-55 North
Jackson, MS 39211 (601) 321-6970 - Office
(601) 321-6955 - Fax

or

Mailing Address:
P.O. Box 12685
Jackson, MS 39236

Once the application is approved, your information is forwarded to the testing company.

A letter will be sent to you from MREC notifying you to contact the testing company and schedule the exam.

There is a testing fee.

The Testing Company
PSI
www.candidate.psiexams.com
PSI licensure: certification
3210 East Tropicana
Las Vegas, NV 89121
Licensure Phone 1 – 800 – 733 - 9267
Certification Phone 1 – 800 – 211 - 2754
Fax 1 – 702 – 932 - 2666

Real Estate Training Institute – Leslie Clauson

Real Estate Training Institute

1636 Popps Ferry Road, M1
Biloxi, MS 39532

228-354-8585
www.goreti.com
www.msrealtycourses.com

The Testing Company
PSI
www.candidate.psiexams.com
PSI licensure: certification
3210 East Tropicana
Las Vegas, NV 89121
Licensure Phone   1 – 800 – 733 - 9267
Certification Phone 1 – 800 – 211 - 2754
Fax 1 – 702 – 932 - 2666

Made in the USA
San Bernardino, CA
21 July 2015